W9-AFQ-905

Banking and Economic Development

Banking and Economic Development
Brazil, 1889–1930

Gail D. Triner

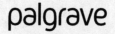

First published 2000 by
PALGRAVE™
175 Fifth Avenue, New York, N.Y. 10010 and
Houndmills, Basingstoke, Hampshire, England RG21 6XS.
Companies and representatives throughout the world.

PALGRAVE™ is the new global publishing imprint of St. Martin's Press LLC Scholarly and Reference Division and Palgrave Publishers Ltd (formerly Macmillan Press Ltd).

ISBN 0–312–23399–X hardback

Library of Congress Cataloging-in-Publication Data
Triner, Gail D.
    Banking and economic development : Brazil, 1889-1930 / Gail D. Triner.
       p. cm.
    Includes bibliographical references and index.
    ISBN 0-312-23399-X (cloth)
       1. Banks and banking—Brazil—History.   2. Brazil—Economic conditions.
    I. Title.

HG2884 .T75 2000
332.1'0981—dc21   00-040519

A catalogue record for this book is available from the British Library.

Design by Westchester Book Composition

First edition: December, 2000
10 9 8 7 6 5 4 3 2 1

Printed in the United States of America

For Carter Kaneen

Contents

List of Tables and Figures

Conventions Used in the Manuscript

Currency
Brazilian currency during the First Republic was the mil-réis. Brazilians denominated 1000 mil-réis as one conto. In keeping with the practice of the period, exchange rates are quoted as pence per mil-réis (p/m-r).

Spelling
Proper names of individuals, organizations, and titles are spelled in keeping with their contemporaneous spelling. When multiple spellings of personal names were used, I have tried to select the most common. Titles of organizations and publications are shown as they appeared, resulting in some inconsistencies of spelling among titles.

Data Sources
Sources for figures and tables are discussed in the Data Appendix, unless otherwise noted.

All translations by the author, unless noted otherwise.

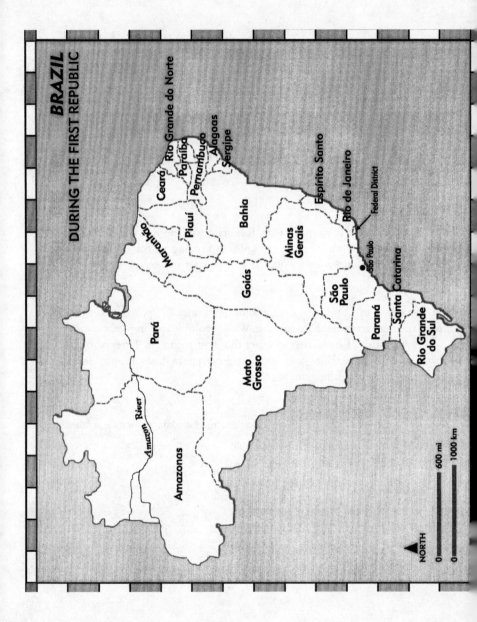

BRAZIL
DURING THE FIRST REPUBLIC

Rio Grande do Norte
Paraíba
Pernambuco
Alagoas
Sergipe
Ceará
Piauí
Bahia
Maranhão
Espírito Santo
Rio de Janeiro
Federal District
Minas Gerais
São Paulo
Goiás
São Paulo
Pará
Santa Catarina
Paraná
Mato Grosso
Rio Grande do Sul
Amazon River
Amazonas

NORTH

0   600 mi
0   1000 km

Acknowledgments

H erbert Klein has guided and encouraged this work from its earliest stage as a dissertation. He also has guided my way into Brazilian history and has generously introduced me to many others interested in my endeavors. Professor Klein has taught me the professional standards, and the excitement, of academic research.

In Brazil, many people contributed to my work. Their help came in the form of long conversations or debates, suggestions for source material and background historiography, and encouraging or friendly words to a newcomer who was captivated and perplexed by what she found. These people made my work easier, and they helped me to better understand and appreciate daily contemporary Brazilian life. Some, but not all, of those whom I want to thank are: Zuleika Alvim, Geraldo Beauclair, Nelson Eizerik, Gustavo Franco, Winston Fritsch, Carlos Gabriel Guimarães, Maria Antonieta Leopoldi, Douglas Cole Libby, Eulália Lobo, Francisco Vidal Luna, Teresa Marques, Walter Ness, Nancy Naro, Mitiko Okazaki, Anderson Pires, Lígia Prado, Luis Carlos Prado, Fernando and Elisa Reinach, and Flávio Saes.

Others who have read portions of the work and have provided guidance, insight, and encouragement include John Coatsworth, Roberto Cortés Conde, Alan Dye, Marshall Eakin, Michael Edelstein, Stanley Engerman, Jeff Freiden, Steve Haber, Anne Hanley, Jeff Lesser, Colin Lewis, Carlos Marichal, Rory Miller, Akira Motomura, Leonard Nakamura, Kerry Odell, Rich Sicotte, Dick Sylla, Steve Topik, Catalina Vizcarra, and Barbara Weinstein.

Rutgers University has provided an extraordinarily receptive professional home. In the Economics Department, Michael Bordo, Hugh Rockoff, and Eugene White have always been generous and enthusiastic with ideas and help. Many of my colleagues in the History Department have helped me to make one of the largest transitions from the dissertation to this book—integrating the "economic" and "history" portions of my work. Sam Baily, Rudy Bell, Paul Clemens, Jim Livingston, Matt Matsuda, and Mark Wasserman have been especially instrumental and encouraging, by reading drafts of papers and chapters.

Historical research cannot be conducted without the help of archivists and librarians. In Brazil, many archivists and others contributed their expertise and good will to help me find materials. André Luis da Rocha e Silva at the Banco do Brasil, Marisa Pereira Guimarães at the Banco do Commércio e Indústria de São Paulo, Geyza Rocha Pereira at the Instituto Brasileiro de Mercado de Capitais, Rosely Curi Rondinelli and Laura Xavier at the Fundação Casa Rui Barbosa, the museum staff at the Banco de Crédito Real de Minas Gerais, and the staff at the Biblioteca Nacional were among those who guided my access to the materials that went into this project. All were anxious to contribute their professional skills and provided friendly companionship through days of research. And, I suspect that the stranger who showed up in their midst offered them a certain amount of bemusement.

Many of the ideas in this book have seen earlier expression in conference papers and journal articles. Work from publications that reappear here, with permission, include: "Banking and Money Markets in Brazil, 1889-1930" (in *Latin America and the World Economy in the Nineteenth and Twentieth Centuries,* edited by John Coatsworth and Alan M. Taylor [Harvard University Press, 1998], 223-70); "Banks, Regions, and Nation in Brazil: 1889-1930" (*Latin American Perspectives* 26: 1 [February 1999]: 129-50); "The Formation of Modern Brazilian Banking, 1906-1930: Opportunities and Constraints Presented by the Public and Private Sectors" (*Journal of Latin American Studies* [February 1996]: 49-74); and "Banking, Economic Growth and Industrialization: Brazil, 1906-1930" (*Revista Brasileira da Economia* 50: 1 [February 1996]: 135-53). Participants in seminars at Universidade Federal Fluminense, Universidade Federal de Rio de Janeiro, Michigan State University, University of Pennsylvania, Rutgers University, Yale University, and Harvard University offered many ideas and suggestions while this was a work-in-progress. The ideas developed here have also benefited from numerous discussions in the University Seminar on Economic History at Columbia University.

Funding for international research is difficult to arrange. Generous support has come from Rutgers University (the History Department and the

University Research Council), Columbia University (the Graduate School of Arts and Sciences, the Presidents Fellowship Fund, the Institute of Iberian and Latin American Studies, and the University Seminars), the Danforth-Compton Foundation Fellowship for Minority Graduate Studies, the Ford Foundation Doctoral Fellowship Program for Minorities, and the Economic History Association Arthur H. Cole Research Grant-in-Aid. Marc Italia of Geografx.net contributed his time and expertise to produce the map. A year spent as a Fellow at the Bunting Institute, Radcliffe College, Harvard University, provided incomparable conditions and companions for productive writing.

Maria Bárbara Levy's encouragement, enthusiasm, and help were indispensable at the early stages of the dissertation. She offered institutional affiliation with the Universidade Federal de Rio de Janeiro and cheerfully helped to shape my ideas and to guide my research. I only hope that a modicum of her graciousness and spirit have found their way into my efforts.

In the face of such extensive intellectual, personal, and material support, any remaining inadequacies of fact or logic are mine.

Carter Kaneen has participated in and lived with this project from the beginning; simply recognizing his support is inadequate. If he thinks that this odyssey has been worthwhile, then it has.

Chapter 1

Introduction

This book examines, through the prism of the banking system, the economic transformation of Brazil during the First Republic from 1889 to 1930. Banking is an especially useful lens through which to view economic change. By observing Brazilian banking, we can better understand broader-ranging issues of economic development, the consolidation of an economy of national scope, the dynamic between the public and private sectors. These are the major themes of this book.

Why Brazil and why banking? The Brazilian economy is currently the eighth largest in the world. Its economic history is a study in extremes. Cycles of booms in commodity production for export have, since European settlement in the sixteenth century, produced wealth for a few and sustained expectations for many. The country has long suffered one of the most disparate distributions of wealth experienced by any country. By the middle of the twentieth century, the significant presence of the State in productive enterprise both benefited and hindered the large modern industrial sector. Further, the means by which Brazil evolved from a loose aggregation of local markets to a large, complex, and strongly centralized economy by the middle of the twentieth century merit better understanding.

Banking history in other countries suggests it as a fruitful field of inquiry for understanding Brazilian experience. In order to understand the full importance of banking, a study of its history needs to incorporate political economy, as well as political, social, and economic history. Banks and their institutional systems have filled pivotal roles in such important aspects of development as state formation, industrialization, and the creation of markets in many countries. Further, banking serves as an important mirror, reflecting the significant transformations that reshaped Brazilian society during the early twentieth century. The development of a dynamic banking system both required and supported the increasing specialization of activities and scale of endeavor that resulted in urban growth, the emergence of the middle class and professional occupations, and the construction of the physical infrastructure needed for these changes.

At the same time, the prescient reader of newspapers today will recognize many of the issues with respect to financial crisis that arise in this book. Themes similar to those that Brazilians faced at the beginning of the twentieth century have accompanied debates about Brazilian (and many other) financial crises at the end of the twentieth century and the beginning of the twenty-first. Some of the common issues and choices related to financial crisis presented in the First Republic and the current world are: the trade-offs between meeting international financial obligations and domestic social welfare; the desirability of economic growth generated by participation in global trading systems as compared to internally supported growth; the stringency of monetary and fiscal policy; and shifting areas of comparative advantage and shifting centers of political strength.

This book explores the ability of governing authorities to negotiate and implement solutions to financial crises. And, it considers the impact of financial crises on the productive sectors of the economy. Banks are the common nexus through which many economic agents operate. Studying them offers an innovative and broad perspective on fundamental issues of development. Therefore, Brazilian banking offers insight on the economic and political history of an important and large country at the same time that it offers a rich historical study of the roots of problems that still have no definitive solution.

To anticipate, this study results in two overall conclusions. The first is that a "modern" banking system, one that intermediated resources between economic sectors and responded systematically to the competing forces affecting the supply and demand for credit and deposits, emerged in Brazil in the early twentieth century. The "modernization" of banking was consistent with change occurring throughout the economy, and indeed, throughout Brazilian society. The nature of banking in Brazil became very similar to commercial banking systems of more "advanced" economies. Nevertheless, its effects on the economy were different than would be expected from experiences in other cases. The second conclusion is that the State constructed and used the banking system in efforts to support its political legitimacy. In doing so, the banking system became important in an economy that was increasingly national in scope. Delineating the trajectory of banking development with these results is the major task of this book.

BANKING AND DEVELOPMENT IN HISTORY

Existing research on banking history is pertinent to Brazil and provides useful theoretical and historical context. A large body of historiography considers the importance of financial systems generally, and the banking system more specifically, in economic and political change.[1] Despite the multiple conclusions that earlier studies have produced about the importance of banking, common themes emerge. The research has followed two paths that reflect the scope of widespread fundamental social change in which banks participate.

First, scholars have studied banking as an important tool in early stages of state formation.[2] Keeping with its emphasis on economic history, this study uses a traditional economic model of the State. In this model, the main activities of the State are to provide public goods and to define and protect property rights (the rules of property ownership and transfer).[3] State formation, or state-building, refers to the complex activities of defining and protecting the provision of public goods and property rights.[4] These efforts require the construction of effective institutions of governance. The provision of money and the rules by which money is created and circulates are public goods and, simultaneously, the locus of fundamental questions of allocating property between private agents and the State. As banks generate an increasing proportion of an economy's money, in the form of deposits, they are increasingly at the center of these issues. Further, banks require early and important enforcement of the definition and protection of property rights among private economic actors.[5]

State-building requires its practitioners to capture resources from ever-widening sources. Establishing bodies and institutions of governance typically incurs heavy costs of warfare, negotiation, accommodation, and inducement. These efforts are often the largest-scale undertakings of their times, and they require innovative strategies to accommodate them.[6] They have led many state builders to establish organizations that capture resources from an expanded pool, by collecting taxes or by promising to compensate constituents in the future. The latter mechanism entails issuing debt and establishing organizations—banks—to monitor them. As the complicated business of constructing governing bodies requires resources beyond the means of individuals, the demands of public finance have given impetus to banking. Simultaneously, the ability of a centralized political entity to command resources from constituents through taxation (coercive or consensual) effectively demonstrates the ability to govern. The Bank of England and the First and Second Banks of the United States offer well-known examples of the intricate ties between state building and the origins of banking, as well as the dynamics between early state organizations and the private sector.[7] With the fullness of time, the dynamics between the State and the private sector express themselves through many activities integral to banking, such as monetary policy, regulation of private enterprise, and the entrepreneurial endeavors of the State. The institutions and practices of these processes contribute to establishing the nature of governance, forming the economic role of the State and the structure by which agents in the private sector conduct their economic transactions.[8]

The potential of banking to connect markets through the medium of money has provided the second major thrust of existing research, which focuses on the role of money in private commercial enterprise. Money has unique properties that make it an especially interesting source of economic cohesion. Money serves many purposes simultaneously. It is a store of value, a "numeraire" (a means of keeping track of value), and a medium for facilitating the exchange of goods and services. Money has prices as measured by interest, exchange, and inflation rates. It can be bought and sold at prices that reflect its value in its different forms. While its most well-known form is currency in circulation, bank deposits are also an important part of the money supply. As any form of money becomes widely accepted, it acquires the characteristics of a commodity. It becomes more easily interchangeable between its forms (currencies, bank deposits, and government-issued notes). Its commodification enhances the ability of money to integrate previously independent markets (networks of individuals, locations, and institutions in which the exchange of goods and services occurs). The State invokes monetary policy to control the value of the currency that it issues. Doing so has the potential to control the price level of goods and services available in the domestic economy as well as to redistribute wealth between the economic sectors. The tools of monetary policy include controlling the exchange rate (the value of a currency relative to other currencies) and defining the rules for the creation of money domestically in the forms of currency and bank deposits. As they become a larger proportion of the money supply, deposits and the banks that manage them become increasingly important.

Credit, the use of deposits by bank borrowers, contributes to market formation and commercial development. Banks accumulate resources from depositors and investors for the purpose of lending (investing) according to criteria of profitability and security.[9] As intermediators of financial resources, banks allocate funds among competing uses. The winners and losers in the allocation process and the uses to which banks put the resources of their depositors/investors reveal much about both finance and economic change. The financial system connects all sectors of the economy; it also connects the State with private interests. By creating organizations that pool resources of wider groups of investors and allocating them among investment options (presumably) based on criteria of profitability and security, the system allows more economic agents to gain access to mechanisms that support the introduction of innovative enterprise to meet the evolving needs of modernizing societies.[10] One could think of banks as offering the potential for economic democratization, both enhancing efficiency and offering access to economic resources according to depersonalized criteria. Looking at the formation of markets through the perspective of money and banks elucidates the emergence of a national economy from relatively unconnected regional economies. Viewing the banking system within the framework of market formation highlights its ability to link previously unconnected markets for goods and services and to serve as an agent of growth.

Much of the historiography concerned with the role of banking in economic development conflates industrialization with market formation and growth. Inconclusiveness is perhaps the most notable feature of this research. Most scholars have agreed that banking is important. However, the "causal nexus"[11] connecting banking with development has remained elusive. Schumpeter may have been the first to hypothesize a direct link between bank credit and economic growth.[12] Gerschenkron's now-classic research schematized the relative chronology of development (as connoted by the onset of industrialization) and the nature of financial entrepreneurship required for economic advancement.[13] Looking at specific European cases of the nineteenth century, Gerschenkron concluded that the later the onset of industrialization, the larger scale and more technologically advanced its efforts needed to be. As a result, later industrialization needed financing from successively larger and more formal sources in order to accommodate larger-scale capital bases. Personally based and internally generated financing gave way to commercial banks with short time horizons, then to universal banks for longer-term investment and to the State. Although subject to subsequent challenge, Gerschenkron's research pointed to the inextricable connection between the private and public sectors of the economy that banking embodies.

Cameron and his collaborators subsequently examined the interactions between the formation of banking systems and industrial development in economies with diverse institutional settings and economic structures.[14] Many other authors have also examined the ability of banking to aid or impede early industrial development.[15] Differences in structure between commercial banking (banks funded with deposits and committed to extending only short-term credit in support of commercial transactions) and universal banking (with long-term funding that allows the bank to make long-term and equity investments) has received much attention in trying to explain different outcomes experienced by various countries.[16] Recent research has questioned whether differences in organizational structure translated into important practical differences in outcome.[17] In Europe, commercial bankers easily renewed short-term credit, converting short-term instruments to long-term financing, and universal banks generally extended the majority of their credit in short-term instruments. Institutional environment and the manners in which markets functioned may hold additional valuable keys to understanding the importance of banking.

In addition to connecting markets among different economic sectors, researchers have considered the ability of banking to create linkages between geographic regions, and in doing so to consolidate economies of increasing size. This line of research asks the question: How do small and localized market areas integrate to become large, seamless markets? Whether because of its size or data availability, most of the research on regional integration focuses on the United States. It considers the roles of banks and credit in the integration of the early economic centers in the Northeast with the expanding frontier of the mid-nineteenth century, the post-bellum South, the industrializing North, the West, and the Pacific Northwest.[18] Although it also arrives at diverse explanations, this body of historiography points to the importance of converging interest rates for bank credit among regions, regulation, transactions efficiency, and information in money-market formation. The underutilized intellectual attraction of this line of inquiry is its contribution to understanding the conjunction between the formation of economic markets and nations.

Extending the questions of finance and banking to other economies, the discipline of development economics has provided both theoretical and empirical work toward understanding the contemporary relationship between finance and economic development.[19] Early research by development economists focused on the allocative function, decreased transactions costs and increased transactional efficiency that banking provided for other economic agents.[20] Goldsmith and, more recently, King and Levine[21] found statistically significant relationships between the size of banking systems and the growth of per capita income. These findings are empirically important, but they shed little light on the causal relationships that explain them. Recent work on institutions and economic development has begun to address some of these issues in manners that have interesting historical application.[22] The research arising from both history and development theory points to an important, if amorphous, relationship between a dynamic banking system and overall economic well-being.

Debates about the historical role of banking have focused on developed economies that achieved sustained industrial growth prior to the middle of the twentieth century. Notably absent from this work are the experiences of underdeveloped economies: those that failed to achieve self-sustained growth before the middle of the twentieth century. The literature on banking and financial history in Latin America has traditionally engaged a different set of topics than those of interest here. As expected, given its visibility, the role of international capital investment has received much attention, and Brazil has been prominently represented in this work.[23] Monetary histories of nearly all countries examine the development of money supply and the formation of central banks; many follow the classic model provided by Friedman and Schwartz for the United States.[24] Business history of Latin American banking, with a small but growing literature, has focused on the politics of banking and social group formation as well as histories of specific organizations.[25] The interplay between finance and the institutional dynamics affecting structural economic change is only beginning to receive attention.[26] All of these strands of existing research on Latin American banking and the experiences of Latin American economies with financial instability, the formation of banking systems, and private-sector development through the twentieth century suggest the broad applicability of findings in the Brazilian case.

If we are to understand the importance of financial systems, the experiences of underdeveloped or late developing countries need deeper consideration.[27] Brazil offers an important, interesting, and rich opportunity to extend our insight on these issues. Exploration of these dynamics with respect to Brazilian experience is important for understanding a country that has emerged as one of the most rapidly growing and complex economies of the late twentieth century. Beyond their importance to Brazil, these issues help to illuminate the historical roots of underdevelopment and development.

BRAZILIAN BANKING AND DEVELOPMENT

Questions about the nature of development and economic aspects of state formation are particularly trenchant for the Brazilian First Republic. Structural change and modernity increasingly impinged on all aspects of economic, political, social, and cultural organization. The structural changes wrought by banking occurred in conjunction with the simultaneous dynamics of industrialization, urbanization, immigration, and the development of a middle class. All generated fundamentally new organizing principles for Brazilian society. Changes in social structure and relations among groups required new financing mechanisms in order to support growth and participation within the formal economy. In another realm of activity, the newly restructured State used banking to enhance its credibility and economic role, in its efforts to establish legitimacy as a governing authority. It needed organizational and financial support for such endeavors as constructing the physical infrastructure of railroads, urban water, sanitation and transport facilities, and electric networks. Accommodating special interests also required new financial networks, as the example of price-support programs for coffee demonstrated. More than representing one type of modernizing force, banking both reflected and shaped structural change throughout Brazilian society, politics, and economy. Its roles in market formation, in providing financial support for entrepreneurial innovation, and in intermediating between investors and entrepreneurs and between the public and private sectors were the means by which banking attained its pivotal position during the First Republic.

Existing research on Brazilian financial history concentrates on the importance of the global coffee commerce and the burden of international debt on national government.[28] In contrast to the attention lavished on the export sectors and their complex integration into the international economy, domestic market formation remains unexplored. A general appreciation of the interrelationships among the coffee sector, global capital flows, the State, and the domestic private-sector economy does not extend to an understanding of the specific mechanisms by which those interrelationships functioned. Traditional Brazilian historiography portrays the economy as comprised of weakly connected autonomous regions, and it describes the State as economically liberal and noninterventionist prior to the mid-twentieth century.[29] Historians and economists have recently rethought the economic role of the State in the First Republic. Recent work questions the presumption of a weak federal government and strong liberal currents. These avenues of research suggest that the State's immediate financial needs often dictated monetary, financial, and industrial policies, in order to accommodate debt service and infrastructure investment obligations in the absence of effective powers to access other resources.[30]

Further, regional economic autonomy had effects that were equal to, if less studied than, those of the hierarchical system of local oligarchies hindering political cohesion.[31] Some argue that the scarcity of exchange between regions entrenched small markets and slowed economic growth.[32] The difficulties of forging a national polity from regionally autonomous groups riddled Brazil in the nineteenth and early twentieth centuries. By looking at the national consolidation of factionalized economic activity, this project contributes to our understanding of how and why effective "nationality" took form.

This book finds that the emergence of Brazil's modern banking system during the first three decades of the twentieth century produced a system that worked efficiently, rationally, and productively. For this to happen, a wide array of activities needed to occur that, together, resulted in the formation of markets. The most important developments included evolution of property rights, corporate structures, and management practices; responsiveness to supply and demand; technological adaptation and the depersonalization of access to economic resources. As in other endeavors of fundamental change, these transitions were not easy, linear, or even complete.

Developments in banking did not have the long-term results of equalizing conditions across economic sectors or regions, as existing theory and historiography from other settings anticipate. The political economy of banking at the national and regional levels, and preexisting patterns of production and wealth, seem to account for these differences of outcome. The experience of the banking system during this period both reinforced incipient patterns of concentration and presaged the mechanisms that allowed the State to emerge as a strong agent in centralizing the economy during subsequent years. As a result, this study finds that the Brazilian banking system forming at the beginning of the twentieth century was dynamic and progressive; but it also suggests that banking simultaneously served to concentrate rather than diversify wealth among individuals.

The analysis relies on a wide range of quantitative and qualitative data. In a study such as this one, quantification offers substantial advantage. Banking exercises its influence through the cumulative effects of a multiplicity of undramatic actions and decisions, large and small. Systematizing information across agents (whether individuals or organizations) is fundamentally democratizing; it recognizes and gives weight to each agent in proportion to its participation. Quantification allows its practitioner to aggregate the activities of many actors in meaningful ways and to analyze *systems.* Consideration of any given agent's actions can be assessed relative to the standard for the system. Specific examples that may be atypical become evident and the cumulative importance of many actions comes to light, in preference to dramatic events of indeterminate long-run importance. Descriptive and analytic uses of data provide very succinct ways of communicating the issues that give banking its significance. That said, the text concentrates on narrative and interpretation. Detailed discussion of the data and their treatment are relegated to the Data Appendix, to the extent possible. The tables and figures in the text illustrate specific points; the Data Appendix tables contain general descriptive data and are referenced in the text, as appropriate.

The most important quantitative sources of information are the financial statements (semiannual balance sheets and income statements) of the domestic and foreign banks operating in Brazil during the period and data on federal debt yields. These data allow for assessments of what banks were doing during the First Republic, their importance for national economic development, and the effects of federal monetary policy. The firm-level financial data for banks begin in 1906. Prior to the restructuring of the banking system in that year, bank financial data were sufficiently dissimilar that aggregation would be misleading. Archival holdings from the major Brazilian and British banks, the financial press, government documents, and a wide array of contemporary economic and financial tracts provide additional information. These materials illustrate case studies and provide rich insight on the political economy and on the motivations of the actors of the period.

A few words are necessary about the concept of agency and the historical actors of this book. With respect to banking, this study involves three levels of agents engaged in its activities. First, individual banks undertook actions in the conduct of their businesses. Second, the collective actions of banks, in response to specific circumstances or conditions, produced generalized results that had widespread effect beyond those possible by individual organizations. Third, the banking system, comprised of bank regulators and political interests as well as banks, at times acted or responded to circumstances cohesively in manners that were specific to the dynamics of banking, rather than to the actions of individual actors. These units are kept distinct in the narrative by referring, as appropriate, to banks by name, or to "banks" and banking collectively or to the banking system.

Similarly, especially in Chapter 3, this book considers the State as an agent with independent interests and actions. While political and economic interests coalesce to bring its representatives into governing positions, the State also has interests that distinguish it from, and sometimes put it in competition with, its constituent interests. This book pays close attention to the difference between specific interests acting through the State and the State as an agent with its own agenda. It assumes that politicians represent their constituencies. However, once a politician becomes a governor, s/he acquires a powerful new constituent, the State, with interests that require satisfaction. Two characteristics of all States serve to demonstrate this point. In incurring debt, States take on the obligation to repay their borrowings. Changes of political regime do not mitigate prior debt or the need for revenues to meet their obligations. States do not abrogate these obligations lightly. States also develop professional bureaucracies of technicians and managers with interests in maintaining administrative structure, without regard to changes of political regime.

Finally, this project emphasizes the collective and systemic logic of economic (as well as political and social) dynamics to explain the development and importance of the banking system. Individual historical actors undertake specific actions. They do not, however, have exclusive identification with single interests. The actions and beliefs of individuals reflect the competing demands of their interests as consumers, producers, entrepreneurs, ideologues, exporters, importers, representatives of family history, and idiosyncratic personalities. Their multiple interests mitigate and belie an over-personalization of processes that are systemic in nature. Therefore, in order to understand the causality of actions, the narrative attempts to find a comfortable, but appropriate, balance between individual actors and the processes that they undertake.

The chapters of this book are organized thematically, rather than chronologically, in order to maintain the clarity of its topics and to use its data most effectively. After this introduction of the study's theoretical context, six chapters make the book's arguments. The second chapter establishes the environment within which banking developed. This overview situates the banking system within the economic and political setting of the Brazilian First Republic. The remainder of the book focuses on the roles of banking.

Chapter 3 delineates the manner in which the federal government employed banking as an important tool for constructing mechanisms of governance. In doing so, the chapter considers monetary policy and its effects on the emerging system of public- and private-sector banks. Focusing on the actions of interest groups pursuing their desired outcomes, the chapter demonstrates that the State constructed a banking system of national scope in response to its monetary and financial needs. Monetary actions were important tools for the State in its attempts to establish governing authority and its role within the economy while it simultaneously managed (or attempted to manage) its participation in global capital markets. The chapter develops the scenario by which the Banco do Brasil became important for the State in constructing its domestic economic role. A relatively safe and responsive banking system allowed the State greater flexibility in making policy choices of accessing international or domestic markets for capital. Although the Federal Treasury made sophisticated decisions about the trade-offs required by domestic and foreign capital, the chapter also finds that the cumulative effects of monetary policy ultimately limited the State's opportunities in international capital markets. In making these arguments, the chapter challenges existing understanding of economic policy by positing greater agency and independence than is normally recognized on the part of Brazil's Treasury relative to international investors.

Banks are the focus of Chapters 4 through 6. Chapter 4 considers the business of banking, its early failure and then the successful reorganization of banking during the First Republic. Rampant monetary and banking expansion in 1889-90 marked the beginning of the Republic and led to a spectacular financial crash in 1891-92. This experience, known as the Encilhamento, constituted an important financial disruption that ultimately led to a restrictive international debt renegotiation and widespread banking failure. Growth conditions did not return for more than a decade. Despite the massive financial failures that the State and the banking system suffered, both private and public actors incorporated the lessons of these years into subsequent policy and business activity. Its restructuring in 1906 marks the successful emergence of the modern banking system. The chapter identifies the successful rechartering of the Banco do Brasil as the change that propelled a revitalized banking system. It also examines the nature of private-sector banking. The businesses of private-sector foreign and domestic banks reflected the evolution of production and markets within Brazil. Using financial ratios to assess the types of business conducted by banks, the chapter explores the hypothesis that, both individually and as a system, banks conducted businesses that demonstrated a logic similar to banking businesses in many other economies. Understanding the nature and composition of the banking business provides a new perspective on the "golden years" in the middle of the Republic.

Chapter 5 establishes the connections between banking and the private productive sectors. Examinations of the banks and bankers who became active during the Republic and statistical evidence converge to demonstrate that financial intermediation took effective, if circuitous, routes. Although its formal business transactions were concentrated most heavily in extending short-term commercial credit (often in the coffee trade), the influence of banking was most heavily felt in emerging sectors of the economy, such as industry and urban real estate development. This finding highlights the multidirectional causality of the influences between economic and banking development. Despite the dynamic intersectoral relationships that supported growth and development, the chapter also recognizes that banking remained small relative to the size of the Brazilian economy. The remaining chapters explore the question of why a dynamic, successful, and rapidly growing banking system in the private sector would not ultimately result in a system that could sustain its dynamism to achieve the scale and scope that would magnify its transforming effects on the economy.

Chapter 6 focuses on institutional limitations to banking. It begins by establishing a framework for understanding institutional structures and property rights with respect to banking. Using this framework, the chapter delineates the comprehensive efforts by which bankers attempted to minimize the risks imposed by their institutional constraints. Management and business practices evolved as banks learned to balance their risks against their profits. Banks limited their businesses to borrowers and forms of credit that they considered safe. However, Brazilian business and legal structures compounded the risks of loss by insufficiently defining property rights. This chapter examines bankers' abilities to define and protect their claims to property (in the form of intangible financial assets) in cases of credit defaults. It highlights the unresolved constraint that the prevailing treatment of property rights imposed.

Chapter 7 returns the focus to the political economy and the establishment of effective governing bodies in order to explore another important aspect of the constraints on banking. State governments regulated banks (with the exception of the Banco do Brasil). This chapter explores the conflicts and tensions that state-level banking presented for a system of national scope. Regulation and politics at the level of individual states reflected both the federal structure of government and the geographically defined nature of banks' early markets. In contrast, both the increasing interrelations of regional economies and the national network of banking infrastructure that the Treasury and the Banco do Brasil constructed in order to facilitate national monetary policy supported the evolution of a banking system of national scope. The inherent conflict in this situation became evident in the 1920s, when state governments began to participate in the ownership and management of banks. State-owned organizations increased the presence of banking facilities in regional economies. They established mechanisms by which states effectively implemented monetary policies that could compete with and offset federal policy. State government banking had profound impact on economic fluctuations of the 1920s and on the structures of governance at the state and national level.

The chapters that engage topics of political economy, Chapters 3 and 7, bracket the chapters on banking and economic development in the private sector. This organization reflects important outcomes of the project. The confluence of the effects of banking in the public and private sectors contributed significantly to the competition between federal and state economic authority. It also reflected the ambiguities of defining the public and private realms in Brazilian social organization.

The concluding chapter serves two purposes. First, it returns to the book's organizing themes. Pulling together the political economy arguments with respect to Brazilian participation in global capital markets and with respect to the domestic competition between states and State, the conclusion highlights the role of banking in attempts to legitimize governing institutions. It also brings together the themes of insufficiently defined property rights for the private sector and the ability of government bodies to establish rights to capture resources, i.e., to allocate property to itself. By linking these themes in a chronological format, the conclusion illuminates the underlying constraints of Brazilian banking that prevented its successes in the First Republic from generating the expansive and distributive effects that theory and other countries' experience suggest would have been possible. The second purpose of the conclusion is to consider briefly the influence of the experiences of the First Republic on subsequent Brazilian economic development. The banking system's development during the First Republic provided both a precedent for the subsequent economic role of the State and the financial infrastructure for constructing that role within an industrializing economy. These findings highlight an experience that conforms with historiographic and theoretical expectations, while they simultaneously generated a fundamentally different outcome for the Brazilian economy.

The Brazilian experience adds new insight to understanding the relationships between banking and broader issues of development. Banking history of the First Republic is an indispensable starting point for understanding Brazil's experiences with extreme financial fluctuation through the twentieth century, the depth of the public sector's role in the economy, and the difficulties of forging an economy of national scope.

Chapter 2

The Setting: Ushering in the Republic and the Twentieth Century

The First Republic (1889-1930) encompassed critical years for establishing the nature of the Brazilian political and economic systems for the twentieth century. Brazilian slavery ended in May 1888 and a republican government replaced the monarchy eighteen months later in November 1889. Historians often typify these two changes to Brazilian life as the roots of fundamental transition.[1] Change in the form of government from monarchy to republic was the most obvious political transformation of these years. Its implementation was slow and painstaking. As late as 1924, financial advisers to British lenders found that "Brazil is not yet a political unit."[2] The importance of the political transition lay in the long struggle that it ignited to establish new forms and practices of governance. Building the institutions of republican government reflected, and contributed to, wider change throughout all aspects of Brazilian life. Competing interests continually struggled to gain representation and benefit from the reconstituted State at the same time that the State struggled to establish new forms of governance. Simultaneously with political transition, Brazilians attempted to convert their expectations of rapid economic growth into sustained reality. The effort proved more difficult than anticipated. Banking emerged during the First Republic as one important new institution that aided in establishing new forms of governance and structural economic change. In doing so, banking also became an essential means of connecting the public and private sectors. This chapter establishes the political and economic environment and the historical context from which modern banking developed.

THE NINETEENTH CENTURY

The economic setting from which the First Republic arose defined many of its possibilities. Brazil had won the commodity lottery[3]; producing primary goods for export was the most notable wealth-generating activity of the economy prior to the second half of the twentieth century. From the earliest years of European settlement, primary commodities had tightly integrated the most visible portion of the Brazilian economy into the international markets for goods and finance. Cycles of intense production of brazilwood dyes, sugar, gold, cotton, cacao, and other commodities created wealth for a few Brazilians during the first four centuries of European settlement—and sustained the hopes of many.[4] By the end of the nineteenth century, coffee formed the core of Brazilian participation in international trading systems, and coffee production expanded significantly at the same time as the Republic began.[5]

In the minds of many Brazilians, the monarchy symbolized the intense export-agriculture regime that had long defined their social and personal relationships. Oligarchic political networks paralleled patriarchal extended families in establishing hierarchical relations among individuals, within social groups, and throughout the political system.[6] In traditional interpretations of Brazilian history, these systems defined the privileges, responsibilities, and obligations accorded to those occupying each rung of their hierarchical ladders. Slaves and plantation owners occupied the extreme positions. But hierarchies also extended to the organization of work and privilege between household and field labor; overseer, artisan, and worker; slave and freedman; male and female; adult and child. Outside of the household setting, hierarchies governed relationships between planter and merchant; landowner and tenant; priest and layperson; administrator, judge, tax collector, and private individual; judge, victim, and criminal; elected official and voter; national, provincial, and municipal government.[7] While hierarchies connoted privilege and prestige, their maintenance required personal loyalties, negotiation, contestation, coercion, bribery, and occasional violence.

Evidence and logic suggest many challenges to this stylized social system. The large plantation was the ideal of planters—and of many historians—more than it was the norm.[8] The unending requirements to maintain oligarchies offer reasons to question their strength. Nevertheless, kernels of reality remain in the paradigm of the hierarchically functioning society. A few large-scale planters, merchants, and bureaucrats did build vast networks of personal, political, and economic influence.[9] Economic and political power was narrowly held. If hierarchical arrangements were less controlling than much research would have us believe, the alternative was not a wide distribution of wealth, power, and participation in political and economic processes. Rather, viewed from the perspective of later generations, the reality of Brazilian life at the end of the nineteenth century was widely distributed deprivation, hardship, and only a very slowly spreading sense of participation in an articulated political system. From a contemporary perspective, some may have welcomed the vagaries of impersonal market dynamics that economic change promised, as contrasted with the realities of slavery and its highly personalized mechanisms of exchange.

Economic historians have identified the nineteenth century as the period during which Brazil, and other Latin American economies, fell behind in comparison with the material well-being of North Atlantic economies.[10] Some attribute economic malaise to bad government policy.[11] Others find that an economy of increasingly national scope did not coalesce. The conclusion of this trajectory of research is that geographically isolated and small domestic consumer markets both reinforced and were reinforced by widespread poverty.[12] Institutional arrangements and slow responsiveness of the nation's organizing institutions provide yet other explanations for falling behind.[13]

THE STATE

The First Republic was a period of change in nearly every social endeavor for Brazilians. The overriding concerns of transition important to this study are state-building and structural economic change. Contemporaries saw these activities as central to defining the Brazilian nation. The political forces constructing an effective national government offer the most traditional perspective for assessing the strength of the State. The struggle to establish the State was always very important to the conduct of public life in Brazil during the First Republic as well as, more narrowly, to the development of banking. Historians of Brazil have considered the question of state formation in several manifestations beyond the cohesiveness of a national government. But they have not developed a consensus on the elements or extent of nationality and statehood. Where some analysts see cohesion, others see fragmentation.[14]

The political regime of the Republic was one of the most obvious efforts to construct new institutions,[15] as well as one of the most important means for promulgating change throughout all endeavors. The difficulties of forging a national unit from regionally autonomous groups permeated nineteenth- and early twentieth-century Brazil. The contradictory tendencies of simultaneously centralized and locally defined power structures generated continuous conflict and shaped the emerging Brazilian system of government.[16] Regional political and administrative autonomy in governance resulted in a hierarchical system of local oligarchies that hindered national cohesion.[17] Many historians of the Republic conclude that the State was weak to the point of being ineffectual.[18] Certainly, if one fundamental indication of an effective State is the transfer of political power by constitutional means, the introduction and demise of the Republic by military-supported coups and continual overthrow attempts in the intervening years support that assessment. Other analysts have shifted their focus from a static conclusion to the ongoing efforts to construct the State through political means.[19] One criterion has not received the attention it merits in determining whether an effective Brazilian State existed. Political actors and interest groups continually sought to gain political and bureaucratic influence within the apparatus of the national government. These competitions took the forms of policy debates, legislative and electoral jockeying of political parties for position in government, violent uprising, and military rebellion.[20] Presumably, those choosing to undertake such struggles expected that they had reason to gain influence within a national government.

The constitution of 1891 codified the political and administrative organization of the federal government. It also defined the allocation of powers between federal and state governments. A *política dos governos* implemented in the mid-1890s furthered the practical limits in the distribution of governance between State and states.[21] Within the federal government, a fairly centralized structure concentrated power in the presidency. The legislative branch, or Chamber of Deputies, elected the president. The Chamber provided a forum for debate and negotiation of policies.[22] Executive policy had to find ways to accommodate strong opposition views in the Chamber of Deputies, but the powers of the presidency also often were able to circumvent challenges. At the same time, the constitution staked out important areas of state autonomy. These included abilities to impose export taxes and negotiate the terms of interstate commerce, as well as the rights to contract foreign loans and to organize state-level militias.

National political organization of the First Republic did not overcome regional divides. State-level politics and economies demonstrated distinctive characteristics. Political parties remained identified by their state of origin, and state-level political elites were well defined.[23] Interests of different states combined or competed on specific issues, as the need arose.[24] Interstate political alliances were ephemeral in nature and limited to specific issues. They did not lead to lasting national political alliances. One effect of the power-sharing arrangements was to enhance the concentration of political and economic power within the already-dominant states, since they could both afford and organize to exercise these rights. The strength of state political power imposed severe constraints on the federal executive's ability to forge national policy. As one analyst has trenchantly summarized, "the State preceded the nation, creating a paradox, indecipherable at first view, of two contradictory tendencies in the structure of political life, exaggerated centralism and local clientelism [*cacicazgo*]."[25]

Some historians focus on the dominance of the state of São Paulo in this system.[26] Regional political contentions were particularly strong between the two economically dominant states, São Paulo and Minas Gerais. A system of alternating the federal presidency that became known as *café com leite* (or as one analyst revised it to recognize the profound competition: *café contra leite*[27]) emerged from their competition. By this arrangement, control of the national government alternated between political leaders of São Paulo and Minas Gerais, except when irreconcilable contention offered occasional opportunities for other regional representation. This characterization, while a reasonable description of political activity, includes an embedded inconsistency: it relies on an underlying assumption of a weak State, simultaneously with a State worthwhile of political contention among local elites. Even if the realities of political maneuvering and negotiation were such that some historians have ameliorated the interpretation of the strong defining axis of governance at the level of individual states,[28] its conceptual hold on contemporaries was strong.

Nevertheless, a consolidated State with effective governing authority over the geographic territory of Brazil did make progress during the Republic, even if slowly and in an uneven fashion. States' rights had constraints that mitigated their effectiveness. For example, while states contracted foreign loans, international lenders were only willing to issue such loans when they also had repayment guarantees from the Federal Treasury.[29] Also, states raised local militias, but the development of a cohesive national military was one of the important features of the Republic.[30] As a last resort, the federal government had intervention rights to install a state president (governor) to circumvent rebellion. Analysts have found that states' autonomy from the federal political system eroded during the course of the Republic.[31] Further, interrelated studies by Wirth, Levine, and Love find substantive change in the nature of political organization that served to cohere into a single system, if not into a commonly agreed set of interests.[32] Those active in organized politics were geographically mobile across state boundaries. With time, mobility of politicians and political managers enhanced a common awareness of political processes and issues despite the persistence of state-level political parties. Political operatives and activities became increasingly professionalized and less personal through the course of the Republic. These changes in political operation constituted important steps toward the establishment of depersonalized governing institutions and state-building.

Without overemphasizing the strength of the State, the findings of political competition for the benefits available from a national government, constitutionally defined federal powers, and a slowly cohering national political system suggest that the State established reasonable credibility for its authority during these years. Nevertheless, the difficulty of the endeavor persisted through the Republic.

ECONOMIC DEVELOPMENT DURING THE FIRST REPUBLIC

Effective statehood extended to concerns well beyond politics and the strength of a national government. Fundamental restructuring of the economy was another crucial aspect of the transformation of Brazil at the end of the nineteenth century.[33] Industrialization, the vast expansion of coffee production, international immigration, migration to cities, and the extension of physical infrastructure required that formal markets increasingly govern the material aspects of Brazilian life. Factors indicating a modern and national economy gained prominence during these years. Brazilians increasingly lived in cities, worked in factories and offices, purchased factory-produced food and clothes, went to school, and engaged in many other activities that came to connote the modern.[34] Even so, the importance of coffee to the economy continued throughout the Republic. From 1889 to 1930, while Europeans and North Americans became addicted and demanded ever-increasing amounts of the stimulant, Brazil produced 71 percent of the world's coffee.[35] Although a traditional agricultural business venture, the scope of coffee operations increased and its management professionalized; even coffee became modern.[36] The industrial base and formal domestic markets that used money to orchestrate the exchange of goods and services took greater hold on the daily lives of Brazilians. The State began to articulate more specifically its role in an economy that became increasingly national in scope. As in the political sphere, these changes did not emerge quickly, easily, or even completely.[37] Nevertheless, they required new institutions and organizations—new ways of conducting everyday life.

Banking was important to both political and economic interests, but its influence was not unique. Other activities of synergistic economic and political development during the First Republic that have received more attention from researchers include coffee price-support programs and the construction of infrastructure, physical (railroads, shipping, electrification) and social (such as public health and education).[38] The political and economic dynamics affecting the trajectories of these activities grew out of their histories during the Empire.

During the last years of the Empire and the early years of the Republic, economic expectations changed dramatically—at least in selected regions. In particular, São Paulo was poised for the expansion of its coffee frontier, and economic potential appeared strong in Rio Grande do Sul and Minas Gerais. (See map; regional economies are a topic of Chapter 7.) Paulista coffee planters believed the only thing holding them back was the need for additional labor, and they relied upon European migration to solve that problem.[39] Indeed, between 1881 and 1942, 4.2 million people migrated to Brazil; they accounted for a minimum of 15 percent of the total population increase during these years.[40] The concentration of immigrants from 1880 to 1920 in São Paulo and Rio Grande do Sul[41] was perhaps the strongest testament to economic expectations for those states. The expansion of the railroad network was another sign that Brazilians expected to transport an increasing volume of goods.[42] Businessmen benefiting from modernization convinced public authorities to share their costs, as subsidies from both national and provincial/state authorities demonstrated the blatant conjunction of political and economic power.[43] The exuberance of these years ignited ambitions for rapid industrialization.[44] For many, the desire to capitalize on agricultural and industrial potential provided much of the motivation to modernize the economy. These expectations carried many Brazilians through the First Republic.[45]

Using the estimated trend of per capita income as a simplified assessment of the trajectory of economic well-being suggests a dichotomized experience for Brazilians during the early twentieth century. In the economically and politically dominant states of São Paulo, Minas Gerais, and Rio Grande do Sul, real (price-adjusted) per capita income increased at an average annual rate of 2.5 percent per year for the thirty-three years from 1898 to 1930. Elsewhere, real per capita income was stagnant or declining slowly (calculated at an average annual decline of 0.3 percent, in Table A.9. These estimates are necessarily very approximate, but they are in line with the equally rough findings of others). Many of the findings with respect to regional banking and economic development in this book will support the implication of these data that success begot success. Overall, real Brazilian per capita income increased at the average rate of 1.4 percent per year. Simply stated, this rate was not sufficiently high or widely distributed to change the reality of deep-seated poverty for most Brazilians.[46] For economic history, the importance of the period was the effort to implement the activities and institutions to effect structural change, rather than the successful remedy of widespread poverty.

The concerns of state-building and economic development converged as both the State and private economic agents paid attention to the consolidation of an economy of national scope. An integrated national market offered advantages of scale and scope to both producers and governors. The confluence of private- and public-sector interests in the efforts to consolidate a national economy resulted in complex relationships. The monetary policy of the federal government and agricultural exports, especially coffee and rubber, continued to receive more attention in public policy than did manufacturing or domestic agriculture.[47] Coffee price-support (valorization) programs were the most visible manifestation of public-sector support of agricultural exports. São Paulo implemented the first coffee price-support program in 1906.[48] Subsequent programs began in 1917 and 1921, with increasing levels of support from the public sector at federal and state levels. Policies and institutions to offset their monetary effects accompanied each of the valorization programs.[49] Contention among state governments within the political system, and the difficulties of coalition building, prevented Brazilians from quickly and effectively maximizing their dominance in the international coffee market.[50] While coffee price supports are well studied (and often referred to as the world's first successful international commodity price-control program), the government also attempted to influence rubber prices.[51] Supporting the rubber commerce proved unsuccessful and expensive; but it confirmed the Brazilian government's interest in protecting its producers' positions in international markets.

Absent the ability to marshal direct subsidies similar to those supporting agricultural exports, monetary policy provided an alternative venue through which the economic sectors concerned with domestic markets pursued public-sector support. Manufacturing and industrialization received little direct or sustained support from the public sector during the First Republic.[52] Tax policy encouraged domestic manufacture through its reliance on trade tariffs, the main source of government revenue.[53] In addition, subsidies and capital for related physical infrastructure (railroads, ports, housing, electrification, etc.) became widespread.[54] More important, domestic demand and capital accumulation supported sufficient manufacturing for industrial development to be sustained in Brazil during the First Republic.[55] The value of the mil-réis, the target of monetary policy, was the factor most affecting the viability of industrial development prior to World War I.[56] As we shall see in Chapter 3, specific monetary policies supporting industry tended to be ineffectual and short-lived. They only worked if they were carefully constructed to balance the well-being of international trade interests.

A fundamental shift occurred in the Brazilian economy in the mid-1910s, associated with the dislocation of international economic relations of World War I. Economic exigencies of the war forced international financial centers away from the open flows of goods and capital. Abandoning the gold standard to maintain currency values was the most dramatic manifestation of this change. Peripheral economies, such as Brazil, suffered severe disruption due to the withdrawal of the core countries from their commitments to openness.[57] For Brazil, this disruption was the impetus to develop self-contained domestic markets in manufactured goods. In doing so, the national reach of markets attained heightened importance, relative to the more limited possibilities of localized networks of exchange.

Economic historiography has a peculiarly ahistorical aspect in its acceptance of industrialization as a beneficial goal for Brazil. Contemporaries (as before and since) rigorously questioned this assessment. Vociferous ideological and policy debates opposed the benefits of diversification of the country's economic base through industrialization, implicitly subsidized by monetary policy, with those of maximizing wealth through the exploitation of its existing comparative advantage in primary commodities such as coffee. Support for developing industrial capacity, from either the public or private sector, was not automatic,[58] though it increased with time. Throughout the period, specific methods of wealth maximization and the role of the State in the economic sphere framed the terms of the economic and financial debates. The conflicts surrounding monetary policy that contributed to shaping early republican forms of governance actively engaged the debate about the desirability of industrialization. Urban development, labor, immigration, and trade protection provided additional arenas for contesting the merits of industrialization. Even so, contemporaries committed to industrial development and diversification clearly appreciated the need for both general prosperity and enhanced banking capability to support their goals.[59]

Despite sluggish overall economic growth and strong financial and monetary fluctuations, the 1920s were years of industrialization and economic diversification. The volume and diversity of factory-produced goods increased notably. Although the relative size of the industrial sector remained small, Brazil was basically self-sufficient in the manufacture of consumer goods and many intermediate industrial products by the end of the 1920s.[60] Conscious import substitution policies and the growth of domestic markets for manufactured goods slowly began to support industrialization after World War I.[61] During the 1920s, the interplay between economic sectors intensified. Government deficits, import requirements (for consumption and capital formation), domestic manufacturing expansion, and continuing demands for coffee price supports competed for economic and financial resources. The direct policy tools at the disposal of the government to encourage private-sector growth were coffee price supports, development of physical infrastructure, and monetary management. Economic priorities during the Republic required that new modes of finance accommodate change.

BANKING

Dynamism and evolution in financial activities broadly paralleled the course of economic change. Throughout the nineteenth century, borrowers obtained domestic credit through personal connections.[62] Investments requiring finance in amounts larger than entrepreneurs could raise within their personal networks were opportunities foregone. Banks did not begin to serve private interests until the last third of the nineteenth century. The first attempts of Brazilian banking in the mid-nineteenth century were in Rio de Janeiro (the Federal District, during the First Republic), reflecting its early position as the commercial and government center, prior to the emergence of São Paulo. Three separate charterings of organizations called the Banco do Brasil facilitated the financial transactions of the monarchy and initiated the State's first attempts to use monetary policy to finance itself.[63] The Banco do Brasil contributed to early inflation and monetary insecurity more than to stable state finances.[64]

Private domestic banks had even less success. The first such endeavors started in the middle of the nineteenth century. Most of the earliest private banks concentrated their business in note-issuance and holding government bonds, activities not directly tied to private-sector growth. None had extended lives.[65] The most serious attempt to provide large-scale private domestic finance during the nineteenth century was the Visconde de Mauá's merchant bank, which had opened in 1854 as an extension of his trading house.[66] Overextended with unprofitable investments and without much flexibility in its ability to raise funds, the bank failed in 1875 and Mauá declared personal bankruptcy.[67]

British banks established their presence in Brazil from the 1860s, serving the business interests of their compatriots. The first British bank, the Bank of London and Brazil, opened in 1863; the Bank of London and the River Plate and the British Bank of Brazil opened thereafter. Until the fourth Banco do Brasil had demonstrated its viability as a national bank in the early twentieth century, British banks offered one of the strongest geographic linkages of financial mechanisms. They focused their activities on foreign exchange trading and financing the agricultural export trade.[68] These financial arrangements did not challenge the economic and social institutions prevailing in the nineteenth century.

The turbulent political and economic activities associated with the beginning of the Republic had their analog in the financial system. The types of businesses that banks conducted changed substantially during the First Republic. A wide array of banks variously issued notes, speculated and/or invested in corporate securities (equities and bonds), and speculated in foreign exchange; some maintained narrowly defined businesses of short-term credit to finance commercial transactions. By 1905, after the failures of the Encilhamento, narrowly defined organizations with short-term commercial focus prevailed. (Chapters 3 and 4 consider this transformation.) While conservative in their approaches to business, these banks became the first in Brazilian history to survive for sustained periods.

The establishment of more solid financial institutions and practices contributed to the increasing sophistication of monetary policy. In addition to the banking system, a private-sector securities market gradually made it more viable for companies to issue stocks and bonds as a means of accumulating capital. A shift of organizational structure toward the limited-liability joint-ownership corporation was notable during the First Republic.[69] The absence of a secondary market for trading the securities after they had been issued may indicate that the change was one more of form than substance.[70] Nevertheless, underestimating its importance would be dangerous. The effects for establishing institutional structures, depersonalizing finance, and creating specialized markets were similar to the effects found in this study for banking. Indeed, financial development economics might hypothesize that markets for long-term private capital and money in its public and private forms (currency and bank deposits) could be successful in the First Republic because they evolved together.[71]

Monetary policy and banking became active tools of state-building and of economic development during the First Republic. The tensions and complications of both endeavors became integral to the conduct of monetary policy. The division between federal and state monetary responsibilities evolved in an unanticipated manner. The federal Treasury chartered a bank with national powers. The Treasury also licensed foreign banks doing business in Brazil. States chartered domestic banks doing business within their states. The result was an example of the paradoxical coexistence of centralized federal powers and highly effective state-level governance. The interplay of monetary policy between federal and state may have exacerbated regional disparities of wealth, since the larger and wealthier states, especially São Paulo and Minas Gerais, could marshal greater resources to conduct such policies. The ambiguities embedded in the exercise of governing powers at the national and state levels offer an excellent example of the complications of the political process that arose while that exercise was simultaneously defining the republican system of governance, as Chapter 7 demonstrates. The modern Brazilian banking system emerged within this environment.

The banking system of the Brazilian First Republic was usually the conduit for changes in monetary policy; it also was the linchpin between money, public finance, and the private productive sectors. Political and economic elites understood the potential of the banking system to assist their causes through two mechanisms. First, as the agents and storehouses of money, banks transmitted its changing value throughout the economy. Second, as accumulators of deposits and allocators of credit, banks increasingly intermediated the flow of funds across economic sectors and regions. Many Brazilians also saw a banking system as an indicator of being modern—like the developed world to which they aspired. Even Joaquim Murtinho, the Treasury minister of the Republic (1898-1902) perhaps least receptive to banking expansion, believed that credit and banking "undoubtedly had a role of great importance in the transactions of the advanced societies and this importance grows with the development of these societies,"[72] a goal appropriate for Brazilian aspirations. The controversies about banking and money were as diverse as the controversies surrounding all aspects of the transformations shaping the First Republic; they reflected both ideology and personal interest.

The effects of monetary change in the private and public sectors governed the value of money. Monetary shifts marked all of the major economic, and most of the political, turning points of the First Republic. These changes shaped, and increasingly were shaped by, the system of banks serving the public and private sectors. The specific mechanisms, economic dynamics, and political motives that determined the course of banking development, along with their effects on economic structure and the formation of the State, are the focus of the subsequent chapters. This analysis suggests banking as an important confluence of private and public, of politics and economics, and of the traditional and the modern. As such, the development of the banking system played an integral role in shaping the modern Brazilian nation that marked the beginning of the twentieth century. Its participation in the structural changes to modernize the economy and in state-building puts banking at the core of processes by which Brazilians were constructing their society.

Chapter 3

State, Money, and Banking

The role of banking in consolidating the mechanisms of governance during the First Republic through its role in the monetary system is the topic of this chapter. An appreciation of the fluctuations of monetary policy and its underlying politics is essential for understanding the structure of the banking system. This approach gives a political economy interpretation to traditional monetary histories of Brazil, with their focus on money supply and its determinants,[1] in order to highlight the interrelated processes of monetary policy and the emergence of a banking system. It demonstrates that the use of banking derived from efforts to manage the tension between supporting economic growth and ameliorating the Brazilian economy's vulnerability from its heavy exposure in international markets. Using monetary policy as a financing mechanism,[2] the Treasury constructed a banking system of national scope that responded to its needs, leaving consideration of the private sector a secondary priority. Out of these processes, a modern banking system emerged during the First Republic that was strongly concentrated within one institution of national scope. The centralized nature of the national banking system differed from the federal political structure, and often decentralized political and economic processes challenged its character. This banking system increasingly served both the private and public sectors. Nevertheless, its public-sector origins determined its nature and scope through their effects on the size of the banking system and their influence in the allocation of resources. Subsequent chapters address additional components of the role of banking, most importantly, its effects on economic structure (industrialization) and geographic integration of local economies. The use of banks in national monetary policy determined the framework in which these additional activities took place.

Fundamental changes of political regime, such as the shift from monarchical to republican government, often necessitate that new political practices and governing mechanisms emerge in order for the newly restructured State to establish its credibility and authority. Monetary policy is one of the most important political and economic tools available to the State, and it is within the framework of the monetary system that banking develops. The historical and theoretical importance of banking in these practices of state (re)formation has a long acceptance. The financial requirements of early state formation have routinely furthered the transformation of small-scale merchant-based banking into large-scale institutions to influence economic change. State building is an expensive endeavor, entailing such actions as war, security, accommodation of the demands of interest groups, and repression of the demands of opposing groups. Typically, these activities have required that political actors construct financing mechanisms allowing access to a larger pool of resources than previously available.[3] Early economic analyses of banking history demonstrate the importance of the State to the emergence of banking systems; in doing so, they illustrate the importance of State entrepreneurialism.[4]

Recent concepts in the political economy of money provide a theoretical framework for understanding the relationship between financial and state development. As the institution that codifies and enforces property rights, the State can serve the property accumulation goals of its leaders.[5] At the same time, control of the means to accumulate and allocate resources through financial systems constitutes one important demonstration of political power. Further, relationships between State and private agents require redefinition during changes of political regime. Political actors need to establish institutional structures that convince private agents of their permanence and enforceability. One of the most important components of an effective state is its ability to structure a monetary system that enforces exchange transactions among all economic agents under its sovereignty. Classic studies demonstrate the importance of financial systems and the emergence of central banking in this process in Britain and the United States.[6] Understanding the relationship between central banking and state building in Latin America remains at an early stage.[7]

Throughout the First Republic, the State faced a problem that was easy to specify, but that proved nearly impossible to resolve. Without regard to the specific political interests controlling the State apparatus at any given time, demands on State resources exceeded the ability to meet those demands. Competing economic and ideological groups perceived sufficient benefit to controlling the State that they coalesced into political interests, and efforts to construct permanent institutional structures made slow progress. As was commonly the case in other experiences with state formation, the process of economic consolidation was an important component in the Brazilian experience. Not only was political competition for control of government always present, but the ability to structure and manage governing institutions was continually under contention. Consolidating the authority to accumulate resources in order to establish and maintain government was an important early goal to demonstrate the authority of the State. Managing the distribution of resources allowed state builders to accumulate power and wealth, while simultaneously responding to the requirements of their supporting constituents and interest groups.

Meeting these goals was problematic. The State had a very limited ability to raise revenues. Trade tariffs funded from one-fifth to almost two-thirds of expenditures between 1900 and 1930. Basing revenues on tariffs rendered them vulnerable to the fluctuations of international trade. The weakness of the State as a governing authority severely constrained its ability to tax the Brazilian population.[8] An income tax was introduced in 1924; by 1930, income taxes funded less that 3 percent of federal expenditures (Table A.12). At the same time, efforts to consolidate political power and build constituencies required that each political party or coalition that attained political power incurred an expense structure that eluded its control. Federal expenditures in excess of revenues for 30 years out of the 41 years of the First Republic demonstrated the State's inability to balance the demands on it relative to resource constraints (Table A.12). Absent the discipline to control expenditure or the ability to raise revenue, the State borrowed to meet its resource requirements.

Given the difficulties of controlling revenues or expenditures, the most direct means of fiscal management, monetary policy became a means of economic management for political regimes that dynamically mediated competing interests. Because it became an additional arena in which the divergent demands of power formation contended, federal monetary policy was always subject to fervent and highly visible political debate. Viewing monetary policy as a tool of governance demonstrates how it served interest groups in their competition for control of State resources. From the additional perspective of the banking system, monetary history reveals the tight interconnection that helped to determine both the course of monetary policy and the development of mechanisms of governance. These dynamics were instrumental in creating a highly politicized banking system.

This chapter situates the emergence of modern Brazilian banking within the economic imperatives of governance, as viewed through monetary history. Using concepts relevant to the economic dynamics of political economy,[9] it documents the effects of shifting monetary policy on the institutional structures of banking. The following section contextualizes monetary policy and banking within the framework of interest groups. The succeeding section applies this context in a survey of the broad contours of monetary history during the First Republic,[10] to demonstrate the effects of the shifting weight of interest groups on the banking system and to delineate the interrelationship of political economy, money, and banking. At the same time that this approach somewhat modifies our perspective on monetary history, it allows for the development of more coherent understanding of the formation of the banking system than was previously available.

The argument the chapter develops is that, during the course of the Republic, the federal Treasury actively used the tools of financial management available to it in order to manage its precarious economic situation while balancing political interests. These actions provided the monetary framework from which the banking system evolved. Monetary policy changed in response to interest group strength (usually manifested by changes in government), State need, and external circumstance. These factors often operated jointly. Lacking a strong and credible State structure, monetary policy fluctuated often and violently in response to the struggles for political control. The vicissitudes of monetary policy governed the size and many activities of the banking system. In 1905-06 financial reform to put Brazil on the gold standard successfully provided the framework to initiate a modern banking system, with the Treasury determining the issuance of money and regulating the interaction between public and private interests. However, with a prolonged period of monetary policy closing Brazilian financial markets to outside investors and favoring domestic banking growth from the mid-1910s, the ability of banks to benefit from an expansionary monetary system ultimately became a force limiting the range of policy options available to monetary officials.

This perspective explicitly develops an argument rarely articulated in Latin American historiography. The argument is that the State was an entity *sui generis*. The State fell within the control of varying governments, representing changing interests. Simultaneously, the State had interests of its own to accommodate. These interests included meeting its debt obligations, establishing the parameters and tools of governance, and maintaining an increasingly professionalized bureaucracy. Determining whether a governmental action reflected the interests of a political regime's constituency or those of the State, if those interests conflicted, can be critical in under-standing the political economy.

These issues can best be demonstrated through an examination of the major actions of monetary history and policy. The relationships of both the exchange rate and the yield differential with the domestic cost of bor-rowing incurred by the Brazilian and British governments (apólices and consols, the domestic debt issued by the Brazilian and British governments, respectively) are the important variables for understanding the effects of changes in monetary policy. (Figure 3.1, on page 41. See the Data Appen-dix for further discussion of these data. For reference only, Figure 3.1 also shows the differential between the cost of debt to the Brazilian and U.S. government debt from 1919).[11] The British financial market was the core of international finance during most of this period.[12] The comparison of the two governments' domestic interest rates encapsulates the total risk pre-mium that investors attached to lending to the Brazilian government—the differences of their domestic creditworthiness and exchange rate risk. Thus, the differential in the yields on these instruments provides a good benchmark comparison of the cost of borrowing attributable to circum-stances specific to Brazil as distinct from global interest rates. The terms "risk premium" and "interest rate differential" refer to this measure. In this context, the risk premium represents the relative costs of borrowing and creditworthiness of the Brazilian government.

Under normal circumstances, an inverse relationship between the yield differential and the exchange rate (quoted as pence/mil-réis) prevailed. That relationship simply reflected that when Brazilian standing in interna-tional capital markets was favorable, the Treasury incurred a low yield dif-ferential, and its currency was also highly valued, commanding a high exchange rate. The growth and contribution of bank deposits to the money supply demonstrates the evolving role of banking.[13] These are the data invoked in the survey of monetary experience. The growth of the money supply, and its changing composition of currency and bank deposits, communicate the necessary monetary information (Figures 3.2 and 3.3, pages 42 and 43).

MONETARY REGIME AND INTEREST GROUPS

The goals of monetary policy to control prices and manage the State's debt structure competed continually during the First Republic. Debates about monetary policy were concerned with two related (and often conflated) dimensions.[14] The first dimension was the value of the mil-réis[15] and the second was the type of monetary regime that governed State financial activity, i.e., the extent of State commitment to maintain the value of its currency. Monetary policy competition was, ultimately, about the distribution of resources. This section delineates the interests and the economic agents involved. The subsequent section applies this model to the monetary history of Brazil in the First Republic in order to situate the emergence of modern banking within its larger context.

By determining the type of monetary regime that it would follow, the State committed to either maintain a fixed value of the mil-réis (exchange rate) or to allow the mil-réis to fluctuate in value, responding to market conditions.[16] In an "open" economy (with a high proportion of economic exchange conducted in international markets), currency policies strongly influenced price stability. Orthodox monetary goals of stable exchange rates and prices combined with disciplined government expenditures vacillated with those of expansive domestic monetary policy that limited the incentives for long-term investment by foreigners or Brazilians. At the end of the nineteenth and beginning of the twentieth centuries, adherence to a gold standard represented, for many countries, an attempt to balance these concerns. As a small open economy, access to European capital markets and the incremental resources that they made available required the gold standard to convince investors of the intention to maintain the value of capital in Brazil.[17] Establishing a gold exchange standard for their currency committed Brazilian monetary authorities to maintaining the value of the mil-réis relative to gold (and for practical purposes to the pound sterling) at a fixed rate of exchange. To maintain the exchange rate the central monetary authority bought or sold the mil-réis on the open money market, or at times, operated through credit markets by "rediscounting" (purchasing) credit from banks' portfolios.[18] New money could not be created without affecting its value. Therefore, the domestic money supply fluctuated relative to the exchange transactions; the gold standard constrained the money supply and the range of policy initiatives available to federal authorities. The extent of the constraint depended on the level of the exchange rate that the Treasury committed to maintain. The gold standard signaled a commitment to stability that encouraged investment and lending.[19] Whether the gold standard prevailed because of the exchange rate mechanism, its associated fiscal austerity, or simply the belief that it worked,[20] the strength of Brazilian adherence to the gold standard determined its reception in international capital markets. Because of its traditional reliance on international trade and on international credit, continuing access to that capital required that the Brazilian economy "play by the rules of the game."

The alternative strategy of avoiding the gold standard allowed the value of currency to move in response to its domestic supply and demand. This strategy signaled an acceptance of fluctuating value for money (exchange rates and price levels), as well as the value of debt.[21] When money was inconvertible the State did not commit to exchange the mil-réis for foreign currency at a fixed rate. An underlying assumption that, absent a fixed value, the mil-réis would depreciate (i.e., lose value) reflected economic thought of the early twentieth century equating depreciation and inflation.[22] The resulting instability and, in periods of rising prices, the declining value of debt deterred the inflow of foreign investment. As this chapter demonstrates, history supported the expectation that currency and price fluctuations in the First Republic would be in the direction of devalued currency and price inflation. Nevertheless, when not maintaining a commitment to the value of money, floating exchange rates lessened the constraints on money creation. Its proponents also believed that expansive domestic monetary policy encouraged economic modernity from two perspectives. First, financial growth contributed to deepening money markets, allowing money to flow more easily to productive uses.[23] Further, expansive money freed the State to direct resources to uses that market forces may not have supported, and thus to invest in capabilities that shifted productive capacity away from existing comparative advantages and toward new capabilities. In Brazil during the First Republic, this entailed support for constructing industrial capacity and physical infrastructure.

Important considerations mitigated domestic economic debates about monetary policy for the Brazilian State during the Republic. Conditions in international financial markets had a very strong influence on the feasibility of monetary strategies. The chronology of monetary history presented below demonstrates that, under some circumstances, fixed exchange rates were not viable for reasons unrelated to Brazilian actions. At other times, financial markets required a commitment to fixed exchange rates as a condition for investment in Brazil. The rhetoric of expansionary domestic policy also often differed substantially from its practice. The rhetoric supporting monetary expansion emphasized the construction of new productive capacity, to expand and diversify the goods Brazilians made for themselves. It focused on the need to encourage industrialization and economic independence. Its practice supported government expenditure and resulted in inflation.

Monetary regime debates, on the value of the mil-réis and whether its value should be maintained by the federal Treasury or allowed to fluctuate, engaged all participants of the political and economic system.[24] Decisions on the trajectory of monetary policy reflected both economic circumstance and the shifting strength of each interest group. The primary dichotomy of interest groups in this context was between producers of internationally traded goods and producers of domestic goods—tradables and nontradables, respectively.[25] This division crystallized the important concerns motivating the major groups coalescing for the purpose of influencing government policy. The direction of anticipated change of relative prices defined this division. Succinctly summarized: "The depreciation of the currency [from floating exchange rates of inconvertible money] shifted relative prices in favor of the producers of exports and importable products; by the same token, it shifted relative prices against those in the 'untraded' sectors. . . ."[26] Exchange rate dynamics established money as the economic link between the international and domestic sectors.

Producers of goods traded in international markets benefited from a low value of the mil-réis, by virtue of the higher domestic income generated from overseas earnings. The assumption that the absence of a formal commitment to maintain the value of the mil-réis would result in currency depreciation induced support for floating rates among agricultural exporters. This scenario intensified when international prices of traded goods declined. Depreciation served to maintain the incomes of trading groups, when measured in mil-réis.[27] Eichengreen has found, as a generalization, that "[f]armers, who were both debtors and producers of traded goods [agricultural exporters], were usually in the vanguard of those pressing for devaluation. . . ."[28] This benefit from devalued currency was most compelling when international prices for the traded commodity were low. High prices allowed producers of agricultural commodities more flexibility. Throughout the First Republic, the coffee sector was the strongest private-sector interest group. Coffee prices suffered severe and long declines (Table A.10); the fluctuation of coffee prices was an important determinant of monetary policy.[29] As a result, inconvertible currency often benefited the coffee sector. Producers of other agricultural export commodities, such as sugar, rubber, and cacao, also belonged to this monetary interest group, though they exercised less political strength than did the coffee sector.

Industrial interests divided. Import-substituting production benefited from floating rates and inconvertible currency, with its anticipated depreciation, because of the implicit protection provided by increased prices of imported goods. During the First Republic, the State provided no explicit protection to most industrial manufacturing. Import-substituting producers actively favored depreciated currency and low exchange rates to suppress competition and enhance the profitability of their businesses.

Subsequent analysts have concluded that promoting the construction of industrial capacity to reduce their traditional reliance on agricultural commodities in the productive structure could be an effective strategy,[30] though not one that maximized current income. Alternatively, nontradable production included the domestic agricultural sector and manufacturers of goods for the domestic market that were not import substitutes. The latter producers, generally, made simple goods that consumers otherwise would have made for themselves (basic textiles, food products, housewares, etc.) or done without. The markets for these products relied on a steady and strong value of the mil-réis for their growth.

Other groups had monetary interests that aligned with these categories for the productive sectors. Investors in Brazilian public-sector debt and private enterprise favored the fixed currency value caused by the gold standard, since it ensured that the value of their investment and its revenue stream (interest and dividend payments) would remain constant. Depreciating currency caused by floating exchange rates deteriorated their value. Attracting and retaining foreign investment received significant attention from those favoring fixed currency values (both during the Republic and since then) because it introduced capital that was incremental to domestically generated resources in the Brazilian economy. However, the decisions to invest in or withdraw from Brazil did not depend on the nationality of investor. Investors could mitigate monetary policy decisions by liquidating Brazilian assets and moving their resources to more hospitable locations. The retention of capital in Brazil required both that money retain its value (at least compared to trends in alternative locations) and that investors believe that monetary policy would continue to support the currency.

Consumers also had interests in maintaining monetary stability. Consumption patterns shifted with the value of the mil-réis. Appreciated currency supported domestic consumption, reflecting the price decline of locally produced goods relative to imports; the reverse dynamics applied for depreciated currency. However, consumers had an intrinsic interest in the value of money that extended beyond consumption patterns. In essence, consumers extended credit to the State by holding and using money. Changes in the price level were equivalent to a transfer between money-issuers and money-holders. To the extent that individuals participated in the market economy, they held money. In a floating-rate regime, by holding and using money, the public transferred wealth to the State through its acceptance of fiduciary money.[31] In the event of the depreciation of money (inflation of prices), the transfer was from the money-holder to the money-issuer, or from consumers to the State. Therefore money-holders had an unambiguous preference to avoid inflation, for currency value to be stable and high. Few consumers were also able to make other investments, and therefore, did not have the flexibility that investors had to transfer their assets in the event of a depreciating mil-réis. As a result, consumers disproportionately bore the cost of inflation.

Two important, but smaller, groups also participated in monetary policy debates, with less commitment to monetary stability. With open capital flows, bank shareholders benefited by a high value for the mil-réis. However, when international capital markets were closed, Brazilian banks could mitigate the declining real (price-adjusted) value of their assets by increasing their interest rates and credit volume, in nominal terms. Therefore, the banking system's size and depth could increase during periods of inconvertible floating currency.[32] When money creation occurred through the mechanism of rediscounting (bank sales of notes to a monetary authority), banks became even more direct participants in the process by developing business that was tied to note distribution for the Treasury.

Finally, the economic interests of the State were unique in this debate, and distinct from its role of implementing policy. The State, by virtue of its monopolies on issuing money and foreign debt, could shift the relative distribution of its obligations from local currency to pound sterling (or other "hard" currency) with more ease than other borrowers, in the event of increasing currency value. Therefore, it could mitigate its costs during periods of currency revaluation by shifting its debt to international markets when the value of the mil-réis was high. Similarly, a depreciating mil-réis could lessen the domestic debt burden of the State, even while depreciation also entailed a transfer from consumers to State.

The dynamics of interest group behavior and the specific course of Brazilian economic circumstances mitigated against consumers and other interests rooted in domestic markets, and to the advantage of policy targeting domestic expansion, with an inflationary bias. Since consumers included all participants in the organized economy and nearly all interest groups could benefit from stability under certain conditions, price stability could be seen as a public good.[33] However, while all consumers benefited by price stability, each specific (and smaller, more focused) interest group had an opposing goal. Their goals included command of specific resources of the State. Each group benefited by economic policies sufficiently expansive to accommodate their interests. Theories of interest groups suggest that, under these circumstances, the public good (relatively low and stable prices, in this case) would be difficult to maintain in the face of more specific challenges for resources that would have a higher marginal value for their recipients. The stronger the political weight of an interested group and the stronger its preference for a specific outcome, the more likely was that outcome.[34]

Two features of the State were relevant in the context of interest group behavior and monetary policy. The first was its ability to minimize the cost to itself of monetary policy by virtue of its flexibility in borrowing. Depending on the relative prices of money and debt, the State's interest fluctuated between a strong mil-réis, to ease the value of its international debt service obligation and give incentive to buyers of its debt, and a weak mil-réis to minimize the value of its debt. As with both banks and the coffee sector, the State's interest in a strong currency could shift. During most of the First Republic, all international borrowing was either directly incurred or guaranteed by the State.[35] As such, the State incurred a significant portion of its debt obligation in pound sterling, and it had a strong financial interest in being able to maximize the value of the mil-réis to ease its debt-repayment obligation.[36] Simultaneously, the ability to alter the form of its borrowing, based on relative costs, gave the State a flexibility that others did not have. The second important characteristic of the State was that, simultaneously, it was the object of contention among interest groups and was, itself, an interest group that negotiated for its best advantage, often in competition with other groups. Because the State had financial obligations, it had economic and financial interests that it constantly strove to accommodate. As its major agent in the monetary arena, the Treasury had a similarly dual character, executing monetary policy that reflected the outcome of political process while simultaneously having an interest in shaping the outcome.

This division of interest groups differs somewhat from the traditional categorization in Brazilian historiography, which posits coffee and industrial interests as the important groups. The approach does not challenge traditional monetary history, focused on the volume of money and its components.[37] Rather, it adds a different perspective to the political economy of monetary history that helps to clarify some actions at the same time that it adds to understanding of the emergence of the modern banking system. This perspective has the advantage of characterizing groups according to the criteria of the debate under consideration. Most important, it recognizes fundamental differences among industrial producers and can explain competition between the State and coffee interests. This framework casts interest groups in terms of the consideration of the domestic distribution of wealth, which was the core of the debate. Another feature of this categorization is that it identifies economic interests rather than individuals involved with the various components of monetary debate. Individuals often, and the State always, had multiple economic interests. While individuals, economic sectors, and geographic regions coalesced to represent their prevailing interests, reconciling specific individuals or political actors with monetary actions can obscure the particular dynamics that dominated coalitions and decisions.

The matrix in Table 3.1 summarizes the positions of the major groups with interests in the conduct of monetary policy.

The modern Brazilian banking system emerged from this complex matrix of competing interests. It developed a prominent role in the political debates and as a tool of monetary history. After early and severe monetary failures caused its demise, the banking system reemerged in 1906. The requirements of the prevailing monetary regime determined its growth and changes in its organizational structure. The structure that the banking system took reflected its origins in public finance. The Banco do Brasil served as a central monetary authority while also maintaining the nation's largest credit and deposit portfolios. A central bank with authority independent of political influence did not form. The Brazilian banking system mirrored the political dynamics that governed monetary policy. Expansive domestic monetary policy both required and encouraged a dynamic banking system. Simultaneously, bankers generally believed that the monetary expansion served their purposes. With each expansionary experience after 1906, the banking system became larger in order to support the Treasury's need to distribute an increasing volume of its notes more widely. As the banking system grew, its own interests for expansionary monetary policy gained additional strength. Banking became strong enough both to support and to influence monetary policy that was increasingly oriented toward

Table 3.1 Monetary Interest Groups in Brazilian Policy Debates

| | Exchange rate preference: | |
Monetary regime	*Appreciation*	*Depreciation*
Fixed exchange rates (gold standard); encouraging capital inflows	Domestic producers Consumers	
Ambiguous commitment to fixed exchange rates	Investors State	Banks
Floating exchange rates (inconvertible currency); discouraging capital inflows		Agricultural exporters Import substituting producers

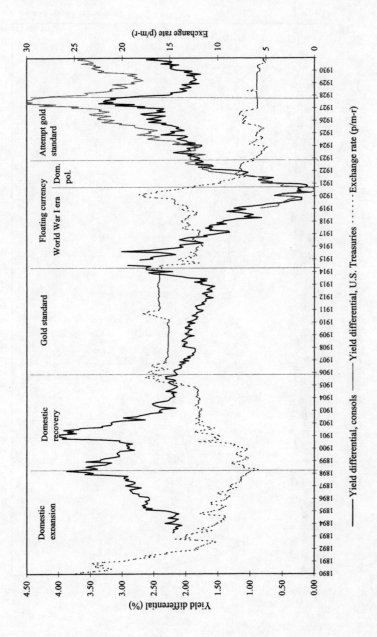

Figure 3.1 Regime Change and Capital Cost

Figure 3.2 Real Money Supply & Banking

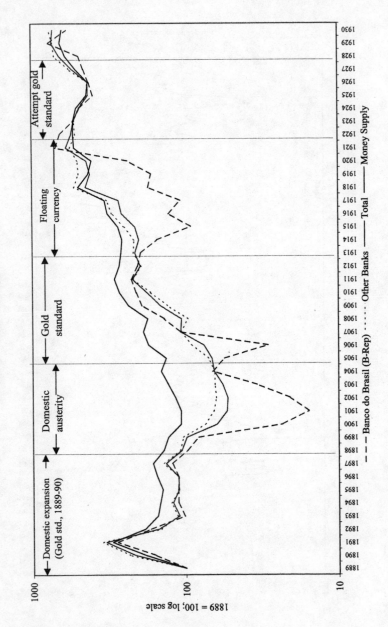

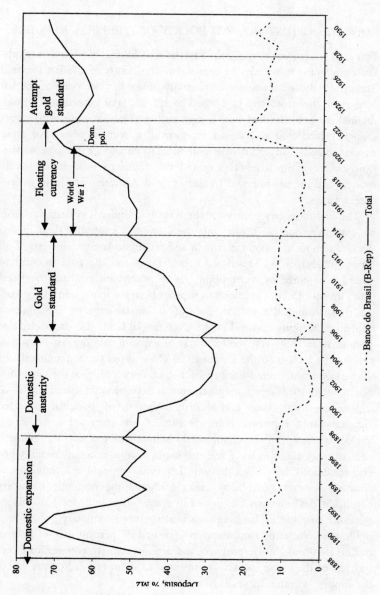

Figure 3.3 Bank Deposits in the Money Supply

expansionary domestic interests. As a result, the banking system contributed to the increasing viability and entrenchment of domestic monetary expansion, with decreasing regard to maintaining currency values.

MONETARY HISTORY AND POLICY OF THE FIRST REPUBLIC

Financial reform was virtually the first order of business for the first republican government in order to consolidate the efforts of the last imperial Treasury. New, and inconsistent, monetary policy had been one of the last actions of the monarchy in 1888. The last imperial government implemented the gold standard, with a high exchange rate, as a means to attract foreign capital into a Brazilian economy that seemed poised for rapid expansion and change.[38] At the same time, to encourage domestic expansion, twelve regional banks acquired the rights to issue notes (create money) and the last imperial Treasury provided interest-free loans to seventeen banks.[39]

The first monetary policies of the Republic, under Rui Barbosa's short but eventful tenure as Treasury minister (1889–91), continued these inconsistent attempts to maximize growth and accommodate the interests of all economic sectors.[40] Unrestricted capital flows and the gold standard to ensure fixed currency convertibility (at an overvalued exchange rate) targeted investor interest in efforts to support both the expansion of the coffee frontier and the construction of industrial capacity.[41] Significant reforms of banking laws and of the Commercial Code (Lei das Sociedades Anônimas) in 1890 were the hallmarks of expansionary domestic financial policies.[42] Changes to the Commercial Code eased the requirements for the formation of limited-liability joint-stock corporations at the same time that it established capital requirements and financial disclosure rules to address the information and security concerns of potential investors. Simultaneously, expansive domestic finance was intended to meet the transactions needs of the commercial community. New laws consolidated note-issuance rights to three regional banks to issue notes under fairly liberal conditions, but they otherwise left banks unregulated. Subsidies to remotely located agricultural banks furthered the domestic monetary expansion.[43] These laws, developed in conjunction with local financiers, were the first use of banking in a broadly based monetary policy. As a result, the volume of bank deposits increased 77 percent and 44 percent during 1890 and 1891 respectively, and deposits came to account for three-quarters of the money supply, as compared to about one-half at the end of the Empire (Figures 3.2 and 3.3).

The Treasury could maintain the exchange rate for slightly longer than a year before abandoning these policies. One measure of the disparity between market conditions and the value at which the Brazilian Treasury tried to sustain the mil-réis was its continuous decline in value from almost 25 pence at the beginning of 1890 to about 12 pence at the end of 1891 (Figure 3.1). Increasingly reluctant creditors caused the Treasury to suspend the gold standard in preference to unrestrained money creation. Expansionary ideology, promoting the financial needs of diversifying production while allowing for the easy circulation of money to all sectors and regions, underpinned the rhetoric and ambitions of the reforms.[44] These policies were divisive and tested the strength of the federal executive.[45] Domestic price inflation had reached politically contentious levels.[46] With coffee prices still high (averaging U.S.$0.20/pound in 1891, proving to be a high price for the period, Table A.10), the coffee sector aligned with other interests for exchange stability and monetary markets that challenged the Treasury's concern for money creation and financial circulation. In 1891, the first president of Brazil, Marechal Deodoro da Fonseca, invoked martial law in order to dissolve the Chamber of Deputies and its efforts to contain unbridled monetary expansion.[47]

Contemporaries dubbed this period of rapid corporate formation and frenzied share trading the Encilhamento, a racing term for the moment the gates holding horses at the starting line open.[48] The phrase connoted the fast-paced, free-wheeling speculative spirit that pervaded the financial system. In this environment of easy corporate formation and note-issuing rights, banks formed more prolifically than did organizations in the productive sectors.[49] Widespread bank failures followed, as sudden and massive as their incorporation.[50] By the end of 1890, two of the three note-issuing banks merged in order to create one larger bank, the Banco da República.[51] Accompanying the sustained decline of the exchange rate, the (real, i.e., adjusted for changes in the price level) volume of bank deposits declined 30 percent and the share of bank deposits in the money supply also decreased from 74 percent to 52 percent between 1890 and 1892 (Figures 3.2 and 3.3).[52] Notwithstanding the very sharp increase in the first two years of the Republic, within three years the aggregate volumes of money and bank deposits returned to their levels at the end of the Empire.

Despite the generalized collapse of banking, the move toward consolidating a central banking system began with the formation in 1890 of the Banco da República.[53] By 1893, the Banco da República concentrated note-issuing rights within one organization and expanded its capital to accommodate public-sector financial needs, while still maintaining its reach into the private sector. The Treasury granted it a monopoly of note-issuing rights (with gold backing one-third of their value[54]), maintained an administrative role in the organization, and provided for the withdrawal of Treasury notes from circulation. The Banco da República also provided a safety net to other banks; it often acquired assets of failing smaller organizations. The elevated use of banking to manage more complex monetary policy during the immediate transition from Empire to Republic was a significant change from the more lackadaisical approach to banking during the Empire.[55] These shifts represented an extension of the State presence into private-sector financial activities.

Monetary and economic recovery were major tasks that began in 1892, but they were not fully achieved until 1906. Efforts by the Treasury to reverse declining currency values and rising prices and interest rates in order to restore confidence of both international and domestic investors met with constant challenge.[56] Until 1898, the Treasury tried to maintain a floating exchange rate policy and to simultaneously reverse the decline of the mil-réis by managing its foreign exchange operations. Earlier experience with inflationary finance rendered the expressed intentions of the Treasury incredible. Unsuccessful in its inconsistent policies, the exchange rate continued to decline and the risk premium on Brazilian debt increased until 1898 (Figure 3.1).

Financial recovery competed with other dramatic challenges to the State's legitimacy. During the last decade of the nineteenth century and the first decade of the twentieth, the federal government also dealt with continual military revolts, a civil war in the south, and urban and rural uprisings of the poor and the newly emerging working class.[57] Asserting the authority to quell these uprisings required a balance of military strength[58] and concession to the demands of rebelling groups. At the same time, the coffee trade entered a period of prolonged decline. Coffee prices fell precipitously between 1891 and 1898, from U.S.$0.20 to U.S.$0.065 per pound (Table A.10). With coffee output increasing steadily, the declining profitability was widespread. Coffee interests searched for ways to restore their prosperity.[59] The price depression aligned the interests of the coffee sector more closely with the currency depreciation associated with floating exchange rates. The shift in the monetary preferences of the coffee sector had long-term importance. It helped to sustain, even during these years, the political demands for domestic monetary expansion,[60] despite the political and financial demands of the more visible challenges to governance.[61]

After the Encilhamento, until the Funding Loan of 1898 rescheduled the federal government's international debt, overseas lenders could not resolve a manner in which their investment in Brazil would receive adequate protection from declining exchange rates. In order to consolidate financial reconstruction from 1898 and to promote antiprotectionism, fiscal austerity and high exchange rates were the primary goals of the Treasury Ministry of Joaquim Murtinho (1898–1902) and the president of Brazil, Manuel Ferraz de Campos Sales.[62] The funding loan carried a number of conditions that coincided with Murtinho's ideological goals for monetary policy and his desire to provide the conditions to induce investment in Brazil. In doing so, the loan approximated the circumstances of the gold standard, without the formal commitment to exchange maintenance.[63] The conditions of the loan established the first steps to enforce, and make credible to investors, the Treasury's commitment to monetary stability. From 1898, the exchange rate enjoyed a sustained revaluation (Figure 3.1).

One condition of the Funding Loan was to simply withdraw notes from circulation to induce monetary deflation.[64] As a result, by 1900 the (real) volumes of the money supply and bank deposits were 23 percent and 41 percent, respectively, below their levels in 1898 (Figure 3.2). In 1900 the Banco da República failed, when the Treasury refused to support it through a liquidity crisis that arose because of a short-term decline in the exchange rate.[65] After a sharp, but short, increase to 4 percent at the beginning of 1901, the yield differential on Brazilian Treasury borrowings quickly resumed its declining trend, and the exchange rate remained relatively stable throughout the disruption (Figure 3.1). When the Treasury took administrative control of the bank it ceased the conduct of the bank's ongoing business with the private sector. As a result, generalized failure among banks ensued. Monetary management consisted of note withdrawal to meet the terms of the Funding Loan of 1898. Deflationary policies responded to the needs of investors, who were not buying Treasury bonds, and the State in its attempt to attract capital. By 1905, ten banks remained in operation in Rio de Janeiro, compared to 68 banks open in 1891.[66]

The Treasury's circumstances improved significantly beginning in 1902; recovery occurred in two stages. From 1902 until 1906, neither a functioning banking system nor improvement for the coffee sector accompanied the recovery of public finance. Nevertheless, the international standing of Brazilian finance clearly improved; with federal expenditures in balance or running a slight surplus from 1902 (continuing through 1907), reserves accumulated and credit conditions improved.[67] The risk premium required on apólices, as compared to British consols, declined to 2 percent at the end of 1906, offering the strongest evidence of Brazil's improved financial standing (Figure 3.1). The monetary contraction was concentrated in the banking failures; from 1902 to 1904 the contribution of bank deposits to the money supply had collapsed to 28-29 percent (Figure 3.3).

At the end of 1905, three interrelated reforms consolidated the slow recovery after the Funding Loan of 1898 and subsequent deflation. The coffee sector, facing very low international prices, had not responded to deflationary policies favorably and was very cognizant of the conflict between their interests and the Treasury's. The press in São Paulo complained that "The presidents of the Republic and of the state [governor of São Paulo], although farmers, find themselves in their positions not as farmers but as prominent politicians. In this character, the farmer has little hope from them . . . ."[68] Beginning in 1889, São Paulo legislators annually proposed federally sponsored coffee valorization (price supports).[69] One analyst attributes their lack of success to the "difficulty of forging domestic political coalitions that spanned both states and branches of government."[70] However, with the return of Brazilian credibility in the international capital markets, coffee interests and the federal government found mechanisms to support both of their interests.[71] Coffee price supports, the implementation of a gold standard of currency exchange, and the reorganization of the failed Banco da República into the (fourth) Banco do Brasil reoriented both domestic and international finance. The changes achieved relative stability of exchange rates and prices. Although fiscal deficits reappeared, access to international capital sustained the Treasury's ability to finance expenditures and wider-spread growth (Table A.12). From 1906, the Federal Treasury borrowings and Treasury-guaranteed state and municipal foreign loans grew notably.[72]

Significant institutional reform accompanied the gold standard. The Caixa de Conversão (Conversion Office, or, in late-twentieth-century terminology, a currency board to buy or sell mil-réis at the fixed price of 15 pence) provided the organizational structure through which the Banco do Brasil implemented the gold standard and gradually retired notes issued by other organizations.[73] The Conversion Office was motivated by the Treasury's desire to access international capital.[74] Two characteristics of its organization demonstrated the limits of the policy's concern to balance stability with growth. First, the inflow of reserves due to its creation "automatically translated into an expansion of the monetary base."[75] Second, the funding limit for the office (initially 320,000 contos, or £20 million) established the limits of the Treasury's commitment to buy currency, and by extension to sustain the exchange rate. The Conversion Office operated entirely through market operations and exercised no short-term policy discretion.

Upon reaching its limit, the Conversion Office had no option other than to allow currency to float in value.[76] The exchange rate of 15 pence/mil-réis was sufficiently low to satisfy exporters, though they abandoned expectation of further depreciation. Producers of nontradable goods and consumers benefited from the increase in the value of the mil-réis and the commitment to maintain the exchange rate. Investors, with the Treasury's commitment to sustain a stable (if somewhat less favorable) exchange rate, continued to extend credit. As a result, these reforms supported a gradual decline of the risk premium from 2 percent during 1905 (Figure 3.1).[77]

The reconstitution of the Banco da República into the Banco do Brasil, as the final component of the 1905 reforms, marked the beginning of modern Brazilian banking. The needs of public finance, while simultaneously supporting the coffee valorization, rather than the expansion of the private-sector banking system, motivated the rechartering of the bank.[78] Nevertheless, the effects of establishing a national monetary authority were pervasive for the private financial system. The Banco do Brasil provided the core of a highly centralized banking system that linked public and private sectors. The bank had multiple goals, and it was successful in instituting fundamental changes in banking. It gave the Treasury a direct presence in banking. Treasury Minister Leopoldo de Bulhões (1902–06) took an active role in structuring the Banco do Brasil in order to move toward creating an institutional framework to manage monetary affairs balancing the needs of the State with productive sectors. With the Conversion Office within the Banco do Brasil's administrative organization, the bank acquired the responsibility to act as federal monetary authority and fiscal agent.[79] Officials expected the bank to maintain high levels of liquidity in order to both meet the Treasury's needs and to lend to other banks on a counter-cyclical basis.[80] However, the commitment to the gold standard defined the limits of the bank's expansionary capabilities. Further, the Banco do Brasil was the only domestic bank with national banking powers.[81] Because of the importance of these activities, the president of Brazil appointed the bank's president and director of foreign exchange (which were immediately very important political positions).[82]

The Treasury owned 32 percent of the bank's equity.[83] Joint private and public ownership was an important feature of the new Banco do Brasil. Private shareholders included prominent business people.[84] The ownership structure served two purposes. Most obvious, it provided capital for the bank. At least as important, the joint commitment of capital by the financially active private sector with the federal Treasury signaled to outside investors an agreement on monetary policy that clearly had been absent during the

1890s. It tied the success of the bank's policy to the major business and political interests of the time. The arrangement served to enhance the credibility of the Treasury's adherence to the gold standard. The presence of private directors, although not as president or foreign exchange director, provided oversight to Treasury activities, ensuring exchange maintenance. Through joint ownership and legislation, the restored Banco do Brasil institutionalized the procedures, initiated by the Funding Loan of 1898, that established Brazilian credibility in open capital markets.[85] Although the last two decades of the First Republic would demonstrate their limits to the policy consensus and the fragility of monetary credibility, these reforms were initially successful. The Treasury could both operate fiscal deficits and easily borrow in international financial markets.[86] For the remainder of the First Republic, monetary policy, the Banco do Brasil, and the scope of activities available to all other banks were intricately intertwined, giving the Treasury an important platform for its economic activities.

For private-sector banking, the institutional structure provided by the Banco do Brasil had two profound effects.[87] The bank recommenced the private-sector commercial banking activities of the Banco da República. Upon opening, it was immediately the largest private-sector bank in Brazil, and as such, it set the standard for much subsequent banking practice. In the short run, these circumstances eased the supply of commercial credit as the economy emerged from the long period of deflation and instability. With greater confidence of stability and institutional support, private-sector banks were able to expand their own portfolios for the first time in fourteen years (Figure 3.2). The banking system became confident of the Banco do Brasil's counter-cyclical lending function to aid in smoothing credit availability. Even with the established leadership of the Banco do Brasil, however, from 1906, for the first time since the Encilhamento, deposits of private-sector banks accounted for an increasing share of the total money supply. This trend continued through the remainder of the First Republic (Figure 3.3). Their increasing representation in the money supply demonstrated a stability and dynamism that banks had not exhibited prior to 1906. From its beginning, the reorganized Banco do Brasil served to link private and public sectors and commercial and central banking, while it provided the framework to concentrate a national system of banking within one organization. The initial effect of the bank had been to establish institutional stability for groups with interests in monetary affairs; its own interests in monetary policy developed over time.

From 1905 to 1912, high exchange rates (supported by the Treasury's financial commitment) offered economic stability simultaneously with growth. Investors rewarded Brazilian commitment to the gold standard with an increased willingness to extend credit, while requiring a gradually declining risk premium on the apólice relative to consols (declining one-fifth, from about 2 percent to about 1.6 percent, Figure 3.1). The coffee valorization program succeeded in halting the decline in international prices. Coffee interests partially compensated for this benefit by accepting the negative effect on their mil-réis-denominated revenues, caused by the gold standard's increased exchange rate in 1910 (to 16 pence). Investors remained satisfied with a declining risk premium. General prosperity funded the State expansion without requiring deficit reduction, and the banking system experienced a significant regeneration.

This felicitous period of stability, prosperity, and an increasingly effective domestic financial system ended in 1912, as the economy suffered serious setbacks in international commodity markets and then through the massive disruptions of World War I. These changes fundamentally unbalanced the State's ability to accommodate financial interests. Capital inflows to Brazil began to slow as early as 1912, due to the trade and capital restrictions that European governments imposed during the Balkan Wars.[88] When the Balkan Wars escalated into World War I, the results intensified. The governments in major international capital markets suspended their adherence to the gold standard. European governments established capital and import controls and they commandeered merchant ships for war purposes, causing trade flows to plummet. Wartime capital controls in European countries made the extension of new credit to Brazil infeasible.[89] As Homero Baptista, the future president of the Banco do Brasil (1914–18) and minister of the Treasury (1919–22), subsequently recognized, the war caught "Brazilian finances completely unprepared and incapable of meeting its [augmented] needs."[90] Summary statistics tell a tale of unrelieved difficulty. In 1914, the nominal value of Brazilian exports and imports were 67 percent and 60 percent, respectively, of their values in 1912.[91] In the same years, the risk premium attached to Brazilian government debt increased to a peak of 2.9 percent. The exchange rate fell from 16 to 12 pence/mil-réis. The federal deficit rose from 28 percent to 81 percent of total revenues, even as the volume of expenditures declined slightly for the same three years (Figure 3.1 and Tables A.10 and A.12).

Brazilian authorities had no alternative to suspending their adherence to the gold standard.[92] This was an "acceptable" suspension of the gold standard. It conformed with the experiences of other countries, either because of the demands on their wartime economies or, for other peripheral economies in similar circumstances as Brazil, because the disappearance of capital flows rendered the gold standard inoperable.[93] Because the financial collapse was global, and all capital-receiving countries suffered, the increased risk premium required on Brazilian debt quickly returned to its previous declining trend after the short disruption of 1912 (Figure 3.1). The Brazilian Treasury renegotiated the terms of its existing international debt in 1914, but it was unable to secure additional resources.[94]

Sharing the expectations of Europeans at the beginning of the war, most Brazilians initially believed that these problems would be of short duration, and they did not immediately abandon the ideal of the gold standard. When the Treasury closed the Conversion Office in August 1914, they anticipated its reopening upon settlement of European hostilities.[95] With time, however, adjusting to the new environment required a reliance on domestic economic policy and a significant shift in the relative importance of economic interest groups. The closing of international markets caused Brazilians to reconsider the vulnerability of their economic prosperity to those markets.[96] Within the Treasury, the experience resurrected attention to modernizing industrial capacity that had prominence in the early 1890s and the role of the State in redirecting resources to develop new productive capacity.[97] It aggressively constructed alternative domestic structures to adapt to the loss of international markets as a source of investors in its bonds and as a market for the output of the private sector. It actively used the new banking system to do so. The Treasury began to establish institutional arrangements that made it increasingly reliant on the domestic banking system for its operations. In doing so, the State's direct intervention in the private sector escalated. From 1914, expansive domestic monetary policy became easier to sustain and increasingly difficult to reverse. The State's use and development of the domestic banking system significantly contributed to this experience.

Three fundings of the money supply between 1914 and 1921 signified the State's intent to spur domestic sources of expansion, with increasing focus and scale. In 1914, the Treasury lent 100,000 contos to banks simultaneously with its suspension of the gold standard. In order to fund this action and to finance its own budget deficit, the Treasury issued inconvertible currency for the first time since 1891.[98] Controversy accompanied the return to domestic money issuance. The *Jornal de Commércio* suggested that "paper money is the most pernicious and vexing of all loans."[99] The Rio de Janiero Associação Comercial (Chamber of Commerce) expressed its concern for the inflationary potential of domestic note issuance.[100] Even so, a year later, in 1915, additional aid to banks took a more systematic form that indicated increased centralization of banking. The Treasury established a fund of 50,000 contos at the Banco do Brasil to rediscount (purchase) commercial notes that other banks held.[101] For the first time, industrial manufacturing was a specified target of support in a counter-cyclical policy action.[102] Using the Banco do Brasil as the conduit through which to channel financing to other organizations represented a move toward the financial system envisioned with its reorganization in 1905. It also presaged further centralization and reinforced the desires to establish a central bank. One supporting argument for a central bank was that they had saved rich countries from inflation, while simultaneously responding to private-sector credit needs.[103] That rich, industrial, and modern countries had central banks to manage money growth was a recurrent argument in Brazil.

For many Brazilians, losing access from 1914 to both trade revenues and the imported goods they had come to rely upon emphasized their vulnerability to international markets. The experience reinforced the desirability of economic independence and the need to diversify production in order to produce what previously had been imported. Constructing and diversifying industrial capacity was one of the major goals of that strategy. Establishing financial mechanisms independent of international capital was another.[104] Interest groups in support of monetary expansion, especially import-substituting industrializers, exploited this opportunity to emphasize their interests. In 1921, their monetary interests in depreciating currency coincided with those of the export agriculture sector, which was suffering from low commodity prices in the international markets. The need for a more permanent organizational arrangement for managing monetary policy impressed itself on public officials.[105]

The establishment of the Rediscount Office in the Banco do Brasil in 1921 was the third expansionary domestic funding and the next major step that simultaneously defined a centralized banking system, deepened its involvement in public finance, and escalated State involvement in the private economy. A sharp global recession after a very brief and spectacular post-World War I rise of international commodity prices during 1919-20[106] rendered Brazil's return to global capital markets expensive. The risk premium, which had fallen briefly as low as 0.1 percent during 1920, increased to 1.1 percent at the end of the following year (Figure 3.1). The Rediscount Office signaled the increasing strength of groups with interests in low currency values and the Treasury's willingness to forego easy access to international capital. By opening a Rediscount Office within the Banco do Brasil to purchase treasury notes and commercial paper in January 1921, the Treasury aggressively committed to monetary expansion, developing domestic money markets in preference to accommodating investors' interests of stable exchange rates and freely convertible currency. This move was one component of widespread support to protect domestic production. As with the major reforms of 1906, the banking actions of 1921 were coordinated with the introduction of a new coffee valorization program. The enabling legislation of the Rediscount Office also had specifically mandated support to domestic industry. The Treasury minister ushering in the Rediscount Office, Homero Baptista (1919-22), had long experience as an architect of expansive domestic monetary structure to support domestic development. As early as 1892, when he was a deputy representing the state of Rio Grande do Sul, Baptista actively promoted protectionist trade policy.[107] As president of the Banco do Brasil from 1914 to 1918, he presided over the major expansion during the World War I years. The president of the Banco do Brasil when the Rediscount Office opened, José Maria Whitaker (1920-22), had been a coffee merchant-turned-banker.[108] The combined experience of Baptista and Whitaker strongly supported domestic banking to promote new industrialization while also protecting the profits of the coffee sector with expansionary monetary policy. In 1916, Baptista advocated the creation of an independent central bank.[109] They intended the Rediscount Office to be a major advance in that direction.

The reality of the Rediscount Office contrasted with the goals of providing institutional support for the private sector. The State's desire for an alternative financing mechanism, in light of the rapid increase of yield differential during 1921, prevailed. As an indication of the political nature of the rediscount program, the director of the Rediscount Office was a position appointed by the president of Brazil. The coffee sector received the protection of a price-support program. Nearly all of the notes rediscounted with the Banco do Brasil had been issued by the Treasury or were notes supporting the coffee valorization, rather than industry and its supporting sectors. In October 1922, nearly two years after the Rediscount Office opened, treasury notes presented to the Rediscount Office accounted for 89 percent of the total notes it held.[110] Issuing notes for discount at the Banco do Brasil became the tool by which the Treasury supported budget deficits that were one-third to one-half the level of federal revenues.[111] Emphasizing the political nature of the office, the president of Brazil rebuffed efforts to raise the rediscount rate, in line with precepts of market-oriented commercial banking.[112]

Even with its origins in public finance, the rediscount program's use of the banking system expanded bank deposits from the private sector, in real (adjusted for price level changes) terms, by 21 percent between 1920 and 1923 (Figure 3.2). Further, the rediscount program reinforced the shift in the composition of money from currency to bank deposits (Figure 3.3). The purchase of coffee warrants, through the price-support program, accounted for much of the increase and significantly affected the banking system. The increased concentration of the Treasury's banking intervention through the Banco do Brasil heightened the centrality of the bank in the economy and organized the means by which the Treasury could distribute its notes throughout the financial system. As these notes found their way into transactions of the private sector, banks developed large and profitable businesses. The increased size of the banking system also enhanced the interests of banks in maintaining policies that supported this form of growth.

The opening of the Rediscount Office consolidated Brazil's transition from open to closed capital markets. It was the State's largest commitment to increasing the volume and institutionalization of domestic monetary expansion.[113] International money markets did not view this commitment to domestic money issuance with the same equanimity with which it had accepted efforts during World War I. The interest rate premium on Brazilian debt increased dramatically over the life of the Rediscount Office (from the low of 0.1 percent in 1920 to about 2 percent by the end of 1923), and the exchange rate declined by half (from 10 pence at the beginning of 1921 to 5 pence in 1923, Figure 3.1). For the remainder of the 1920s, efforts to reestablish monetary austerity, in reaction against price inflation and the inability to access international capital markets, repeatedly failed.

By 1923, trends in international markets, public dissatisfaction with inflation and the overall debt service burden combined to change political direction and financial policy to once again meet the conditions necessary to reestablish the gold standard and attract foreign capital. A new government took office at the end of 1922. President Artur da Silva Bernardes (1922-26) based his political platform on price stability and the fiscal austerity to support currency appreciation.[114] Reflecting his political background and constituency as the president (governor) of Minas Gerais, a state with fairly strong economic roots in domestic agricultural commerce, antiprotectionism and monetary orthodoxy reemerged as strong themes in the debate against expansive domestic monetary policy through the 1920s.[115] Based on the rhetoric of orthodox monetary policy, the Treasury closed the Rediscount Office and reorganized the Banco do Brasil in 1923, allocating to it the term central bank, with monopoly rights on note-issue. Hoping for a relatively painless and gradual transition, new policy fell short of the strict rules of monetary orthodoxy in fundamental ways. The commitment to full convertibility of currency would become effective only after sustaining a market exchange rate of 12 pence/mil-réis for three years—almost twice the market rate at the time of implementation. Gold reserves would back one-third of bank notes issued.[116] The provisions establishing the Banco do Brasil as the central bank did not put controls on Treasury-issued notes. Further, after acquiring half of the incremental capital issued to expand the bank, the federal government owned almost 45 percent of the bank's equity.[117] The central bank office was not independent of political control.[118]

These organizational arrangements did not achieve the short-term political priorities of currency appreciation and fiscal control.[119] Absent legislation to constrain the use of the banking system, the possibility existed to use the same political platform to support competing goals. Sampaio Vidal, the Treasury minister (1922-25), and Cincinato Braga, the president of the Banco do Brasil (1923-24), used the transfer of note-issuing responsibility to the Banco do Brasil in an attempt to instill independence of monetary authority from the political requirements of the Treasury. They were in agreement with the goal of impeding the State's use of monetary policy as a financing mechanism. However, rather than advocating complete austerity, they were committed to allowing the banking system to liberally support the growth and diversification of domestic production.[120] This experience brought to a head the conflict between financing real growth in the productive sectors and using monetary policy to control political activity that had been building since the beginning of the efforts to promote domestic monetary expansion in 1914. The effort to introduce orthodox monetary policy would have significantly shifted the benefits accruing to the favor of investors. During the previous nine years, Brazilian commercial banks had accommodated expansionary finance and had grown significantly (10 percent annually on average, in price-adjusted terms. See Figure 3.2). When Bernardes attempted to induce deflation, groups interested in managing the nature of productive growth through monetary mechanisms were able to circumvent stated policy.

As a measure of the weakness and low credibility of this compromised attempt to introduce deflationary policy, the changes halted the declining exchange rate, but not the increasing premium required of the Brazilian government's borrowings (Figure 3.1). Given Brazil's long history of large budget deficits and lack of effective constraints on money creation, as well as strong evidence of opposition to the policy parameters, without changing the underlying rules by which monetary policy operated, changing the policy framework was not sufficient to attain the goals of the government.[121] During 1923, the exchange rate continued to decline; the risk premium continued to increase until it reached 2.6 percent at the end of 1925, and debt service obligations consumed 30 percent of federal expenditure in 1923 and 1924, an increase of one-half over the course of one year (Table A.12). With Brazil having neither a legislated institutional commitment to orthodoxy nor a specified ceiling on money supply, and in the face of policy controversies,[122] it took two years and further policy change, aided by foreign intervention, to bring about the original goals of credit contraction and exchange control.[123]

In keeping with trends in international financial markets and with the assistance of a British mission assessing financial conditions in preparation for a new loan, Bernardes used the new organizational structure—and new officials—to implement strongly deflationary policies in 1924. During the 1920s, the use of financial missions to lend a seal of approval and credibility to orthodox policy spread through net borrowing countries as a mechanism to bolster public acceptance and the confidence of investors.[124] By this time, arguments in favor of austere domestic monetary policies explicitly invoked the interests of previously underrepresented interests, such as "workers, civil servants, the armed forces who live on fixed incomes."[125] Deflation had the desired effect on prices (after 1924) and budget deficits (although they were not eliminated until 1927).[126] The monetary deflation contributed to a serious recession, as the banking system contracted by 20 percent between 1923 and 1926 (in real volume, Figure 3.2) without lowering the risk premium required of the State.[127] Neuhaus concludes that the recession in the private sector was the result of bank credit contraction associated with diminished money supply.[128]

Without meeting its political goals for managing public finance and prices, the Treasury's closing of the Rediscount Office caused the only serious contraction of the banking system since its revival in 1906. Bank deposits declined in real (price-level adjusted) terms. At the Banco do Brasil, deposits (from the private sector, and after adjusting for price changes) declined 19 percent in 1923 and another 11 percent in 1924; among all other banks, deposits fell 8 percent in 1924 (and had been steady in 1923, Figure 3.2). The composition of the money supply experienced a short reversion toward currency this time (Figure 3.3).

The relative cost of borrowing continued to increase, as investors became no more accommodating and the risk premium on Brazilian debt reached almost 3 percent by the end of 1927 (Figure 3.1). Washington Luís Pereira de Sousa's new government from the end of 1926[129] again attempted to establish policies amenable to price stability and the interests of investors, by reinstituting the gold standard, with procedures that did not allow for discretionary operations by the Treasury. Getúlio Vargas gained experience in implementing orthodox financial policies during his tenure as Treasury minister from 1926 to 1928; historians of subsequent time periods can assess its effects on his regimes as head of the State from 1930 to 1945 and 1951 to 1954.

An important aspect of the strategy of implementing orthodoxy during these years was to diminish the size of the domestic banking system. The Treasury revoked the Banco do Brasil's note-issuing rights. To replace the monetary authority, the Stabilization Office (Caixa de Estabilização), established at the Banco do Brasil, reinstituted a gold standard to enforce exchange stability with automatic purchases and sales of mil-réis in the open money market. The Stabilization Office used the same procedures and statutes as the Conversion Office had from 1906 to 1914. Now the Treasury committed to maintain the exchange rate at 6 pence/mil-réis, in contrast to 15 pence under the arrangements of 1906 (and 27 pence of 1888 and 1846). Further, the Stabilization Office's goal was to withdraw money from circulation, rather than to maintain a steady volume of currency. The price of coffee on international markets had rebounded strongly and commanded more than U.S. $0.20 per pound from 1924 through 1926. Therefore the major agricultural exporters could forego continued mil-réis depreciation associated with monetary expansion in preference to the interests for an appreciated mil-réis to accommodate increasingly influential domestic interests. The inability to create money forced budget constraints on the Treasury. Even so, full convertibility remained elusive. Reflecting that the Treasury remained weak, the premium attached to Brazilian debt continued to increase until late 1927, when it was greater than 3 percent (Figure 3.1). A domestic recession that was prolonged by the Depression short-circuited economic recovery.[130] With this recession and international capital flight, Brazil again abandoned the gold standard in 1930.

The Banco do Brasil no longer had an explicit role in monetary matters from 1927, and money market management issues were completely separated from the bank's commercial concerns. Absent public-sector and note-issuing responsibilities, the bank quickly responded to the profit-maximizing goals of a completely private-sector organization. Decreasing its credit portfolio entailed diminishing its support of the financial system.[131] Simultaneously, domestic recession began in 1928.[132] The public-sector influence of the Banco do Brasil and its connection to the private-sector financial system had become sufficiently strong that its national effects did not depend on its official roles. By 1929, the bank undertook a strong counter-cyclical credit policy, in an unofficial capacity, to offset the effects of domestic recession, then global depression.[133]

A brief effort to reestablish economic stability and to improve access to foreign capital took place in 1930.[134] However, the closing of international capital markets during the Depression diminished the rewards for such discipline. The overthrow of the Republic in 1930 did not change the fundamental problems of establishing political legitimacy or of the Depression. Neither did the change of political regime appear, at first blush, to usher in fundamental financial change. Vargas, with extensive political experience, including his stint as Treasury minister from 1926 until 1928, initially voiced concurrence with the prescriptions of the recent financial advisory mission (led by Otto Niemeyer) for monetary and fiscal orthodoxy. However, in the midst of the Depression (though shorter and less severe in Brazil than in many industrial countries[135]) and given the need for the new regime to consolidate its constituency, rhetoric and policy soon diverged. The federal government implemented a series of expansive counter-cyclical programs. In October 1930, the Banco do Brasil again gained note-issuing responsibilities in a reconstituted Rediscount Office. The federal government also reestablished programs to support the coffee sector and promote industrialization. Continual threats to the new regime of Getúlio Vargas required finesse and expenditure to offset. Economists have credited counter-cyclical policy for the comparatively limited effects of the Depression in Brazil. By 1932, financial crisis proceeded further than it had since 1891, and the Brazilian Treasury declared a moratorium on international interest payment obligations.[136]

Even during the contractionary second half of the 1920s, under various policy regimes and credit conditions, banks extended their realm of operation as part of their reaction to monetary conditions. Each substantive change of monetary policy required a change in the use to which policy makers put the Banco do Brasil. The banking system was sufficiently established that privately owned banks continued to increase their share of the money supply (Figure 3.3). The banking contraction from deflationary policies of 1926 was entirely concentrated in the Banco do Brasil. Banking contracted to a smaller extent than the money supply and served to offset the effects of contractionary monetary policy.[137] By the end of the Republic the strength of the system had transformed from its being a creation of the State to its having a trajectory that could be independent of the State's goals.

CONCLUSION

The continual competition for the benefits of monetary policy between producers of tradable and nontradable goods, and their allied groups, resulted from the inability of fiscal means to accommodate demands on the Treasury during the First Republic. Successive political regimes expanded their support of their constituencies, and the claims on public resources outstripped the State's claim on the resources of constituents. The monetary fluctuations reflected the struggle in meeting persistent fiscal deficits. The reliance on expansive domestic money issuance became self-reinforcing and increasingly difficult to reverse. The banking system's development in support of these policies helped both to entrench them further and to shape the nature of banking in the twentieth century. The long-term result was to support a banking system whose size and strength were intimately connected to a large presence of public finance.

Two conceptual issues embedded within this framework need to be articulated. First, the monetary regime, subject to fiscal austerity and committed to fixed exchange rates, served consumers both by maintaining relative price stability and by providing incentive to foreign investors, attracting incremental capital into Brazil. These gains were offset by expenditure control imposed on the federal government, inhibiting its economic activity, and controls on currency issuance that constrained the volume of money and credit. Therefore, the benefits to consumers of orthodox monetary and fiscal policies (measured by the level and fluctuation of prices) competed with the targeted beneficiaries of expansive policies. Second, issuing money served as a means of redistributing resources from the private to the public sector. When the Treasury shifted the distribution in meeting its financial needs from debt to money, it constrained the total volume of capital in Brazil and accumulated resources from the general population by virtue of increasing the money supply.

The ideological framework underlying monetary debate positioned protection of the value of Brazilian currency in order to attract the incremental wealth of foreign investment and to maintain domestic price stability against a commitment to structural transformation of the domestic economy that could ultimately free Brazilians from the vagaries of international markets. This perspective formulated monetary expansion as a means of accommodating the needs of local commerce. Its proponents spent much energy and experimentation during the First Republic to find the mechanics that would allow for such a policy, without being subject to overly easy money creation. As its beneficiaries—agricultural exporters, import-substituting domestic producers, and allied groups—gained strength, the benefit of low and stable price levels to the general population of Brazilian consumers became increasingly difficult to forward. The realities of monetary experience indicated that, during these years, money creation was a tool to shift the distribution of public debt from international to domestic origins, thus fueling price inflation and limiting the import of incremental capital.

The strength of the coffee sector in the Brazilian economy in the early 1890s, during a period of declining coffee prices, initiated the Republic's experience with expansionary monetary policies. Alignment of strengthening groups of import-substituting domestic producers with the coffee sector depended on the level of exchange rates and prices. The Treasury, banks, and other economic agents were able to accommodate the growing strength of inflationary interests. Given this shift against open capital flows with fixed exchange rates, the continuing rhetoric of the federal government to establish such a policy suggests its perceived benefits to maintaining price stability and to attracting incremental capital.

Pursuit of the orthodoxy of maintaining the value of the currency offered the promise of stability and access to foreign capital during an era when capital (mostly) flowed across borders freely. During the First Republic, Brazilian commitment to orthodox monetary policy was not credible without the institutional structure and automatic mechanisms of a currency board to maintain the exchange rate. In 1898 and again in 1923, the Treasury made its strongest efforts to institute monetary policies that encouraged creditors. The policies could not be successful without the establishment of the Conversion and Stabilization Offices in 1906 and 1926 respectively; and in 1926 stability remained elusive. That Brazilians pursued this goal for so long, with so little success, testifies to its promise to maximize investment and stabilize prices, and to their inability to marshal the discipline or authority to meet the goal. At the same time, the costs of orthodoxy were high, and they did not always serve the goals of important special-interest groups. Each foreign loan required guarantees and collateral that often appeared to Brazilians to reduce sovereignty or to claim national wealth.[138]

The realities of international capital markets, and their importance in the economy, also severely constrained the ability of Brazilians to implement monetary policy. In 1890, 1914, and again in 1929, for reasons outside of their control, Brazilians could not access international financial markets. Or, if capital could be made available, its scarcity would have imposed very restrictive conditions.[139] At these times, domestically expansive monetary policies were effective, if only because of the diminished viability of alternatives. The experience of each of these periods reinforced the desire for economic independence among many Brazilians.

The Banco do Brasil, Conversion Office, and Treasury divided the activities and responsibilities of monetary authority in the absence of a fully independent central bank. During the 1906–12 experience with the gold standard, the arrangement worked well. Coffee price supports and liquid international capital markets contributed to the conditions allowing this success. The years subsequent to World War I demonstrated the weaknesses of central banking responsibilities distributed across agencies without a politically independent central bank. Because of its strength within the domestic economy, the increasing benefit to the coffee sector from low mil-réis values, as international coffee prices remained low, significantly realigned economic interests away from protecting international capital to protecting domestic producers of import-substituting goods. The response of the Treasury, to rely increasingly on domestic inflationary finance, reflected the limited range of options available to it. Absent independence from political processes, monetary policy fell to the inconsistencies of political demands. The divergence between political reality and the monetary goals of the Treasury (and Banco do Brasil) in 1923 was the most obvious example of this problem, which had been building since 1914.

During these years, banks became fundamental to the implementation of monetary policy in manners that supported expansion with floating exchange rates, and in turn, policy shaped the nature of the banking system. After its failed efforts during the early 1890s, the Treasury learned some of the techniques to monopolize note-issuance. With each turn toward expansionary domestic policy, the Treasury actively supported the development of banking facilities in order to ease the domestic distribution of its debt. Periods of monetary austerity induced banking contraction. In 1892 and 1900, bankruptcies were the primary result of contraction among banks. After 1906, monetary contraction was accomplished in the less dramatic and more organized manner of note withdrawals. Note withdrawal altered the size, but not the nature, of the banking system, and it did not challenge the centrality of the Banco do Brasil. Therefore, each expansionary period contributed to building the size and presence of banks, without a fully offsetting reversal during contractionary periods.

At two important junctures, monetary policy was fundamental to shaping a new banking system. The reorganization of the Banco do Brasil in 1906 was the most important and successful effort in this endeavor. The bank provided the mechanisms to implement the gold standard on a credible basis. Joint financial commitment, in the form of the bank's capital, demonstrated the consensus of the public and private sectors to the policy's monetary constraints. The Banco do Brasil was instrumental in effecting changes in monetary policy and money supply. However, its reconstitution also addressed needs important for domestic banking. This organizational change provided a structure for the emergence of a more stable banking system, after the system's earlier failures. The Banco do Brasil was at the core of the private-sector banking system. It was the largest bank and the only domestic organization with a national network. As a result, it was both highly centralized and intimately linked to the circumstances of public finance. These characteristics came to define Brazilian banking. In 1921, the formation of the Rediscount Office further strengthened the Banco do Brasil as the center of a politicized network and simultaneously enhanced the importance of the banking network to the State as a means of building domestic money markets.

The self-sustaining dynamics of banking notably gained strength during the 1920s. After the closing of the economy that had been an effect of World War I, economic agents restructured in order to benefit from changed monetary (and therefore profit) dynamics. It did not prove possible to accommodate the interests of diverse sectoral groups within the constraints of monetary orthodoxy. Both the interest groups favoring closed financial markets and the means for sustaining them had strengthened. Brazilian banks were prominent among the economic interests that took advantage of the inflationary effects of expansive domestic monetary policies from 1914. The institutional impetus of the Rediscount Office to inflationary dynamics outlived its operations. The growth and increasing share of the money supply originally resulted from the Treasury's use of the banking system to accommodate the expansion of the monetary system. It ultimately increased the difficulty of reopening the economy to international capital flows. Making the Brazilian economy more attractive to international capital increasingly had to contend with expansionary domestic monetary interests. Incremental investment required domestic austerity, the sanction of an international advisory mission, and the removal of discretionary policy through the implementation of a currency board. These efforts had a very different effect in the 1920s than they had produced in 1906. Stabilization could only be achieved at a much lower value of the mil-réis and with higher risk premia on debt than had been experienced since the Encilhamento.

The goal of a central bank independent from the political influence of the Treasury and Presidency made little progress during the First Republic. Ultimately, the combined public and private ownership of the Banco do Brasil gave the Treasury a tool for channeling the resources of the private sector, rather than maintaining currency-valuation commitments and controls on the political garnering of resources. However, a strong national bank acting as a central monetary authority linking public and private finance advanced significantly. Just as each change of monetary regime came about after intense debate and a change of political regime, it was implemented by fundamentally altering the Banco do Brasil's (or its predecessor, the Banco da República's) organizational structure. Changes in organizational structure, the significant proportion of State ownership, and the reservation of the bank's top positions for political appointments rendered the bank a political institution as much as an economic one. Its complementary role as the linchpin of the private banking system resulted in the efficient transmittal of public-sector financial activities to the private sector. Precisely because of its importance in connecting public and private finance and in mediating between international and domestic, the Banco do Brasil became a political prize. As their strength increased through the 1920s, representatives of producers of tradable goods gained greater control of the institutional mechanisms of the bank, reinforcing the pressures for closed monetary policy.

These policies, debates, and experiences reflected and shaped the nature of the Brazilian economy, as it emerged in the twentieth century. Through its use and ownership of the Banco do Brasil, the State gained a strong position within the private-sector credit system in a manner that served to link inextricably private finance to the Treasury. The same ties, putting the Banco do Brasil at the core of the monetary system, reinforced the highly concentrated and politicized banking system that developed from 1906. The manner in which policy-makers organized themselves intricately interwove public and private. Banking provided a model for a sector concentrated within a single large-scale organization, with multiple and sometimes competing goals. Banking became a crucial tool through which Brazilians struggled to shape the nature of their domestic economy and their role in the world economy.

These policy actions were not esoteric conflicts and machinations among economic elites. The ability to implement changes in monetary policy, with widespread effects throughout the economy, demonstrated the authority and increasing legitimacy of governing bodies. At least as important, the struggles between interest groups for the benefits attainable through monetary and financial policies reflected the broader shifts and compromises of economic and social class balances that were fundamental to the First Republic. The vicissitudes of monetary policy reflected contention among all sectors of society about the nature of modernity and economic growth. At the core was the question of whether Brazil could grow and become modern while operating within the established economic system that had been intimately tied to international trade and capital. The alternative strategy was to attain the benefits of modernization and development by abandoning the traditional reliance on external forces and capital in order to develop domestic capabilities and goods that they had previously imported from European sources. While navigating these conflicts, the State made use of monetary tools to establish its legitimacy, accommodate constituent interests, and extend its role within the economy. The very pragmatic results sacrificed price levels and stability for Brazilians. By the end of the Republic, a wider array of social classes had firmly established efforts to gain benefit through the tools of the financial system.

Chapter 4

The Business of Banking

Building responsive entities to conduct the ongoing activities of everyday life commanded as much effort as the struggle to construct new forms of governance during the First Republic. In this regard, banks developed increasingly dynamic activities within the private sector at the same time that they responded to the opportunities and constraints presented by monetary policies. The evolution of the banking business served two purposes. From the perspective of the banks, the need to establish their credibility and profitability after the widespread failures in the first years of the Republic required that they incorporate remedies to the early problems into their business practices. From a broader perspective, the demand for a banking system that could accommodate the needs of a changing economy provided the incentive for banks to evolve. At the end of the Republic, the business of banking was very different than it had been in 1889. Institutions and businesses had changed in nature. In restructured form, they were more solid, more mature, and more responsive to their environment than they had previously been. Their stability and responsiveness to a wider array of circumstances signified the transition from an early system of narrow reach to a more modern one that functioned much as both late-twentieth-century banking analysts would expect and as many Brazilians wanted. This chapter focuses on the business of banks and its evolution during the First Republic by assessing the financial structure of the banking system. Subsequent chapters will explore the motivations and actions of individual banks and the means by which they affected economic development.

Banks suffered extreme disruption and massive failure during the financial and monetary chaos of the first years of the Republic. The sharp break in monetary and banking history at the end of 1905 marked the beginning of modern banking in Brazil. While monetary history defined this transition, changes in the business of banking were also important. Bankers adjusted their business practices in response both to the prior experiences of the sector and to their ongoing circumstance. Despite the heavily politicized nature of the monetary superstructure, banks consolidated their emphases in specific business activities and maintained conditions for organizations to operate on more solid ground. Conservative business practices enhanced the capacity for growth and dynamism among banks in support of private-sector development. These changes occurred within the context of a political economy that increasingly relied upon banking for developing domestic markets for goods and services. In this sense, the modernization of banking reflected its politicized importance.

The business of banking evolved with its role in the economy. However, because of their visibility in the political economy, banks as business enterprises often receive little attention. Though the State became an important investor in the largest bank in order to meet political goals, other economic agents also committed capital to these endeavors. In the First Republic, the Federal Treasury committed capital only to the Banco do Brasil (and its predecessor, the Banco da República). State governments also invested in the major banks in their states. However, these organizations derived much of their capital from private investors; most banks were fully owned by private entities. Two objectives for banks motivated their owners: to earn profits and to establish mechanisms of financial intermediation.

The types of financial transactions that banks undertook and their business structures demonstrate their evolution. The data available for this analysis change during the period in a manner that paralleled the shift in the business of banking. Prior to the reorganization of the banking system at the end of 1905, estimates of the size of the entire banking system provide the only data available. Problems with the comparability of business structures and short-lived organizations mitigated the value of aggregating firm-level data. However, with the banking system's reorganization, financial data reported by individual banks appeared consistently in terms of the regularity of publication, the duration of bank existence, and the reporting of balance sheets in standardly defined categories and comparable structure. Financial data from bank balance sheets and income statements trace the nature of the banking system from 1906, providing systematic standards for assessing the nature of banking. (The Data Appendix explains this information.) Using data from individual firms, rather than previously published estimated and summarized data, allows for aggregation of the total banking system,[1] and of relevant groupings of organizations, to trace the consistent trends by which it became increasingly modern.

EARLY REPUBLICAN FAILURE

The financial chaos of the first years of the Republic, the Encilhamento and its "crack," was the most obvious result of the State's attempts to use banking in response to multiple needs simultaneously. Its monetary characteristics have been the focus of scholarship on the Encilhamento.[2] Although the issue remains underexplored, some historians have alluded to the effects of the Encilhamento on industrial development and restructuring of business organization for the productive sectors of the economy.[3] Banks were the locus combining the monetary and real characteristics of the Encilhamento. The detriment to banking was among the most notable features of the Encilhamento.

The disruption caused to the development of the banking system occurred in three stages. The Encilhamento, a bubble of bank-led corporate formation, preceded two stages of banking collapse before economic recovery and organizational reform supported fundamental banking growth. Chapter 3 considered the growth of the banking system in conjunction with monetary policy and regime changes, and it documented a massive expansion of banking from 1888 to 1891, followed by an equally massive collapse in 1892 (Figures 3.2 and 3.3). The attempts to enforce economic and monetary orthodoxy did not permit an immediate recovery. The deflationary conditions enforced by the Funding Loan of 1898 are often held responsible for a second collapse of banking in 1900-01. At its trough in 1901, the volume of bank deposits (in real, price-adjusted terms) and their contribution to the money supply were about half the level they had reached at the beginning of the Republic. The number of banks whose equity shares traded on the Rio de Janeiro Bolsa de Valores increased from 13 in 1888 to 21, 43, and 68 in 1889, 1890, and 1891 respectively. In 1892, the shares of 14 banks were traded, and of 10 in 1905.[4] These numbers dramatically illustrate the collapse of banking; they do not address the questions of what banks did during these years, or of whether banking addressed the financial needs of the private sector. Did the nature of the banking business exacerbate or ameliorate its problems deriving from public policy?

Commercial code and bank reform in 1890 supported the increase in banking at the beginning of the Republic, when Brazilians expected economic growth to require a quantum increase in financial services. The ability to form limited-liability corporations, without legislative approval for individual firms and with some steps toward financial "transparency," enhanced corporate formation in all sectors.[5] Published statements allowed shareholders and potential shareholders to monitor the financial positions of firms and made information on their financial conditions more accessible to the public. Changes in laws affecting banks moved to constrain bank note-issuance rights (though not volume) but otherwise did not impose constraints on their business activity.[6] Loans to banks by the Treasury also encouraged their expansion. The eased ability to form limited-liability corporations, combined with the encouragement of banking, had strongly encouraged the opening of new banks in these years. Certainly, the business press conveyed the perception that banks accumulated capital in advance of the identification of investment opportunities:

> In view of the excessive growth of banks, there was an immediate need for support from the managers, and they naturally responded to all classes of individuals, those without the necessary means and even to adventurers, without hesitating to take on operations beyond their means.
>
> The madness in the market had only one lucid moment . . . before relapsing to excitation and mind-numbing expansion. . . .[7]

Without constraints on the nature of their investments, bankers committed their funding from capital, deposits, and Treasury loans to a variety of activities. They extended credit for commercial transactions, some financed real estate development through mortgages, and they made long-term investments by purchasing corporate bonds and equity shares.[8] Their traditional reluctance to extend long-term credit (in excess of a year, or often as short as six months) had not prevented banks from making significant investments in the stocks and debentures (bonds) of corporations— often of dubious financial worth. With otherwise unused funds, they bought large volumes of Treasury apólices (domestic debt issued by the federal and state treasuries).[9] Foreign exchange trading was also an integral part of banking. Banks used their funds in order to arbitrage currencies, buying and selling foreign exchange to exploit price differentials in various marketplaces.[10]

The Encilhamento cracked during 1891-92, when the value of the mil-réis collapsed.[11] Since the value of apólices and many of the other securities relied on the value of the mil-réis, and since banks were also speculating in the value of the mil-réis through their foreign exchange operations, currency decline generated massive bank failures. As their investments lost value, banks could not meet the obligation to redeem deposits. Investors lost the capital that they had committed to acquire bank shares. Partially paid-in capital for subscribed shares was a common arrangement that affected bank safety and the extent of investors' losses.[12] To prevent failure, banks called in additional portions of the unpaid capital subscriptions from their shareholders. The success of capital calls depended on the perceived viability of the bank and the ability of shareholders to meet their capital obligations.[13]

Failed banks used a variety of mechanisms to close their business obligations. Some unscrupulous banks, usually founded with purely speculative motives, simply defaulted on their obligations and did not redeem deposits.[14] One possible case resulted in the forced liquidation of remaining assets of the Banco de Crédito Commercial.[15] More often, extended families and groups of close associates had combined their capital to establish organizations in order to take advantage of investment opportunities and to attract still further resources from depositors, perhaps to capitalize new business ventures, as well as to speculate in foreign exchange and corporate securities. Built upon the combined resources of family and social groups, these banks were less inclined to unscrupulous activity and more concerned with minimizing their losses while maintaining their social and commercial reputations. Simultaneously meeting their legal obligations and failing, banks had two avenues they could pursue. They could liquidate their investments to the extent possible, use capital to redeem deposits, and sell any remaining illiquid assets to the Banco da República.[16] Alternatively, stronger private organizations could acquire failing ones.

The major regulatory change affecting the businesses of banks following the Encilhamento's crack was that, from 1893, foreign exchange trading by banks (other than the Banco da República) that did not support underlying business transactions was illegal. Brokers on the securities exchange successfully interpreted the law regulating their activities to impede banks from engaging in speculative foreign exchange transactions.[17] This regulation was a clear response to the Encilhamento. Many believed its severest effects to have been speculative frenzy that depreciated the mil-réis through excessive currency speculation.[18] The regulation did not prohibit licensed brokers on the securities exchange from trading currencies.[19]

Banks received no ongoing support from the Treasury during the years that it attempted monetary orthodoxy subsequent to the crack of the Encilhamento.[20] Deflation served to keep the volume of money, and therefore bank deposits, low. Surviving banks operated at a low level of activity and within very narrow confines. With coffee prices in secular decline (Table A.10), however, the demand for banking in support of either international trade transactions or domestic endeavor was also low. The economic activities that might have required banking were, themselves, in long-term decline. While banks remained in a weakened position, the Funding Loan of 1898 triggered the second round of deflation. The Treasury, under the Ministry of Joaquim Murtinho, assumed strong antiprotectionist positions.[21] Formulating policy based, in part, on the conviction that banking should rely on a "real bills doctrine" that supported existing economic activity,[22] the Treasury was sympathetic to maintaining a weak banking system at this time and was not inclined to help banks survive further pressure. These became the most sustained and effective deflationary policies for the duration of the Republic.

The Banco da República (and Banco Hypothecário[23]) failed in 1900, as an immediate result of one of the periodic foreign exchange speculation crises that Brazil had suffered throughout the second half of the nineteenth century. The bank had been in increasing difficulty for about eight months prior to the Treasury assuming control of it, and supplemental funding advanced from the Treasury postponed the bank's closing for four months.[24] Analysts have attributed the failure of the Banco da República to either a lack of liquidity during the foreign exchange crisis, or the withdrawal of Treasury support during the crisis.[25] Both conclusions can be supported in limited senses. A shortage of immediately available cash was the event that triggered the failure.[26] The refusal of the Treasury to increase its special funding of the bank determined the timing of the failure. In the political efforts of assigning responsibility for the failure, supporters of the bank noted that it had purchased large volumes of federal apólices in the past, leaving it with an inflated balance sheet that had served the Treasury's financing needs, rather than the bank's interests.[27]

Beyond the immediate crisis, the detritus of the Encilhamento left many banks holding in their portfolios worthless loans to, and the shares and debentures of, failed enterprises.[28] The Banco da República held assets from the time of its formation that had declined substantially in market value during the eight years since the Encilhamento.[29] These were the remaining assets of the two original banks that had merged in 1892 and those acquired from other failing banks in the early 1890s. The Banco da República held these investments because they could not sell them.[30] A substantive weakness of accounting practice accentuated the 1900 crisis. The bank's balance sheet reported all assets at their original (par) value and did not restate them to reflect changes in their value in the current market. This practice masked the significant decline in the value of the assets that the bank had owned since the 1890s. As a result, its financial statements substantially overstated the value of the bank's assets. In the face of rapidly deteriorating currency values, the bank could not liquidate its assets for amounts approximating their stated value in order to meet its obligations. At the time that the Banco da República closed, the market value of major categories of the bank's assets was only slightly more than half of their stated value.[31] The Board of Directors represented to its shareholders that these assets were a major factor in the failure.[32] Sustained Treasury support could have continued to mask this problem. However, the prevailing orthodox and antiprotectionist ideology of policy makers and the perceptions of capital markets mitigated against such support. In the ensuing failure, the Treasury assumed administrative control of the bank and disbanded its commercial operations for approximately five years.[33]

By 1903, with severe inconvenience to its commercial transactions, the business community had begun to anticipate a new banking system.[34] Ideas for the restructuring of banking arose in conjunction with concerns about the effects of credit shortages and problems encountered by coffee producers:

> Some proclaim the re-creation of banks in new form, supported by large official favor, that furnish abundant resources, others want indirect support, such as tax exemptions and rate reductions for railroads, other services, and goods necessary for farming. The coffee planter complains of the lack of credit and monetary resources . . .[35]

The more flexible orientation of Treasury Minister Leopoldo de Bulhões supported the more expansive commercial community. He identified a need for a "central bank" that would rediscount the notes of other banks in order to improve the circulation of resources through the economy and to meet the needs of economic agents while avoiding the conditions of the 1890s.[36] Without following a directly expansionary monetary policy to subsidize its constituency of coffee planters in São Paulo, the presidential administration of Campos Sales,[37] with Bulhões, put in place a policy that maintained monetary orthodoxy, while providing for the rejuvenation of financial flows and private banking facilities. Attempts to arrange for coffee valorization highlighted the need for an organization with resources greater than existing banks in order to place the notes that the price-support program would issue. Restructuring the Banco da República offered a solution to the note-circulation challenge of the coffee valorization program as well as the administrative problems of implementing the gold standard (in the Conversion Office). It established the basis for restructuring private-sector banking. Ambitious plans for a new organization to contribute to stable financial markets and serve as a central bank indicated a role for the emerging bank larger than administering foreign exchange transactions and coffee notes.[38]

At the time of the reorganization, the nominal value of capital invested in the banking system had fallen to one-ninth its peak level in 1891.[39]

THE EMERGENCE OF MODERN BANKING

The monetary reforms of 1905 encouraged the emergence of the banking system after the financial chaos and the slow recovery that characterized the first sixteen years of the Republic. The establishment of the (fourth) Banco do Brasil supported the development of banks' businesses in a dynamic and logical manner. For the first time, a system began to coalesce in which relationships among banks, and between banks and other economic agents, experienced self-sustaining growth. The increased importance of banking in the money supply clearly identified this turnaround, initiating a dynamic banking system (Figure 3.3). Although indications arose of structural characteristics that sometimes weakened the long-term effectiveness of the system, banking proceeded successfully by historical standards. The business structure of banks also needed to evolve to sustain the potential of the restructuring.

The construction of a responsive banking system was slow and difficult; in many ways, it did not completely succeed. Certainly, complaints about the inadequacy and conservatism of banking came from a wide range of economic interest groups, and they did not stop throughout the period. In 1917, the *Retrospecto Comercial* (which usually articulated mercantile interests) complained that "[i]n matters of banking organization, it is incontestable that our situation compares unfavorably to that of neighboring countries. In Brazil, agricultural credit does not exist, notwithstanding the irony of being primarily an agricultural country."[40] In 1923, Treasury Minister Sampaio Vidal, while promoting further reform to open a central bank facility and reintroducing restrictive monetary policy, emphasized, "What most impresses those who study the financial situation of Brazil is the malfunctioning of its financial machinery. Our financial organization leaves much to be desired . . ."[41] And, as late as 1930, Roberto Simonsen, Brazil's most influential industrialist, both echoed complaints from the late nineteenth century and anticipated those later in the twentieth:

[W]e do not have stable or elastic money. We do not have an efficient organization of credit . . . So, how can we create the productive apparatus to aug-
ment Brazilian acquisitive capacity when the monetary disorder and credit
shortages create anarchy for production . . . ?

We do not have sufficient circulating [working] capital, which our
improvidence and the permanent cycles of successive inflations and defla-
tions that we have lived with have destroyed.[42]

Even accepting these complaints, the transitions during the early twentieth century were significant. The change in banking did not occur sud-
denly in 1905 and 1906. Rather, the banks that survived the crises of the
1890s and 1900 were the ones that had, or adopted, both responsive and
cautious portfolios. As new banks incorporated, they embraced similar
practices. The structure of the banking system that emerged and its evolution for the remaining twenty-five years of the First Republic demonstrated that, although uneven, difficult, and contentious, by 1930, a
relatively stable banking system began to serve the Brazilian economy.

For domestic banking, the opening of the Banco do Brasil in December 1905 marked the significant change of the 1905–06 financial restructuring. The size and special functions of the Banco do Brasil became
central to shaping the banking system. Enhancing the State's financial interests (in particular, to maintain stable exchange rates) and providing a financial agent to execute the Treasury's business transactions motivated the
resurrection of the failed Banco da República into the Banco do Brasil.
The bank also quickly became the largest bank serving the private business
community, while it simultaneously served as a "national" bank by implementing monetary policy and opening a national network. The structure
and role of the Banco do Brasil enhanced institutional stability and provided a model for the operations of the entire banking system.

Private-sector banking also became more dynamic and responsive to
economic change. To many, its progress was one component of the widespread modernization that was improving Brazil: "One of the large indices
of the modernization of our commercial practices is the expansion of
banking."[43] Progress, modernization, and growth took place within narrowly defined constraints; prudence and conservatism accompanied
dynamism. Bankers engaged in more constricted activities than they had
prior to the two decades of crisis. Organizations limited their activities to
commercial banking and left merchant (or investment) banking to private,
unchartered parties.[44] Practices that had been common at the beginning of
the Republic had been abandoned as they proved unsound or as regulation

required. In particular, banks no longer issued notes on their own credit-worthiness, arbitraged foreign exchange, or undertook unsubsidized and unfunded long-term investment. For the banks entirely in the domain of the private sector, these constraints remained firmly in place through the last twenty-five years of the First Republic.

The prohibition against long-term investment was the most fundamental constraint on the banking business that resulted from the financial crises of the 1890s.[45] Their experiences in these years reinforced bankers' well-established aversion to long-term credit.[46] By 1906, renovated operating statutes codified banks' prior reluctance to extend credit on a long-term basis, typically establishing six months as the maximum duration for loans and four months for discounted notes.[47] However, the practice of continually renewing credit as it matured could effectively transform short-term instruments into long-term investments, while maintaining some flexibility for the bank.[48] Because banks reevaluated credit at each renewal (reflecting current market value at the time of renewal), they were able to minimize the accounting problem of reflecting the current market value of its business on its balance sheets. Bankers' knowledge of the current real value of their business reflected a more fundamental benefit of short-term lending. They retained the option to change the allocation of their assets according to prevailing conditions (or any criteria they chose). Bank statutes also now routinely prohibited banks from purchasing the stocks or debentures of business concerns, as a new and strong limitation on the long-term commitment of resources. The conservative response of adopting strict commercial banking constraints against holding such securities prohibited banks from directly investing in productive enterprises.

Their specific business concerns justified banks' prohibitions against long-term investments. However, bankers also responded to pressure imposed by the Banco do Brasil. The bank's short-term orientation was explicit; its statutes prohibited it from accepting long-term notes from other banks.[49] As a result, banks required short-term notes in order to take advantage of the Banco do Brasil's facilities. With the Banco do Brasil serving as *de facto* central banker, other organizations could only rediscount the notes structured to conform with the bank's short-term orientation. The incentive to manage their portfolios by selling notes to the Banco do Brasil diminished the willingness of banks to accept long-term credit exposure. The organizers of the Banco do Brasil and private-sector bankers clearly understood the inhibition this constraint created on long-term credit. Indeed, it was one of the goals of the Treasury to structure a short-term commercial banking system: "The regulatory action of our new credit institution will not be felt only in the exchange market, but equally and with extraordinary result in the market for discounted bills."[50]

The other significant business constraint, restrictions against foreign exchange trading from 1893, remained a constant source of tension between bankers and securities brokers and between domestic and foreign bankers. In addition to concentrating the foreign exchange business with brokers on the Bolsa de Valores and the Banco do Brasil (in transactions for the Treasury, primarily to manage the exchange rate), it created a division between foreign and domestic banks. Foreign banks could, and actively did, engage in currency trading (including obviously speculative trading for their own profits or losses). Their businesses in Brazil were directly tied to the international trading activities of merchants of their home nationalities. Thus foreign banks routinely had commercial transactions that underpinned currency trades, and regulators could not distinguish the nature of specific currency exchanges. Further, regulating currency trading of foreign organizations was simply not feasible, since the banks could conduct foreign exchange transactions in their country of origin, rather than in Brazil. In particular, British banks actively arbitraged differentials in currency values between the London and Brazilian exchange markets with continual trading.[51] They routinely earned a sizable portion of their revenues through currency trading.[52]

Foreign banks were among the major dissidents to protest the monopoly that the newly chartered Banco do Brasil had on conducting the foreign exchange transactions for the Treasury, despite capabilities more expansive than their local counterparts.[53] This monopoly was also an important component of federal monetary policy, since it was the mechanism by which the Treasury managed the value of the mil-réis foreign exchange markets (when policy mandated). The function was sufficiently important that the bank's director of foreign exchange remained an appointee of the president of Brazil.[54] Substantial currency transactions to manage the exchange rate and to effect international debt payments and state-subsidized trade translated this privilege into a profitable business for the bank.[55] By regulating foreign exchange transactions, the Banco do Brasil had a large protected monopoly. Other financial intermediaries could invoke their ongoing business to engage in currency trading. Only domestic banks were prohibited from a type of business that proved profitable to its competitors.

The constraints against long-term investment, foreign currency transactions, and issuing debt to raise funds for extending credit left banks with a narrowly defined range of business transactions. Banks financed commercial transactions undertaken by merchants, extended short-term loans that could be plentifully protected with secure collateral or personal wealth, and often bought and sold ("rediscounted") among themselves credit extended to commercial borrowers.[56] Many large and prominent borrowers did not appreciate this conservatism. Roberto Simonsen's complaint, quoted above, about banks' rigorous commitment to short-term credit based on deposit taking reflected this sentiment.[57]

From the perspective of the banks, however, the narrowed and better-defined focus of business was attractive.[58] Commercial banks responded to their economic environment and constraints in constructive manners. The conservatism of banking from 1905 enhanced its stability and allowed its growth. Bankers and regulators remained sensitive to their earlier experience with massive and disruptive failures. The changes in the business of banking after the 1890s responded to the perceived sources of inordinate risk that had contributed to the instability and losses during the monarchy and the early years of the Republic.

THE COMPOSITION OF THE BANKING SYSTEM FROM 1906

Its increased conservatism, maturity, and intricately interrelated public and private business structure became obvious in the banking system's financial characteristics after 1905. Banks varied widely in their business structures, reflecting the peculiarities of each organization and of local markets. However, their aggregate financial structure reflected the development of banks into a cohesive banking system. The characteristics of broadly defined categories of banks revealed consistent patterns. Ownership status most usefully categorized banks for these purposes: privately owned banks of domestic and foreign ownership,[59] banks subsidized and accorded privileges by state governments,[60] and the Banco do Brasil. Aggregating the financial data of individual banks into these groups illustrates the evolution of the banking system through patterns of concentration, growth, liquidity, and interest rates.

Participation and Concentration

Increasing stability supported the gradual opening of new privately owned banks. They opened in a fairly smooth progression, with at least ten domestic and nine foreign entrants into the formal banking system between 1906 and the end of the Republic in 1930. As a result, the sector became progressively less concentrated. An index of market concentration,[61] based on deposits, reveals that the increasing dispersion of banking activity was most marked among privately owned domestic banks (Figure 4.1). For these organizations, declining concentration occurred fairly steadily from 1908, after the consolidation of banking reforms, through the remainder of the First Republic.[62] For the entire banking system, the reversal of monetary policy and expansion of public-sector banking resulted in the sharp disruption of the early 1920s. Not only did concentration decline, but the identity of the five largest banks (excluding the Banco do Brasil) changed regularly, signifying an emerging dynamism among organizations (Table A.7).

With its opening, the Banco do Brasil quickly became the largest bank serving the private sector of the economy. After its first year, it held more than 10 percent of the banking system's deposits (from the private sector); during the years when the Rediscount Office was open, the bank's market share reached one-third (Table A.6). Along with structural reforms to address concerns about previous weaknesses and failure, both the Treasury and the bank strongly highlighted the importance of the revamped organization in order to establish its credibility in the financial community.[63] The federally financed policies that affected the availability of credit at the Banco do Brasil encouraged many business endeavors of substantial size to use the bank as their financial intermediary. Its geographic scope and size allowed for a range and volume of transactions that exceeded other organizations.[64] However, its market position was not an aspect of its business upon which the Banco do Brasil could rely. The bank was usually—but not always—the largest holder of private deposits. For example, in 1918 and 1919, it ranked second in size of deposit base after a major organization for trade finance and immigrant remittances, the Banco Nacional Ultramarino. The combined share of deposits in the five largest banks other than the Banco do Brasil fluctuated inversely with the share of deposits held by the bank.[65] Other large banks offset the Banco do Brasil's counter-cyclical policies with significant results for both mitigating monetary policy and tempering the bank's position in the commercial community.

The last twenty-five years of the Republic also saw a significant change in the composition of foreign banking. The commercial banking businesses operated by foreign and Brazilian organizations were very similar in nature, and they responded to similar dynamics. Nevertheless, the share of total deposits in foreign banks declined from 30 percent in 1907 to 19 percent in 1930[66] (Table A.6). The indigenization of banking occurred exclusively in the growth of public-sector banks, the Banco do Brasil, and the state-subsidized organizations. Foreign banks retained their overall share of private-sector deposits, with 37 percent in 1907 and 39 percent in 1930.[67] This apparent stability masks an important shift among foreign banks.

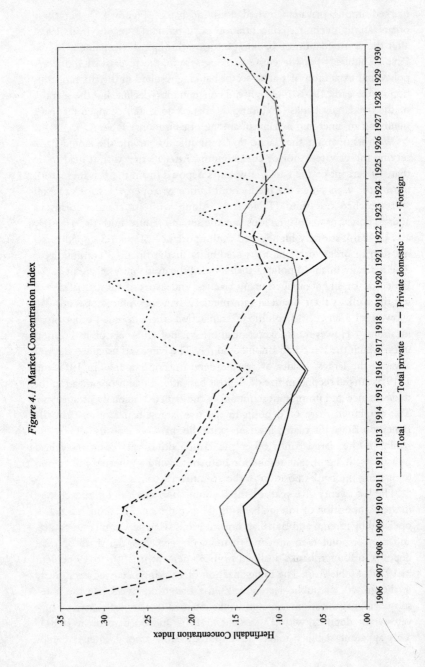

Figure 4.1 Market Concentration Index

British organizations lost their predominant position, with their market share declining by about half over these years. The changing market share reflected specific organizational dynamics.[68] By the early 1930s, the Bank of London and South America (the major British bank) assessed its weakening position in the Brazilian market and emphasized a need to shift its business focus to offering local credit and lessening its reliance on foreign exchange transactions.[69] The shift in the composition of the foreign banking community reflected the increasing ease and interest with which these organizations could do business in Brazil.

Growth

After the earlier years of stagnation, the restructured banking system quickly realized very rapid growth. In 1930, the banking system was about thirteen times the size it had been in 1906, measured by real (price-adjusted) deposits (Figure 4.2 and Table A.11). Organizations receiving public sector support—the Banco do Brasil and state-subsidized banks—fueled the expansion at rates greatly in excess of the private-sector organizations (Table 4.1).

The periods of exceptional growth for the Banco do Brasil's private-sector deposits—its early "start-up" years prior to World War I and the expansionary period from 1921 to 1923, when the Treasury funded large rediscount operations—paralleled federal monetary policy. Monetary policy and Treasury action motivated the bank's growth during both periods. Among private organizations, quite different dynamics characterized each of these periods. During the first period, until 1912, policies that simultaneously stabilized the value of the mil-réis and promoted domestic expansion also supported strong growth among all components of the banking system. In contrast, from 1921 to 1923, the Banco do Brasil's growth, rooted in its rediscounting function, resulted in a shift toward the bank and away from other organizations, rather than overall growth. During the course of 1921 both private domestic and state-subsidized banks contracted their real (price-adjusted) deposit bases, while the Banco do Brasil's nearly doubled. (Table A.2 shows the annual growth indices depicted in Figure 4.2.)

The exponential increase of state-subsidized banks after 1926 was the result of an injection of capital and assumption of ownership by its state government in the Banco do Estado de São Paulo (Banespa). Although the political economy of this move was important (and it is explored in Chapter 7), Figure 4.2 demonstrates that its short-term impact on overall growth remained relatively small. Beyond the strong shift that this event generated,

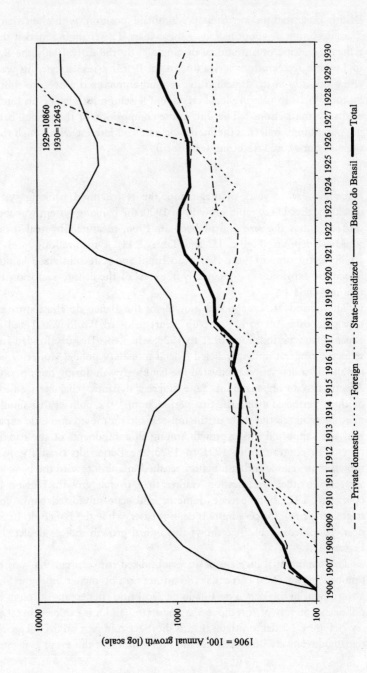

Figure 4.2 Deposit Growth Index, by Type of Bank (1906 = 100)

- - - Private domestic   · · · · · Foreign   - · - · State-subsidized   —— Banco do Brasil   —— Total

the state-subsidized banks tended to grow in a pattern that countered the growth of privately owned organizations. The dichotomized growth rates between public and private organizations clearly demonstrated the beginning of the similarly bifurcated banking system.

Privately owned domestic banks grew at significantly lower rates than the public-sector-related organizations. Nevertheless, they still experienced average, price-adjusted growth of almost 9 percent per year for the entire twenty-five years. In 1930, domestic banks' real deposits had increased eight and a half times from their 1906 base; foreign banks had grown almost fivefold (on a price-adjusted basis). By contrast, according to the best measures available, the real national product increased at a rate of about 4.8 percent annually for the same period; so that, by 1930, the economy was only about two and a half times its size in 1906 (Table A.10). The privately owned banks experienced significantly smoother growth than did the public-sector organizations (as evidenced visually in Figure 4.2 and by their lower standard deviation of the annual growth rates in Table 4.1). The banking system advanced consistently in its importance in the economy with its high and fairly steady growth. Nevertheless, at the end of the 1920s, the recapitalization of Banespa and the counter-cyclical actions of the Banco do Brasil with the onset of the Depression resulted in a strong shift of source of growth toward the public-sector organizations.

Liquidity and Leverage

While the banking system was expanding rapidly, its overall business structure reflected enhanced stability and confidence, simultaneously with conservative attitudes toward risk. One of the most consistent indicators of

Table 4.1 1906-1930 Deposit Growth Experience

	Annual growth	
Type of bank:	(% per annum)	Standard deviation
Private domestic	8.9	14.8
Foreign	7.0	20.7
State-subsidized	20.2	35.2
Banco do Brasil	17.5	41.2
Average of total banking system	10.7	14.7
Total production	4.0	4.5

Source: Derived from Tables A.2 and A.11.
Note: Growth rates based on real, price-adjusted annual average deposits.

banks' increased stability through the period was declining liquidity, as measured by the reserve ratio (of cash as a proportion of deposits, Figure 4.3 and Table A.1). Safely declining reserves indicated that banks could allocate an increasing proportion of their funds to productive and profitable lending, rather than holding cash in reserve, without jeopardizing their ability to redeem deposits. As important, depositors did not perceive an increased risk to their deposits. This trend clearly signified both improved risk management on the part of banks and the increasing confidence of the public. Contemporary concern and existing historiography have emphasized the high levels of cash held by banks and their constraint to credit availability,[70] despite the sustained declining trend of the reserve ratio. Measured by late-twentieth-century standards, banks did hold high levels of cash. However, assessed against the perception of a liquidity crisis as the cause of banking failures from 1900 to 1905, and thin capital markets at the time, it is possible to conclude that the banks were behaving in a manner that was rational for them and for the economy.[71]

The reserve ratio history yields three significant findings. First, in the aggregate, between 1906 and 1930, reserve ratios increased only during three short periods, when economic contraction magnified the risk attendant to banking. The economic contractions that severely constrained private productive activities—in 1914, 1920, and 1927 to 1929—quickly caused banks to increase cash balances relative to their deposits. These respective contractions were due to the decline of international trade at the beginning of World War I, the collapse of international commodities markets in 1920, and the severe domestic recession that preceded the 1929 global depression. During these periods, rapid declines in economic activity severely limited investment opportunities for banks.[72] However, each contraction saw a successively smaller increase in the reserve ratios; after these periods, reserve ratios immediately fell below the levels preceding the contractions.

The reserve ratio history's second important finding is the similarity in the experience of foreign and domestic privately owned banks.[73] During World War I, the liquidity of foreign banks increased more sharply than did that of domestic banks, in reaction to European capital controls and the freezing of German assets imposed by the Brazilian government. More important, foreign bank liquidity increased again during 1921 and 1922, the years that the Rediscount Office was in operation. Because their capital resided in their home countries, foreign banks did not meet the capital requirements to access the Rediscount Office. The rapid deterioration of the exchange rate (from 9.72 pence/mil-réis to 6.28 pence/mil-réis

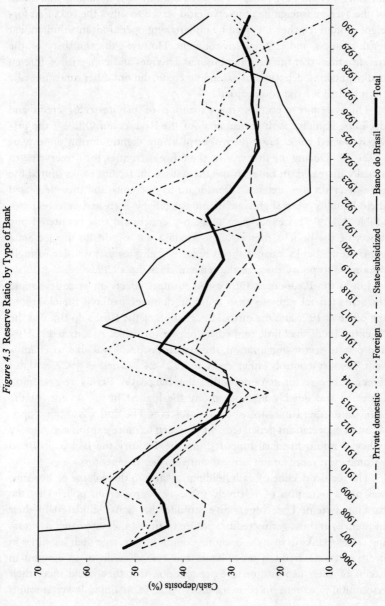

Figure 4.3 Reserve Ratio, by Type of Bank

- - - Private domestic   ····· Foreign   -·-·- State-subsidized   —— Banco do Brasil   —— Total

between January 1921 and December 1923[74]) also decreased the value of profits, denominated in the home currency. These two periods interrupted the longer trend only briefly. The persistent, though declining, increment of the average foreign bank reserve ratio served to offset the risks that foreigners often felt they incurred by undertaking operations in an unfamiliar legal, business, and cultural environment. However, the similarity of the trend testifies that the ongoing business activities and concerns of foreign banks, in taking deposits and extending credit, did not differ fundamentally from their domestic counterparts.

Third, despite espousing the expansion of private-sector credit and declining liquidity as rhetorical goals of the Rediscount Office,[75] the privately owned banks grew (in real terms) only slightly during these years (1921-23). During the first year of the office's activities, their reserve ratios actually increased. In order to use the rediscount facility, banks shifted the type of credit they extended from loans to discounts, and they decreased their liquidity very slightly, as demonstrated by increased reserve ratios (Table A.1).[76] This experience suggests a conclusion that countered one aspect of the policy's rhetoric. The funding was a move to finance State expenditure. Banks' balance sheets reflected behavior that was decreasingly responsive to policy through the remainder of the 1920s.

Just as the Rediscount Office had stronger effects on price levels and financing federal expenses than it did on domestic banking, the closing of the office in 1923 and the official designation of the Banco do Brasil as the "Central Bank" had little immediate impact for banks. As a mixed public- and private-sector organization, the Banco do Brasil was able to circumvent Treasury controls rather easily in 1923-24.[77] Then in 1927, without direct public-sector responsibilities, the Banco do Brasil's reserve ratio increased and quickly became among the highest in the system. At the same time, other banks decreased their reserves. The shift was also in opposition to expectations generated by the return to more expansive monetary policy. Without financial support from the Treasury, the Banco do Brasil became even more conservative than its smaller competitors.

The secular decline of cash holdings, relative to the volume of deposits, was not a reflection of relatively more aggressive credit policies by the banking system. The conservative attitude that banks displayed in their insistence on short-term credit exposure mirrored their approach to creating credit. Banks in many economies commonly leverage their liabilities in order to create credit. That is, banks can extend credit to an amount in excess of their deposits, on the presumption that they could meet their responsibility to redeem their liabilities while maintaining lower amounts in reserve for potential losses.[78] During the last twenty-five years of the First Republic, banks did not aggressively expand their liabilities in order to create credit. Bankers could have chosen to increase credit by aggressively soliciting deposits or by extending the risk to which they submitted their capital.[79] Instead, banks lent only against their deposit bases. The relatively steady and low leverage experience of the private-sector banks reinforces the suggestion of Chapter 3 that they actively served as note-distribution agents for the Treasury during periods of expansive domestic monetary policy.

Indicating their conservative credit practices, the ratio of short-term credit to deposits remained fairly steady, and close to 100 percent, for the entire period (Figure 4.4). The two brief periods when short-term credit reached beyond 105 percent of deposits were from 1913 to 1914 and again in 1924. Both were periods of contraction in banking and in the economy, following periods of strong growth, discussed above. The banks with public-sector orientation led the leverage experience during these years. Counter-cyclical lending of the Banco do Brasil or the state-subsidized banks partially offset the contractionary economic periods. Monetary policy discouraged banks from expanding their credit during either contractionary period. Especially in 1924, the Treasury worked hard to induce a contraction of the money supply (and therefore of deposits).[80] Further, at these times, bank deposits in private organizations could decline more rapidly than credit, reflecting the banks' inability to reduce credit as rapidly as depositors withdrew their funds.[81] Nevertheless, the stability and non-expansive relationship between bank credit and deposits among privately owned organizations through expansive periods as well as contractions suggests that either the demand for, or the structural conditions to support, more expansive and risky lending did not exist. An alternative perspective could emphasize, however, that the volume of credit increased at about the same—substantial—rate as deposits. Therefore, although it did not create incremental financial resources by leveraging deposits, the banking system executed an increasing share of the transactions undertaken by the economy and actively managed its risk exposure.

Cost of Money—Interest Rates

One succinct indication of a dynamic and increasingly responsive banking system would be found in the trend of the cost of money—interest rates. Banking theory expects that, abstracting from the short-term fluctuations of economic cycles, as banking becomes more efficient at attracting and allocating funds and managing risk, and as banks become more competi-

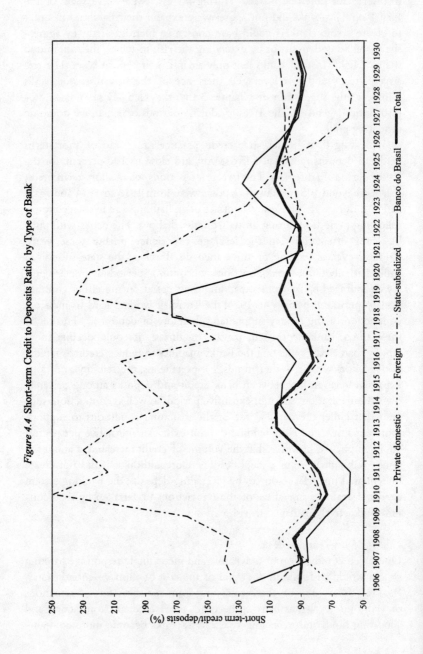

Figure 4.4 Short-term Credit to Deposits Ratio, by Type of Bank

- - - Private domestic   · · · · · Foreign   – · – State-subsidized   ——— Banco do Brasil   ——— Total

tive among themselves, the interest rates they charge on credit should decline. In the absence of a direct measure of interest rates that banks charged on loans, a proxy rate, based on the net profitability of banks' earning assets, traces the average return on bank investments. This proxy interest rate assesses the perspective of banks, rather than the cost of credit incurred by their borrowers.[82] These data also include only a subset of banks from the entire sample; complete data are available for the private domestic banks in Rio de Janeiro and São Paulo, the state-subsidized banks, and the Banco do Brasil. (Details and a discussion of constraints on the data and the measure of the proxy interest rate are in the Data Appendix.) Figure 4.5 presents the trend of proxy interest rates for private domestic and state-subsidized banks, as well as the Banco do Brasil, from 1906 to 1930. The data and methodological constraints of these trends suggest caution. Nevertheless, their results are unambiguous.

Proxy interest rates varied for each type of bank. Their relative ordering conformed with expectations. With only short exceptions, the private domestic banks extended credit more profitably than did others. Investors with solely private-sector interests required higher returns than would be acceptable for organizations with public mandates and subsidies and with goals additional to profitability. From 1906 until 1918, the private domestic banks also experienced higher degrees of fluctuation. The secular decline of proxy interest rates at both the privately owned domestic banks and the Banco do Brasil were firmly entrenched by the 1920s. These results should be representative of the entire banking system. From its reopening, the private domestic organizations and the Banco do Brasil never accounted for less than half of the banking system. Their combined market share usually ranged between 65 percent and 75 percent of the entire system (Table A.6).[83] The sharp and apparently permanent decline in the rates that privately owned domestic banks earned from the mid-1910s offered the most dramatic evidence of the successful banking development, from the perspective of nonbank economic agents (if not from the perspective of diminished bank returns, Figure 4.5). Strong cyclical fluctuation did not interrupt the trend of declining interest rates for the private domestic banks and the Banco do Brasil, as the correlation coefficients of the proxy interest rates with an index of time demonstrate (Table 4.2). These results reflect a system of increasing volume and maturity that eased the flow of money from its sources of supply to uses of greater productivity and security.

The tumultuous credit and money circumstances of World War I that had prompted reversals of monetary policy also generated the very sharp

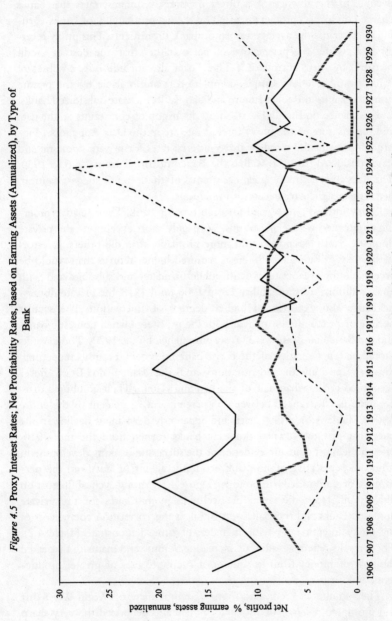

Figure 4.5 Proxy Interest Rates; Net Profitability Rates, based on Earning Assets (Annualized), by Type of Bank

Table 4.2 Bi-variate Correlation Coefficient

Proxy interest rates of:	Time correlation with
Private domestic banks	-.70**
State-subsidized banks	.51*
Banco do Brasil	-.66**

Source: Derived from Table A.5.
Notes: Time is a trend variable, with its value set equal to the entry number of the observation. Correlation (2-tailed) is significant at:
**   1% level.
 *   5% level.

turnaround of declining private-bank interest rates from 1914. The increased risk premium on sovereign debt and the plummeting exchange rate due to shocks in international capital and money markets at the beginning of World War I (as examined in Chapter 3) were transmitted to domestic money markets through interest rates in the banking system. Anecdotal evidence and contemporary complaints of diminished credit availability were other expressions of this experience.[84] This disruption of the longer-term rate decline was short-lived. The lower interest rate scenario returned by 1917, as both monetary and bank credit policies adjusted to the sharp change in financial circumstance.

Rates also reversed their pattern of fluctuation simultaneously with their sharp declines from the mid-1910s. The rate trends at domestically owned private banks became more stable, while fluctuations increased at the Banco do Brasil. Proxy interest rates at the Banco do Brasil in the 1920s directly mirrored its role in monetary policy. Rates fell dramatically during domestic monetary expansion, with only short increases during the 1924 attempt to induce contraction and when the bank was without any formal or informal monetary responsibility in 1927-28. As monetary policy more aggressively pursued domestic monetary expansion, the effects of economic fluctuation shifted from the domestic financial system to exchange rates and capital flows. Given such dramatic monetary changes through the 1920s as the Rediscount and Stabilization Offices, the comparatively small changes in proxy interest rates for domestically owned private banks signified their emerging stability. A combination of increasingly dynamic competition among the private banks and the post-World War I trend of expansive monetary policy resulted in lower proxy interest rates.[85]

The extreme fluctuations of interest rates for the state-subsidized banks resulted from the aggressive expansion of public-sector banking among states, as explored in Chapter 7. The increased rates of state-subsidized banks and the apparent inverse relation between these organizations and the Treasury-supported Banco do Brasil will provide much of the evidence for that argument. However, these two state-subsidized banks only accounted for 1-2 percent of the banking system prior to 1926. Their small size constrained their impact on the average cost of credit.

The Banco do Brasil's impressive set of privileges and responsibilities gave the bank a role that transcended its private-sector credit and deposit-taking activities and was at odds with the profit-maximizing and risk-minimizing goals of (at least some) shareholders. From its beginning, its public and private orientations conflicted with the bank's commercial operations, as interest rates lower than those of the private banks demonstrated. The experience of the Rediscount Office made this most evident. Although the funding and the financial management of the Rediscount Office were separate from the bank's commercial activities, the separation was never complete. In June 1921, the president of the Banco do Brasil, José Maria Whitaker, negotiated directly with the president of Brazil, Epitácio Pessoa, in an unsuccessful attempt to reverse a reduction in the rediscount rate from 6 percent to 5 percent. The interest rate that banks paid to attract (interest-bearing) deposits ranged from 3 percent to 6 percent at the time.[86] The bank argued for the higher discount rate in order to protect shareholder interests and to maintain a positive differential between the rediscount and deposit rates. Although the deposit and rediscount rates were separate decisions, the bank had difficulty accepting a situation in which it was lending funds (through its rediscounting) at rates lower than it acquired funds from public sources. Other banks, its competitors in commercial markets, could raise funds by borrowing money from the Banco do Brasil at lower rates than they paid to depositors. In practice, the argument regarding the competitive and economic logic of the rediscount rate simply represented an attempt to enhance the bank's profits from its financing of Treasury operations.[87] Shareholders paid a price for this policy, documented by the very low return on their earning assets.[88] The bank further demonstrated the extent to which its State sponsorship affected its private-sector credit portfolio in 1927, the year after closing its central bank facilities and formal public-sector responsibilities. Immediately, its interest rates increased and the bank was increasingly conservative with increased reserve ratios and declining leverage of its deposit base (Figures 4.3 and 4.4). Its financial structure quickly began to approach those of the private domestic banks when it no longer had either the responsibility or automatic backing of the Treasury. Finally, these trends reversed slightly again at the end of the decade, as the Banco do Brasil took on an informal counter-cyclical role with the onset of the Depression.

CONCLUSION

The banking system in 1930 had little in common with its antecedents at the beginning of the Republic. From 1889 until 1898, uninhibited ambitions for growth, competing economic ideologies, and inexperience with the dynamics of financial markets contributed to financial chaos. The slow and painful reconstruction lasted until 1906. After the Encilhamento, regulation prohibited banks from issuing their own notes and trading in foreign exchange. Markets for long-term investment, either in loans or stocks and debentures, were not liquid. Therefore long-term investment became a risky strategy. Banks adopted conservative business practices both out of prudence and necessity. By the time that Brazil was able to access significant new international loans, valorize coffee, go on the gold standard, and reestablish a national bank, bankers and financial authorities had structured a financial system that was both safe and dynamic.

After its reorganization at the end of 1905, the banking system developed many characteristics of stability and maturity that strengthened through the remainder of the First Republic. The entire banking system grew, while also exhibiting conservatism. The variation in the experiences of different types of banks corresponded with the differences of their ownership structures and economic interests. The types of business transactions in which banks engaged became more strongly focused, as they learned from past problems and as regulation required. Declining returns for lenders (proxy interest rates) indicated the increasing efficiency of money, while still reflecting economic fluctuation and the distinction between public and private in predictable manners. Declining market concentration was another indication of dynamic fluidity among privately owned organizations. Characteristics of dynamism combined with conservative business strategies of banking enterprises resulted in a system that did not experience generalized failure for the remainder of the First Republic, even if it suffered strong fluctuation. These changes also indicated that economic agents increasingly perceived banking as a viable and desirable activity that responded to economic circumstance in manners consistent with their financial structure. This represented a significant improvement from previous bank experiments throughout the nineteenth century.

The results for the banking system corresponded to expectations derived from modern banking theory and the experiences of other economies. Under conditions of general economic growth with reasonably steady monetary policy and a strong international position from 1906 to 1912, a strong system emerged with a stability that continued through the remainder of the First Republic. The financial and economic reversals of World War I encouraged the economy to turn inward, creating domestic financial instruments in the face of closed international markets from 1913-14. Restructuring and accommodation characterized the remainder of the 1910s. During the 1920s, institutional mechanisms more overtly attempted reconciliation between domestic and international financial circumstance. Through these vicissitudes of government intervention, the banking system continued to function, and with increasing success.

Simultaneously with this positive evolution, the banking system demonstrated characteristics that raised questions about its long-term effectiveness and substantiated some of the complaints of contemporaries. Although diminishing, reserve ratios remained high. Combined with the low rate at which banks leveraged deposits into credit, the widely publicized opinion in the commercial community that banks could have been more expansive in creating credit deserves consideration. While the trend was clearly toward increasing expansiveness, bankers also weighted the risk factors very heavily in their lending decisions and in the types of transactions they were willing to undertake.

Further, the relationship between public and private sectors provided one of the strong dynamics for banking. Because of its size and the politicized nature of the federal government's role, the State's use of the banking system through the Banco do Brasil was an active avenue by which it constructed influence in the economy. Its combination of public and private ownership injected an important ambiguity in the definition of "public interest." The opposition between the state-subsidized banks and the Banco do Brasil was evident in the inverse relationships between them with respect to growth, reserves, and interest rates. Additionally, the strong dichotomy of the growth experiences of public- and private-sector banks suggests that a two-tiered banking system began to emerge at the beginning of the twentieth century. This tension between the federal government and individual states in banking developed into a very strong economic and political force through the twentieth century. Incipient evidence of the opposing dynamics became obvious from the earliest days.

These transformations of the banking system did not require any of the fundamental conditions associated with the introduction of the Republic.

However, it is difficult to imagine an environment in which banking could have arisen without the structural economic change that was integral to the Republic. The transition from slave to wage labor, the reconstitution of governing mechanisms, and the vast expansion of the labor force in commodified agriculture and industry created the demand for responsive and dynamic banking in the private sector. Even in light of this dynamism, though, this chapter has also indicated potential constraints to the ability of banks to maximize their contribution to long-term economic growth and development. This picture of an energized banking system in the wake of the early failures of the First Republic lays a foundation for understanding the interactions of banks with other economic agents, as well as the opportunities and limits of banking for transmitting economic change.

Chapter 5

The Productive Sectors, Banking, and Bankers

B razilian banks did not extend long-term credit that financed the construction of new economic capabilities, such as industrial manufacturing. They limited their activities to financing the traditional activities of commercial exchange. Then, how could banking be important to the fundamental economic transformations in the private productive sectors of the economy during the First Republic? And, what might have been important about banking? These are the questions that this chapter addresses, and they have been central to the study of banking history in other settings.

One of the persistent interests of banking historians has been the connection between the development of banking systems and industrialization. As with state-building, the scale of capital required for sustained industrialization and the risks involved in the innovation of new production technologies have typically induced its practitioners to look for new financial methods. The goals motivating financial development have included attracting increasing volumes of capital, involving new participants, devising new methods to control and share risks, and enhancing efficiency. Existing research on the effects of banking on economic structure focuses on industrialization in currently developed economies.[1] That body of work comes out of the desire to understand the origins of industrial development and its attendant financial requirements for capital formation and easing the conduct of transactions. Historians and economists had long noted the (approximately) simultaneous development of the two processes. History and logic have contributed to the belief that they depended upon each other. In the classic typology of banking development, delineated by Gerschenkron, the scale of banking evolved from small organizations that maintained short, relatively risk-free time horizons, to organizations of larger scope able to absorb the increased risk of long-term investment, and ultimately to include the State as entrepreneur-banker with an economy's later onset of industrialization. Gerschenkronian logic related the scale of banking and the nature of its entrepreneurialism to the scale, capital intensity, and technological complexity of prevailing industrial practices at the time the process began.[2] Despite many challenges by specific cases, economic historians have generally retained this framework for understanding banks and development.

More broadly than industrialization, however, the functions that banking fulfilled facilitated market building: the formal, depersonalized exchange of an increasing diversity of goods and services among larger groups of individuals. Because commercial banking systems limit their activity to short-term transactions, they did not participate directly in capital formation as economies began to industrialize. Focus on this constraint has minimized attention to their significant contribution to mercantile exchange. Banks broadened the scope of accumulation and allocation of resources and facilitated the financial aspect of commercial exchange. As consumers increasingly met their daily subsistence needs by purchasing goods in the marketplace, and as domestically manufactured goods represented a greater proportion of their consumption, banks responded to the need for credit that supported the expanded production and distribution of goods.[3] They provided working capital to producers and to the distribution network of wholesalers and retailers. In doing so, they smoothed the timing differentials of payments between the beginning and end of each step from the production to the consumption of goods and services. The concentration on commercial finance both allowed goods to flow more freely and it allowed entrepreneurs to direct their wealth to the long-term capital formation required to sustain these developments. These were among the transformations necessary to sustain industrialization, beyond the construction of manufacturing concerns in which to expand the production of goods.

Such transformations were of crucial concern to shaping the society of the First Republic as it anticipated changes that were as profound as industrialization. Simultaneously with the implementation of the processes of industrial manufacturing, population and urban growth, the formation of an industrial and urban labor system based on wage compensation, the commodification of domestic agriculture, and significant territorial expansion of export agriculture challenged traditional life. All of these processes were mutually reinforcing and they required new financial mechanisms.

Some of the better-studied manifestations of these changes at the beginning of the twentieth century have included the formation of an industrial workforce, race relations, physical infrastructure, and the organization of workers and employers.[4] Although slow to spread, the shift from subsistence- to market-based consumption was one of the underlying fundamental economic and social transitions that restructured lives during the Republic.

The increase of industrial production is a useful indicator of the widespread attendant changes in consumption, labor, and commerce. Brazil remained, relatively, an agricultural economy throughout the First Republic, with about 17 percent of national income deriving from industry in 1930.[5] Nevertheless, industrial growth was rapid during the first years of the twentieth century. Available sectoral indices suggest that industrial production increased at an average rate of about 5.4 percent per year from 1906 to 1930, and agricultural production (including coffee) grew at a rate of about 3.2 percent annually.[6] The construction of industrial capacity has received wide attention,[7] as has the economic sociology of industrialization.[8] The development of banking proceeded in conjunction with other fundamental adjustments in social organization that supported industrialization and other forms of market building. In order to accommodate the financial aspects of change, Brazilian entrepreneurs looked for new methods of financing innovative endeavors, both to expand their reach and to share the risks inherent in innovation, just as their peers in other locations did. Banking responded to this need.

This chapter explores the extent to which, and ways that, the growth of banking and industry, or economic transformation, were related to each other. Building on an understanding of the banking business, the chapter focuses on the effects of banking within the private sector. It approaches the topic in a manner different from that typically applied in Brazilian historiography. Rather than emphasizing issues of money supply, this chapter highlights questions about the demand for money—and specifically that portion of money housed in banks. It addresses the basic questions of: How large was the banking system relative to the economy? Did its growth correlate with economic growth generally, or with the increase of industrial output (as a rough approximation of industrialization)? How did banking, especially of the short-term commercial variety, affect industrialization? Why did entrepreneurs become bankers? Two bodies of evidence provide information to pursue these questions. Quantitative data on banking derived from aggregated firm-level bank balance sheets covering the period from 1906 to 1930, as in Chapter 4,[9] combine with the available information on sectoral economic growth to explore statistical relationships between the growth of banking and production. In addition, an examination of the formation of privately owned banks provides useful insight into the motivations of bankers and their intersectoral connections.

THE SIZE OF THE BANKING SYSTEM
RELATIVE TO THE ECONOMY

Traditional literature represents Brazil as historically "under-banked." The characterization reflects the low volume of banking services.[10] Relative to criteria that financial historians have applied, this conclusion stands. The most commonly accepted measure of the extent to which banking serves an economy is the ratio of bank credit to national income.[11] This measure of financial depth indicates "efficiency in the performance of one of [the banking system's] two essential functions: securing control of disposable funds,"[12] and leveraging those funds into productive investments. The most conservative estimate of financial depth excludes the public-sector banks—the Banco do Brasil and the state-subsidized organizations. (Excluding these banks overcorrects for the role of public treasuries, since these banks undertook a significant portion of their business as normal commercial transactions.[13]) Comparisons of financial depth confirm that the banking sector had a lesser presence in Brazil than it did in other economies during the initial construction of their industrial structures (Table 5.1).

Despite its low level, the rate of the banking system's increasing involvement in the economy is impressive. Banking grew much more rapidly than did other components of the economy. Previous chapters have demonstrated the significant growth of the banking system relative to total output and its incursion in the money supply (Table 4.1 and Figure 3.3). A similar pattern of the enhanced economic importance of banking appeared in the trend of financial depth, increasing from 3 percent of national income in 1906 to almost 18 percent in 1930 (Figure 5.1). Relative to sectoral growth, its record was also impressive. The size of the banking system (real, price-adjusted deposits) increased thirteenfold from 1906 to 1930, with privately owned domestic banks growing by a factor of 8.6. During this period, industrial output increased by a factor of only 3.7 and agricultural output approximately doubled (Figure 5.2 and Table A.11).

In addition to growing more rapidly than the productive sectors of the economy, after the reorganization of banking in 1906, bank deposits constituted a steadily increasing proportion of money.[14] The share of bank deposits in the money supply more than tripled, from 20 percent in 1906

Table 5.1 Financial Depth

	Bank credit as a % of national income:	
	Total credit	Privately owned banks
Brazil, 1906-1930:		
1906	3.4	3.0
1930	17.5	9.4
maximum (1922 for total; 1921 for private)	17.6	12.4
Comparative points of reference:		
Argentina		
1905		27
1930		43
England & Wales		
1775	15.2	
1844	34.4	
France		
1800	1.5	
1870	15.6	
Russia		
1914	61	
United States		
1871	29.8	
1899	62.0	

Sources: Brazil: see Data Appendix. Argentina: della Paolera & Taylor, 1997: 8-9 and Table 1. Other country data: Cameron, 1967: Table IX.1.
Notes: The European and U.S. comparative points of reference represent periods that economic historians have found to cover early industrializations.

Mortgages are included in this measure of Brazilian bank credit, consistent with the comparative data.

to 68 percent in 1930.[15] The money supply's increasing composition of deposits had three potential benefits for the economy. First, the increase of the deposit base created a larger capacity for the banks to extend credit. Although they did not aggressively create credit, it grew in parallel with deposits (Table A.1). Second, the willingness of Brazilians to place deposits with banks, rather than holding currency as a store of resources, implied increasing stability of and strengthening confidence in banking institutions. Third, having a larger share of money in the form of bank deposits improved the efficiency of commerce by settling a larger share of transac-

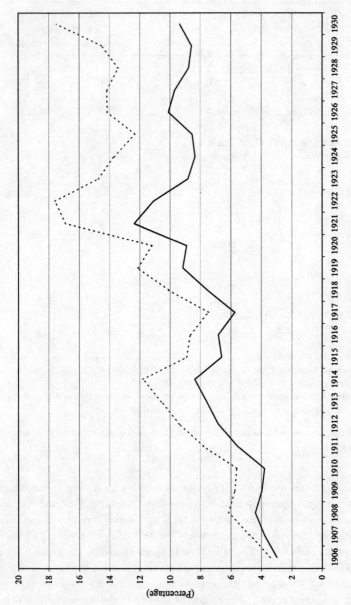

Figure 5.1 Credit as Share of National Income (Percentage)

—— Private-sector banks ‥‥‥ Total banks

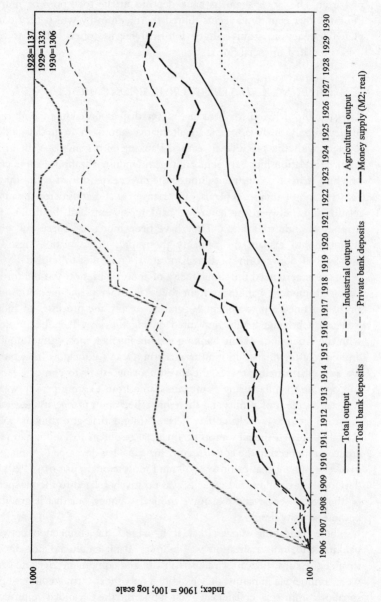

Figure 5.2 Aggregate Economic Growth Measures (1906 = 100)

1928=1137
1929=1332
1930=1306

— Total output
······· Total bank deposits
- - - Industrial output
-·-·- Private bank deposits
······ Agricultural output
— — Money supply (M2; real)

Index; 1906 = 100; log scale

1906 1907 1908 1909 1910 1911 1912 1913 1914 1915 1916 1917 1918 1919 1920 1921 1922 1923 1924 1925 1926 1927 1928 1929 1930

1000

100

tions within the banking system, without the actual exchange of currency or barter. The larger share of bank deposits in the total pool of money indicated that economic agents shifted the medium by which they completed transactions from cash or informal means (often barter) toward bank-mediated financial flows.

BANKING AND STRUCTURAL ECONOMIC CHANGE

Assessing the demand for banking, rather than undertaking a traditional money supply analysis, offers an alternative approach to understanding linkages with the productive sectors. Banking historians have identified empirical relationships between banking and industrialization, even in cases in which structural constraints limited the direct extension of credit for the construction of industrial plants. Historians have also considered the interrelationships between the nature of banking systems and the timing and manner of industrialization. They have been much less successful when attempting to explain the causality motivating these relationships. The problems of doing so in the Brazilian case are no easier to resolve.

Brazil experienced the simultaneity of industrialization and the formation of a modern banking system found in other economies. Although Brazil remained a predominantly agrarian society, the processes of industrialization became firmly implanted during the First Republic,[16] along with the emergence of the banking system. Further, most studies imply a limited role for finance in industrialization. Dean[17] concluded that industry was self-financing; that is, the investment necessary to construct, man, and operate manufacturing companies came from existing private wealth and reinvestment of profits and therefore relied upon prosperity generated in other sectors, notably coffee. Peláez[18] found that government policy actively impeded the allocation of financial resources to industry in preference to supporting the coffee sector. Suzigan[19] has developed a more persuasive argument that prior to 1930 (and most strongly prior to 1920) the development of industrial capacity was positively related to the prosperity of the coffee sector and expansive monetary policy, but that it gradually became self-sustaining.

These indications suggest that, if it existed, the connection between banking and industrialization was indirect. Bank credit did not directly finance the construction of industrial plant and equipment. Because banks were commercial in nature, they extended only short-term credit with personal or commercial collateral. Credit supported the expanded volume and range of ongoing commercial transactions and freed investors' wealth for long-term capital investment. Banking and industrialization were mutually supportive.

The data allow a test to establish the presence and significance of this relationship in the Brazilian economy. A simple model of the supply and demand for banking following elementary economic principles postulates that the demand for banking within an economy should move in the same direction as production and vary inversely with price fluctuation. The available data also allow for sectoral disaggregation to test the connection with increasing industrial production, as a succinct indication of its importance to banking development (Table 5.2;[20] the Appendix to this chapter on the Model of Demand and Supply of Banking discusses the methodology and Appendix Tables A.13a and A.13b present a wider array of tests). The results of these regression tests conform to expectations about the relationships between the real (inflation-adjusted) size of the banking system and the levels of output and prices. The interdependent relationships between banking and growth by sector and by type of bank provide more nuanced interpretations. The results also substantiate a stronger relationship of banking with industry than with agriculture.

The size of the banking system as a whole fluctuated in the same direction as production, and it fluctuated inversely (and more strongly) with the price level.[21] The positive correlation between banking and production and the stronger negative correlation with prices held for both the industrial and agricultural sectors separately, as well as for the total economy. The consistently stronger relationship with prices than with production confirms the importance of money and international finance for the domestic Brazilian economy. The transmission of the international environment to the domestic economy occurred through the mechanisms of money and prices. In this specification, the relationship between the fluctuation of banking and prices expresses the monetary linkage created by the fluctuation value of the mil-réis. These tests concur with all expectations and demonstrate the importance of price level fluctuation to the banking system. The strongly negative connection between prices and demand for banking supports the developmentalist hypothesis that monetary policy favoring domestic financial mechanisms and price inflation spurred the construction of manufacturing capacity because of the implicit price barriers impeding imports due to low value of the mil-réis.[22]

Banking growth showed no significant empirical relationship with coffee. The relationship between fluctuations in banking and the coffee sector, to which contemporary bankers and later historians[23] assign a predominant presence in banking transactions, was statistically insignificant (as indicated by the low proportion of explanatory value, responsiveness, and reliability—the values of R^2, correlation coefficient, and t respectively in Table 5.2). The valorization (price-control) programs, which both provided exogenous control of coffee prices and initiated demand for bank transactions for much of the period, significantly impeded the market-driven relationship between coffee prices and money or the banking system. While this result supports a conclusion that coffee support programs were successful, it does not indicate who benefited from the programs.[24] The total agricultural sector also demonstrated a relationship with banking that was statistically insignificant (Table A.13a).[25]

The development of banking and industry demonstrated a convincing relationship, despite the limited opportunities for banks to directly finance industrial production. The correlation with banking was stronger for industrial production than for other segments of the economy.[26] The significant correlation between the (price-adjusted) size of the banking system and production suggests that bank financing capabilities were related to the rate of industrialization. This influence derived from the cumulative effects of the banking system in freeing up capital for long-term investment and in financing the distribution of goods and services, rather than the direct route of participation in constructing industrial capacity.

Privately owned banks also had a closer connection with industrial growth than did the public-sector organizations. From this perspective, foreign and domestic banks did not differ significantly. (Total private banks are shown in Table 5.2 and the disaggregated results are presented in Table A.13a.) In light of the importance of monetary actions for the banking system and industrialization, and the conduct of monetary policy through the Banco do Brasil, the stronger relationship between private-sector banking and industry is interesting. At the Banco do Brasil and the state-owned banks, supporting industrialization competed with public-sector and monetary goals. Supporting the hypothesis (in Chapter 7) of their similar purposes, the regression results for the Banco do Brasil and the state-owned banks were similar in direction, order of magnitude, and significance. The very different growth trends of these banks (Figure 4.2) suggest that they served distinct markets, again anticipating the analyses of Chapter 7. For current purposes, their comparison with private-sector banks is most revealing. Without the concerns of exercising monetary authority or mediating political interests, private-sector banks responded closely to economic impetus.

These findings, especially the lack of a correlation between fluctuation in the coffee sector and the growth of banking combined with a strong

Table 5.2 Banking, Growth, and Prices

							Dependent variable: (Real) bank deposits:		
	Total Brazil		Total private		State-subsidized		Banco do Brasil	
	β	(t)	β	(t)	β	(t)	β	(t)
Total prices	-2.40	(-2.85)***	-2.03	(-2.54)**	-9.53	(-1.66)	-11.58	(-1.42)
Total production	1.27	(1.23)	0.96	(1.03)	7.71	(1.66)	5.83	(0.89)
Constant	0.14	(2.53)**	0.12	(2.28)**	0.24	(1.10)	0.37	(1.16)
R²	0.28		0.24		0.14		0.09	
Total prices	-2.45	(-3.04)***	-2.14	(-2.78)***	-14.31	(-1.18)	-10.58	(-1.59)
Industrial production	1.25	(1.95)*	1.16	(1.98)*	5.82	(0.98)	4.61	(1.20)
Constant	0.13	(2.53)**	0.10	(2.10)*	0.41	(1.19)	0.31	(1.18)
R²	0.31		0.28		0.06		0.11	
Coffee prices	1.32	(1.15)	1.35	(0.96)	3.36	(1.05)	3.41	(0.72)
Coffee exports	0.05	(0.11)	0.07	(0.16)	0.32	(0.27)	0.28	(0.22)
Constant	0.00	(0.03)	-0.02	(-0.15)	-0.01	(-0.04)	-0.12	(-0.29)
R²	0.07		0.05		0.05		0.03	

Source: Derived from Table A.2.

Notes: See Appendix, "Model of Demand and Supply of Banking" for an explanation of the data and the two-stage least squares regression model. Regressions cover the period 1907-30. All variables are measured as rates of change. Rates of change of bank deposits are calculated after adjusting for price inflation; they are based on the aggregation of firm-level data (see Data Appendix). "Total private" includes privately owned domestic and foreign banks. (See the Table A.13a for foreign and domestic banks, individually. They do not produce significantly different results.) "State-subsidized" are Banespa and Crédito Real (MG).

N=24.

*   significant at 5% level.

**   significant at 1% level.

***   significant at .05% level.

β: Correlation coefficient.

relationship between industry and banking, confirm that the effects of bank intermediation were circuitous, working through the avenues of distribution rather than production. Nevertheless, they also substantiate the empirical relationship between banking and the productive economy that existing historiography and theory anticipate. The regressions demonstrate that banking and production were linked through real, as well as monetary, mechanisms. The statistical exercise does not explain the causes or nature of that relationship. The regression statements specified the direction of causality as running from production and prices to banking; i.e., that changes in monetary policy and production generated fluctuations in the size of the banking system. Econometric tests to determine the antecedence of banking or output growth (if not the direction of causation) yield indeterminate results,[27] supporting the assumption that banking and industrialization relied upon each other to become self-sustaining, rather than sustaining a unidirectional causal relationship.

For insight on the causal factors underpinning the connection between banking and industrial development, one must consider issues subtler than identifying the sectoral distribution of credit. As a practical consideration and reflecting the concerns of bankers, banks' balance sheets did not identify credit by its destination sector. Bankers intended their funds to support a specific type of transaction, mercantile exchange, without regard to sectoral allocation. The cumulative outcome of the daily conduct of individual banking transactions was to create a web of financial flows between businesses and between sectors. The result was that banks intermediated the intersectoral accumulation and allocation of resources. In this process, they contributed to larger and more dynamic markets within which commercial exchange took place for a wider variety of goods and services. Exploring how banking supported, or deterred, structural change in emerging sectors and processes of the economy gives additional perspective to understanding the nature of intersectoral intermediation of financial resources.

THE MULTIFACETED BUSINESS TIES OF BANKERS

Examining individual banks and bankers who became active during the First Republic helps to illustrate the underlying nature of banking's intersectoral relationships and the web of connections that their transactions created. Specific cases demonstrate the mechanisms of bank-supported economic change. Observing the formation of new banks is especially useful for this purpose. Five joint-stock limited-liability banks that formed after the abolition of slavery provide interesting examples. Reflecting their increased stability, the newer organizations had long lives. Four of the banks survived into the late twentieth century. These banks began their lives as privately owned domestic organizations; listing their equity shares on the public securities exchanges was an important step, denoting limited liability and freely transferable ownership. Four of the banks became large and influential, and their senior managers were important in a wide array of activities. (A group of foreign owners took over one of the four surviving organizations.) The common elements of the cases elicit the means by which these organizations intermediated growth and structural change.

In January 1890 (two months after the end of the monarchy and the declaration of the Republic), Antônio Prado took over the small Casa Bancária Nielson & Comp.[28] In doing so, Prado opened and became the first president of the Banco de Comércio e Indústria de São Paulo (Comind).[29] He remained president of the bank until 1920, by which time it had become the largest bank in São Paulo and one of the largest in Brazil. The Prado family had established itself prominently in the economic and political elite of both São Paulo and Brazil by the beginning of the nineteenth century. Tax collection and exporting (but not producing) sugar provided the family's early wealth. By the middle of the nineteenth century, the Prados had diversified their activities to become major participants in the burgeoning coffee complex; they were both *fazendeiros* (plantation owners) and exporters. The baron of Igauape, the patriarch of the Prado clan, began the family's association with banking in the 1850s, as the president of the São Paulo affiliate of the (second) Banco do Brasil; the Prado family held about half of the affiliate's capital.[30] At least one family member[31] was also involved in the formation of the short-lived Casa Bancária da Província de São Paulo in 1885.[32] Other business endeavors of the family during the last quarter of the nineteenth and beginning of the twentieth centuries extended to widespread holdings of coffee plantations, livestock and hide-tanning, the first Brazilian-owned refrigerated meatpacking plant (jointly owned with Alexandre Siciliano, an important Italian immigrant entrepreneur), and a glassworks plant. The family also had large equity positions in the Rio Claro and Paulista Railways; Antônio Prado served as president of both. The Prado family extended its activities to banking because it diversified their economic holdings toward new activities, while still supporting its traditional sources of wealth. Toward these ends, they took advantage of the eased Commercial Code reforms of 1890 to incorporate a joint stock bank. During the 1890s the bank had significant share holdings in Prado family enterprises.[33]

Comind became a large and influential bank in the paulista economy and the national banking system. The bank maintained a very conservative business profile during the First Republic. Its reserve ratio was always above the average reserve ratio of private domestic banks, reaching 60 percent in 1910 and 55-57 percent in 1915-16 (years of recession and unstable financial situations).[34] Throughout the period, Comind was one of the largest banks in Brazil; usually it was either the largest or second largest (excluding the Banco do Brasil, Table A.7). Reflecting its size by 1906, it grew more slowly and steadily than the banking system as a whole. Even so, at its largest in 1928 (before the recession beginning that year), Comind's real (price-adjusted) deposit base was almost four times its size in 1906. The bank became a crucial nexus for early industrialists. During the 1920s, such major industrial entrepreneurs as Jorge Street (primarily textiles) and Roberto Simonsen (construction and engineering) served as directors of the bank.[35]

In another example, Francisco Matarazzo exemplified the paulista immigrant-merchant-turned-industrialist.[36] Matarazzo arrived in São Paulo from Italy in 1881, slightly in advance of the massive, post-abolition wave of European immigration that was important to all of Brazil, but especially to São Paulo and its coffee expansion.[37] Beginning as a dry goods merchant, Matarazzo soon expanded into the production, canning, and distribution of lard. He then diversified to other consumer goods such as milled flour and rice, canvas sacks, soaps, and oils. Initially he banked with the Bank of London and Brazil. But, by 1900, Matarazzo joined forces with other Italian immigrants to open the Banco Commerciale Italiano di São Paulo. In 1905, he participated in the formation of a second bank, also with Italian immigrant partners, the Banco Italiano del Brasile. The two banks appear to have merged shortly after the opening of the Italiano del Brasile.[38] Then, in 1910, the Banque Francesse et Italiano, headquartered and managed in Paris, took over the Commerciale Italiano.[39] Matarazzo remained an important shareholder. His banking interests remained organizationally separate from the incorporation of the family industrial conglomerate. By the end of the 1920s, family enterprises had further diversified to include successively more sophisticated industries. They established monopolies in producing rayon, and in refining and deodorizing cottonseed oil. The family-owned conglomerate also owned equipment-maintenance and tool-and-die plants. From an early stage in building what became the country's largest industrial conglomerate, Matarazzo constantly maintained a presence in the banking sector to ensure his firms' access to working capital.

The Francesse et Italiano was the largest foreign bank in Brazil, after it became French-owned. For some years in the early 1920s, it was the largest bank in Brazil, after the Banco do Brasil (Table A.7). Its size reflected the combined markets that it served, of both merchants and Italian immigrant workers. Even so, its growth experience and financial structure, as demonstrated by the reserve and leverage ratios, were not substantively different from the norm of foreign banks. In contrast, prior to 1910, when the ownership transfer occurred, very high reserve ratios (70-95 percent) and leverage ratios (175-290 percent) could indicate a strongly personalized use of the bank. These ratios, significantly higher than the average for domestically owned publicly traded banks (Table A.1), document that the bank did not rely on deposits to fund its operations. By implication, the bank invested its large base of capital, relative to assets held as cash and credit, without the necessity of accommodating depositors' concerns. The change in ownership and management seemed to immediately restructure the bank's financial orientation toward that seen in the foreign banks.

In Rio Grande do Sul, the Banco Pelotense opened in 1906[40] as a commercial bank. (In an important experiment, its amended statutes in 1910 allowed the bank to extend mortgage credit; it did not do so to a significant extent.) The Pelotense was one of three substantial banks in Rio Grande do Sul. The other two major banks, prior to the opening of the Banco de Rio Grande do Sul in 1928, were the Banco da Província de Rio Grande do Sul and the Banco de Comércio. These three firms held 70 percent of riograndense bank deposits in 1927, immediately prior to the formation of the state-owned bank. Lagemann finds that the two older banks, located in the town of Porto Alegre, confined their businesses to traditional commercial relationships. By contrast, in Pelotas, the Pelotense was heavily involved in ranching and the production of jerked beef, as those activities became more highly commercialized during the early twentieth century. The bank participated in the expansion of refrigerated shipping (with *frigoríficos*) to enable the export of beef to Europe. And, it extended the geographic reach of banking in the south away from the established commercial center of Porto Alegre. The Pelotense had highly concentrated ownership and management. One hundred and forty-three shareholders founded the bank; only five individuals initially held one-half of the shares.[41] Through the remainder of the First Republic, only eight shareholders served as directors; and with minor exceptions the economic interests of the directors were concentrated in cattle ranching and processing.

The Pelotense quickly became large. By the mid-1910s, it was among the five largest (excluding the Banco do Brasil, Table A.7). The bank was also notable for its practice of maintaining very low reserves, by Brazilian standards of the time. From 1910, the bank consistently maintained less than 20 percent of its deposits as cash. In the high growth years of 1919 and 1920, its reserve ratio was 11 percent, and in the recessionary years of 1929 and 1930, when other banks aggressively increased their holdings of cash, the Pelotense's declined. During the 1910s and 1920s, the bank established a branch system throughout the state. Based on the geographic distribution of credit and deposits by branch, Lagemann concludes that the Pelotense served to transfer resources from traditional to newer ranching interests.[42] By unexplained arrangements, the bank also established the first interstate branches of a privately owned domestic bank.[43] The bank located its out-of-state branches in ranching areas. The Pelotense had the shortest life of these banks. The bank failed in 1931, during the Depression (although Lagemann specifically does not attribute the failure to the Depression[44]) and within four years of the state government's opening the Banco do Rio Grande do Sul.[45] It appears that the Pelotense failed when the state treasury transferred deposits to the Banco de Rio Grande do Sul in a move that had the political support of Getúlio Vargas as he was establishing the "revolutionary" government.[46] Since the Pelotense was the only bank in which the state government had placed deposits that failed (from among all three of the large riograndense organizations), its experience may indicate the continuing importance of maintaining reserves of cash to protect against rapid withdrawals.

More successfully, in the Federal District (the city of Rio de Janeiro), a group of Portuguese immigrant merchants and industrialists combined their capital to form the Banco Português do Brasil in 1918 (merged into Banco Itaú in 1973).[47] The original investors included important business names in Rio de Janeiro, such as its first president, the Visconde de Moraes (real estate development and industrial ceramics), Zeferino de Oliveira (textiles, candles, soap, and beer), and the Sotto Maior family (textiles, import/export). The bank's original statutes specified the bank's intent to service the Luso-Brazilian community and to serve the economic and financial interests of both Portugal and Brazil.[48] Almost immediately upon opening, the bank replaced an older Portuguese organization, the Banco Nacional Ultramarino, as the organ through which immigrant workers remitted funds to their families in Portugal.

The Português do Brasil was somewhat different from other banks in its widely distributed share ownership. Within its first year of operation, the bank's stock registered 529 Brazilian owners, representing 73 percent of its capital. Portuguese shareholders controlled the remainder. The five largest shareholders owned 22 percent of the firm. Even with its diversified ownership, the bank's activities seemed directed toward the business interests of its major shareholders. The Português do Brasil was also unusual in that its 1919 amended statutes and capital increase specifically allowed for the bank to extend long-term credit. Although this provision was seldom used, Marques finds an instance of the bank extending long-term credit to the Companhia Fiação e Tecidos Corcovado (a textiles firm, owned by one of the bank's major shareholders, the Sotto Maior family). In 1920, the major shareholders also used the bank as a conduit for investment in the Empresa Melhoramentos da Baixada Fluminense (a waterworks company in the lowland suburban area surrounding the city of Rio de Janeiro), a major recipient of federal financing for urban improvement. The Empresa Melhoramentos' eight largest shareholders, accounting for 77 percent of its capital, were the major investors of the Português do Brasil, including the Visconde de Moraes and five individuals or companies of the Sotto Maior family. Further, the Português do Brasil was an important creditor to the Manufatura Nacional de Porcelanas (industrial ceramics); the Visconde de Moraes was president of both organizations. Both the Melhoramentos da Baixada and Porcelanas became unprofitable activities for the bank; and, according to the bank's own analysis, they significantly contributed to severe difficulties it suffered during the Depression years.[49]

Although the Português do Brasil served the specific needs of its directors and owners, its financial structure was unremarkable. The growth pattern and liquidity and leverage ratios of the bank were not significantly different from the average experience of privately owned domestic banks. The bank became large and important, but during the First Republic it was not among the largest in Brazil.[50] The use of deposits to fund directors' other business initiatives did not cause the Português do Brasil to compromise its business structure; the conservative financial structure, while supporting new entrepreneurial investment, appeared in line with other organizations.[51]

Banco Boavista became publicly listed on the Bolsa de Valores in 1924, when two established Rio de Janeiro business names, the Guinle family and Alberto Teixeira Boavista, combined their interests.[52] The Guinles were established merchants, hoteliers, and textile manufacturers.[53] Boavista was a professional banker. He learned banking through his work experience with the Banque Francesse et Italiano before opening his eponymous *casa bancária*. In 1922, Alberto Boavista was instrumental in the founding of the Associação Bancária de Rio de Janeiro, and in 1931 he became a director of the Banco do Brasil. A Portuguese immigrant, the Barão de Saavedra, was the third participant in the Casa Bancária Boavista. In 1927 the three investors recapitalized the *casa bancária,* raising its capital from 4 contos to 15,000 contos (approximately U.S.$1.7 million). In order to raise the capital, the Guinle family sold its electric company, Companhia Brasileira de Energia Elétrica, to the Canadian Traction, Light, and Power Company.[54] Initially, 93 owners held Boavista stock; the Guinle family owned 62 percent of the firm and the nine largest shareholders controlled 93 percent of the stock. Boavista was one of the few banks to raise funding by issuing long-term bonds. Therefore, its shareholders were able to raise capital without divesting their control of the firm. Interestingly, Marques finds an absence of direct relations between Banco Boavista and the nonbanking firms of the original shareholders.[55]

In manners similar to these specific examples of the new domestic banks, foreign banks responded to the circumstances of both international financial circumstances and to economic conditions within Brazil. As mentioned earlier, the French Banque Francesse et Italiano assumed the portfolio of Matarazzo's Commerciale Italiano, and it became a major lender to coffee planters.[56] This bank became very large after its transfer in 1910. For some years during the 1910s and 1920s, it was among the five largest privately owned banks, measured by deposits. With a different business emphasis, another French financial interest, Crédit Foncier, became a major investor/manager in state-subsidized banks before states became majority owners of the firms. Notably, Crédit Foncier provided the original capital and management personnel for the Banco de Crédito Hypothecário e Agrícola de São Paulo before its conversion to Banespa.

However, the more typical mode by which foreign banks entered Brazil in the 1910s was to follow commerce and other businesses from their country of origin.[57] By the end of World War I, the diminution of the early importance of British banks and the dynamic interaction between banks of other national origins and Brazilian had become obvious.[58] The entry of foreign banks of a wide variety of national origins was one consequence of the changes in financial techniques and the national distribution of capital investment that followed World War I.[59] During the 1910s and early 1920s, Brazilian commerce experienced a notable expansion of foreign banks of diverse origins. At least nine foreign banks opened offices in Rio de Janeiro or São Paulo: two new German bank names appeared in 1911 (Allemão Transatlântico and Deutsch Sudamerikansche[60]); two U.S. banks (First National City of New York in 1915 and the American Banking Corporation, which opened in 1919 and was acquired by First National City in 1921); Español y Rio de la Plata in 1909; Hollandez-America do Sul in 1917; the Norwegian Banking Amalgamation in 1918; Royal Bank of Canada in 1919; and Yokohama Bank in 1923. They initially built their business and sectoral interests around nationally defined client bases. Once chartered, laws, regulation, and taxation did not consider foreign banks differently from their local counterparts.[61] Although not all of these organizations had long or successful lives, they increased the sense of competition and dynamism for commercial banking during the 1910s and early 1920s. Those foreign banks that remained diversified their activities to clients and businesses far removed from their national roots as they became more deeply implanted within the local business culture.

The appearance of these foreign and domestic organizations crystallizes many of the salient points of banking, from the perspective of the entrepreneur. Although many of the domestic organizations developed a large and diversified base of shareholders,[62] a small group of original investors often controlled their management and business focus. The formation of the domestic banks explored here brought together small, cohesive groups of investor/managers with interests in wide-ranging endeavors. As Comind and Boavista exemplified, informal unlimited-liability partnerships often converted their structures to joint-stock limited-liability organizations, as they grew in size and diversity of operations. The new legal structure reflected the *casa bancária*'s increasing scope, as well as the associated need for capital and formal business structure.[63]

The investor groups that combined to open these banks defied the stereotypes offered by existing historiography. The Português do Brasil was the only one of this group to have a well-defined immigrant focus; original investors of the others combined immigrant and native Brazilians. Commonly, banks combined "old" with "new" family elites, and they meshed "foreign" with "domestic." Of the bank-forming entrepreneurs involved with these organizations, only one (Boavista) concentrated his business activities primarily in banking. Clearly, it would be misleading to consider the formation of banking elites. Bankers, elite and otherwise, were businessmen with diversified interests, trying to rationalize their commercial operations. In doing so, the banks offered an organizational linkage that connected the interests of diverse economic sectors.

Often, these new banks were responding to the needs of emerging economic agents and interests, whether the recent entry of multinational companies or immigrants or the modernization of economic activity (such as water supply or construction companies). The Pelotense was the only bank with an, apparently, sharply defined sectoral focus; its commitment to livestock targeted technological advances that extended the geographic reach of markets. As the circumstances of the new domestic banks highlighted, banks offered important sectoral diversification of their holdings to investors.[64] With the exception of Boavista and (perhaps) Pelotense, the banks and the other enterprises of the initial investors were explicitly interrelated, through both interlocking directorships and their credit portfolios.[65] Most interpretations of interlocking relationships between banks and other enterprises focus on the outcome of "insider lending," narrowing the pool of creditors to small and closed groups of investors who combined their funds in order to borrow from themselves.[66] From the investors' perspective, organizing as joint-stock limited-liability banks constrained their risk of losses (in the bank) to the value of their investment; they did not risk the full amount of their personal wealth in the event of the organization's failure. Joint-stock organization also offered the possibility of capital accumulation from a wider pool of small-scale investors, who otherwise had limited investment alternatives. Therefore, banks allowed individuals to diversify their investments through the mechanisms of accumulating and allocating (shared) resources in a manner that both enlarged the pool of resources and limited their exposure to failure. Comind, the Português do Brasil, and Boavista offer clear examples of bank portfolios safely linked to their founders' business endeavors during the First Republic.

From the perspective of the increasing pool of prospective borrowers, the predominantly short-term nature of credit limited the scope of operations for which they could use banks. Some entrepreneurs were critical of this limitation. Roberto Simonsen (who also held significant banking interests in Comind and a regional paulista bank) was the most influential and vocal, but ultimately unsuccessful, critic of banking's short-term horizon and its inability to extend long-term credit:

> Our banking apparatus does not favor the financing of production, as we need. Composed of deposit banks, by their nature they cannot employ their cash for the long term. In circumstances of crisis, the deposit banks are the first to suffer and they aggravate the commercial and production situation by the restrictions that they need to apply to their business. In the advanced countries there are merchant banks [*bancos de negocios*] and the public that finances production for the long term through the intermediation of stock markets [*mercados de valores*] where shares and short-term industrial and agricultural credit [*titulos de crédito mobiliário da indústria e da agricultura*] are placed.[67]

Even so, many of his counterparts appreciated that banks, by safely and increasingly supplying short-term finance for ongoing operations, freed an accumulating portion of their wealth for innovative ventures.[68] During the early twentieth century, the banking system provided important opportunities to private-sector entrepreneurs to facilitate their business activities. Among the most important was the ability to diversify the scope of their business interests. Diversification often included investing in industrial manufacturing. By doing so, they facilitated both intersectoral transfers and risk minimization.

CONCLUSION

Throughout the First Republic the growth of banking reflected its increasingly dynamic interaction with the private productive sectors. From a low level of representation in the economy, banks grew more rapidly than the economy. The banking system supported overall growth and structural change. Because banking developed concurrently with significant industrialization, traditional historiography would support a presumption that the two processes were significantly intertwined. The direct evidence of a causal relationship between banking and industrialization suggests that the relationship manifested complicated dynamics. A more secure interpretation is that banking strongly supported a shift in the balance between economic sectors. Industrial manufacturing benefited from this process.

Both the empirical evidence on the banking system and the anecdotal evidence from individual organizations demonstrate the effective, if indirect, manners in which banks contributed to the fluid movement of resources between different sectors of production and reinforced growth. For entrepreneurs and investors, participating in bank ownership provided a number of advantages that served well within an economy experiencing significant structural shift. As investments, banks diversified the holdings of their owners in a manner that limited risk in new ventures. As borrowers, entrepreneurs took advantage of the fungible nature of money. They used banks to provide short-term working capital for their ongoing ventures, freeing resources for other endeavors and facilitating an increasing range of distribution. While historians tend to classify entrepreneurs by their sectoral interests, the entrepreneurs themselves did not do so. By the twentieth century, they exhibited strong tendencies for multisectoral diversification, with banking an integral component of their portfolios. Further, the financial infrastructure that banks created allowed investors to flexibly meet the requirements of an expanding volume of commercial transactions. One long-term result was to facilitate the exchange of a wider array of goods among an increasing proportion of the population. In this manner, banks contributed to building markets that functioned with increasing ease and for a widening array of participants.

The banking system's rapid growth was the result of two fundamental shifts that occurred simultaneously. Economic growth generated a larger volume of commercial transactions for which banks executed the financial exchange. In addition, the trend of financial deepening demonstrated the banking system's intermediation of a growing proportion of economic activity, by serving as an important mechanism by which investors used the profits of more mature businesses to develop activity in new sectors and enterprises. The growth and pattern of banking evolved with economic development and they fluctuated with changes in monetary conditions in predictable manners. The privately owned banking network and the process of industrialization were closely associated with each other. In many respects, privately owned banks in Brazil were similar to early banking systems found among some early industrializers. They limited their activities to conservative commercial banking, with closely held ownership among small groups of partners, and operated within small geographic markets. Private-sector organizations organized funds on a relatively small scale.

However, the Brazilian banking system also demonstrated an important difference from the model of early industrializers. Despite the substantial evidence of strong growth and increasingly firm connections with the productive sectors of the economy, the empirical relationship between banking and other aspects of the economy depicted in Figure 5.1 raises an important question. Although the private-sector banks accounted for an increasing share of the system until the early 1920s, the public sector (through both the Banco do Brasil and, beginning in the 1920s, state banks) exerted countervailing influence within the private system. Their growth trends (Chapter 4) and the economic dynamics associated with their growth (Table 5.2) reflected fundamentally different behavior. Divergent growth trends between the private banks and the public-sector organizations began with the 1921 Banco do Brasil rediscount program and became attenuated in 1928, with the vast expansion and transfer of ownership at one organization, Banespa. In addition, as large-scale entrepreneurial managers, public banks set the stage for a dichotomized system, dominated by a few large-scale organizations, with many smaller banks in less prominent positions.[69] These experiences highlight the need to explore the role and effects of the public-sector banks. They also suggest the need to identify activities not met by private banks, and thus, filled by the public sector.

The successful maturing and increased stability of the banking system after its reorganization in 1906 allowed for its growth and entrenchment as a viable economic force. Nevertheless, the contributions of the banking system did not develop easily; throughout the First Republic they continued to face limits in the extent to which they could facilitate growth and development. Further, compared to those in other economies, Brazilian banks intermediated a small share of financial resources. Therefore, despite the rational and rapid manner in which the banking system evolved and despite its contribution to efficiency, questions arise about important structural factors that may have limited the scope of its effects. Two approaches address these questions in the following chapters. The next chapter explores the means of and limits to banking's development, by focusing on the character and evolution of institutional factors that affected the development of the banking system. Then, Chapter 7 examines the limitations and opportunities deriving from regional factors and the effect of state governments on banking.

Appendix: Model of Demand and Supply of Banking

I n order to determine the relationship between the banking system and the real (the nonfinancial) economy, Chapter 5 presents results from a very simple model to estimate demand and supply functions for changes in the real (adjusted for price-level changes) volume of bank deposits.[1] The bases for this model are the elementary principles of economic theory that supply and demand are (different) functions of quantity and price, and that the supply of real deposits equals their demand. Changes in the demand for real bank deposits can be expressed as the result of changes in income (quantity) and interest rates (price). Fluctuations of income, measured as the annual change of output, are expected to result in changes in the demand for real deposits in the same direction. The rate of change in the price level approximates the effect of deposit price change (in preference to the limited interest rate data that are available). The demand for real deposits is expected to be inversely related to prices. As its price increases, the demand for money, in the form of deposits, should decline. Idle funds on deposit in banks carry an increased opportunity cost to depositors as interest rates increase and alternative investments earn higher returns. That is, as prices increase, depositors are expected to direct funds toward uses more profitable than bank deposits. Reduced borrowing is an important use of funds during periods of increasing interest rates since interest rates for deposits change less and more slowly than loan rates. Obviously, in a scenario of declining prices (and interest rates), the inverse dynamics are expected to hold, with the result of increased demand for bank deposits.

Further, the model hypothesizes that the fluctuation of the supply of real bank deposits is a positive function of their price, reflecting the benefit to banks of increasing size as interest rates increase. An increasing deposit base translates into higher profits during periods of rising prices for money, again assuming that the cost of attracting deposits increases less than the interest rate that can be earned on credit. The fluctuation of bank cash balances should also move in the same direction as deposits since banks hold cash reserves primarily in order to redeem deposits. These concepts can be specified as:[2]

$$Dep_D = \alpha_1 + \beta_1 Y + \beta_2 P \qquad \beta_1 > 0;\ \beta_2 < 0 \qquad \text{(Equation 1)}$$
$$Dep_S = \alpha_2 + \beta_3 C + \beta_4 P \qquad \beta_3 > 0;\ \beta_4 > 0 \qquad \text{(Equation 2)}$$
$$Dep_D = Dep_S.$$

where: Dep_D = demand for real bank deposits, annual rate of change

Dep_S = supply of real bank deposits, annual rate of change

Y   = output, annual rate of change

P   = prices, annual rate of change

C   = real cash balances, annual rate of change

The demand side is of most interest for questions about the relationship between the productive economy and the banking system. Therefore, this model is most useful for estimating the demand of deposits.

An advantage of this specification is that it allows for a certain amount of disaggregation. The model measures the responsiveness of the total banking system to major overall economic variables. Since output and price indices for the industrial and agricultural sectors are available, the model can also test whether the banking system responds more strongly to one sector or the other.[3] This provides a succinct test for hypotheses of the relationship between banking and industrialization. In addition, the bank data can be disaggregated by various geographic and structural features, and the model can be used to test whether banks with certain characteristics were more or less responsive to different economic variables.

This model of the banking system also has some drawbacks that need to be recognized when assessing its results. The first is its simplicity. In an economy with price fluctuation as rapid and severe as that experienced during the First Republic, both experience and economic theory support the expectation that prices and nominal interest rates moved together, and that fluctuations in prior years would have little effect on the current year, or on price expectations for the current year. The rate of price change reflects fluctuation of nominal interest rates (as compared to real interest rates); therefore, the rate of price fluctuation captures the change in the opportunity cost of holding deposits. Further, the model incorporates only three variables: income, prices, and cash balances. A wide variety of exogenous variables may be missing from the model that could be important in explaining the growth of the banking system. The statistics that measure the reliability of the regression statements can reveal whether variables are missing, but they do not identify what those variables are. Some likely factors not included in the equations are the requirements of international debt servicing and international trade and the funding policies of the state and federal governments. Another drawback of this model is that it assumes that the direction of causation is from the economy to the banking system. This model specifies the growth of banking as a result of economic change. It does not take into account the likelihood of two-way causation. That is, growth of the banking system could have an effect on the fluctuation of output or prices. While the regression statements measure the statistical relationship between the variables, it should be recognized that causation probably ran in both directions.

The model is a set of two simultaneous equations (Equations 1 and 2) that estimate the same variable, the change in the volume of real deposits. One independent variable, prices, appears in both equations. Because of the simultaneity problem, the two statements cannot be estimated independently of each other. I have solved these equations by using two-stage least squares estimation[4]; and price-level changes are determined endogenously in the first stage. The statistical integrity of the results for the model is sufficient that they can be usefully analyzed. In most instances, the results are statistically valid.[5] The comparison of when these regressions generate statistically significant information (and when they do not) also reveals useful findings. The directions of correlation are as expected (with the important exceptions of the functions using agricultural output to estimate deposits and when the population measured was the Banco do Brasil). The indices providing the information for the sectoral and total growth rates (the input data for the regressions) are in Table A.11; Tables A.13a and A.13b show the full set of estimated demand and supply functions, respectively, for the change in the volume of bank deposits.[6]

Chapter 6

Institutional Development in Banking

In January 1911, the president of the Banco do Brasil fired the bank's branch manager in Pará, the center of the Amazon rubber commerce.[1] The manager had extended credit beyond the limit of his responsibility and taken undue lending risks. The price of rubber had plummeted and rubber merchants could not repay their debts. In November the bank brought a lawsuit against the former manager.[2] In 1911, the bank recognized losses of 1,936 contos (approximately U.S.$625,000), or about 30 percent of the bank's net profits for the year.[3] This situation revealed changes in the manner of conducting banking that were important in its evolving role in the Brazilian economy. A branch manager, who was a full-time employee (but not a shareholder) of the bank, was held accountable for a defined volume and risk-structure of business. Being able to be sued by the bank represented a heightened level of personal responsibility assigned to bank managers. In the branch manager's defense, exceeding the authorized credit exposure only became a problem when rubber prices declined precipitously.

Until the early years of the twentieth century, the lack of established procedures, protections, and regulation enhanced the risk of bank failures. With institutional development to address these weaknesses, individuals and firms began to see banks as increasingly secure conduits for their business endeavors. The increasing share of the money supply that the public held in bank deposits, rather than currency, was the most succinct demonstration of this development. Enhancing its safety and credibility, given its unstable history, required that the banking system actively establish the parameters of its business. Banks needed to address the internal causes of previous failures and anticipate new threats if the business community were to develop confidence in their ability and if banks were to turn themselves into attractive investments for potential shareholders. They could not remain viable conduits of commerce if the experience of the Banco do Brasil in Pará were common. The challenge to banks was to identify and manage their risks. They did so by investing effort and money in means of accumulating and using information, developing management controls, and limiting their business when necessary. As a result, other economic agents gained confidence in the banking system, and banks could sustain rapid growth even while facing serious constraints.

Recent research within the framework of institutions and development economics examines the role of banking in "development" using measures and concepts that have interesting historical applications. Coining the term "contract-intensive money" for the share of bank deposits in the money supply, Clague et al.[4] conclude that the ratio indicates the extent to which economic agents have confidence in the contracts that routinize and depersonalize their activity. The contracts that banks maintained with their borrowers and depositors were among the earliest and most common to develop. Banks routinely entered into contracts for taking deposits and extending credit. Their prevalence suggested the extent to which economic agents accepted that the contracts effectively protected their rights to the property underlying their transactions.[5] Therefore, the proportion of contract-intensive money serves as an indication of the extent of institutional stability and evolution. These concepts help to understand the importance of the long-term increase in the share of the money supply composed of bank deposits and the increasing efficiency and stability that identified the beginning of the modern banking system (as found in Chapters 3-5).

This chapter explores how Brazilian contracts and financial property became more secure during the early twentieth century, and it considers the limits to their increased security. It finds that evolving management procedures created the framework for depersonalized and decentralized decision making and increasingly managed the risks of banking with improved information, technology, and operating procedures. However, the chapter also explores aspects of the conservatism governing banking in the early twentieth century that impeded their ability to engage in more expansive practices. Conservative procedures protected banks against risk. While these procedures evolved in manners that allowed banks to expand and to simultaneously maintain their stability, risk protection remained a high priority to Brazilian bankers. One important reason for their continuing conservatism was that prevailing legal and regulatory structures limited the improvements that banks could bring about of their own accord.

The chapter outlines important considerations that enabled banks to function more effectively within the Brazilian economy. It also serves as an important case study for the economy as a whole. There is no reason to expect that the evolution toward a depersonalized framework for conducting economic endeavors should have been limited to banking. In fact, logic suggests that these developments applied broadly to the business community. The parties with whom banks entered into contracts understood, and often shared, the concerns of bankers. Because bankers engaged in a wide variety of business undertakings, successful practices in one endeavor had a natural conduit to others. One would expect them to spread to additional endeavors, as the need arose. The findings of this chapter have broad applicability for understanding changes in the underlying rules by which economic agents functioned in the early twentieth century. Nevertheless, given the ambiguities of defining and enforcing financial transactions, these protections may have arisen earlier within banks than in other businesses.[6]

INSTITUTIONS, PROPERTY, AND BANKS

"Institutions" is one of the most amorphous terms in the social scientist's lexicon. The term applies to the general structure of formal and informal rules by which society functions.[7] Institutions come in various forms, including government (by consensus or coercion), organizations, individuals, abstract understandings, and codified law. Institutions, and their development over time, fundamentally affect material well-being. Among the most important uses of institutions have been to define what constitutes property, who can own it, and the manners in which property can generate additional wealth. At least as important, institutions also protect the rules of property ownership. They determine the extent to which owners of property enjoy and control its use, including the transfer of its ownership, and they reveal the extent and security of property rights. Systems of property law codify the rules of ownership and exchange, and their enforcement.[8] Protecting property incurs significant costs "associated with the transfer, capture and protection of rights";[9] these are often called transactions costs. The most important costs of transacting are those of managing the risk of the exchange: gaining and using information, policing the value of exchanges, and ensuring contract enforcement.

Transactions costs for banks are the costs of gathering and monitoring information about its clients—especially borrowers—managing the risks of bad investments, and ensuring contract enforcement when investments fail (i.e., when a borrower does not repay credit as scheduled). In banking, property is less tangible than is often the case in other endeavors. Bank assets (primarily credit) and liabilities (deposits and investor capital) categorize the property concerns of banks. Unlike real property in land and goods, bookkeeping entries evidence their existence. Although their application may arise earlier and more strongly in financial transactions, the issues and concerns with respect to property rights were not different in banking than in other economic activities. Therefore, exploring the specific concerns about property rights, and how banks dealt with them, contributes to understanding the development of banking, as well as the interactions between banks and other economic sectors.

Brazilian banks needed to institutionalize procedures and standards of operation to support their enhanced scope and scale. Institutional shortcomings continued to impede the ability of banks to extend credit more expansively. Nevertheless, during the First Republic their successes at institutionalizing their practices were significant. Banks tried to minimize their risks of lending by maintaining accurate and timely information on their borrowers. In fact, for the business community one of the benefits of banking was that it facilitated the depersonalization of commerce by serving as a repository of information. When a bank intermediated the financial aspects of transactions, by securing financing or even by simply holding documents, the principle parties could engage in commerce with a wider array of agents. Merchants and producers did not need to know each other or rely on their webs of personal networks to have confidence that their counter-parties would fulfill their obligations. The banks took that risk.[10] In response, however, bankers needed to accumulate information about their clients and their clients' businesses. Banks were especially concerned with gathering information regarding the creditworthiness of specific borrowers and the general economic conditions affecting their clients' businesses. Banks needed to be able to make informed credit decisions in order to provide investors (shareholders and depositors) with safe profits. One of their key functions was to centralize knowledge and information of financial and credit risk. The basis for banks' specialized knowledge was their exposure to a wide variety of borrowers and investment opportunities. Banks continually assessed their borrowers' business and financial conditions. By doing so, they accumulated a wide familiarity with investment options and business circumstances. This advantage was cumulative; as the scope of bank activities widened, so did their access to information.

Banks provided some of the most informed analyses of economic conditions, and they became quite skilled at using their own transactions to gauge general trends.[11] Annual reports and Board of Directors' minutes continually assessed the effects of crops, production, money supply, and international market and political conditions for their business implications.[12] As their client bases grew beyond the range of closely related and well-known borrowers, banks' expertise in sectoral business analysis and their advantage in accumulating information across a wide selection of borrowers became more important. This knowledge helped them to offset the problems of asymmetric information that they faced with any given client. That is, banks continued to suffer disadvantages with respect to understanding specific borrowers, since any party would always have a better understanding of its circumstances and intentions than its counter-party (the bank). However, bankers' wider attention to the competitive and market conditions of borrowers offered perspectives on the general risk level of a total portfolio that individuals could not match.

More so than smaller, informal financial agents, banks developed an advantage in that they centralized information about their borrowers and the specific uses of credit that allowed them to make the risky decisions to extend credit. They generated consistent information about a wide range of investments and borrowers, giving them a privileged perspective on the full range of economic activities underway in their market. In addition to specific borrowers, banks also monitored the value of the businesses that they financed. For example, pledges to the ownership of coffee beans often guaranteed credit to a coffee merchant. As a result, the lending bank needed to understand the international coffee market, both to ensure that the value of the guarantee remained constant and to monitor the financial prospects of its client, the coffee merchant. For investors, banks offered significant economies of scale with respect to accumulating information. Without having to attain an equivalent base of knowledge to make efficient investment decisions, shareholders and depositors could benefit from a bank's information and expertise in specific businesses.

For banks, gathering information was crucial in order to maximize these benefits and to minimize the risks of adversely selecting bad investments. Even so, bankers were continually aware of their risk of loss. They required collateral to guarantee loans in order to ensure that if a loan failed, the debtor had property that the bank could repossess in lieu of payment. The judicial system was available to mediate the resolution of failed contracts. In the most extreme manifestation, bankruptcy courts mediated the settlement of debts of companies and individuals that failed financially. As a final resort, banks maintained reserves to cover debts that were not repaid or fully collateralized.

MANAGING RISKS

Brazilian banks were acutely attuned to the problems of protecting their property and managing the risks attendant to their credit contracts during the First Republic. Concerns about property protection and efforts to implement procedures to minimize risk were common to all banks. The composition of ownership was irrelevant. Whether owners were foreigners, state governments, or small, closely knit groups of individuals, the problems of protecting their investments were universal.

The best means available to bankers to protect their property was to minimize their credit problems. Credit was the source of both their revenues and losses. Bankers had more control over their ability to meet their responsibilities to redeem deposits than they had over ensuring the repayment of credit commitments.[13] Balancing returns against the risks of lending was, perhaps, the most sensitive concern of bankers. They often looked for ways to expand their credit portfolios, while minimizing their risks. At the same time, potential borrowers used every opportunity to complain about the lack of credit. However, neither of these positions demonstrated that the banking system was ineffective or that credit was in short supply. The business and profit interests of banks motivated them to expand revenues while minimizing risks; and borrowers decrying the availability of credit were actually complaining about the prevailing interest rates.

In managing the total level of credit exposure and allocating it among alternative uses, Brazilian banks actively took account of risks and potential returns. As early as 1901, the financial community recognized the difficulties of allocating credit to productive uses, as opposed to applications perceived to be less risky. At that time, interest in using the banking system to facilitate the circulation of currency and manage the exchange rate superseded its potential application for productive investment, because of the inability to control "speculation":

> If the banks realized their business, trying to harmonize their interests with those of the nation which gives them such generous concessions, they could always find gainful revenues distributing the notes that appear during the harvest season; thus transforming to a continuous circulation the current intermittent circulation of letters of exchange, regularizing the supply and demand, and finally achieving the exchange rate. . . . Unfortunately, this does not occur, thus facilitating a high level of speculation.[14]

Banks continued to explicitly reassure their shareholders of their concern in balancing profit and risk throughout the First Republic.[15]

Banks created a variety of methods to minimize their lending risks. The four most important protections invoked by the banking system were to limit the universe of acceptable borrowers, to extend credit only for short periods of time, to obtain sufficient collateral to protect against defaults on debt, and to develop personnel and professional skills that improved the information available for each credit decision. These protections also constrained banks from innovative or expansive uses of funds.[16]

Selecting Borrowers

Perhaps the most common form of choosing borrowers occurred when small, closely knit groups of individuals owned banks as conduits for their own business activities. The business group based on kinship and social association provided the organizational basis for much financial innovation.[17] In the previous chapter, the formation of Comind, the Banco Italiano del Brasile, Banco Português, and Banco Boavista offered examples of this sort of arrangement. New domestic banks incorporated during the First Republic were often recapitalizations of previously existing, informal *casas bancárias*. These organizations often increased their capital and changed the form of their legal organization without enlarging their group of participants (as in the cases of Comind and Boavista). The close relationship between banks and their entrepreneurs could take complicated forms. In addition to linking their fortunes, interlocking directorships of individuals simultaneously on the boards of banks and borrowing entities could tighten creditor/borrower relationships, rather than contribute to depersonalizing the credit relationship.

Imprudent lending was not the only possible outcome of these relationships in which close ties influenced credit decisions. Banks were in business to make money. If advancing credit to their own enterprises were not profitable, they would shift the use of their resources, or go out of business. Entrepreneurs generally found severe limits to the willingness of their partners to finance ventures that revealed themselves to be flawed. Insider lending could also offset the fundamental problem of asymmetric information that underlay any credit decision.[18] Bankers understood that financial disclosure by their borrowers offered useful, but only limited, information. Borrowers would always know more of their circumstances and future prospects than their financial statements revealed, and they could share additional information selectively. Relying on reputation and social relationships, close organizational and personal ties between borrower and banker served to minimize information asymmetries and to lower the transactions costs of monitoring the circumstances of borrowers. Therefore, while the bias toward insider lending occurred, it is unlikely to have distorted the allocation of credit toward demonstrably inefficient or risky uses on a consistent or large scale.

The attitude of foreign banks with (perhaps) less access to local personal ties in credit decisions revealed the importance of those ties. British commercial banks assessed their risk somewhat more severely than did their domestic competitors, describing much of the credit extended by Brazilian banks as accommodation notes (short-term credit extended to borrowers based on the personal relationship between the borrower and the banker).[19] They characterized this form of lending as an expression of inefficient or uneconomic personalism. This type of complaint may have reflected the relative disadvantage that foreign banks faced in extending the domestic reach of their business. When concerned about its dealings with a failing bank, the first information the head office of the Bank of London and Brazil requested of its Rio de Janeiro office was the lists of names and occupations of the bank's directors.[20]

During the early years of the twentieth century, bankers viewed lending to limited-liability, publicly registered corporations (of which they were not participants) as particularly uncertain.[21] They believed that the risks in lending to these organizations were different from traditional lending to individuals because the liability of each of the investors (shareholders) was limited to the amount of his investment.[22] Further, in practice, the value of a corporation's capital fluctuated severely. In essence, bankers remained uncertain that they could rely on the contracts between their organizations and other corporations. Oversight and understanding of corporate financial affairs were new, complicated, and not always well understood. It was not always clear how the law could hold corporate entities to the same standards and requirements as individuals.

Therefore, one of the early means of protecting against the risks of corporate lending was to lend to the principal individuals participating in an enterprise, rather than to the enterprise itself: "At times the share of debt based on purely personal credit, including some accepted for commercial firms, translated funds administered by the Bank to individuals for commercial uses that developed business with little or no capital . . . ."[23] In at least one instance, the Banco do Brasil declined to extend credit to an incorporated entity in Bahia (the Companhia Light & Power de Bahia) because its shares traded on the exchange in Salvador, rather than Rio de Janeiro.[24] Such practices as lending to the individuals rather than their corporations or only to companies listed on certain exchanges defeated the purposes of incorporation, since one of the major benefits of incorporation was to limit the personal risk of the organizers while investing in new ventures. Limited-liability companies undertook large industrial enterprises and infrastructural development. To the extent that banks viewed this form of organization cautiously, corporations were disadvantaged in credit markets.[25] Therefore, without sufficient legal and institutional development, modernizing economic activity of organizations was not encouraged in bank credit markets.

However, over the course of the First Republic, limited-liability corporate organization appears to have gained acceptance among Brazilian bankers. In cases in which an enterprise, rather than an individual, guaranteed credit, public registration of the company was an important substitute for personal relations in providing financial information.[26] Publicly chartered corporations were subject to conditions of disclosure of financial condition that did not apply to individuals. Provisions for public incorporation required the minimal collection of 20 percent of the statutory capital, the public disclosure of trading volume and prices for equity shares on a securities exchange, and the publication of semiannual financial reports. These requirements helped to communicate that the corporations were legitimate, adequately capitalized, and had viable ongoing business concerns.[27] The mandatory disclosure of corporations' balance sheets and the ongoing publication of share prices offered information about their financial standing that banks turned to their advantage, as they became confidant in the legal form of organization.

Duration of Credit

A more mechanical method available to banks to protect themselves against credit risk was to maintain a series of short-term contracts with borrowers to minimize the duration of their exposure.[28] Bank statutes established the maximum maturity of credit instruments.[29] The exclusive reliance on short-term credit mitigated the need to monitor information about the changing financial conditions of individual borrowers, since lenders could simply stop lending at the first sign of a problem.[30] However, viable borrowers could easily have their credits renewed upon maturity.[31] In fact, at the time of its formation, one of the concerns about access for private-sector credit to the Banco do Brasil Rediscount Office was the impetus it could give to undue continuation of debt: "Money in circulation [*dinheiro em gyro;* currency] is not useful, because notes that need to be paid are only renewed. . . . The Rediscount Office served to give resources to the banks with large sums in circulation, but does not receive payment. . . ."[32]

Despite the importance that bankers attached to this protection, banks often experienced difficulty if they tried to exercise their right to withdraw credit from individual borrowers when credit quality deteriorated. Withdrawing credit from a deteriorating borrower could precipitate default by disrupting an already-precarious cash flow. In these cases, a bank could choose to continue its credit exposure, rather than forcing the borrower into bankruptcy.[33] Although its risk increased, a bank could avoid a loss, at least temporarily. Frequently, financial conditions improved sufficiently to avoid bankruptcy. In addition, a lender would often have more than one credit instrument extended to a borrower at any one time. Therefore, a bank's total credit exposure could be significantly greater than the single defaulted instrument. By law, a default declared on one instrument put the borrower in bankruptcy; all of the credit outstanding would be in default and at risk. While efforts to avoid bankruptcy could provide financing to commercial concerns during difficult periods, it could also put a bank in a position of providing funds on a long-term basis under unfavorable circumstances:

> The decline of coffee and of the exchange, reflecting the general course of business, led commerce almost to a paralysis in its receivables and sales. In turn, it made the situation of the banks extremely difficult; the more so since commerce and industry generally come to consider the bank as a[n equity] partner, whose capital remained permanently in the companies, and not as a reserve which they drew upon provisionally. Restricting credit, even in reasonable proportions, the lives of these companies became impossible. So, in this regard, the action of banks has to be monitored with great caution.[34]

Considerations with regard to continuing credit extended to all manner of distressed borrowers. Whether it was a widow struggling to settle her deceased husband's debts or the national shipping line (Lloyd Brasileiro) in financial straits of a heavily politicized nature, Banco do Brasil directors kept close, and not always polite, track of renewals on questionable borrowers.[35] Contingent on the ability to maintain close oversight, the Bank of London and Brazil continued lending to J. P. Wileman, who was often in financial trouble during the years he published *Wileman's Review,* a newsletter on economic circumstances in Brazil.[36] Similarly, Comind and the Crédito Real de Minas Gerais closely monitored troubled coffee merchants.[37]

Continuing short-term credit to a distressed borrower gave banks opportunities both to withdraw credit within a fairly short time horizon and to monitor the creditor's situation frequently (at each credit "roll-over" date). Although these provisions did not offer perfect protection, bankers strongly opposed giving them up, since they believed that ". . . there is no greater danger to a credit establishment than the immobilization of its funds in long-term operations. . . ."[38] The flexibility of extending short-term credit, with the possibility of continual renewals, could effectively convert short-term obligations into medium- or long-term capital, while preserving the legal form of protection for the bank.

Collateral

Ample collateral requirements to secure credit were a related protective mechanism that bankers routinely used. By pledging collateral, borrowers assigned to the bank the legal right to take ownership of specified property (the collateral) in the event that credit was not repaid. Banks clearly saw this as an important protection. Collateralization standards were rigorous and banks followed them strictly. Bank statutes detailed the requirements, and transactions entailing varying degrees of risk carried corresponding amounts of collateral.[39] Beyond the statutory requirements, if the risks appeared to merit additional protection in specific cases, borrowers had to pledge incremental collateral.[40]

Collateral could take a variety of forms. For discounted notes, individuals could personally guarantee the credit, or borrowers could pledge goods as collateral. Loans required the specific guarantee of precious metals or diamonds, Treasury notes (apólices), marketable goods, stocks, or bonds. Bankers had learned the risks of depreciating market value of assets that had cost them dearly during the 1890s. When assessing the adequacy of collateral, banks valued all goods and financial assets substantially below their current market value in order to protect against a decline in prices of the collateralized goods. Usually, banks applied a discount of 20-25 percent to the market value of the goods, as specified in their statutes.[41] In some cases, the appraised value of collateral was two to three times the amount of the loan.[42] Banks could refuse to advance loans upon discovering that the promised collateral fell short of their expectations. Once, on doing so, the president of the Banco do Brasil justified his action to the president of Brazil and refused to modify it.[43] At least once, a borrower collateralized a loan with its own debentures.[44] This offered the (insecure) protection that, in the event of a bankruptcy proceeding, claims on the debentures would receive more favorable consideration than credit. Banks carefully structured these provisions to ensure that they could recover the full value of the original credit, should the collateral be liquidated to remedy a default.

The difficulty in structuring credit instruments to accommodate mortgage lending on rural real estate was the most obvious and serious collateralization problem facing banks. In fact, the long history of Brazilian property rights and their difficulties may have roots in the problems of collateralizing rural real estate.[45] The intertwining of plantation and commercial finance had proven extremely disruptive to the viability of sugar plantations from the earliest colonial days.[46] Portuguese imperial law responded to these difficulties by preventing the breakup of plantations for the purpose of collecting on defaulted debt. In practice, this meant that during the colonial period and the Empire, creditors could not take possession of land, slaves, mills, and other large-scale equipment in order to settle failed debts, if the repossession seriously diminished the productive value of the remaining estate. Schwartz identifies this, logically enough, as a major explanation for the credit shortages that he believes impeded settlement and expansion.[47]

These concerns did not abate for the few banks undertaking mortgage lending during the First Republic. Bank statutes included procedures for valuing real property and establishing appropriate collateral. They did not permit nonpartible collateral to guarantee mortgages.[48] For example, the statutes of the Crédito Real in Minas Gerais included the constraint that: "The bank will not lend: . . . for real estate 'pro indiviso', unless the mortgage is established for the whole, and with the unanimous consent of all co-owners. . . ."[49] This serious limitation in lending to an agricultural concern meant that any part of an estate could not be possessed if it made the entire holding less productive. Further, banks required a high level of collateral when extending mortgages. The Crédito Real would accept the rights to mortgaged urban buildings[50] to guarantee the credit, but they would only do so if the mortgage had a maximum duration of five years, and they valued the collateral at one-third the current market value of the buildings.[51] Alternatively, they often accepted railroad bonds as mortgage collateral, because of their more secure value.[52] Concerns about the possibility of issuing bad mortgage credit were strong enough that the Banco de Crédito Hypothecário e Agrícola do Estado de São Paulo proudly published in its annual report of 1925 that "[a]t the moment the bank does not own a single fazenda."[53] The problems of collateralization perpetuated the attraction of personal guarantees for credit and inhibited the potential for depersonalizing the benefits of banking. To compensate, bank operating statutes typically simply prohibited agricultural credit; when provided for, onerous collateralization requirements governed its terms.

The long-term reliability of property rights was also a factor in banks' continual inability to raise the long-term funding necessary to finance mortgage loans. Since mortgage credit represented a commitment of funds for five to ten years, banks required that they have a source of funds that matched the duration of the loans. Prior to the financial crises of 1900-01, banks that undertook long-term lending did so either without matching sources of funding or by issuing long-term bonds to the public (finding few purchasers). Whether because of credit or funding problems, these banks did not survive. Failed banks with mortgage portfolios during the First Republic included Banco de Crédito Real de São Paulo, Banco União de São Paulo, and Banco Rural e Internacional. After the 1906 restructuring of banking, the only banks to routinely engage in mortgage lending did so with funding from state-issued bonds. As a result, the state governments' creditworthiness was ultimately at stake, beyond the banks', for the mortgage portfolios. Banespa and Crédito Real of Minas Gerais were the most prominent examples of this mechanism providing for the entrée of state governments into the banking system. Recognizing the pervasive problems of providing mortgage and agricultural finance, the Federal Treasury continually assessed the prospects for opening an agricultural bank of national scope (or an office within the Banco do Brasil). Each banking reform during the First Republic included unsuccessful efforts to create a national institution to promote mortgage and agricultural lending.[54] The 1905 rechartering of the bank anticipated such a facility, as did the statute amendments of 1923.[55] These, and a separate effort to open a national mortgage bank in 1913, failed because of the Treasury's inability to find a sufficiently large market to purchase the notes that it would have issued to fund the long-term credit.[56]

The problems of valuation and protection that inhibited mortgage lending also applied to other credit instruments. The cost and procedural complications of valuing assets and collateral were important considerations in commercial lending. Difficulties in establishing and maintaining the value of collateral impeded financing of both mortgage lending and credit for export commodities with rapidly fluctuating prices. Extremely rapid declines in coffee and rubber prices made bankers very nervous for this reason. As the most dramatic example, the average price of coffee on international markets in 1920 was 57 percent of the average price in 1919 (measured in mil-réis[57]). Therefore, banks extending a constant amount of credit to a coffee merchant during this period, without adjusting collateral, would have lost an equivalent amount of protection (57 percent, since the collateral would have been coffee). In addition, the likelihood of a problem with the merchant's creditworthiness would have increased, since his revenues declined commensurately with the fall of coffee prices. This problem also reinforced the role of short-term credit instruments in the banker's portfolio. Each renewal of a note offered an occasion to recalculate its underlying collateral. Bankers' attention to collateral and its valuation in the early twentieth century suggests that they had learned from the failures of 1900-01, when many failed banks held overvalued assets of defaulting borrowers. The inability to protect against credit risks remained pervasive throughout the First Republic and justified bankers' insistence on strong procedures.

The Professionalization of Bankers

As the volume of business and available information increased, banks adjusted their procedures for making lending decisions. In the early years of the Republic, bank boards of directors met weekly, at a minimum, and decided on each credit proposal, including each renewal of existing credit instruments.[58] With time, directors concerned themselves with the credit approval process, rather than individual credit requests. Directors adopted the practice of establishing credit authorization limits for branches and individual bankers. They adjusted lending limits either as economic conditions changed or as an employee advanced in rank.[59] As banks expanded in size and geographic reach, directors delegated credit authority to their bankers in the offices geographically nearest the borrower. Banks maintained better knowledge of their borrowers' financial conditions by keeping the decision to extend credit with a source close to the borrower. The banks that opened branches (the Banco do Brasil on a national basis, and other banks within their state of charter) relied on branch managers for credit decisions.[60] They recognized that the success of the branches in distant locations depended on having accurate and timely local information: ". . . in order to disperse bank credit to regions of the interior, it will always be preferable to create local organizations to support the branches of the credit institutions in the [regional] capitals and principal production centers."[61]

By the mid-1910s, at least the Banco do Brasil and Banco de Crédito Real de Minas Gerais had introduced an important accounting innovation. They applied transfer prices to deposits in order to promote an efficient allocation of deposits throughout their branch networks.[62] Branches that accumulated deposits in excess of their credit lent their funding capacity (deposits) to other branches, allowing the credit of the borrowing branches to exceed local deposits. However, the borrowing branches paid for the use of the transferred funds, in a manner that was analogous to paying interest on deposits from the public.[63] Applying a cost to the funds, with the attendant necessity to earn an interest rate above that cost, created an incentive to extend credit only when a minimum threshold of profit could be earned. This procedure both protected against unwise credit risk and reinforced the connection between deposits and credit.[64] In effect, branch managers needed to decide whether it was prudent to borrow money in order to expand. These banks applied many of the criteria to their branches that they used for their borrowers and depositors.

Decentralization, depersonalization, and professionalization of banking did not proceed smoothly. In 1910 and 1911, the Banco do Brasil suffered heavy losses from its first efforts to expand services to new geographic and sectoral markets, servicing the rubber commerce in Pará. In addition to firing and suing the branch manager, the bank began to implement controls over the lending functions that it had decentralized. Initially, the directors imposed new restraints to lending in support of the rubber trade. They tightened collateral requirements, valuing the rubber pledged as collateral at 50 percent of the market price (reduced from 75 percent), and they imposed a maximum credit limit of five contos per borrower.[65] After that experience, the Banco do Brasil and other banks began to implement procedures to monitor their delegated managers, and to more rigorously define the limits of managers' authority. By 1912, bank directors addressed the delegation of authority on a routine basis. The Banco do Brasil and Banco de Crédito Real de Minas Gerais implemented accounting procedures and centralized management procedures that were intended to enhance and monitor the delegation of authority.[66] By 1920, at the Banco do Brasil, personnel were chosen on the basis of examination (public *concursos*), rather than purely on the strength of personal recommendations and judgments. Exceptions to the rule of personnel decisions (both hiring and promotions) by examination may have continued after their introduction. However, some individuals who thought they had influence with the president of the bank did not gain employment because of insufficient exam results.[67] After its 1926 restructuring, Banespa instituted public *concursos*. It is not clear if, or when, other banks used competitive *concursos* for hiring. But, by the 1920s, the responsibilities of bank directors had shifted from the approval of specific transactions to the definition of bank policies.

The development of a profession of bankers arose during the First Republic from the simultaneous requirements of growth and protecting banks' claims on their property. Employees gained responsibility for credit decisions, and they required skills and the confidence of bank owners to commit the resources that the banks commanded. Further, the Commercial Code of 1890[68] mandated that incorporated enterprises maintain internal audit committees of accountants responsible for monitoring and reporting the financial condition of corporations. Two specialized middle-class professions emerged from the growth of banking and its attendant requirements for information and financial accountability.[69] Full-time bankers and accountants developed specialized skills and commitments to particular professional activities that coexisted with personal ties to companies. They engaged in a wide range of activities that required sophisticated information and judgment. Among the responsibilities of these employees were: to assess potential borrowers' creditworthiness, to forecast economic prospects for all businesses to which the bank lent, to continually monitor and update collateral requirements, to keep track of the banks' own financial circumstances, to guard against internal defalcation, and to maintain detailed, accurate accounting systems.

These employees depicted the emergence of new, prosperous, educated, specialized, urban professions with standards of meritorious performance. In short, they were white-collar, middle-class occupations. Individuals entering these professions formed professional associations. For example, in 1922, the Bankers Association of Rio de Janeiro organized. It was a forum for bank owners to orchestrate their common interests (often with respect to influencing regulatory and monetary policy actions) and for professional bank employees to develop their skills and common interests.[70] The formation of the Bankers Association constituted one example of the closely knit business groups and newly emerged professionals coming together to form professional technocracies and interest groups into powerful associations.[71]

Costs of Risk Management

The cost of borrowing money (the interest rate on loans and the effective discount rate applied to purchases of commercial paper) included three components. The cost of money was the most important. The average cost of money combined the rates that banks paid to depositors to attract their money and the cost of raising funds in open money markets. An analogy with other businesses would be that money was the major factor input that banks purchased. The second component of bank costs was the cost of maintaining bank operations (commonly known as overhead). Under this rubric falls the transactions costs that banks incur to institute sound business practices and to protect against risks. Finally, bank shareholders required a return on their investment, their stock dividend, to compensate them for the use of their funds and the risks they incurred. The return on borrowing needed to be sufficient to generate profits for the banks' owners.

Transactions costs of gathering and using information must have been expensive for Brazilian bankers in the early twentieth century. Brazilian banks did not, for most of this period, publish itemized income statements that distinguished between the costs of funds and operations expenses.

Therefore, the data are not available to determine banks' transactions costs.[72] Listing the nature of these costs, however, both suggests their extent and reveals that their major component was in developing a cadre of professional, full-time bankers with the expertise to exercise finely attuned judgments. Decentralized and depersonalized banking procedures required the employment of increasing numbers of educated, trained, and concomitantly expensive professional staff. For concrete financial protection against problems that did occur, all banks also maintained reserves to mitigate possible credit losses, and they left cash uninvested in order to protect themselves against large deposit withdrawals. Both practices incurred significant opportunity costs since they diminished the income-generating capacity of their resources. Banks also tended to be early users of communications technology. The geographic spread of telegraph and telephone lines deeper into the reaches of Brazil often came at the initiative of banks, in their efforts to improve the timeliness of their information.[73] Banks made the investments necessary to protect their risks in order to protect the third component of the creditors' cost: profits to bank shareholders. To shareholders, profits represented the return that they needed in order to commit their capital to the wealth-creating endeavors, and to absorb residual risks that would not disappear from banking, despite increasingly elaborate protective practices.

LEGAL PROTECTION OF PROPERTY; DEFAULTS

Bankers recognized that short-term exposure, collateral, credit management procedures, and information were not sufficient protection against their risks. Despite rigorous procedures, borrowers still defaulted on their debt obligations, either because bankers had misjudged circumstances or because of unpredictable changes in circumstance. Further, banks realized credit losses when the value of collateral was not sufficient to repay the full amount of credit or when the total capital of the defaulting company was less than its debts.

As a last resort, banks tried to rely upon the legal system to enforce their contracts. However, the system of legally defined property rights often compounded the effects of insecure credit. The legal system often jeopardized claims on financial property. Requirements of traditional real property, agricultural producers, and landowners defined the evolution of property rights.[74] Since the colonial period, property rights had developed to reflect the types of property transactions that were most prevalent, those governing land and agricultural production. Complex, and perhaps economically inefficient, practices and law reflected the concerns of transferring and protecting rural, agricultural property. The uncertainty of claims on financial instruments offset the protections of banks' risk-minimizing procedures. Insecurity diminished the ability of banks to extend credit to risky new ventures.

Insufficient protection for the recovery of debt was a serious problem throughout the First Republic.[75] The laws and Commercial Code simply did not address issues involving financial property. The Commercial Code of 1850 (often amended and reformed in 1890), did not explicitly recognize most financial assets as property. Therefore, the characteristics and transferability of equity stocks, debentures, bank credit and deposits received no legal consideration. The lack of clarity in property law extended to the identification of financial assets, the means for declaring bankruptcy, the procedure for settling debts in a default liquidation, and the means for adjudicating ownership disputes in transfers of financial assets. For banks, these shortcomings resulted in increased aversion to risky lending because of the possibility that they would not be able to minimize the losses from a credit default.

In an important example, as late as 1929, current accounts (including bank accounts) had no legal definition. As a result, no consistent procedures were in place to close or settle current accounts in bankruptcy.[76] This had both legal and financial implications. No codified rules governed access to current accounts of bankrupted parties, impeding the settlement of ongoing transactions. It was unclear whether the bankrupted party could claim any funds from the accounts, despite the fact that the bankruptcy laws gave ownership to the creditors.[77] This ambiguity left open the opportunity to settle some transactions outside of the *pro rata* settlement process for all creditors in a bankruptcy case.[78] As a result, no legal basis existed to determine the distribution of financial assets and obligations arising from involuntary transfers of property, such as defaults, estate settlements, or even simple misunderstandings. The conservative attitude that banks had in accepting collateral on loans and the impressive extent to which banks went to avoid default proceedings against borrowers demonstrated the difficulties that bankruptcies entailed.

When extending credit, the most severe manifestation of risk was the bankruptcy of a borrower. Bankruptcy followed upon default of payment obligations. However, a default did not require that creditors declare a bankruptcy. Debtors could be in default on many, or even all, payment obligations for an extended period of time without having a bankruptcy declared. Any single creditor, bank or otherwise, could declare a borrower in default, thus putting the borrower, and all of his credit, in bankruptcy.[79]

Once bankruptcy was declared, the law required that all creditors settled their accounts jointly. Further, if liquidation of the bankrupted party's property settled less than half of the debts, resolving the bankruptcy and distributing remaining assets required unanimous agreement of all creditors. The law protected the role and the interests of the bankrupt party, sometimes in preference to those of creditors.[80] Early during this period, even the ability to declare a default on incorporated entities was questionable. The fact that no individual could be found responsible for the whole entity generated this indeterminacy.[81] The difficulties of liquidation procedures and the likelihood of losses seriously undermined the legal recourse that bankers relied upon to protect against risk.

Creditors recognized their weak position in bankruptcy proceedings.[82] As a result, banks made extreme efforts to avoid declaring defaults. They frequently continued credit to borrowers even while recognizing their deteriorating financial condition, and at times banks continued extending credit specifically in order to avoid a bankruptcy.[83] The tendency to continue credit in order to avoid bankruptcy may have been especially strong during the recession preceding World War I:

> A considerable number of failures occurred and more would have been forced but for the characteristic indisposition of Brazilian business men and foreign merchants engaged in business in Brazil to crowd their customers. . . . Interest rates, to be sure, have advanced, and the merchant pays for all the accommodation he gets. . . .[84]

A bank might become active in the management of a failing firm, in order to avoid declaring a bankruptcy. In one early instance, the Bank of London and Brazil engaged in transatlantic correspondence about the management of a failing textile company's practices of inventorying cotton.[85] In another, particularly graphic, example, the Bank of London and Brazil (and subsequently the Bank of London and South America) maintained an unhappy oversight and management role in the firm of coffee merchant P. J. Nicolson. Beginning in 1923, bank correspondence documents contentious negotiations that included the bank's vetoing the firm's reorganization plans, influencing its business plans, voicing decisive discontent with firm management practices, and threatening the firm with declaring an irresolvable default.[86] These unpleasant exchanges were transatlantic; they occurred in London and Brazil, over a period of years. Nevertheless, at least through 1929,[87] the bank avoided a situation that forced the company into bankruptcy.

Bankruptcy settlements suffered severe delays and difficulty because of the requirements of uniform action.[88] Unanimous agreement on liquidation procedures, and the likelihood of losses, seriously complicated the ability of bankers to protect against the risk of borrowers' defaults. When one creditor was determined to liquidate his position with a distressed debtor, another creditor could try to convince the first to not force a bankruptcy, or he could assume the first creditor's position. The experience of the Companhia de Tecidos de Botafogo provides a good example of the full range of activities a bank could employ to avoid the bankruptcy of one of its borrowers.[89] The Banco do Brasil first tried to persuade banks to not declare bankruptcy in order to avoid the default of the company in 1915. The efforts of a consortium of banks to avoid the company's bankruptcy faltered when the Bank of London and River Plate threatened to initiate proceedings. The Banco do Brasil then tried to acquire the company's debt. Ultimately the bank was willing to make an exception of its operating statutes to become a major shareholder in the firm. The Banco do Brasil's directors authorized the acquisition of up to 60 percent of the stock of Companhia de Tecidos de Botafogo at its original par value, rather than current depreciated market price.[90]

Banks found many resourceful ways to circumvent the need to act in concert during bankruptcy negotiations. In one case, the Bank of London and South America office accepted fifty cases of *goiabada* (guava paste) from a Pernambucan merchant "on condition that we do not embarrass the concordata" and that it be "kept strictly secret."[91] It is not clear what the bank did with the *goiabada*. (Unless the office staff chose to consume it, they would have marketed it to other merchants in an attempt to recover the value of the credit.) The transaction was clearly outside of the *pro rata* liquidation procedures. Later in 1929 the same bank used its private information on a distressed client in Pelotas, Rio Grande do Sul, to liquidate its credit prior to the announcement of an impending default.[92] These examples ought not suggest that the Bank of London and South America was more aggressive than other banks at circumventing bankruptcy negotiations. More likely, distance from higher-level management required written communication in matters that others may have preferred to leave undocumented.

During the severe recession of the late 1920s, resistance to "throwing good money after bad" became more pronounced. One of the largest banks published in its annual report: "The firms that are not punctual almost entirely do not merit the credit that had been conceded to them; and there is only advantage in their disappearance, although the losses they caused have been high."[93] The Banco do Brasil (at this period, without responsibilities as a monetary authority) was very specific to its shareholders that the bank was not jeopardizing its business during the recession. The bank reduced its willingness to renew or increase credit. Notably, it took physical possession of real estate acquired in defaults.[94] However, even during these conservative and contractionary years, the Banco do Brasil continued credit to avoid bankruptcies in specific instances,[95] while forcing failures in others.[96]

Bankruptcy laws and the Commercial Code were not amended during the First Republic to accommodate the difficulties presented by financial property.[97] To the extent that property law did not evolve to recognize new forms of ownership, it constrained the ability of financial instruments, such as bank credit and deposits, to represent ownership or indebtedness. Brazilian law did not recognize financial property until the monetary and commercial reforms of 1946, and it was only fully recognized with the banking reforms of 1964.[98] Under these circumstances, traditional, informal channels of credit, with their security based on personal relations, proved more certain and retained their advantages relative to bank borrowing. Traditional sources of funds may not always have allocated capital to its highest earning or most productive use. However, as long as social and personal relations were the primary channels for allocating capital, the constraints imposed by those relations served the same effective purpose as codified property law.

REGULATION

The inability or disinterest of state and federal governments to protect the property of banks extended beyond the concerns of bankruptcy. Ongoing bank regulation and oversight of business activities were slow to develop in Brazil. At the national level, the Treasury Ministry recognized early the desirability of maintaining a centralized oversight function for banks for the purposes of regulating monetary policy. The laws of public incorporation required that all corporations publish their balance sheets monthly in their local financial press; and they published audited semiannual financial reports with their annual reports to stockholders.

Regulations passed in 1918 mandated that banks report financial data to the Treasury.[99] The decree was only implemented in 1922, with the creation of the position of national banking inspector.[100] An earlier attempt, in 1907, to impose a reserve requirement of 15 percent on bank deposits went unenforced.[101] With the formation of the Banking Inspectorate, the Ministry was defensive about instituting any reporting requirements. The Treasury explicitly stated that the banking inspector did not require any data in excess of the securities-exchange standards, and that the new regulations would give the Ministry enhanced abilities to track the activities of foreign banks.[102] It remains unclear how the Treasury enforced and maintained its regulations, and how it verified the reported data. Neither did the Inspectorate develop regulatory oversight to establish minimal standards of bank safety, such as responsive capitalization, during the First Republic. In essence, private-sector banks were left to determine, establish, and maintain their own credibility. For the public, such oversight could have provided valuable information about the viability of the banks themselves, easing decisions to deposit with or invest in specific organizations. Further regionally specific studies would illuminate whether state governments were more aggressive regulators of banks. But little suggests that to be the case. Parenthetically, it should be noted that such a situation could serve to reinforce the dominance of the Banco do Brasil and the state-owned banks, since their privileged positions with governmental authorities enhanced the perception that they would not be allowed to fail. Privately owned banks relied on more informal and less comprehensive procedures to convey such information to their clients and investors. From all perspectives, risk protection was an area in which the State did not involve itself in private-sector concerns.

CONCLUSION

By organizing banks, entrepreneurs took advantage of legal opportunities that limited their risks of diversification, and they established increasingly secure and depersonalized mechanisms of financing that subsequently could be applied broadly to wider groups of clients. Although the banks began from small and closely knit business networks, they paid close attention to establishing codified and routinized operating procedures. These procedures applied to all operations the banks undertook, providing the mechanisms to expand their interests and exposure beyond those of the original investors. Statutes specified permissible operations, collateralization requirements to protect the safety of individual transactions, management structure, and the distribution of profits. These means allowed banks to expand safely during the First Republic. By creating organizations that economic agents "knew," they established organizational structures that with time, confidence, and success could gradually expand their scope of operations. From the early twentieth century, banks policed and protected their property with increasing care. Specific management practices evolved for improving information about clients and economic expectations. These tools allowed the safe expansion of banking in dynamic response to economic growth. As a result, contract-intensive money became more secure.

Even so, structural and legal constraints continued to hinder the effect of banking in private-sector development during the First Republic. Banks' continual and rigorous evolution of practices to ensure the integrity of contractual obligations created serious limitations. Efforts that banks undertook to mitigate their credit risks and enhance their legal protection constrained the extension of credit and imposed complicated and expensive procedures. Changes in management practices were more evident than improvement to the legal protection of bank property rights. The slow change in legal code and practices served as a constraint against more dynamic banking. The question arises: Why did these protections not develop? Two possibilities are that strong interests impeded the development of a dynamic banking system, or that the demand for bank credit was not yet sufficiently strong to merit substantive institutional and legal changes. No systematic evidence supports the hypothesis that specific interests impeded the development of the banking system in this regard. The second, and more likely, possibility suggests that traditional private financial channels often could continue to serve their original purpose effectively. While traditional small and closely aligned groups may have continued to serve the best interests of investors and entrepreneurs, much economic development theory considers them less than optimal for long-term development of capital markets.[103] Depersonalization proceeded slowly.

Notwithstanding these experiences, by the end of the 1920s, an appreciation of the symbiotic relationship between economic and banking well-being reflected the growing importance of banks. The financial community recognized that bank restraint was important in controlling financial crisis: "The failures in November [1928], although they affected a limited circle of businesses, provoked a general retrenchment. They caused much apprehension and losses to some banks."[104] But, at the same time:

> Had it not been for the calm, the proverbial honor, the secure action displayed by large firms and banks, the situation would have been much worse.
>
> The directors of many banks were quick to re-establish confidence. The retrenchment of the principal institution [the Banco do Brasil] imposed the expected prudent attitude.[105]

Its institutionalization was an important component of the confidence and prudence that the business community recognized by its increased use of the banking system. Banks both implemented standards of depersonalized and decentralized practices and maintained the protection afforded by personal networks. They focused very intently on establishing their claims to ownership of assets and on determining the limits of their business when they could not protect their claims. They invested in the physical- and human-resource capabilities. These efforts manifested themselves in the evolving identification of acceptable client bases for banks, in the short-term and collateralized characteristics of their business transactions, and in the active development of professional skills. As a result, the contractual obligations, representing banks' business transactions, became increasingly secure. When banks confronted the competing institutional constraints that compromised their notions of property ownership, they both took protective measures and restrained their exposure to potential risks. The evolution and broader application of formal and informal criteria defining the institutional framework of the banking system allowed it to became more firmly embedded within the web of economic transactions.

Chapter 7

Regions, States, and Banks

B razil occupies approximately one-half of the Latin American land-mass. Its size and geographic, economic, and cultural diversity resulted in abiding regional tensions. Some historians have argued that a corresponding lack of national economic unity hindered growth by restricting market formation.[1] Economic managers of the First Republic were keenly aware of this problem. The State continually struggled with the difficulties of consolidating diverse geographic regions into an economy of national scope. With strong orchestration by republican governments, regional money centers began to integrate into a national market during the First Republic. Equal efforts by states challenged this process.

This chapter considers the role of banking in regional consolidation into a national economy from three distinct perspectives. First, it describes the construction of a national infrastructure for banking transactions and relationships, primarily through the agency of the Banco do Brasil, that provided the capacity to intermediate money throughout increasingly large geographic areas. Then, the chapter questions whether a single national monetary market was beginning to emerge from separate local markets. In the states where banking had its strongest presence, surveys of local economies and their banking structures examine the effects of regional economic differences on local banking systems and money-market formation. Finally, the chapter considers the conversion of major regional banks into state-owned organizations and its effects on national economic consolidation and the political economy. Just as competition among interest groups defined political and economic struggle at the national level, these contests also dominated the role of state governments in local economies.

During the First Republic, interest in constructing a loosely federated

State, in which states retained broad powers, competed against the interests of a strongly centralized system of governance. Regional tensions reflected economic interests as well as political ambiguities. Regional economies during the First Republic have received the attention of scholars, but the relationship between regional economies and the structure of the national economy remains relatively unstudied. This chapter, focused on the banking aspect of that relationship, finds close parallels with the political associations between State and states.

The allocation of powers between State and states in the economic realm gave states a great deal of latitude. Their rights included taxing interstate and export commerce, borrowing in international capital markets (though investors required that the Federal Treasury guarantee borrowings), and chartering banks. Although offsetting federal powers tempered all of these rights, the states had the potential to act quite independently of federal direction. That these same tools had proven to be effective for the Treasury recommended them as interesting avenues for viewing economic aspects of federalism. The strength of the states relative to the State in governance was in constant flux. The State was able to centralize some interstate commerce and taxation powers during the Republic, and it retained its power to veto international borrowing, by withholding its guarantee. This chapter also demonstrates that the Treasury helped to construct the infrastructure for a centralized government with the Banco do Brasil's national network of banking services. Nevertheless, economically strong states used their abilities to enhance their positions within the federation, both politically and economically.

Some observers have also noted that the states' capabilities reinforced the positions of strong states, because they could take advantage of them with greater ease and effect than could weaker states.[2] This chapter offers support to that perspective. At the same time, because states had these powers, policy innovations often originated at the state level. The coffee valorizations in São Paulo were the most important example.[3] But other agricultural finance efforts also offered arenas in which the states implemented economic policies when federal policy could not do so, with the crucial involvement of banks.

The competing tensions between State and state (or regional) interests found one of their outlets in banking. Regional conditions defined the ability of banks to establish themselves in given locations, and the use of banks by the political system often overshadowed the progress of the individual organizations. Local banking systems were an indicator of regional economic strength. They also became an important arena for working out the contradictory forces of centralized organization in contrast to loosely defined structures that permeated political controversy during the First Republic. The use of banks in the competition between states and State created the largest challenge to their role in forming a national economy.

Although it solidified slowly and with difficulty, a banking system of national scope emerged during the first three decades of the twentieth century. It began to connect regions and sectors of the economy with each other, smoothed out seasonal bottlenecks for money and credit, provided the conditions for a continuously operating and homogenous financial system, and assisted in defining the role of the State in the economy. Economic and political forces shaped the particular nature of banking's consolidation. Complicated dynamics of regional economic patterns, the intricate, pervasive reach of the Banco do Brasil, and state-level politics in contention with national authority defined the national banking system. The outcome was a banking system of national scope with two dominant— and competing—characteristics. First, interactions among banks developed in a hierarchical pattern, with the Banco do Brasil at its apex, rather than in support of an increasingly dense interweave of transactions among organizations. Second, state governments developed a presence, through their ownership of banks, allowing them to effectively establish monetary policies that challenged national policy and probably accentuated regional disparities.

THE NATIONAL DISTRIBUTION OF FINANCIAL SERVICES AND BANKING INFRASTRUCTURE

Seasonal fluctuations in the demand for currency had been among the earliest concerns of financial authorities in the Republic with respect to constructing a national banking infrastructure.[4] In an economy heavily reliant on expanding agricultural commodity exports for its dynamism in the formal sectors, the transition from slave to free labor created a significant new demand for money. Wage payments incurred during harvests defined fluctuations of demand for currency. The seasonal component of the demand for money had been one of the major considerations in allocating note-issuing responsibilities on a regional basis at the beginning of the First Republic. In response to these needs, expansion of the geographic reach of banking was a consistent goal of republican governments.[5] The first post-abolition efforts to provide for local monetary needs through regional banks met with the inability of the regional economies to support them. The concentration of banking services within the central monetary authority began with the consolidation of regional note-issuing rights into the Banco da República in 1892. Although less intense, the difficulties of seasonal fluctuations continued throughout the period. As late as 1927, the Banco do Brasil still expressed concern that money did not circulate freely enough to meet the seasonal requirements.[6] Meeting the seasonal demand, important as it was for the smooth functioning of the commodity-export markets, was a subset of a more fundamental problem, that of providing liquidity for an expanding range of market transactions.

In the absence of an enduring national bank, the network provided by foreign banks had been the closest alternative for the distribution of financial services. Foreign banks operated with national charters in Brazil. They negotiated the extent of their branch system at the time of entry.[7] During the collapse of the banking system from 1900 to 1906, when a bank of national scope did not operate, British banks offered the closest approximation of a national network. With the early national expansion of the Banco do Brasil, the Bank of London and Brazil did not initially expect competitive pressure on its local commercial business from regional Banco do Brasil branches.[8] Nevertheless, the Banco do Brasil did construct a national network.

From the time of its charter in 1905 through the remainder of the First Republic, the Banco do Brasil succeeded the Banco da República in serving as the proxy for the federal government in the banking system. Complementing its role in monetary policy, the bank also acquired a dominant position in the national distribution of financial services. After its opening, the Banco do Brasil actively pursued regional expansion. In doing so, it constructed a well-defined hierarchy of services to connect the smallest participants into a centralized financial system. The means for undertaking these efforts included establishing a national network of branches, serving as correspondent for regional banks, as well as interbank note rediscounting. Efforts to expand the geographic reach of the banking system through the Banco do Brasil franchise had ambiguous results. The low volume of financial services needed in regional locations constrained the viability of local banks. By the same token, however, the absence of financial services hindered the development of local commerce.

With its new charter, the Banco do Brasil was the only domestic bank with the rights to establish a national system of branches. Its interstate branch network was one of the few explicit institutional expressions of a national financial or economic system during the First Republic.[9] Other domestic banks had only limited opportunity to expand beyond their states of incorporation.[10] The first Banco do Brasil branches outside of the Federal District (the city of Rio de Janeiro) opened in 1908, two years after its new charter. The bank established branches in Pará for the purpose of easing financing in rubber commerce. While rubber was a thriving export for Brazil, these branches in the towns of Manaus and Belém were successful. They opened financial flows and allowed for the smoother functioning of an export industry that had not previously had sufficient financial infrastructure.[11] Santos, the coffee port in São Paulo, was the next area of expansion for the Banco do Brasil interstate branching.[12] By the early 1910s, new branches opened regularly. The bank often chose its branch locations in support of local business conditions, rather than solely to serve the needs of the export trade. In 1915, the bank's annual report described its branches as "true regional banks with the necessary autonomy to serve local commercial and industrial interests. . . . The first benefit of the emergence of banking will be the reduction of [local] interest rates to a natural level."[13] One aspect of the continuing efforts to create a central bank had been to "regularize" transactions and "ease economic communications" nationally.[14] In 1922, "the intensification of banking in the interior of the country continued as one of the major preoccupations of the Bank."[15] Even so, the bank had branches located in every state by 1921;[16] by 1928, 73 branches were operating.[17]

Banking activity outside of the Federal District quickly became a substantial share of the Banco do Brasil's total portfolio. From 1908, the proportion of the bank's deposits undertaken in branches increased steadily, reaching 21 percent of the total volume by 1916.[18] The head office often subsidized the opening of branches by transferring funds to the new locations. As a result, branches could lend in excess of the deposits they collected locally. In the early years of the branch system, from 1908 to 1916 (when these data are available), funding from the head office to the branches marked a significant transfer of the bank's resources. The net transfer of funding to branches was the equivalent of almost 20 percent of the Banco do Brasil's deposits from the private sector during the years 1909 through 1916.[19] In some years, transfers to branches were almost three times the level of deposits that they accumulated locally.[20] The Banco do Brasil effectively transferred resources from the Federal District. Nevertheless, the total volume of activity in the branches remained relatively small in the context of the banking system. Except during the years when the bank carried a large, unprofitable, and involuntary rubber portfolio (1910-13), total credit extended by the branches remained at approximately 5 percent of total private-sector credit in Brazil.[21] The volume of transferred funds may have been sufficient to significantly increase available resources in specific locations. However, it was not enough to substantially divert the course of Brazilian financial development. These transfers were important in establishing banking services where they had not previously been available, but they did not substantially define Brazilian banking.

One of the goals of the Banco do Brasil's Rediscount Office from 1921 was to reinforce the distribution of credit outside the major financial centers of Rio de Janeiro and São Paulo.[22] However, changing the geographic distribution of credit in practice proved difficult. The geographic distribution of the Rediscount Office's activity reflected its primary purposes of financing the Treasury and the coffee price-support program. In 1921, 23 percent of note purchases originated in São Paulo for coffee valorization, and 54 percent of notes rediscounted were in the Federal District (preponderantly rediscounts of treasury bills). The concentration in the Federal District increased to 63 percent in the following year.[23] During the Rediscount Office's first year of operation, the president of the Banco do Brasil, José Maria Whitaker, orchestrating its expansion, complained to the president of Brazil about the limitations imposed on these resources:

> The valorization operation, even though currently suspended and in spite of the recent increase to its limit, absorbs all of the resources of the Rediscount Office. . . . The Rediscount Office offers an immense service to the national economy, but currently its resources are employed almost totally by the Treasury. By the attached note [not available], you can see that all of the banks in the country are responsible for only 23,752 contos, while the Banco do Brasil is responsible for 88,757 contos. The Banco do Brasil only needs rediscounts to meet the needs of the Treasury account [including coffee valorization notes].[24]

A similar method by which the Banco do Brasil also served as a conduit for facilitating the flow of resources nationally was through acting as a correspondent for other banks. By this arrangement, local banks established accounts with the Banco do Brasil in order to facilitate their transactions between the financial center and the more remote hinterlands. In 1923, private-sector bankers decided that a separate central clearing facility was not needed because they deemed the Banco do Brasil's role as correspondent adequate to meet their needs.[25] Even so, between 1922 and 1930 (the years for which data measuring this activity are available), the volume of balances in domestic correspondent accounts (on the asset and liability sides of the balance sheets) remained less than 1 percent of the bank's total volume of credit and deposits.[26]

Through its branch, rediscount, and correspondent capabilities, the

Banco do Brasil constructed a network of financial services that expanded the geographic reach of banking to areas otherwise unserviced. Given the limited size of many local financial markets responding to private-sector credit demands, additional centrally orchestrated facilities could neither create nor redistribute private-sector credit. However, the modest volume of transactions belied the importance of these facilities. They defined the infrastructure for banking development that prevailed for the remainder of the twentieth century. For the first time in Brazil's history, a national bank provided important institutional stability to the banking system in a manner that established a common network of services to (substantially all) commercial centers. This network further consolidated the role of the Banco do Brasil as a centralizing force for the national banking system. The construction of an infrastructure of national scope to conduct finance was the Treasury's major tool to develop a cohesive and monetized economy; the effects spread unevenly. While these facilities enhanced the movement of resources from the regions to the center, it is not clear that they fostered mobility among regions.

REGIONAL ECONOMIES AND BANKING

The regional and sectoral integration of the Brazilian economy was necessary to consolidate the national scope of the economy. National financial consolidation addressed the interrelated concerns of geographic and sectoral integration in Brazil by facilitating the exchange of a wider variety of goods and services through ever-larger markets. As markets expanded, the need to finance those transactions also became more acute. Exploring the evolution of regional economies and banking systems reveals the nature of their integration.

To what extent did regionally specific conditions enhance or impede the centralizing and integrating influences of the Banco do Brasil's national financial infrastructure? This section, after a short digression to address theoretical and methodological issues, surveys regional economies and banking systems in São Paulo, the Federal District (Rio de Janeiro), Minas Gerais, and Rio Grande do Sul in order to explore the effects of regional economic differences on local banking systems. Together, these three states and the Federal District accounted for the vast majority of the formal economy, if only about 15 percent of the country's land and half of its population.[27] They also offered a diversity of economic activity. To the extent that regionalism was important, differences among these regions should reveal it. The political boundaries of states define regional banking systems because, with few exceptions, domestic banks were confined to their state of incorporation and because state economic structures were reasonably distinct. Nevertheless, the structures of the businesses and transactions that banks conducted were similar across all regions. Their common characteristics allow comparison among state banking systems. Two interrelated questions assess the extent to which banks reflected regional economies and the manners in which they contributed to the integration of a national system: Did banking differ among regions in manners that corresponded with variances in regional economies? During the First Republic, did banking evolve toward a national norm, thus indicating national economic integration of diverse regions?

Financial distribution on a national scope and increasing interrelations among regional markets generate expectations of an equalization of the cost of money across regions. An established literature, instigated by Lance Davis's controversial article in 1965, on the formation of a national money market in the United States compares interest rates on short-term bank credit across regions in order to consider the extent and methods of financial integration.[28] This material hypothesizes that, in an economy that is in the process of integrating financially, resources shift from resource-rich to resource-scarce areas and uses. Increased interaction both requires and reinforces commensurate improvements in information flows, ease of conducting transactions, and broadening groups of economic agents. Such conditions should lead money to respond to opportunities throughout an enlarging geographic region with greater facility and to reflect conditions of supply, demand, risk, and transactions costs that become increasingly similar. As a result of financial integration, the conditions affecting interest rates (the prices of money) become more uniform.[29] Consolidating information networks over larger areas should diminish the costs of assessing risks.[30] In addition, larger market areas enhance competition and erode local monopolies.[31] These were the circumstances that Brazilian authorities hoped to achieve in building an effective national banking system in Brazil at the beginning of the twentieth century.

Analysis of interest rates and examination of bank financial ratios provide the bases for the exploration of regional issues. They use the firm-level financial data and interest rates introduced in Chapter 4, aggregated by banks' state of incorporation, in conjunction with the existing historiography on state-level economies, to test the validity of the integration hypotheses in Brazil and to explore the extent to which local banking systems reflected the structures of their regional economies. The same observations made in Chapter 4 and the Data Appendix apply here.

Two characteristics should identify a money market that enlarges by consolidating markets that had previously been smaller in scale. The first is convergence of bank financial structures and the returns on their business activities (proxy interest rates) toward a national norm, as transactions and the mobilization of resources become more efficient. Second, recognizing continuing underlying regional variation, fluctuations in banking would become increasingly similar as changes increasingly affected different regions in like manners. The trend of proxy interest rate differentials reveals much about the trajectory toward an economy's unity, and persistent differentials should demonstrate underlying regional and institutional variation.

These hypothesized relationships between local interest rates, fluctuations, and differentials,[32] for the Brazilian case, can be expressed as:

$$\Delta r_{it} = \alpha + \beta_1 (\text{CONVERGE}) + \beta_2 \, \Delta BB_t \; ; \qquad\qquad \beta_1 < 0; \; \beta_2 > 0$$

where: Δr_{it} = proxy interest rate for bank or region i, change from prior period (proxy interest rate = semiannual net profit return on earning assets)

CONVERGE = differential between the local and the central (Banco do Brasil) rate, with a lag of one period ($r_{it-1} - BB_{t-1}$)

ΔBB_t = proxy benchmark money market (Banco do Brasil), change from prior period

The Banco do Brasil proxy interest rate connotes the "national rate," against which to measure convergence and uniformity of fluctuation. The lagged differential between the rates specifies the convergence relationship (CONVERGE) over time, recognizing a delay in the transmission effect. A negative relationship between CONVERGE and individual rate change ($\beta_1 <$ 0) suggests that rate changes (Δr_{it}) were mitigated by the extent of the previous period's rate differential, influencing movement toward more uniform rate structure. A positive coefficient relating contemporaneous rate change, β_2, would confirm that the given regional rate fluctuated in tandem with the Banco do Brasil proxy rate. In a perfectly integrated money market, a single interest rate would prevail for money instruments of similar structure and rate fluctuations would be uniform throughout the market (CONVERGE = 0 and β_2 = 1). Available data allow this test of market integration in Rio de Janeiro and São Paulo. The proxy interest rates of public-sector banks are identified separately, because of their substantive difference in structure, and they inform the discussion of the emergence of state banking in the following section. The results are in Table 7.1. The overall findings of convergence, without simultaneous direction of rate

Table 7.1 Interest Rate Integration Tests

| | (Based on proxy interest rates, 1906-1930) | | | | | |
	Constant	CONVERGE	BB CHANGE	R^2	D-W	n
Interest Rate Change in:						
Rio de Janeiro	0.30*	−0.66***	0.21	0.29	2.66	35
	(1.67)	(3.54)	(0.76)			
São Paulo	0.04	−0.22**	0.06	0.09	2.01	40
	(0.43)	(1.88)	(0.45)			
Banespa	0.13	−0.11	−0.04	0.04	2.57	32
	(1.02)	(1.00)	(0.21)			
Crédito Real—MG	−0.06	−0.03	−0.19**	0.13	2.89	38
	(0.83)	(0.54)	(2.23)			

Source: Derived from Table A.5. See Data Appendix for information on sources and methodology.

Notes: *   significant at 10%.

      **   significant at 5%.

      ***   significant at 1%.

      D-W: Durbin-Watson statistic to test for autocorrelation; all statements are sufficiently free from autocorrelation to pass statistical tests.

Absolute value of *t*-statistic in parentheses.

change, for private banks and a lack of convergence for the state-owned banks demonstrate the complex dynamics of banking and the money markets.

The best-studied aspect of Brazilian regional economic structure during the First Republic is the expansion of coffee cultivation and trade in São Paulo. Throughout these years, paulistas asserted coffee as the "basis of Brazilian wealth."[33] The expansion of coffee was massive, rapid, and usually profitable for its participants.[34] More important for future development, the growth and transition of the coffee sector from slave to free (largely immigrant) labor transformed the demand for goods and services in São Paulo. It propelled the early construction of industrial manufacturing capability for consumer goods (processed foods, textiles, and clothing). By the end of the First Republic, industrialization based on consumer demand was evolving to include industrial production of intermediate goods that previously were imported. Considerable research convincingly situates the sources of dynamic industrialization with success in the São Paulo coffee sector.[35] Further research also suggests that the early concentration of wealth and development in São Paulo resulted in the evolution of a system by which other regions capitalized on linkages between paulista growth and the goods they could efficiently produce. Much development in other regions occurred in support of paulista development.[36]

Reflecting its economic weight, the São Paulo banking system was the largest state banking system in Brazil, representing one-half of total deposits in 1906 and 35 percent in 1930[37] (Table A.6). Accompanying its development, which was earlier and stronger than in many other regions, the state banking system appeared relatively mature and conservative. These banks demonstrated a slower willingness to increase their risk exposure or credit portfolios. That is, their average reserve ratio (of cash to deposits) declined more slowly and remained relatively high in comparison to other areas (Figure 7.1). Until 1928, shortly after the establishment of state ownership of Banespa, paulista banks also grew notably more slowly than others (Figure 7.2). The proxy interest rate history of private domestic banks in São Paulo loosely conforms with the expectations outlined above for an area with financial systems that increasingly integrated into a larger, emerging money market, while also demonstrating conservatism. Their proxy interest rates declined in both level and rate of fluctuation (Figure 7.3). The convergence test (Table 7.1, the coefficient on CONVERGE, $\beta_1 < 0$ for private domestic banks in São Paulo) indicated that private paulista bank interest rates converged slowly[38] toward the national norm established by the Banco do Brasil. However, simultaneous fluctuation of the São Paulo rates with the Banco do Brasil's was not statistically significant.

From 1910, banking in São Paulo had two distinct components: a relatively mature network of privately owned organizations and Banespa (the Banco do Estado de São Paulo), the agricultural finance bank that opened in 1909. The state treasury acquired majority ownership in 1926. Prior to state acquisition and its expansion, Banespa was a small bank with an agricultural and mortgage focus, incorporated under the name Banco de Crédito Hypothecário e Agrícola do Estado de São Paulo. The state government engineered Banespa's expanded and restructured agricultural financing to meet the needs of the coffee trade in 1926. The levels of their proxy interest rates testify to the difference between Banespa and the privately owned banks (Figure 7.3). From the 1920s, Banespa earned returns on the credit that it extended in a counter-cyclical pattern to those of other banks in São Paulo and to the Banco do Brasil. Banespa also enjoyed exceptional earnings in the early 1920s, which immediately reversed when it became a state-owned organization. Only after the state government's acquisition of Banespa did the conservative profile of the state banking sys-

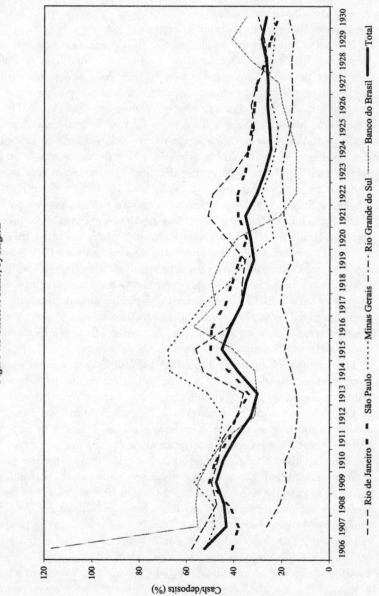

Figure 7.1 Reserve Ratio, by Region

--- Rio de Janeiro ■ ■ São Paulo · · · · · Minas Gerais — · — Rio Grande do Sul · · · · · · · · Banco do Brasil ■■■■ Total

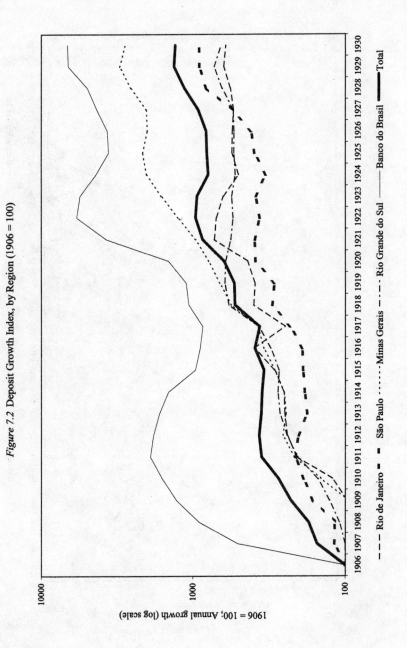

Figure 7.2 Deposit Growth Index, by Region (1906 = 100)

- - - Rio de Janeiro ■ ■ São Paulo · · · · · · Minas Gerais - · - · - Rio Grande do Sul ——— Banco do Brasil ━━━ Total

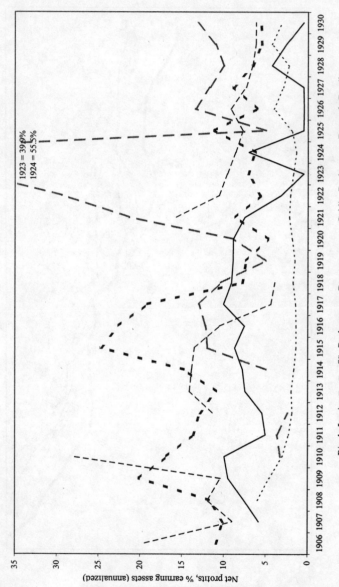

Figure 7.3 Proxy Interest Rates; Net Profitability Rates based on Earning Assets (Annualized), by Region

tem change (Figures 7.1 and 7.2; the political economy of Banespa's ownership structure is considered in the following section). In contrast, the privately owned banks did not change their conservative natures, and their convergence toward the Banco do Brasil rate confirms expectations of a financial axis of increasing strength between São Paulo and the core of the money market.

Two very different dynamics characterized economic development in the state of Rio de Janeiro. Outside of the Federal District, a declining coffee sector coexisted with a rural population that produced for small local markets and urban areas.[39] Rapid urbanization in the bureaucratic and commercial center of the Federal District supported the growth of middle- and working-class occupations and demand for consumer goods distributed through organized market systems. Urban infrastructure and consumer demand for simple manufactured goods supported industrial growth, especially in textile manufacturing.[40] Although São Paulo grew more quickly than Rio de Janeiro, at the beginning of the Republic, the Federal District's port remained the third largest destination of imports in the western hemisphere, after New York and Buenos Aires. During the First Republic, São Paulo firmly supplanted Rio de Janeiro as the source of dynamic growth in export agriculture and industry.[41] Rio de Janeiro was well on its way to becoming the administrative center that it has been through the mid- and late-twentieth century.[42] While urban and rural economic activity were related, they seemed to proceed along different trajectories.

Banking in Rio de Janeiro strongly reflected its connection with the national government and its relatively long history. Privately owned banks experienced declining reserve ratios and modulated growth (though with a short surge in 1921, as rediscounting had strong local effects, Figures 7.1 and 7.2), a pattern similar to that in São Paulo. The history of proxy interest rates suffers from some discontinuity,[43] but its trends are clear. The rate declined and converged toward the Banco do Brasil rate (Figure 7.3 and Table 7.1). As occurred with private paulista banks, the trend of rate convergence happened in Rio de Janeiro without contemporaneous correlation of rate fluctuations.

Development in the state of Minas Gerais differed from other regions during the First Republic. As in São Paulo, coffee was important for the state's economy and it supported some industrial growth.[44] The inland location of the state required that commercial networks with São Paulo and Rio de Janeiro coffee trading houses develop early. Interregional commercial networks between the states supported the export sector and local demand for consumer goods.[45] However, coffee did not define economic well-being in Minas Gerais to the extent that it did in São Paulo. Producers in Minas Gerais also mined for such ores as iron and manganese and exported agricultural products to other regions of Brazil. Notably, mineiros provided grains and dairy products to markets in other regions of the country.[46] Recent evidence confirms that these trends had origins that long preceded the First Republic.[47] Growth, diversification of production to domestically oriented agriculture, and consumer manufacturing appeared strong during the 1920s, a period of slow progress for the country as a whole.[48] Much of the economic diversification and industrialization in Minas Gerais can be traced to a few family groups. The size of both coffee and industrial production units was smaller than those found in São Paulo or Rio de Janeiro.[49] Finally, the government of Minas Gerais took an active role in the state's economic development earlier than governments in other states, and it developed that role through the financial sector.[50]

Banking in Minas Gerais appeared more dynamic than in Rio de Janeiro and São Paulo. In addition to growing more rapidly than the more mature centers (Figure 7.2), banks in Minas Gerais also became more expansive, as demonstrated by their reserve ratios. The mineiro banks realized a precipitous and permanent decline of their average reserve ratio from the mid-1910s (Figure 7.1). Their portfolios, based on more diverse markets of domestic consumer goods rather than highly fluctuating agricultural exports, may have been more predictable and therefore required lower levels of reserves.[51] Banking facilities in Minas Gerais also seemed to take more innovative forms than found elsewhere. The state treasury apparently allowed, under some circumstances, out-of-state banks to establish branches.[52] Banco Pelotense, from Rio Grande do Sul, opened a branch in Minas Gerais and one of the state-government-sponsored mortgage banks opened an early branch in São Paulo.[53] The relative dynamism of banking resulted in nearly a fourfold increase its share of total deposits. Even so, the rapid increase brought the mineiro share to only 5 percent of the total banking system by 1930 (Table A.6). Although the relevant income data are not available, the state's share of banking facilities was clearly much smaller than its contribution to national income.[54] While banks displayed impressive growth, the relative lack of banking facilities in the state motivated the early role that the state government assumed in the banking system (as is discussed in the following section).

In Rio Grande do Sul, as in Minas Gerais, the slow formation and growth of domestic consumer markets had a significant role in determining economic development. As early as the eighteenth century, the economy of Rio Grande do Sul derived its dynamism from producing goods exported to other areas of Brazil. The region provided dried beef to feed the slave population of the Northeast.[55] During the Paraguayan War (1864–70), the military's expanded demand initiated significant growth.[56] Though it remained an important activity, by the First Republic, the demand for dried beef stagnated and production of crops grown for domestic consumption expanded. Riograndense cultivators increasingly produced such crops as rice, beans, wheat, corn, potatoes, and maté for distribution through domestic markets.[57] Industrial capacity for consumer manufactures expanded slowly during the period but remained small and primarily limited to food processing.[58] *Frigoríficos* (for refrigerated shipping of meat) lent some dynamism to riograndense exports and capital flows, but the meat trade did not reach the intensity of Argentina's. Economic growth in Rio Grande do Sul may have remained strong through the 1920s, as in Minas Gerais, because of the state's rapid introduction of crops and goods that served domestic, rather than volatile international, markets.[59]

Reflecting the domestic nature of production that prevailed in the state, banking remained a local business in Rio Grande do Sul. Nevertheless, the state supported a fairly large banking system, accounting for approximately 15–20 percent of total bank deposits during the Republic (Table A.6). The three largest riograndense banks were among the largest in Brazil (Table A.7). Throughout the early twentieth century, riograndense banks maintained low and stable reserve ratios (Figure 7.1). As with the rapid decline of reserve ratios in Minas Gerais, this indication of an ability to maintain lower liquidity reserves may reflect the relative stability of economic well-being rooted in domestic markets for consumer staples. In Rio Grande do Sul, the banking system grew strongly in two discrete periods: 1911–12 and 1917–18 (with another small spurt with the formation of the state-owned Banco de Rio Grande do Sul in 1928, Figure 7.2). Outsiders had limited interest or influence in the local riograndense economy. They did not affect national government revenues; nor did they attract the participation of foreign producers or merchants as intensely as in areas more focused on internationally traded commodities. Therefore, foreign banks maintained a minimal presence in the state;[60] neither did the state government become formally involved in banking until 1928.

In summary, among these regions, banking systems differed in accord with the variations of their underlying productive enterprises. Despite business and organizational similarities, the financial structures of banking systems in these four regions reflected the varying levels of risk, innovation, and stability of their economic bases. In these four regions, the organized banking system grew at widely divergent rates beginning in (approximately) 1910, and, though converging, liquidity levels (the reserve ratio of cash as a percentage of deposits) also varied significantly (Figures 7.2 and 7.1, respectively). In Minas Gerais and Rio Grande do Sul, with economic growth more connected with the emergence of production for domestic markets, new forms of financial arrangements showed their most dynamic effects. The growth of domestic markets engendered opportunity for production and distribution on ever-larger scales, with increasing and increasingly complex financial requirements.

In the regions where it established a presence in the commercial community, state banks demonstrated the characteristics expected with increasing interactions in enlarging markets while reflecting the differences of states' economies. The available evidence in Rio de Janeiro and São Paulo found that in the private sector proxy interest rates converged toward a national norm (the Banco do Brasil rate), but they did not fluctuate synchronously with the Banco do Brasil rate. These results reflect the two (sometimes competing) roles of the Banco do Brasil. As the most important financial institution affecting other banks, its roles as rediscounter, correspondent, and money market center transmitted its interest rate patterns to others, with a time lag. At the same time, market integration, relative to the rate set by the Banco do Brasil, was impeded by the bank's role as monetary authority, often exercising counter-cyclical credit policy.

This overview of regional economies and banking abstracts from many nuances and details of the experiences that shaped regional banking systems. Nevertheless, its implications are clear. Where local banking systems were self-sustaining, they showed signs of cohering into a national system. Extending this conclusion to other regions is necessarily speculative (made all the more so by fundamental structural differences among states). Absent the empirical evidence, logic suggests the possibility that convergence among these states, with relatively strong banking presences, combined with the hierarchical system of national banking services could have contributed to increasing disparity between them and other areas that were both poorer (Table A.9) and less serviced by financial infrastructure. The ability of the governments of the strongest states to capitalize their own banks adds to the possibility of this outcome.

STATE-OWNED BANKS

During the First Republic some state governments became intimately involved in banking in order to accommodate local needs that proved difficult to meet at the national level. With time, their involvement in banking transcended their original purposes and created the opportunity for state governments to implement monetary policies within their states that challenged national policy. This extension became a tool in the competition between decentralized federalism and political interests of centralization, and in determining the nature of the Brazilian economy. Ultimately, the evolution of banking and money policies at the state level challenged the credibility of the Federal Treasury's ability to implement national monetary policy.

The interests of state governments in banking originated in the difficulties of financing agricultural enterprise that neither privately owned organizations nor the Banco do Brasil could resolve because of the duration and risk considerations. In some states, the state treasury began to subsidize long-term funding for a bank within the state. The states of Minas Gerais and São Paulo funded facilities to support a range of agricultural needs, including mortgage finance, small-scale production, and the purchase of agricultural stocks (price supports).[61] Initially, they subsidized mortgage banks by guaranteeing dividend payments and by granting monopoly rights for mortgage lending in their states. Issuing long-term debt obligations, known as mortgage notes, required special license from the state. In São Paulo and Minas Gerais these notes proved to be a difficult funding tool for the banks.[62] Few investors were willing to buy the notes because of the uncertainties about interest rates and creditworthiness over a prolonged period.[63]

Direct funding from state treasuries provided an alternative method to accommodate mortgage lending. Both state treasuries also funded agricultural credit by maintaining accounts (which had some characteristics of both equity and deposits) in the mortgage banks of their states.[64] In these instances, the states effectively lent to their mortgage banks, and the transfer from the state treasuries to the banks increased the level of state indebtedness. Ultimately the state treasuries became majority shareholders of the banks, for purposes that transcended the concerns of mortgage funding. The relationships between the banks and state treasuries became close and multifaceted. Through the First Republic, state-subsidized banks continued to justify their special status in the needs of agricultural and long-term mortgage credit. However, their effects began to assume a more subtle form with respect to monetary policy and the political competition between the State and individual states. The growth and interest rate experiences of the banks that came to be state-owned indicate that these organizations were substantively different from banks completely in the domain of the private sector.

The Banco de Crédito Real de São Paulo was the first state-subsidized agriculture bank in São Paulo after the beginning of the Republic. It opened in 1899, and it failed in 1904. In 1909, the state of São Paulo granted the mortgage concession to, and guaranteed the earnings of, a group of French bankers, the merchant bank of J. Loste & Cie. in combination with Crédit Foncier. They opened the Banco de Crédito Hypothecário e Agrícola de São Paulo (Bchasp). The bank provided mortgage and short-term production financing to farmers. It developed a network of branches throughout São Paulo.[65] Bchasp operated as both a commercial and agricultural bank, and agriculturalists often expressed dissatisfaction with the sectoral distribution of the bank's portfolio.[66] The state of São Paulo acquired 30 percent of the bank's capital in 1914. In 1926, after buying the French-owned equity and initiating another capital expansion, the state treasury owned 57 percent of the equity and changed the bank's name to the Banco do Estado de São Paulo (more familiarly, Banespa).[67] By the time of the transfer of ownership, mortgage-lending operations were of secondary importance relative to financing coffee commerce.[68] The bank readdressed this need when it opened a new mortgage affiliate in 1928.

The motivation for the state government of São Paulo to recapitalize and expand Banespa was the transfer of the coffee price-support program from federal to paulista responsibility.[69] The Federal Treasury had terminated its 1921 coffee price-support program in 1924, with its commitment to orthodox contractionary monetary policy. In response, the state government of São Paulo elevated its efforts to support its most powerful constituents. Political rebellions in São Paulo in 1924 made it difficult to abandon support of coffee entirely. Some analysts suggest that the transfer of coffee price supports from the federal to state level was a ploy to accommodate international capital markets and paulista coffee interests simultaneously.[70] However, such a strategy in 1924, two years before exchange stabilization through the Stabilization Office, seems quite unlikely to have fooled international financiers. The failure of the attempt to reintroduce other components of orthodox monetary policy in 1923 and 1924 support the assessment that paulista price supports for local coffee interests conflicted with the intentions of federal policy.[71]

Whether state and federal governments colluded or competed,[72] the federal government had neither the strength nor the authority to prevent the transfer. The state treasury of São Paulo purchased the national coffee stocks, opened the state's Coffee Institute, and continued to support coffee prices.[73] The desire for a permanent means to support coffee motivated the acquisition and recapitalization of Banespa, in order to accept the notes generated by the program, in the same manner that the Banco do Brasil had previously functioned.[74] The state treasury and the Coffee Institute of São Paulo intended to use Banespa as the financial institution to create a permanent program. With its restructuring, the state treasury and the Coffee Institute of São Paulo had positions on the Banespa Board of Directors.[75] This triad of public institutions did not support coffee producers through the Depression; coffee price supports collapsed in 1929.[76] Nevertheless, Banespa and the state treasury of São Paulo demonstrated the potential strength of, as well as the potential conflicts between, state and federal policies. As early as 1930, Banespa went directly to the international capital markets for a loan of £20 million, when the Banco do Brasil declined to participate.[77]

To expand Banespa, the state government of São Paulo used locally derived monetary expansion to replace national support of the coffee sector. The treasury of São Paulo issued bonds that it deposited in Banespa, in a manner analogous to federal money creation. As part of this endeavor, the growth of Banespa in 1926 and 1927 (in real deposits) equaled 65 percent of the Banco do Brasil's growth during the Rediscount Office's expansion in 1921 and 1922.[78] Banespa's growth continued, at only slightly slower rates, through the remainder of the decade. The presidency of a paulista, Washington Luís Pereira de Souza, from 1926 to 1930 created an opportunity to reconcile divergent economic interests, by controlling money creation and domestic inflation while also attending to the needs of the coffee sector. The Stabilization Office (Caixa de Estabilização), operating as had the Conversion Office of 1906-14, attempted to reintroduce the gold standard in order to maintain exchange stability. One important component of this arrangement was that Banespa also gained foreign exchange trading rights for the state treasury to offset the exchange effects of coffee valorization.[79] The structure of these arrangements paralleled the 1906 reforms, but at the level of one state.[80] The creation of a state-owned bank to operate these mechanisms responded to regional economic divisions very differently than had the 1906 arrangements. With foreign exchange trading and money-creation rights in other domestic banks severely constrained, this capability conferred on Banespa an additional influence on the value of money beyond that of other organizations.

Reflecting its state government involvement, the interest rate history at Banespa was more complicated than elsewhere. While the bank remained small, until the early 1920s, its proxy interest rates conformed to the direction of the rest of the São Paulo banking system, at somewhat lower levels. Then, Banespa realized exceptional returns in the early 1920s, and its proxy interest rates moved in an inverse pattern with the paulista rates and with Banco do Brasil rates throughout the decade (Table 7.1 and Figure 7.3). The sharp inversion of proxy rates in the early 1920s was the result of the 1921-23 federal rediscount and coffee price-support programs; rediscounting of coffee notes allowed the bank to expand credit without consideration of its funding obligations. The bank's effective proxy rate of return reached 55 percent during 1924. The exceptional returns ceased immediately with the end of these federal programs. By the late 1920s, the change in ownership structure redistributed the gains that had accrued to Bchasp shareholders through federal rediscounting directly to the paulista coffee sector.

The expansion of Banespa and the 1928 opening of its mortgage affiliate strongly concentrated the paulista banking system. By 1930, Banespa accounted for approximately 60 percent of the São Paulo banking system (excluding deposits in Banco do Brasil branches), as compared to its share of paulista deposits, which remained below 5 percent, prior to the reorganization. This level of growth suggests that the São Paulo program seriously offset the federal government's contractionary goals in the mid-1920s. The interest rate and growth history demonstrated that the effects of the national policies included enriching Banespa shareholders and integrating a financial nexus between paulista banking and national finance that exceeded the experience in Minas Gerais. The debates surrounding the state capitalization of the Crédito Real in Minas Gerais emphasized the belief that Banco do Brasil policies and programs benefited São Paulo in preference to other states.[81] The findings here add specificity to those conclusions.

The relationship between the state government of Minas Gerais and Banco de Crédito Real began in a similar fashion to that between the government of São Paulo and Banespa. The Banco de Crédito Real de Minas Gerais opened in 1889 in the original state capital of Juiz de Fora, and it was more successful than other early mortgage finance efforts. Other states attempted to fund rural credit and mortgage banks at the turn of the Republic; the mineiro bank seems to have been the only one to survive.[82] In 1909, the state of Minas Gerais began to fund special facilities in support of state agricultural production and marketing.[83] Crédito Real was the only publicly chartered bank in Minas Gerais until 1911.[84] The state government retained positions on Crédito Real's Board of Directors and also the ability to appoint the bank's president.[85] The bank attended to its original goals in agricultural finance. Simultaneously, it served the same purpose for the state government, small family-held banking houses (*casas bancárias*), and small joint-stock banks in Minas Gerais that the Banco do

Brasil provided for banks in the financial centers and for other large regional banks. The bank accommodated the financial transactions of large clients and rediscounted notes from smaller financial institutions, maintaining a branch system throughout the state. It also ran a small state-financed program to purchase coffee warrants as a means of price support and other agricultural finance initiatives.[86] In turn, the Crédito Real rediscounted its notes with the Banco do Brasil, establishing a hierarchy through which banks and the state government could manage their finances. The bank also served as a funding tool of the state treasury by taking its notes.[87] By 1924, the state treasury of Minas Gerais owned 67 percent of the bank's equity.[88] Much of the political impetus for expanded state ownership was to counter the perceived maldistribution of the Banco do Brasil's programs toward São Paulo.[89] This expansion took place during the state presidency (governorship) of Antônio Carlos Ribeiro de Andrada, who had gained some of his experience with monetary affairs as Federal Treasury minister, during the expansion of the World War I years in 1917-18. Although the bank's focus was on financing commercial agriculture, it did not develop the large and programmatic exclusivity that Banespa had in the 1920s.

The strong presence of the state treasury through Crédito Real in the regional banking system had a different effect than the analogous activities in São Paulo. From 1911 through the end of the First Republic, Crédito Real extended an average of 45 percent of the credit in Minas Gerais; the bank defined the money and credit conditions in the state. However, rather than concentrating banking in one organization, as occurred at Banespa, in Minas Gerais a strong state-owned bank supported the presence of additional banks. Its share of deposits in the state declined continuously from 1918, as more banks incorporated. In the mid-1920s a number of very small banks opened (or converted from their original structures as *casas bancárias*) throughout the state.[90] Few had long lives, and the most significant was the 1923 opening of Banco de Commércio e Indústria de Minas Gerais (acquired by Banco Nacional in 1975). By 1930, Crédito Real deposits accounted for only 28 percent of the formal banking system of the state. Diversified economic growth combined with financial distribution did seem to contribute to an increasingly vibrant banking system, rather than the concentration seen in São Paulo.

Interest rate fluctuation at Crédito Real correlated inversely with Banco do Brasil rate change, rather than moving synchronously as predicted for an "integrating" banking system. (The correlation was statistically significant, Table 7.1.) The inverse relation between rate change at the Crédito Real and the Banco do Brasil reflected the fundamental growth and relative strength of the mineiro economy during these years. Proxy interest rates at Crédito Real experienced a subtle but important shift; beginning from a persistently low level in the early 1900s, they did not decline during the Republic, as did others. The Crédito Real's proxy interest rates at the end of the Republic were in line with other organizations (Figure 7.3).[91] Although banking in Minas Gerais remained a small share of the total, its very rapid growth (Figure 7.2) coincided with the expansion of coffee and domestic agriculture simultaneously with the involvement of the state in supporting vastly larger bank credit facilities.

These results of rapid banking growth combined with increasing proxy interest rates reflected the long-term increasing value of money in a rapidly developing region.[92] The state government's participation in Crédito Real contributed to strong growth in the size of the banking system. Effective interest rates demonstrated the very small state banking system at the beginning of the period and the scarcity of bank funds, relative to demand. Mineiro banking had only a small effect on nationally aggregated costs of money, but it clearly demonstrated coherence within an evolving national economic unit.

Money markets reflected the interests of competing strategies and agents during the latter twenty-five years of the First Republic. The specific interests of paulista economic agents in maintaining their prosperity from international markets certainly found strong representation in national financial and monetary policy. When that representation was jeopardized, economic agents within the state circumvented and offset national policy. In a similar manner, when national policy did not address the perceived needs of locally influential mineiro economic interests, the state government organized and funded alternative facilities. Though the mineiro actions had much a smaller impact on national policy than did those in São Paulo, they addressed local goals effectively. Republican policy and practice did not overtly discriminate by region. As with monetary policy, Banco do Brasil programs had their largest effects in the geographic area where they had the most opportunity to be exercised. The experiences of Banespa and Crédito Real demonstrated that state-financed banks were able to countermand the Banco do Brasil's activities in deference to local interests. For neither bank did the convergence measures behave in predicted manners (Table 7.1). Proxy interest rates did not converge toward the norm set by the Banco do Brasil. Though correlated in the predicted direction, the convergence relationship was not statistically significant. Neither did their interest rates fluctuate in synchronization with the Banco do Brasil's.

Two results of these activities, which traditional historiography of the political events has not recognized, were important for the evolution of the national banking system. First, they proved an effective, if slow, mechanism for reinforcing the financial nexus between the dominant regional economy of São Paulo and the national government that exceeded the linkages developing elsewhere in Brazil. Second, multiple layers of monetary management limited the importance of privately owned banks responding freely to the demands for banking in the productive sectors. The hypothesis that through the twentieth century the ability of states to exercise monetary policies through the vehicles of state-owned banks significantly deterred the credibility of federal monetary policy deserves further empirical research.[93]

CONCLUSION

The evolution of the banking system offers a concrete example of the difficulties created by the countervailing forces of national consolidation and strong regionalism that were often in contention during the First Republic. The processes of building a national banking system and their effects on consolidating a national economy expressed these tensions. Banking continued to incorporate strong differences due to both local conditions and conflict between state and national political forces. Three distinct processes have demonstrated the difficulties and progress of consolidating a national banking system.

The strongest tool of the Federal Treasury to contribute to the emergence of a banking system of national scope was the construction of infrastructure to effect banking transactions across an increasing geographic area under the auspices of the Banco do Brasil. One of the Banco do Brasil's goals was to establish banking facilities nationally; its effect was to concentrate the national financial system within a single organization. The monopoly of the Banco do Brasil in the transactional infrastructure that connected banks entrenched the bank, and by implication the Treasury, at the center of the banking system. The bank effectively distributed resources among a larger geographic area. A network of similar banking transactions and procedures accommodated differences in regional economic structures within a system that was increasingly national in scope. This system connected state banks in a hierarchical fashion with the Banco do Brasil, and local organizations with state-owned banks, without fostering a dense weave of relationships among banks in closely aligned markets. As a result, financial activity between regions occurred through the intermediation of the Banco do Brasil. The low volume of geographically dispersed transactions that the bank undertook suggests that the supply of financial infrastructure anticipated its demand. Nevertheless, it supported the growth of depersonalized financial arrangements in markets that were increasing in size. Efforts to spread the benefits of banking to wider geographic areas had the ironic result of concentrating and reinforcing incipient regional patterns of distribution within the banking system, rather than mitigating them. The dominance of the Banco do Brasil has not been challenged in subsequent years.

The comparison of banking among states (after reorganization in 1905) reflected their local economic structures. State economies and banking systems demonstrated early, though often weak and inconsistent, signs of increasing interrelatedness. The relatively mature economies of São Paulo and Rio de Janeiro had banking systems that experienced long periods of slow growth and appeared liquid and risk averse (with high reserve ratios). In contrast, in the more dynamic and (perhaps) domestically rooted areas of Minas Gerais and Rio Grande do Sul, through different impetuses, banks grew quickly, accommodated new entrants, and exhibited a higher tolerance for risk. In regions for which data are available, private-sector banks became slowly integrated into a national money market, as proxy interest rate trends moved toward a national norm. Integration occurred through various means, reflecting the initial diversity of integrating regions. Proxy interest rates of private-sector banks in São Paulo and Rio de Janeiro converged toward the Banco do Brasil benchmark. At Crédito Real, rising rates, rather than synchronous rate fluctuation, brought the state's rates toward the national level. These tentative findings suggest the slow unification of a national market for money. Nevertheless, the banking system remained concentrated within a relatively few organizations. The largest of the banks also developed strong political orientations and purposes, as state governments learned to use them to support local purposes.

The national and state governments subsidized the construction of national and state-level financial systems for overlapping reasons of economic exigency and political opportunity. These processes intimately intertwined the political and financial systems at multiple levels of governance. State governments appropriated mechanisms used at the national level to serve their political purposes and the interests of their constituencies. The treasury of Minas Gerais was an early exemplar of subsidizing, using, and finally acquiring a bank to meet its constituents' needs for agricultural and mortgage credit. The treasury of the state of São Paulo adopted similar strategies on a larger scale. The expansion and acquisition of a majority ownership position in Banespa in order to support the paulista coffee trade upon the withdrawal of federal participation in the banking system and coffee valorization programs had two important effects for banking. The funding of Banespa, previously a small bank, motivated a very large, rapid expansion of banking in São Paulo. Although much historiography of federal monetary policy and political history emphasizes the political accommodation of transferring coffee price supports, both interventions of state treasuries also strongly countered national monetary policy. Interest rates of Banespa and Crédito Real, moving in patterns countering the Banco do Brasil rates, demonstrated this oppositional nature. Because the State used monetary policy more strongly than fiscal or development policies to manage its intervention in the economy, the use of the same tools by state governments to offset centralized efforts offers another strong indication of the challenges to the State's authority and legitimacy.

The argument that the areas of greatest strength had the ability to concentrate political power had its analog in the economic and banking realms. Banking concentrated in the wealthiest states, those with economic reason and capability to make use of dynamic banking facilities. The same states also constructed monetary policies through their banks to support their strongest constituents. The Minas Gerais treasury did so early, in order to counter monetary policies that favored interests rooted in international trade, predominantly coffee price supports directing federal resources toward São Paulo. Paulistas followed similar mechanisms later in order to preserve support policies. While the Banco do Brasil's national presence brought financial services to remote locations with commercial potential, it did so on a relatively small scale. If the political economy of state-level participation in banking challenged the ability of the State to manage its monetary policy, it also seemed to have exacerbated the concentration of financial resources in the states of greatest means.

The forces that contributed to constructing a financial system of national scope combined to produce the outcome of concentrating the financial system, even while spreading its services. Financial infrastructure built by the Banco do Brasil spread its geographic coverage and incorporated specific commercial locations into larger markets, but the nature of the services resulted in a highly concentrated distribution of resources. Meanwhile, where the growth of markets was strongest, it impelled active and rapidly evolving banking in response to demand. Within regions of emerging domestic markets, such as Minas Gerais and Rio Grande do Sul, banking became less concentrated as it grew. The political economy of state treasuries entering banking gave added force to regional economic circumstance and political power at the same time that it created a complicated interdependency between state-level and national monetary policies. The concentration of the banking system and the conflicting goals of its participants reinforced its hierarchical nature and contributed to defining the consolidation of an economy of national scope.

The tensions between centralization and decentralization were expressed in distinct arenas. As a result, the Banco do Brasil could both construct a national infrastructure for distributing financial services and confront serious constraints in its role as a monetary authority. The persistent competition between autonomy and integration within banking mirrored their origins in the contentions within the national political structure. Continuing tension in the distribution of federal and state-level policy authority created an opportunity for private-sector agents to pursue their interests at multiple levels of governance simultaneously. The public- and private-sector roles of banking made it a target for state-level governments to develop their autonomy from federal monetary authority. The resulting competition between states and the State for resources and political power did not disappear during the twentieth century, and it has often been channeled through the actions of the state-owned banks in opposition to republican monetary policy. During the First Republic, the use of banks introduced a new forum, and intensified the conflict between region and nation that had found numerous expressions throughout Brazilian history.

Chapter 8
Conclusion

The transformation of the banking system during the First Republic both reflected and helped to shape the transitions in Brazilian society. Banking development facilitated, even if it did not initiate, fundamental change in social and economic structure. This study points to the inseparability of international financial markets from domestic development. The intricate interplay of interest groups, market dynamics, political structures, and economic growth often took place within the banking system, and it defined the evolution of Brazilian banking. Exploration of these interactions within the banking system illuminates the historical trajectory and complexity of development.

Significant synergy marked banking and development in many arenas. A quick catalog of the more notable effects of banking offers concrete examples of major structural changes that historians have ascribed to the Republic. The increasing use of banks made intersectoral flows of funds more fluid, especially those between coffee, industry, and the public sector at the federal and state levels. Intermediating their financial transactions more efficiently allowed greater scope of activity to all economic agents associated with banking. Public policy with respect to money and banking became a prominent forum for competing interests to jockey for influence and to define the emerging structure of governance. The State and states were prominent among these interest groups. Individuals from a wide range of backgrounds, reflecting the increasingly diverse nature of the Brazilian population and their activities, also participated in establishing a modern banking system. Bankers came to typify a new urban middle-class profession. They introduced innovation in their risk-management and operating procedures in order to sustain their growth, while accommodating remaining weaknesses of information flows and legal protection. These were among the most important economic transitions of the Republic. Few aspects of economic organization or development were unaffected by banking.

Transition in banking was incomplete and compromised. The total banking system and the number of economic agents directly affected by banking remained small. Traditional social groups tended to combine their interests within given banks. The competition of interests and the unsettled nature of governance resulted in inconsistent monetary and banking policy. Continuing vagueness about the concept of property deterred a greater tolerance for risk among banks, as it did for all enterprise. Recognizing these constraints sheds light on the complex process of structural economic change that affected Brazilians at the beginning of the twentieth century.

CHRONOLOGY

At the beginning of the First Republic, efforts to accelerate economic change motivated attempts to engineer a larger and more expansive banking system. Under a great deal of pressure to support massive expansion from multiple sources, the financial system underwent a radical experimentation and transformation at the beginning of the Republic. The end of the Republic in 1930 saw financial pressure from the opposite direction— to support the economy through a prolonged and deep-seated recession. Although banking failed to meet the first challenge, it had become strong and viable by the Depression. Treasury Minister José Maria Whitaker[1] declared a bank holiday for two weeks in October 1930, during the political coup ending the Republic and in the midst of the Depression;[2] the banking system avoided a general failure. The roots of the modern banking system had emerged in the early twentieth century, and by 1930, Brazilians realized its benefits. Both the scale and nature of banking were fundamentally transformed. From its earliest stages, the banking system developed along two parallel but interdependent trajectories. Banks intermediated the accumulation and allocation of privately owned financial resources. Simultaneously, the banking system became a crucial arena in forging the political mechanisms of governance. The formation of a banking system was a vital component in consolidating an economy of national scope and determining the participation of the public sector in the economy.

The nature and size of the banking system, its relationship with public- and private-sector growth, and the institutional and managerial principles by which it functioned evolved together. Public finance served as an early impetus for banking. However, both individual banks and the collective practices of the banking system needed to make progress in resolving problems of risk and profitability management as well as procedural efficiency in order to sustain the system's development and growth. During the First Republic, three general phases marked the development of the banking system.

The first period, one of disruption and slow recovery, lasted until 1906. Banking expansion at the beginning of the Republic was an integral component of a larger strategy of rapid growth. Although within only a few years it resulted in bank failures that were as widespread as their formation had been, the earliest efforts signified a substantive change in banking. The causes and sequence of events leading to the Encilhamento, and its effects throughout the economy, deserve more systematic study than they have received. Nevertheless, the experience had two lasting results. The trend toward consolidating a banking system that connected public and private sectors began with the formation of the Banco da República in 1890. At the same time, the private sector, both as investors and borrowers, came to consider banking an integral component of their business strategies. They looked for mechanisms to enhance the safety and viability of banks. Entrepreneurs began to use banks more actively as financial tools to accumulate resources from ever larger pools and to deploy those resources according to increasingly depersonalized criteria. The banks that survived the crises of the 1890s scaled back their scope and ambitions of engaging in a wide variety of financial activities. The deflation that followed was long; it interrupted growth and innovation. However, financial and monetary restructuring ultimately put banks on a firmer foundation than they had previously enjoyed.

Restrictive monetary policy slowly contributed to a long and painful economic recovery that culminated at the end of 1905 and allowed a second phase of banking development. Widespread reforms introduced coffee price supports and the gold standard to maintain the value of the mil-réis. These programs required a stronger banking system to provide administrative support and to realize the wider economic benefits that they promised. After its reorganization, a nationally consolidated banking system slowly emerged in Brazil. Government policies controlling the value of the mil-réis and economic growth supported revitalized banking. The most obvious step was the restructuring of the national bank, the Banco do Brasil. An increasingly stable system allowed banks to become more integrated into the productive economy than they had been previously. In 1914, during a time of international financial circumstances that might have previously led to another collapse, domestic finance and money markets sustained the economy.

The ruptures in international markets caused by World War I ushered in the third phase of the banking system's evolution during the First Republic. Its institutional development continued, allowing the banking system to become a stronger instrument supporting the withdrawal of Brazil from international capital markets. After World War I, increasing reliance on domestic financial mechanisms supported increasing depth and political strength of banking. The successful use of expansionary domestic money entrenched the institutional and political impetus for inflationary finance. The opening of the Banco do Brasil's Rediscount Office in 1921 formalized the Federal Treasury's commitment to expansive domestic monetary policy. Unsuccessful efforts to reimpose monetary orthodoxy from 1923 to 1926 clearly demonstrated the strength of this commitment. At important junctures, state-level governments exacerbated inflationary pressures by implementing monetary policies that responded to local political interests. With each turn toward expansionary domestic finance, the State actively supported the development of banking in order to facilitate the distribution of its debt. Each expansionary period contributed to the influence of banking, with only partial reversals during subsequent contractionary periods.

THE IMPACT OF BANKING

Development in banking was often the result of government influences in response to the burden of federal financial requirements and political uses of monetary policy, rather than of private-sector initiative. The State actively used monetary policy and banking as important tools for establishing new forms of governance, responding to the changes in political regime and economic structure that were central to the Republic. The ideological framework underlying monetary debate positioned protection of the value of the mil-réis in order to attract incremental foreign capital and to maintain domestic price stability against domestic expansiveness and money issuance that might ultimately give Brazilians greater independence from the fluctuations of international markets. The juxtaposition defined many of the conflicts between economic and political interests during the Republic. Through its impact on the value of the mil-réis and the price level, monetary policy determined the size of the banking system and accorded banks a larger impact on economic change than they might otherwise have attained. At important junctures, monetary policy was also fundamental to shaping the banking system. As their deposits became a larger component of the money supply, banks assumed a more complicated role in monetary policy.

Its growing role in the monetary system and its increasing stability allowed banking to become important in the formation of intersectoral and interregional markets for money and goods. The banking system grew more rapidly than other sectors of the economy. The growth of banking reflected both economic growth and the transfer of financial activity from informal networks to formal organizations. Simultaneously, it contributed to widespread economic growth by improving the efficiency of transactions and by providing an increasingly reliable source of short-term credit that released equity for capital formation. The business of banking reflected its increasing stability. Banks behaved in generally predictable and conservative manners. They increased their liquidity during periods of contraction and expanded their willingness to extend credit during growth. By the 1920s, banks were more stable than ever before. The financial system became increasingly sophisticated while it responded to economic circumstance. The conservative business practices of banks and their stability were two sides of the same coin.

Banks supported dynamic aspects of productive economic activity. The growth of private-sector banking was closely related to real economic growth and, more specifically, to the level of industrial production. The coffee sector and banking were linked through monetary mechanisms, i.e., through the impact of international coffee prices and trade on the value of the mil-réis. However, measured in real (price-adjusted) terms, the growth of industrial production had greater impact on the demand for banking. Valorization programs supported coffee when the international markets did not, giving coffee relative independence from market forces. Meanwhile, the increasing importance of domestic markets in determining the dynamics of industrialization after World War I[3] was met in the monetary sphere with an increasing reliance on domestic financial markets. Banks provided the mechanisms to smooth the commercial transactions between sectors. They also centralized the information flows necessary to make decisions about the viability of innovative activities and entrepreneurs. In doing so, they enhanced their ability to attract funds from a widening universe of depositors and investors.

Banks of varying ownership structure undertook activities that reflected their roles within the financial system. New organizations continued to form to meet the specific needs of economic agents, be they entrepreneurs, immigrants, or public agencies. After the reorganization of the banking system in 1905 and during the post–World War I years, when domestic finance gained importance, new banks regularly entered the economy. Small, closely knit groups of investors formed many of these private domestic banks to accommodate needs in other entrepreneurial endeavors. Nevertheless, they expanded their operations judiciously in order to protect their investments and to attract a widening pool of deposits. They reacted to expansionary monetary policies when they were available and functioned strictly in accord with their economic and business interests. In a similarly responsive vein, foreign banking in Brazil shifted in nature. The early predominance of British banks financing coffee and currency trade followed the demise of British control of international capital markets. Moving from a strong emphasis on trade finance, new entrants followed immigrants and multinational corporations coming from diverse national origins. These new foreign banks established closer connections to domestic markets of Brazil.

The performance of banks mirrored the major trends of their regional markets. They demonstrated the shift of importance in the productive sectors from Rio de Janeiro to São Paulo. At the same time, the scale of banking activity and new organizations reflected the relative maturity of these two states, in comparison to the dynamism of Minas Gerais and Rio Grande do Sul. State economies and their banking systems demonstrated signs of increasing interrelations. Comparisons of banking in the states for which data are available suggest that their business practices, financial structures, and interest rates converged toward a national norm during the 1910s and 1920s. Although regional economic differences remained strong, these signs of convergence implied the beginning of a banking system of national scope in concert with the geographic expansion of markets for goods, services, and money. Additional regional studies on the relationships of local banks in remote areas with larger networks would help to fully identify the difficulties and shape of the national money market. Further research could also clarify whether the consolidation of such a market may also have entrenched significant distributional patterns between strong and weak regional economies.

The most obvious banking mechanisms for linking regions emanated from the infrastructure for distributing financial resources that the Banco do Brasil constructed with the sponsorship of the Treasury. The bank's monopoly in the transactional infrastructure connecting banks established it, and by implication the Treasury, at the core of the banking system. The federal government's involvement in the banking system established the long-term dominance of the Banco do Brasil. In providing the public good of financial distribution, the bank developed business opportunities that other banks could not justify because of scale, risk, and profitability con-straints. Doing so imposed long-term constraints on Brazilian financial markets. During the First Republic, this network was only marginally suc-cessful at meeting the Treasury's goal of diversifying the geographic avail-ability of financial services; neither did it intensify relationships among private-sector banks. The expediency of using the Banco do Brasil for both private and public finance may have delayed the development of institu-tions strictly accountable for monetary management, such as an indepen-dent central bank. Further, the bank always had difficulty balancing its interests as a profit-seeking limited-liability commercial bank lending to the private sector and its public role as a monetary authority. However, the infrastructure it provided was influential in reinforcing the Banco do Brasil's position at the core of the system and in the evolution of uniform practices among organizations.

Simultaneously with its progressive characteristics, structural features of banking and its political economy impeded its ability to support economic growth and modernization. The increasing size, complexity, and geographic scope of banks propelled them, as profit-seeking organizations, to adopt more sophisticated management. Avoiding credit defaults required that banks maintain the fullest information possible about their clients and their clients' businesses. Banks actively developed the procedures and incurred the transactions costs to acquire information and to minimize defaults. Even so, they remained conservative in the limits and nature of their busi-ness practices. After their early experiences with overexpansion, few banks expanded the limits of credit exposure by lending in excess of their deposit bases; they did not put their capital at risk. Neither did the banks lend without very secure collateral. Aversion to risk constrained the banking system's expansive effects on the economy.

If the banking system did not support economic transition on a larger scale, the reasons derived from structural features of the society from which it sprang more than from a lack of participation by the banks. The struc-tural constraints that had impact throughout the Brazilian economy were emphasized within the banking system. Important foundations for financial development, such as secure property rights to protect against these risks, were slow to evolve. Legal constraints hindered the banking system's involvement in private-sector development during the First Republic. The law did not provide consistent protection against risks to financial instru-ments. Efforts to mitigate these risks constrained the extension of credit; imposed rigorous, complicated, and expensive procedures; and motivated the development of management practices. The demand for bank credit was not yet of a volume to induce substantive institutional and legal changes. Private financial channels established by personal connections among small groups of investors could still serve their original purpose of guarding against egregious misapplications of funds. Traditional networks could continue to finance much of the industrial expansion because of its limited scale and geographic concentration. However, the movement toward depersonalized banking, limited-liability joint-stock corporate organization, and increasingly interrelated patterns of regional production pointed toward the benefits of more responsive structural arrangements.

The inability to firmly establish property rights for privately owned financial assets constituted only one arena in which the concept of "property" was important in shaping banking and its role in the Brazilian economy. In its use of monetary policy to establish the federal State as an effective governing unit, the Treasury both claimed wealth for itself through expansive domestic finance and distributed benefits to specific sectoral interests by manipulating the value of the mil-réis. The competition among sectoral interests for the direction of monetary policy was, at its core, a competition for the distribution of wealth and an assertion of claims on the value of property connoted by money. For this reason, various groups worked to establish and control the mechanisms of governance. The efforts to control forms of governance constituted a crucial channel to capture resources. By providing a distribution network for money, the development of the banking system furthered these endeavors. The mutually reinforcing interests of the State and banks in expansive domestic money became stronger and more sustainable over the course of the First Republic.

These processes took an interesting form in Brazil. The State and the Banco do Brasil demonstrated relative success at instituting their chosen monetary policies (when agreement existed among them), and the banking system developed in a cohesive manner that supported expansive monetary policy. The response of individual states devised a further consideration affecting the balance of governance. They appropriated similar mechanisms and procedures, sometimes countermanding and sometimes accentuating the effects of the Treasury's practices. This response led state governments to enter into the realm of bank ownership and management as an important component of their monetary strategies. In practice, states undertook expansionary activities in support of powerful local special interests when the Treasury did not do so (or did not do so fully enough to satisfy local interests).[4] The competition between the State and states in the monetary realm helped to embed inflationary biases in the Brazilian economy.

The difficulties of securing rights to financial property and money in the public and private sectors had important implications for Brazil that extended well beyond economic concerns and for much longer than the years of the First Republic. They illustrate two related and pervasive themes of Brazilian history: the hazy distinction between "public" and "private" and the difficulty of establishing institutional structures to organize the conduct of economic, political, social, and cultural interactions.

The lack of a strong and well-defined distinction between "public" and "private" often resulted in each trying to exercise strong claims on the other. General perception categorized banks as organizations with social purpose as much as private businesses with independent profit goals and operating constraints. Of course, such a view was useful, long-held, and explicit in the Treasury Ministry.[5] Private-sector banks also stated such beliefs about their role in the Brazilian economy. As late as 1920, the fourth-largest bank, the Banco de Commércio e Indústria de São Paulo (Comind), published in its annual report that: "This is the role of the large banks: they exercise a social function, and are a means for compounding the economic forces of the country. Their action should be more energetic just when it is necessary for these [economic] forces to assure their maximum profit."[6] The Treasury tried to influence banking in support of its needs and goals through monetary policy and banking regulation. Efforts to accumulate through monetary actions resources that it could not access with fiscal measures motivated the Treasury's forays into the banking system. The State's need for resources and for tools of governance limited the ability of even nominally orthodox ideological interests to restrain money. The position of the Banco do Brasil in the economy solidified during the First Republic, and it provided concrete expression of the confluence between public and private interests. Similarly, banks looked to public authorities for support, and other economic agents turned to public authorities to marshal banks to behave in their interests.

For Brazilian banking, these blurred distinctions had an ironic effect. Banking was an important tool for accommodating special interests within the public sector. Simultaneously, banks actively constructed the principles and procedures to depersonalize the allocation of private-sector credit according to criteria of risk and profitability. From a broader perspective, the difficulties of separating public from private in finance reflected the continuing synergy between patriarchy in personal relations and oligarchy in public ones—two deeply entrenched organizing concepts of Brazilian society. An innovation during the First Republic, and one in which banking was important, was to institute new mechanisms to establish the basis for an effective oligarchy at the national level while not fully destroying traditional underlying concepts. The effects of these mechanisms and institutions on the ability to broaden economic participation and wealth distribution deserve further attention.

The fluidity between public and private contributed to the difficulty of establishing institutional structures. Significant changes of economic circumstance and political power also impeded the establishment of stable institutional structures. Monetary policy was one area that demonstrated policy-makers' inclination to reverse policy by dismantling and reconfiguring institutions and public agencies. Ratcheting the role of monetary policy to a higher level of activity and significance during the First Republic laid the groundwork for continuing fluctuation among economic institutions in subsequent years. As with the problem of defining public and private, the difficulties of institution-building in banking reflected a more general trend within Brazilian society. Other difficult arenas for these issues during the twentieth century included building nationwide political parties and electoral processes, establishing the role of the military in civil society, defining the public goods to be provided by the public sector (such as education, public health services, and physical infrastructure), and establishing standards of juridical equity.[7]

Developments and constraints in banking were important because the modernization of business and industry, the governing effectiveness of the State and states, and the definition of public and private were defining issues for Brazilian society during the First Republic. They were important issues in many other sectors of the economy, such as industry, agricultural exports, transportation, and other physical infrastructure.[8] Banking was more than simply another instance, however important, reflecting fundamental change. The pivotal allocative role of finance ensured that banking was an important influence on shaping and transmitting the particular pattern by which Brazil developed.

The introductory chapter established two criteria for assessing the role of banks in the economic transformation of Brazil. These criteria, which have proven useful in studying other economies, are, first, the contributions of the banking system to industrialization and market formation, and, second, its effect on the economic aspects of state-building. The body of the book demonstrates that, by both criteria, banking was an integral component of the fundamental transitions of the First Republic. The inextricable linkages in banking between state formation and the nature of economic growth suggest that, for the Brazilian case, the predominant models for explaining bank history among early industrializing societies are useful, but insufficient. Brazil, as a late industrializer, did rely on state management and entrepreneurialism in order to accelerate industrialization, as the Gerschenkron model would anticipate. The scale and influence of the State could harness technical and managerial skill and accumulate capital to the extent necessary, and on a larger scale than the private sector, which was left to its own devices. Large-scale state-directed financial tools coexisted with, rather than displaced, a network of small private-sector banks. The influence of banking on industrialization operated through the circuitous route of financing short-term commerce, with a strong emphasis on the coffee trade. That conclusion is crucial for understanding additional findings of this project. Banking served as an indirect intermediary between sectors in response to economic opportunity. In the private sector, banks eased the flow of finance between coffee, industry, and other activities and between the international and the domestic realms.

The effects of intermediation were also central to understanding the role of banking in state-building. As political economists would hypothesize, those struggling to reconfigure the nation-state simultaneously sought to fashion a banking system to further their political goals and economic interests. The construction of the banking system was a response to economic pressures of state-building. They often embedded internal contradictions. Political historians assess specific governments by their ability to manage those contradictions. The goal here has been to demonstrate how they came into play during the formation of the republican state. Both the Gerschenkronian schematization of coordinated stages in finance and industrialization and the political model of banking in state formation are incomplete. Each model requires explanations provided by the other, just as the theoretical models require the support of historical analysis.

BEYOND THE FIRST REPUBLIC

What was the legacy of the banking system to the subsequent course of events in Brazil? The First Republic ended with a political coup in October 1930 that established the regime of Getúlio Vargas.[9] In the following years, a fully articulated economy of national scope with widespread management and participation by the State emerged as one of the dominant outcomes of the Vargas era.[10] The economy became highly centralized and it included an activist State. The State dominated selected major sectors, including steel, infrastructure, mining, and automobile production through such tools as price and trade regulation and ownership of large-scale enterprise. Experience gained from the banking system of the First Republic provided precedents for this expansion into other enterprises. The Banco do Brasil was crucial to economic management in subsequent years.[11] The model of centralized economic management depended upon the State's use of the bank in the private financial sector, and it mirrored strategies of earlier financial consolidation during the Republic. In the following decades, the Brazilian economy became highly industrialized, and for various periods it experienced extraordinarily high growth rates and inflation rates.[12]

The relative merits of growth reliant on international markets as compared to domestically directed development were the topic of increasingly attenuated controversy, as the difficulties of both became ever more obvious in the mid- and late twentieth century.[13] The nature of the prevailing monetary regime and the value of the currency never lost their primacy as economic and political issues. [14] The ability to control deeply entrenched price inflation, and the problems of not doing so, remain among the most serious difficulties of Brazilian society.[15] Some political economists have emphasized the importance of these issues in the military coup of 1964, perhaps the major political event of the late twentieth century.[16] Other important periods in the late twentieth century when these questions came to the forefront of political debate were occasioned by international disruptions in petroleum markets (1973 and 1978) and capital flight from emerging markets (of which Brazil is one of the largest) in 1982, 1988, and 1999. Profound domestic political instability accompanied all of these experiences. The continuing importance of international markets to the Brazilian economy ensures the constant presence of these controversies. Many of the mechanisms of international financial management have changed significantly from the early years of the twentieth century. However, the underlying consistency of the issues and debates is impressive.

After the Republic, the institutional and organizational development of banking facilities continued to reflect simultaneously their history and changing economic and political circumstance. At the federal level, banking regulation and monetary policy became increasingly active tools of governance. The Treasury and the Banco do Brasil carried out federal monetary policy and financial transactions, with specific responsibilities shifting between them, as they had during the First Republic. The separation of central banking, public finance, and monetary policy from private-sector commercial banking proceeded very slowly. In 1946, the Superintendency of Money and Credit (Superintendência de Moeda e Crédito, or SUMOC) was created to coordinate monetary and exchange policy. A separately organized Central Bank did not open until 1964, and then, without full independence from electoral and legislative politics.[17]

The role of state banks in financing state governments, creating claims on the Banco do Brasil, and contributing to the total public debt service burden and inflation emerged through the twentieth century to become one of the most intransigent problems of economic reform in the 1990s.[18]

Until liberalization in the late 1990s, the private-sector banking system retained the commercial orientation that it acquired during the First Republic. Privately owned banks gained importance relative to the Banco do Brasil.[19] A significant innovation that gained strength after the 1964 reforms was the opening of financial markets to a wide variety of nonbank financial organizations. Finance companies, investment banks, the National Housing Bank, federal and state Caixas Econômicas (savings banks),[20] development banks, and credit unions opened to meet specific banking needs that the commercial banks did not accommodate. While some were privately owned organizations, public agencies were prominent in all of these endeavors. The private banking system inherited from the First Republic provided the precedent for developing mutually advantageous business practices with the public sector while it also remained very traditional in its practices. With banking reform in 1964, widespread mergers consolidated the banking system. Privately owned banks could continue to operate as conservative, closely held groups, benefiting from the inflationary trends that their predecessors had been influential in initiating.[21] The private sector's reluctance to lead in subsequent banking innovation reflected the regulatory environment and its ability to continue benefiting from entrenched inflationary trends. Banking did not fail after the Republic, but neither did it continue to evolve to meet the larger-scale and more complex needs of a highly industrialized economy.

Banking emerged as both dynamic and increasingly stable during the First Republic. The emerging system facilitated the ability of money to flow between its various forms, economic sectors, and geographic regions. The stability, credibility, and government support of the Banco do Brasil established it at the system's apex. The low volume of geographically dispersed transactions suggests that the supply of financial infrastructure antedated its demand. Nevertheless, it supported the growth of depersonalized finance in markets that were increasing in size, geographic reach, and interrelations. In doing so, banking contributed to the construction of dynamic markets that an increasing share of the Brazilian population used to meet its needs as producers, workers, and consumers. The federal and state governments subsidized the construction of a national financial system prior to its articulated demand for overlapping reasons of economic exigency and political opportunity. As a result, the political and financial systems became intimately intertwined in a manner that perpetuated the use of domestic finance as a political tool to ever-larger ends. Banking provided a fruitful venue to explore the "public" and the "private" and identify the limits of the State and states. These important state-building aspects did not prevent a system of privately owned banks from emerging that was efficient, rational, and dynamic. Banking dynamically and influentially participated in laying the groundwork for modern Brazilian society during the formative years of the early twentieth century.

Data Appendix

This appendix defines and explains the financial data that the study uses. Financial data are notoriously difficult to accumulate and to derive into comparable format. The data on bank balances and revenues used in this book required manual accumulation from a variety of published sources. The practicalities of data collection have imposed limits on the data. In order to achieve consistency and comparability a number of compromises have been necessary. Even so, data availability constrains the empirical tests and analyses. One major consideration in the use of these data has been to minimize the disparity between the quality of the raw material and overly refined analytic methods. As a result, both data manipulation and methodology remain as simple as possible. These constraints recognized, the significant volume and variety of financial data compiled for this study allow for substantive analysis of the banking system.

BANK FINANCIAL DATA

The balances and revenues of individual banks from 1906 through 1930 are the most important raw data used in this study.[1] These data form the bases for assessing the size, structure, and composition of the banking system. Publicly chartered banks published balance sheets in their local financial press monthly; audited semiannual balance sheets and revenue statements appeared in bank annual reports. The foremost constraint on the use of reported bank balances was that, prior to 1906, data and accounting standards among banks were inconsistent, and their businesses varied substantially. These differences made dubious the value of aggregating the data for the level of detail used in this book. 1906 was an appropriate year to begin firm-level data collection because of the reorganization of banking that became effective at the end of 1905.[2] The availability of financial data by individual banks made possible multiple levels of analysis. The aggregation of the banking system by various subgroups that are relevant to the issues of the study, and the consideration of specific bank behavior, have contributed to the work. Chapter 3 considers the size of the entire banking system from 1889, based on the volume of bank deposits, as reported in the *Estatísticas históricas,* Table 10.2.[3] These are the most reliable of aggregated publicly available data, and for the period 1906-1930, they correspond quite closely to the aggregated firm-level data. Comparison of these data suggests that the firm-level database captures 90-95 percent of bank deposits.

Financial data for banks organized as limited-liability joint-stock corporations (i.e., their equity shares traded on local securities exchanges) from the four largest states comprise the firm-level database. The states are Guanabara (currently, Rio de Janeiro and including the Federal District), São Paulo,[4] Minas Gerais, and Rio Grande do Sul. In 1930, they accounted for approximately one-half of the nation's population, 85 percent of bank assets (broadly defined), 80 percent of industrial production, and 80 percent of government revenues.[5] While these states clearly had populations that were significantly wealthier than the other half of the population, they also represented a very wide diversity of economic bases. Therefore, they represent both the bulk of the banking system and a wide range of the economic activities of importance to banks. The geographic limitation, however, does render impossible a specific examination of the areas in which banking was slow to develop.

When bank annual reports have been found, they provide the original data source for the financial information. However, for all but four of the organizations, the data come from the financial press. In Rio de Janeiro, the *Jornal do Commércio* published bank financial results. In São Paulo, the *Estado de São Paulo* provided the majority of the data, supplemented by the *Annuário estatístico do Estado de São Paulo.*[6] In Minas Gerais, the Minas Gerais: Orgão official do Governo Mineiro[7] was the most important of the financial press. For Rio Grande do Sul banks, the annual balance sheets published in Lagemann, *O Banco Pelotense,*[8] provide the source data.

The format and terminology of bank financial data were fairly consistent from 1906. Unfortunately, however, published accounts were always undocumented and undefined. Reconstructing definitions of the balance-sheet categories has required a significant amount of research, inference from banking discussions in a variety of primary sources, and establishing the logical relationship between different categories as presented on the balance sheets over a sustained period. A contemporaneous accounting text has been useful.[9] Reformatted data from the balance sheets identify those categories that are useful for the purposes of this project.

In order to maintain consistency, this study reports annual bank balances.[10] Semiannual balance data are available for some banks (those in Rio de Janeiro and São Paulo, and the Banco de Crédito Real of Minas Gerais). The decision to only use annual data comes at considerable cost. It diminishes the size of the database. Further, it eliminates patterns of seasonal fluctuation. Anecdotal information of the financial requirements imposed by harvest patterns of agricultural economies suggests that seasonal fluctuations were important for Brazil.[11] The requirements to treat data consistently necessitated not using the semiannual balance data, although they were available for a large portion of the banks in the sample. Again, the practicalities of data collection have been such that collecting the semiannual balances for most banks outside of Rio de Janeiro and São Paulo proved infeasible. The availability of price indices only on an annual basis (see below) further supports the decision to minimize the use of semiannual balance information, and to work with average annual balances rather than year-end data. Since this project is concerned with long-term trajectories of growth, the loss of mid-year balances is regrettable, but not fatal.

The financial ratios and growth rates summarizing the banking system from these data are in Tables A.1–A.4.

BANK BALANCE SHEETS

BANK ASSETS

The asset side of the balance sheets revealed the uses of bank funds. Predominantly, banks used their financial resources in order to extend credit. They distinguished different forms of credit by their repayment and protection terms and the types of risk that the credit engendered. The relevant bank asset categories from original balances sheets were cash, discounted commercial paper, loans, and mortgage-secured loans for real estate. Short-term credit was the combination of commercial paper and loans. Total credit extended by a bank included any mortgages (long-term loans secured by real estate). Total earning assets were all of a bank's assets that generated revenues. A definition and discussion of each of these categories follows.

Banks held cash in their portfolios of assets in order to meet ongoing operating needs. However, cash holdings did not contribute to a bank's revenues, since they did not earn interest. Accounting practices contained an ambiguity with respect to the reporting of cash balances. Prior to the mid-1920s, Brazilian bank balance sheets clearly specified that their cash positions included only "current money" (currency). From the mid-1920s, some banks identified both currency and interbank deposits (deposits that they maintained with other banks, usually the Banco do Brasil, to ease the flow of their transactions). In some cases after the mid-1920s, the category "cash" apparently included interbank deposits. Notably, this was the case for Banespa from 1927.[12] Therefore, in the later years of the First Republic, cash was overstated; this results in an understatement of the decline in reserve ratios. Since the early years of the data did not face this inconsistency, the overreporting of cash did not explain the very high reserve ratios (of cash as a percentage of deposits) in the early years. Therefore, the effect of this data inconsistency was to underestimate one of the project's findings—the decline in reserve ratios, indicating increasingly secure banking. (See Chapter 4.)

SHORT-TERM CREDIT—DISCOUNTED COMMERCIAL PAPER AND LOANS
Commercial Paper. As a common way to extend short-term credit, banks bought "commercial paper" (a promise, usually from an enterprise conducting a business transaction, to pay the holder of the note a fixed amount on a fixed future date). Buyers purchased commercial paper for a price that reflected a discount from the original amount of the note. Usually the note (the commercial paper) represented a promised future payment upon the completion of a commercial transaction. For example, a bank could purchase a promissory note from its client (perhaps a coffee merchant), discounting it at a rate of 8 percent per year from its par value (the value identified on the note), with a four-month maturity. The bank would advance credit to the merchant for 97.4 percent of its par value (100 percent of face value minus 2.60 percent, based on three four-month periods of compounded interest during the year). The merchant undertook to repay the bank its full original (par) value on the maturity date four months hence, based on the expected sale of coffee in the amount of the note. In this transaction, not only was the bank extending credit to the coffee merchant, but both the merchant and the bank were implicitly predicting the international prices of coffee in the period between discounting and repaying the note. In the event that payment was not made, the discount-

ing bank had recourse to the goods exchanged in the underlying commercial transaction. Should the merchant not have met his payment to the bank, and the bank chose to put the merchant in default, it would have had the right to take the merchant's coffee stocks, up to the face value of the note. The bank, then, would face the prospect of selling the coffee in the prevailing markets.

Banks held the notes for short periods; four months was the maximum maturity usually specified in bank statutes. However, as a matter of practice, a creditor would often "roll over" a note (replacing the maturing one with a new note), sometimes with the amount of underlying collateral (coffee, in the case of the example) adjusted to reflect its current value. In these circumstances, the connections between the discounted note and the original commercial transaction became quite remote. By this mechanism, note discounting could be transformed into a method of providing general ongoing credit. This was a means of lengthening a borrower's credit maturity (duration). It was also an important tool for a bank to control its total credit exposure.

Loans. Loans were another form of short-term credit instrument; they had maturities of six months to a year. Loans did not necessarily have a specified purpose, and they were secured by either the borrower's property or by bonds for public-sector debt (*apólices*), rather than the merchandise of commercial transactions. Loans also committed banks to slightly longer credit exposure than discounted notes at each time a credit decision was taken. Bank statutes specified that a borrower's collateral secured the loans, and they identified acceptable collateral. Publicly chartered banks did not routinely advance unsecured loans during the First Republic. Lending also involved the cost and risk of valuing the collateral. For example, a bank lending to a textile manufacturer who wanted to acquire machinery could accept other machinery as collateral. The value of the collateral to the bank would be significantly affected by the bank's ability to realize that value. That is, collateral was only of value to the bank if it could, in the event of taking possession of it in a default, resell the machinery to another manufacturer for the original par amount of the loan. (Assuming, of course, that the bank did not go into the textile manufacturing business as a result of acquiring the collateral.) Public-sector bonds (for federal, state, or municipal debt) were somewhat more secure as collateral; however, they also fluctuated in value. As a result, banks accepted collateral at a fraction of its face value.

MORTGAGES; TOTAL CREDIT

"Loans" as used in this book excludes mortgages, reflecting the distinction that Brazilian bankers maintained with respect to long-term lending guaranteed by real property. Difficult considerations with regard to funding, maturity, and collateralization impeded the ability of banks to extend mortgages. The fundamental aspects of economic structure that shaped bankers' concerns about mortgage lending are discussed in Chapter 6. The few banks that engaged in mortgage lending managed and reported it separately from any other sort of credit. Because of the special issues related to mortgage lending, and the few banks engaged in the activity, comparisons between these banks and the majority of the data base would be distorted if mortgage loans had been included. The narrative of this book clearly labels as "total credit" the instances in which bank credit portfolios, inclusive of mortgage credit, are relevant.

EARNING ASSETS

The category "earning assets" included all of the investments on which banks earned revenues. Besides its total credit, bank portfolios often purchased assets that were not extensions of credit to borrowers. Additional investments could include equity shares or debentures of private companies or debt issues by public authorities (treasury notes). Especially after the reorganization of banking, this was also a relatively small category. Occasionally, property taken in settlement of bankruptcy proceedings fell into this category before its liquidation. Some banks bought treasury notes as an investment choice (usually in small quantities). Banks that extended mortgages funded by state treasuries held these notes as assets, as a part of a funding strategy while building mortgage portfolios.

Bank Liabilities

The liability side of the balance sheet revealed the ways in which banks accumulated the funds that they had available to lend. The majority of resources accumulated by the banking system to create credit were in the forms of deposits and equity. Deposits were the important liability category in considering bank size and funding. Capital and loss reserves belonged to the banks and their shareholders. Third-party accounts and other small accounts constitute the remainder of liability categories. Deposits are the focus of attention in this study. As discussed below, banks reported their equity and reserves in manners that were very limited. Further constraining the ability to analyze the sources of bank funding, typically foreign banks only reported deposits in their Brazilian branches. They did not allocate equity (capital) or reserves to their overseas locations, but rather they consolidated these categories in their home office accounts.

DEPOSITS

Deposits were, in essence, funds that the banks borrowed from the public. Business or individuals placed deposits, providing banks with their largest source of funds for extending credit. The banks' most important business and legal responsibility was to redeem the depositors' funds in full. In exchange for the temporary use of deposits, banks agreed to arrangements by which the depositor could regain access to the funds. Savers could deposit funds in a bank for a specified time period or they could be available to depositors on demand, referred to as term and demand deposits, respectively. Often, banks paid interest on term deposits; demand deposits could be either interest-bearing or interest-free.[13] These characteristics affected the stability and cost of funding credit. In 1910, some Brazilian banks began taking "limited deposits"; these were small deposits of a preestablished size that paid lower interest than larger deposits.[14] For the purposes of this study, funds that banks held without discretion over their uses are excluded.[15]

EQUITY

Equity (or capital) represented the owners' investment in a company. (In joint-stock companies, equity was denominated in stock shares that investors could buy and sell.) Banks distributed profits among their owners in accordance with the amount of equity they invested in the bank. Banks reported equity in such a way that their balance sheets did not reveal their true net worth. The liability side of the balance sheet showed equity at the original level authorized by the banks' originating statutes (and sometimes referred to as statutory capital). Differences between the current market and original statutory value of the stock could be considerable, and they did not appear on bank financial statements. Neither was the difference between statutory capital and the amount actually paid into banks taken into account on the liability side of the balance sheet. Partial payment of equity shares was common. Further, "paid-in capital," often reported on the asset side of most domestic Brazilian banks' balance sheets until the 1920s, appears to not have been defined consistently.[16] Banks considered the statutory level of equity (that amount authorized by bank charter) as a very general tool to manage the financial structure of the banks. The total par value of shareholder equity moved in discrete amounts that did not reflect the true value of the firm. The market value of bank capital could be derived from stock prices. Surprisingly, these price series were not consistently available for all banks for the entire period of the study.

RESERVES

Their statutes also specified provisions for banks to set aside from profits reserves against potential losses. Reserves represented the expected cost of bank risk, usually at a conservative estimate. Special reserves also occasionally protected special liabilities or programs. These could occur when government agencies contributed funding for special purposes, such as coffee valorization programs. However, the provision and dissolution of special reserve funds often appeared quite arbitrary.[17] Because banks accumulated their reserves from profits, the change in reserves is one component of the net-profitability calculation.

Other Balance Sheet Categories

At times, mortgage banks issued long-term notes (*letras hipotecárias*—or *hypothecárias*—debt with 15- to 30-year maturity dates before they would be fully redeemed) to fund their mortgage loans. This funding was very specific and isolated. Therefore, it was not comparable with general bank funding. In addition, the usual mechanics of this funding were such that alternative funding for mortgage lending was from state or federal sources, rather than the general public. Banks issuing mortgage notes typically posted bonds for an amount equivalent to the notes issued. Therefore, these funds were not freely issued or raised. There were also periods during which various federal and state government agencies provided funding for individual banks, usually for specific purposes such as coffee price supports and mortgage or agricultural lending. Public-sector funding was not considered equity, since it did not share in the profits of the bank, but the nature of the investment involved more control of the banks' operations and management than did regular deposits.

This study does not use other categories reported on Brazilian bank balance sheets that do not address the issues of capital accumulation and allocation. For example, banks' real assets (the value of real estate that they owned, such as bank office buildings) are not included.[18] Similarly, the residual category "other" is not considered in this analysis. The balance sheets do not reveal the contents of this category. Various accounts of an operating nature (e.g., provisions for bonuses and pensions) have not been included here because they were not integral to the role of banks as investors (and often are not reported consistently). Most important, Brazilian banks reported assets held for third parties as components of their balances. Offsetting accounts appeared on the asset and liability sides of the balance sheets. These did not involve the extension of credit by banks; their sole purpose was to ease commercial transactions, and the risk of nonpayment remained with the principle parties. This category was significant on the balance sheets: ranging from 30 percent to about 80 percent (for short periods) of the reported sizes of the individual banks. On the liability side of the balance sheet, they were not deposits available to the banks to fund lending, and on the asset side, this category did not involve the banks' investment discretion. Therefore, third-party notes are not considered in the current work, focused on the role of the banks in economic development.[19] However, their inclusion on the balances sheets as assets and liabilities of the bank suggests that banks viewed their role as fiduciary institutions (institutions with the responsibility for safeguarding financial property of other owners) on an equal footing as their roles in accumulating and allocating capital.

BANK REVENUES, NET PROFITS, AND INTEREST RATES

This study only considers revenue and profit data on very limited bases in Chapters 4 and 7, in order to approximate interest rate trends. The data are difficult to derive and they suffer analytical constraints. Interest rate approximations can be based either on gross revenues or net profits. Both data sources are considered below.

Domestic banks reported their gross revenues and net profits semiannually; the annualized compilation requires data for both semesters.[20] Gross revenues were simply the revenues from all payments entering the bank. Public reporting requirements for bank revenues were less comprehensive than for balance sheets. After 1910, only São Paulo banks published income statements in the commercial press. In other locations, banks were not required to publish their revenue streams. Income statements that banks printed in their annual reports became less comprehensive with time. Further, foreign banks did not routinely publish income statements applicable to specific branches or locations. Therefore, on a consistent basis, income statements were available only for private domestic banks in the state of São Paulo, the Banco do Brasil, and the "state-subsidized banks" (for which annual reports covering the period were available: Banco de Crédito Hypothecário de Agrícola de São Paulo/Banco do Estado de São Paulo [Bchasp/Banespa] and the Banco de Crédito Real de Minas Gerais).

The money remaining after meeting all of a bank's obligations (interest payments and personnel salaries and other business expenses[21]) constituted its net profits, or the money left to bank owners to compensate themselves for the use of, and risk to, their capital. Net profits are the sum of the change in reserves, dividend payments, retained earnings, undistributed gains or losses from the prior semester,[22] and fees to bank directors and managers (when identified). Bank balance sheets recognized these accounts semiannually, obviating the need for the income statements. Therefore, net profits can be calculated for the banks for which semiannual balance sheets are available. Without the requirement for revenue data, organizations in Rio de Janeiro as well as São Paulo and the public-sector banks are available. Of the domestic banks in the total sample for bank balances, privately owned banks in Minas Gerais and Rio Grande do Sul were the only ones excluded.[23] Because foreign banks did not report revenues or profits by location, only domestic banks could be considered.

The interest rate approximations presented here represent the first attempt to construct interest rate histories for domestic Brazilian money instruments as early as the First Republic.[24] These are tricky data to estimate.[25] In the absence of published information and standardization of interest rates that borrowers paid for credit, or that investors required as returns on their investments, a proxy bank interest rate provides the information for this study. It reflects compromises that the data mandate. Possible proxy rates are the gross revenues as a share of earning assets and net profits as a share of earning assets.[26] The measure of gross revenues as a percentage of earning assets captures the concept of the cost of money to borrowers.[27] However, given the constraints of gross revenue data, the applicability of that measure is quite limited. The net profits as a percentage of earning assets offers a good approximation of long-term interest rate movements. It reports the profitability of banks' investments, rather than the cost of borrowing to the customer. This measure represents the lenders' perspective, revealing the effective return on banks' investments. Some authors have found this measure more useful because it yields information on the allocation of investors' resources toward banking.[28] Because of its wider availability and its attention to the allocation of resources, the net profitability rate is used to proxy interest rates in Chapters 4 and 7. While the data would benefit from enhanced detail and coverage, they are credible for the limited purposes in this project.[29]

Considerations of data coverage and applications motivated the decision to minimize the manipulation of the data to the extent possible. Overall (national) bank interest rates are not included in this study, because the differences in the results for different groups of banks were sufficient to render overall averages misleading (as Chapter 7 demonstrates). Because Rio de Janeiro and São Paulo banks were dominant (by size) in the Brazilian financial system, their aggregation represents the average interest rate accruing to private domestic banking. While this treatment does not distort the aggregate banking system, it also does not accurately portray the results of any location remote from these financial centers. To calculate the proxy annual interest rate, semiannual net profits as a proportion of the semester's average earning assets[30] are annualized and then averaged for the calendar year.[31] The semiannual rates are weighted by asset volume to take account of rapid fluctuations. Annualizing the semiannual rates prior to averaging accommodates seasonal variation. As is normally the case in interest rate analyses of this type, the calculations are based on nominal, rather than real, values. Table A.5 and Figures 4.5 and 7.3 report the proxy interest rates based on net profit rates.

PRICE INDEX

When considering the volume of bank balances, a price index adjusts for the effects of price-level changes, or to determine the "real" level of balances.[32] Price fluctuations were large and rapid during the First Republic. Increases predominated; but short, strong periods of deflation also destabilized the Brazilian economy. The availability of price indices to quantify these effects is problematic. Therefore, I have resorted to a compromise method of splicing together the two major indices that cover portions of the period. A wholesale price index (with 1913 as base year)[33] covers the years to 1913. From then, the rate of price change derived from a widely published purchasing power index (with 1939 as base year)[34] is applied to the wholesale price index. The rates of change from the constructed index constitute the price-level changes that apply to the series, setting 1906 at 100. The only other price index that continuously covers the entire First Republic[35] is derived from a methodology even more disparate than the one used here. Nevertheless, this method clearly has weaknesses. The change in base years between 1913 and 1939 is significant, as is the difference in methodologies in deriving the indices. However, for the years with overlapping indices (1908-13), they do not show differences in price trends that are out of the range of expectations. And, comparisons with other available estimates[36] indicate that the rates of price changes yielded by this construction reflect rates of change in expected directions and order of magnitude.[37] Table A.10 shows the final price index used.

APÓLICE YIELDS; COST OF GOVERNMENT BORROWING

This project considers the interest rate that the government paid on its domestic debt in Chapter 3. To do so, I have introduced the yield on federally issued apólices.[38] The Federal Treasury issued apólices and the notes traded in domestic money markets. Apólices were analogous to British consols; they were issued with perpetual maturity and fixed (5 percent per year) interest rates. The time series of apólice price data begins in 1893; end-of-month prices are used to calculate the yield.[39] Price data for long-term Brazilian debt traded in London—the more usual comparison—are not consistently compiled for the entire period.[40] Initial comparison of the available foreign and domestic debt data suggest that their differential remained relatively constant. The limited use of this data is simply to construct a benchmark comparison against the cost to the British government of raising funds (through the issuance of consols. The cost of long-term debt to the U.S. Treasury is shown as a point of comparison).[41] The role of London as the center of Brazilian international financial markets (lasting longer in Brazil than in many other Latin American countries) dictated the use of the British consols as a benchmark comparison, in preference over the cost to the U. S. Treasury of raising funds in its capital markets. The yields on the Brazilian and British series are useful for comparative purposes.

Appendix Tables

Table A.1 Bank Financial Ratios, by Type of Bank

	Reserve ratio (cash, % deposits)					Leverage ratio (credit, % deposits)				
	Private domestic	Foreign	State-subsidized	Banco do Brasil	Total	Private domestic	Foreign	State-subsidized	Banco do Brasil	Total
1906	48.38	48.55	51.93	116.95	52.36	104.82	71.28	132.67	122.01	90.69
1907	36.10	47.18	48.03	55.21	43.08	91.67	86.35	139.29	85.57	89.63
1908	35.35	44.55	48.81	56.03	44.07	93.49	104.06	136.64	86.50	94.85
1909	41.66	46.53	56.90	55.07	47.47	81.90	90.04	162.89	74.24	82.67
1910	41.91	41.09	49.71	50.21	44.47	77.10	77.45	249.10	59.02	73.49
1911	35.98	38.86	45.37	43.14	39.22	82.07	86.22	214.51	58.43	78.38
1912	31.31	35.35	37.14	31.22	32.75	90.26	100.10	229.72	71.81	90.64
1913	26.68	33.90	22.59	30.30	30.12	106.21	109.21	210.25	93.39	105.74
1914	31.76	50.67	35.29	31.24	38.27	105.04	104.48	175.54	103.11	106.27
1915	37.40	56.20	41.64	40.36	45.05	90.77	81.39	192.68	102.06	91.88
1916	35.12	45.03	31.37	56.83	41.53	78.98	74.92	205.62	93.30	82.23
1917	33.23	38.79	26.60	47.84	36.88	87.62	70.82	145.68	105.25	85.72
1918	30.32	37.61	24.15	49.41	34.97	92.45	76.97	167.31	173.20	97.59
1919	26.36	36.17	26.31	45.52	31.74	95.02	86.00	234.97	173.50	103.95
1920	24.11	46.56	28.30	38.54	33.12	97.69	86.42	225.87	119.67	98.96
1921	24.57	53.40	38.29	21.10	35.28	100.08	82.88	181.46	89.16	91.44
1922	26.30	51.70	47.37	14.06	30.49	93.99	84.63	156.71	92.18	90.91
1923	26.07	44.62	36.00	14.21	27.12	92.24	92.16	125.68	114.67	100.06
1924	25.41	37.28	31.18	14.02	24.62	94.46	103.81	113.77	127.89	107.11
1925	24.69	32.70	26.44	16.93	25.16	98.19	101.60	102.26	119.53	104.57
1926	24.67	32.39	36.25	19.71	26.03	100.88	97.19	77.33	103.44	99.88
1927	24.19	29.52	35.54	21.39	25.79	100.38	97.91	60.03	92.09	94.14
1928	22.63	24.47	28.88	32.66	26.47	101.65	95.58	57.71	89.49	90.36
1929	24.18	27.43	18.76	41.05	28.48	103.18	91.60	65.42	87.05	89.33
1930	29.07	30.19	9.41	34.91	26.55	104.74	97.41	75.25	91.57	92.93

Source: See Data Appendix.

Table A.2 Bank Growth, by Type of Bank; Index, 1906 = 100

	Deposits					Short-term credit				
	Private domestic	Foreign	State-subsidized	Banco do Brasil	Total	Private domestic	Foreign	State-subsidized	Banco do Brasil	Total
1906	100.00	100.00	100.00	100.00	100.00	100.00	100.00	100.00	100.00	100.00
1907	170.52	97.20	92.76	504.71	152.93	149.13	117.74	97.38	353.96	151.15
1908	161.76	102.05	83.81	907.95	173.49	144.27	148.97	86.32	643.68	181.44
1909	190.96	142.11	95.79	1283.28	226.66	149.20	179.51	117.61	780.86	206.62
1910	223.53	170.36	148.42	1596.10	273.27	164.42	185.11	278.67	772.13	221.44
1911	279.62	245.80	236.79	1906.36	353.33	218.94	297.29	382.84	912.89	305.36
1912	298.14	265.25	242.59	1819.96	366.16	256.73	372.47	420.04	1071.11	365.94
1913	287.65	269.13	265.36	1662.12	354.97	291.47	412.33	420.52	1272.19	413.86
1914	307.69	258.11	400.09	1448.61	350.10	308.35	378.31	529.36	1224.17	410.23
1915	331.19	272.97	412.66	960.52	340.81	286.82	311.66	599.30	803.43	345.27
1916	408.09	313.78	393.09	894.13	390.57	307.48	329.81	609.20	683.73	354.13
1917	401.49	265.04	413.68	857.69	363.17	335.62	263.32	454.22	739.90	343.27
1918	585.40	409.02	521.31	1061.76	527.70	516.35	441.67	657.41	1507.19	567.82
1919	638.97	366.18	454.52	1106.66	532.79	579.23	441.77	804.97	1573.70	610.70
1920	742.53	417.22	412.71	1448.41	621.60	692.01	505.82	702.62	1420.56	678.30
1921	673.71	726.53	362.96	3722.47	861.03	643.25	844.74	496.41	2720.18	868.12
1922	699.52	658.04	358.43	5857.25	959.33	627.27	781.28	423.38	4425.39	961.63
1923	819.98	522.85	509.98	5573.09	938.07	721.61	675.99	483.09	5237.67	1034.98
1924	797.02	372.47	536.82	4365.44	790.54	718.26	542.44	460.33	4575.70	933.64
1925	784.70	509.67	556.70	3604.02	807.39	735.05	726.45	429.08	3530.76	930.92
1926	762.52	529.03	783.02	3677.55	815.78	733.88	721.32	456.36	3117.64	898.40
1927	813.26	500.08	3405.82	4306.52	920.94	778.85	686.92	1540.93	3250.48	955.93
1928	952.21	528.93	7812.43	4973.04	1136.53	923.43	709.24	3398.29	3647.30	1132.40
1929	1002.31	546.42	10859.94	6665.72	1332.26	986.63	702.18	5354.79	4755.77	1312.19
1930	855.03	535.79	12643.24	6743.23	1306.33	854.43	732.18	7170.97	5060.53	1338.57

Source: See Data Appendix.

Table A.3 Bank Financial Ratios, by Region

	Reserve ratio (cash, % deposits)						Leverage ratio (credit, % deposits)					
	Rio de Janeiro	São Paulo	Minas Gerais	Rio Grande do Sul	Banco do Brasil	Total	Rio de Janeiro	São Paulo	Minas Gerais	Rio Grande do Sul	Banco do Brasil	Total
1906	57.85	40.76	51.93	—	116.95	52.36	68.81	103.28	132.67	—	122.01	90.69
1907	52.42	37.81	48.03	26.30	55.21	43.08	75.55	99.22	139.29	89.04	85.57	89.63
1908	47.21	42.06	48.81	20.84	56.03	44.07	91.16	102.87	136.64	94.74	86.50	94.85
1909	49.47	50.48	56.90	18.07	55.07	47.47	92.74	79.16	162.89	92.86	74.24	82.67
1910	46.74	47.57	50.08	18.56	50.21	44.47	86.07	73.09	164.07	84.18	59.02	73.49
1911	44.66	41.97	45.81	14.56	43.14	39.22	97.65	76.61	153.40	83.97	58.43	78.38
1912	38.43	38.89	44.57	13.48	31.22	32.75	111.38	87.17	161.98	86.88	71.81	90.64
1913	35.94	33.53	51.26	13.85	30.30	30.12	115.74	110.24	211.82	91.80	93.39	105.74
1914	52.96	41.91	66.91	16.05	31.24	38.27	113.27	96.88	335.29	92.15	103.11	106.27
1915	56.20	49.86	67.88	18.80	40.36	45.05	85.24	83.21	321.45	84.88	102.06	91.88
1916	42.29	49.44	60.54	17.06	56.83	41.53	70.25	85.11	225.73	82.07	93.30	82.23
1917	36.88	43.74	52.83	20.40	47.84	36.88	75.72	84.27	167.68	80.68	105.25	85.72
1918	36.61	40.79	42.09	19.79	49.41	34.97	79.37	91.85	129.80	90.30	173.20	97.59
1919	35.34	37.79	35.26	15.59	45.52	31.74	85.18	99.15	124.01	98.16	173.50	103.95
1920	43.22	34.64	23.58	16.69	38.54	33.12	82.77	99.64	123.85	103.62	119.67	98.96
1921	51.10	38.33	24.62	19.26	21.10	35.28	78.57	99.04	115.36	108.37	89.16	91.44
1922	48.90	38.59	28.67	19.57	14.06	30.49	80.52	93.82	107.53	103.08	92.18	90.91
1923	40.17	35.28	25.05	20.14	14.21	27.12	84.73	98.46	104.45	97.27	114.67	100.06
1924	33.54	34.05	22.67	18.58	14.02	24.62	97.07	100.20	101.10	94.95	127.89	107.11
1925	31.65	32.48	21.63	16.47	16.93	25.16	99.40	101.57	97.61	97.76	119.53	104.57
1926	32.92	31.46	24.15	15.72	19.71	26.03	95.97	100.29	98.81	100.85	103.44	99.88
1927	30.25	30.54	26.30	15.75	21.39	25.79	95.96	91.12	98.65	99.67	92.09	94.14
1928	26.01	26.81	24.08	16.03	32.66	26.47	93.44	86.03	96.58	96.47	89.49	90.36
1929	27.50	24.74	23.13	15.09	41.05	28.48	91.76	85.94	95.53	96.99	87.05	89.33
1930	30.00	21.39	23.42	17.37	34.91	26.55	98.79	88.43	95.34	99.01	91.57	92.93

Source: See Data Appendix.

Table A.4 Bank Growth, by Region; Index, 1906 = 100

	Deposits						Short-term credit					
	Rio de Janeiro	São Paulo	Minas Gerais	Rio Grande do Sul	Banco do Brasil	Total	Rio de Janeiro	São Paulo	Minas Gerais	Rio Grande do Sul	Banco do Brasil	Total
1906	100.00	100.00	100.00	100.00	100.00	100.00	100.00	100.00	100.00	100.00	100.00	100.00
1907	94.14	117.86	92.76	100.00	504.71	152.93	103.36	113.23	97.38	100.00	353.96	151.15
1908	85.69	117.18	83.81	109.04	907.95	173.49	113.52	116.71	86.32	116.02	643.68	181.44
1909	96.75	163.01	95.79	126.64	1283.28	226.66	130.40	124.94	117.61	132.07	780.86	206.62
1910	121.44	186.78	144.27	150.81	1596.10	273.27	151.89	132.17	178.41	142.58	772.13	221.44
1911	207.18	211.64	215.20	204.90	1906.36	353.33	294.02	156.98	248.82	193.22	912.89	305.36
1912	238.74	202.25	255.45	239.73	1819.96	366.16	386.43	170.69	311.88	233.89	1071.11	365.94
1913	248.53	177.12	243.34	266.97	1662.12	354.97	418.02	189.06	388.50	275.23	1272.19	413.86
1914	251.36	183.96	250.99	276.16	1448.61	350.10	413.75	172.56	634.30	285.79	1224.17	410.23
1915	289.80	188.51	288.55	270.96	960.52	340.81	358.97	151.88	699.11	258.30	803.43	345.27
1916	392.29	190.77	340.66	306.61	894.13	390.57	400.51	157.20	579.60	282.61	683.73	354.13
1917	247.14	228.89	372.73	368.69	857.69	363.17	271.94	186.75	471.09	334.05	739.90	343.27
1918	397.01	300.93	557.18	578.23	1061.76	527.70	457.91	267.63	545.11	586.38	1507.19	567.82
1919	389.17	290.71	663.21	613.91	1106.66	532.79	481.72	279.07	619.91	676.76	1573.70	610.70
1920	436.03	387.50	782.95	608.03	1448.41	621.60	524.50	373.83	730.88	707.53	1420.56	678.30
1921	719.41	391.77	957.86	561.77	3722.47	861.03	821.41	375.68	832.86	683.71	2720.18	868.12
1922	699.38	362.90	1252.64	543.13	5857.25	959.33	818.41	329.66	1015.26	628.72	4425.39	961.63
1923	630.11	386.83	1616.49	554.78	5573.09	938.07	775.88	368.75	1272.57	606.01	5237.67	1034.98
1924	498.94	331.27	2025.00	524.81	4365.44	790.54	703.81	321.37	1543.03	559.60	4575.70	933.64
1925	552.54	393.64	2147.24	535.65	3604.02	807.39	798.18	387.11	1579.73	588.07	3530.76	930.92
1926	548.81	412.48	1998.02	534.72	3677.55	815.78	765.38	400.54	1488.07	605.61	3117.64	898.40
1927	538.71	555.19	2029.04	540.69	4306.52	920.94	751.26	489.82	1508.64	605.23	3250.48	955.93
1928	564.21	814.95	2570.70	640.54	4973.04	1136.53	766.11	678.83	1871.27	693.97	3647.30	1132.40
1929	624.63	905.45	3039.15	722.97	6665.72	1332.26	832.91	753.39	2188.34	787.49	4755.77	1312.19
1930	605.99	907.12	2795.06	649.17	6743.23	1306.33	870.01	776.66	2008.51	721.83	5060.53	1338.57

	By type of bank			By region				
	Private domestic	State-subsidized	Banco do Brasil	Rio de Janeiro	São Paulo	Banespa	Crédito Real	Banco do Brasil
1906	14.57	—	—	19.41	10.91	—	—	—
1907	9.62	—	5.83	9.00	10.08	—	—	5.83
1908	11.85	5.98	7.58	11.97	11.77	—	5.98	7.58
1909	16.31	4.60	9.50	10.40	20.09	—	4.60	9.50
1910	20.64	3.13	9.95	28.23	16.78	3.25	3.03	9.95
1911	14.74	2.93	5.03	—	13.65	3.67	2.26	5.03
1912	12.28	2.08	5.44	11.39	12.86	2.33	1.82	5.44
1913	12.21	1.38	7.46	14.11	10.96	—	1.94	7.46
1914	14.44	3.29	7.76	13.85	14.82	4.99	1.64	7.76
1915	20.59	6.08	8.71	13.53	24.71	11.97	1.39	8.71
1916	17.66	6.18	7.54	10.54	22.57	12.19	1.39	7.54
1917	13.00	6.71	10.07	4.43	19.12	12.99	1.45	10.07
1918	6.05	6.70	9.09	3.94	7.80	10.38	1.76	9.09
1919	9.70	3.63	8.92	—	7.34	5.05	1.53	8.92
1920	7.35	6.04	8.89	—	4.78	8.84	1.86	8.89
1921	9.82	14.05	7.51	15.70	8.61	21.35	2.19	7.51
1922	6.93	18.52	3.19	10.60	5.65	29.40	2.08	3.19
1923	7.78	22.35	0.50	9.61	7.11	39.91	1.74	0.50
1924	6.83	28.51	7.05	8.61	6.29	55.45	1.36	7.05
1925	10.38	2.72	0.50	7.73	11.16	5.00	1.90	0.50
1926	6.67	8.67	0.45	9.20	6.08	13.42	4.06	0.45
1927	8.57	9.13	0.50	7.35	8.85	11.70	2.92	0.50
1928	6.59	8.54	4.29	6.60	6.59	9.99	2.24	4.29
1929	5.64	10.07	2.58	6.21	5.50	11.02	4.31	2.58
1930	5.72	12.14	0.50	6.20	5.57	13.16	3.08	0.50

Source: See Data Appendix.

Note: Proxy Interest Rate is calculated as the weighted average of the annualized six-month ratio of net profits to earning assets.

Table A.6 Market Concentration (%Market Share, by Deposits)

	By type of bank				By region				
	Private domestic	Foreign	State-subsidized	Banco do Brasil	Rio de Janeiro	São Paulo	Minas Gerais	Rio do Sul	Banco do Brasil
1906	45.21	46.90	2.32	5.57	41.53	50.59	2.32		5.57
1907	50.41	29.81	1.41	18.37	25.56	38.99	1.41	15.67	18.37
1908	42.15	27.59	1.12	29.14	20.51	34.17	1.12	15.06	29.14
1909	38.09	29.41	0.98	31.52	17.73	36.38	0.98	13.39	31.52
1910	36.98	29.24	1.26	32.52	18.45	34.58	1.22	13.23	32.52
1911	35.78	32.63	1.55	30.04	24.35	30.30	1.41	13.90	30.04
1912	36.81	33.98	1.54	27.67	27.08	27.94	1.62	15.69	27.67
1913	36.64	35.56	1.73	26.07	29.08	25.24	1.59	18.02	26.07
1914	39.73	34.58	2.65	23.04	29.82	26.58	1.66	18.90	23.04
1915	43.93	37.57	2.81	15.69	35.31	27.98	1.96	19.05	15.69
1916	47.24	37.68	2.33	12.75	41.71	24.71	2.02	18.81	12.75
1917	49.98	34.23	2.64	13.15	28.26	31.88	2.38	24.33	13.15
1918	50.15	36.35	2.29	11.20	31.24	28.85	2.45	26.26	11.20
1919	54.22	32.24	1.98	11.56	30.33	27.60	2.88	27.61	11.56
1920	54.01	31.48	1.54	12.97	29.13	31.53	2.92	23.44	12.97
1921	35.38	39.58	0.98	24.07	34.70	23.02	2.58	15.64	24.07
1922	32.97	32.17	0.87	33.99	30.28	19.14	3.03	13.57	33.99
1923	39.52	26.14	1.26	33.08	27.89	20.86	3.99	14.17	33.08
1924	45.58	22.10	1.57	30.75	26.21	21.20	5.94	15.91	30.75
1925	43.94	29.61	1.60	24.85	28.42	24.66	6.16	15.90	24.85
1926	42.26	30.42	2.22	25.10	27.94	25.58	5.68	15.71	25.10
1927	39.92	25.47	8.57	26.04	24.29	30.50	5.11	14.07	26.04
1928	37.88	21.83	15.93	24.36	20.62	36.27	5.24	13.51	24.36
1929	34.01	19.24	18.89	27.86	19.47	34.38	5.29	13.01	27.86
1930	29.59	19.24	22.43	28.74	19.26	35.13	4.96	11.91	28.74

Source: See Data Appendix.

210

Table A.7 Five Largest Banks, Ranked by Deposits (Excluding Banco do Brasil)

Year	Comind	Comercial-RJ	Província-RGS	São Paulo*	Francessa Italiano	Pelotense	Commercial-RGS	Portugués do Brasil	Com. do Est. de São Paulo*	Banespa	London & Brazil**	London & River Plate**	London & South American**	British Bank of Brazil	Brasiliansche Deutsch	Nacional Ultramarino	National City Bank
1906	1	5									2	4			3		
1907	1		2	5							3				4		
1908	1		2	5							3				4		
1909	1		3								4			5	2		
1910	1		4								3			5	2		
1911	1		2								3			5	4		
1912	1		2		5						4				3		
1913	2		1		4									3	5		
1914	2		1		5						4				3		
1915	1		2		5						3				4		
1916	1		2		3						4			5			
1917	3		2			4					5					1	
1918	3		2			4					5					1	
1919	4		2			3	5									1	
1920	5		2			3		1								4	
1921	1		2			3										5	4
1922	2		3		1	5					4						
1923	2		3		1	4	5										
1924	1		2			4	5		3								
1925	2		5		1	4							3				
1926	1		5			3		4					2				
1927	1					4		3	2				5				
1928	2		5			4		3	1								
1929	2		5			3		4	1								
1930	2		3		5	4			1								

Source: See Data Appendix.
Notes:
 * Neither the Bancos de São Paulo nor Commércio do Estado de São Paulo are related to the related to the Banco de Crédito Hypothecário e Agrícola do Estado de São Paulo/Banco do Estado de São Paulo.
** The London & Brazil and the London and River Plate merged in 1923 to form the London and South American.

Table A.8 Bank Coverage in Database of Balances

	Note	Year data: Begin	End
Domestic banks			
Banco de São Paulo		1905	1930
Boa Vista		1924	1930
Brasil		1905	1930
Commercial de Minas Gerais		1923	1930
Commercial de Rio de Janeiro		1905	1930
Commercial do Estado de São Paulo		1912	1930
Commercial e Industrial de São Paulo		1905	1930
Commércio de Rio de Janeiro		1905	1930
Commércio de Rio Grande do Sul		1906	1930
Crédito Hypothecário e Agrícola do Estado de Minas Gerais		1911	1930
Crédito Hypothecário e Agrícola do Estado de São Paulo	(1)	1909	1930
Crédito Real de Minas Gerais		1905	1930
Crédito Rural Internacional		1915	1921
Iniciador de Melhoramentos (SP)		1919	1928
Lavoura e Commércio		1905	1925
Mercantil (RJ)		1910	1930
Nacional Brasileiro		1915	1925
Pelotense		1906	1930
Portugal do Brasil		1918	1930
Província de Rio Grande do Sul		1906	1930
Foreign banks			
Alemão Transatlántico	(2)	1911	1930
American Foreign Banking Corp.	(3)	1919	1921
Brasiliensche Deutsche	(2)	1905	1929
British Bank of Brazil		1905	1930
Commerciale Italiano de São Paulo	(4)	1905	1909
Deutsche Sudamerikansche	(2)	1911	1930
Español y Rio de la Plata		1910	1922
Francessa-Italiana	(4)	1910	1930
Hollandez-América do Sul		1917	1930
Italo-Belge		1913	1930
London and Brazil	(5)	1905	1923
London and River Plate	(5)	1905	1923
London and South American	(5)	1924	1930
Nacional Ultramarino		1914	1922
National City Bank	(3)	1915	1930
Royal Bank of Canada		1919	1928

Notes: Data beginning 1905, refers to 31 December (beginning point for 1906).

(1) Renamed Banco do Estado de São Paulo (Banespa) from 1926.

(2) German bank activity was frozen from 1917 to 1919, and therefore balances are excluded for those years.

(3) National City Bank acquired the American Banking Corporation in 1921.

(4) Commerciale Italiano was sold and reconstituted as the Francessa-Italiano in 1910.

(5) The London and Brazil and the London and Rio Plate merged to form the London and South American in 1924.

Table A.9 Income per Capita, Estimated

| | São Paulo, Minas Gerais, & Rio Grande do Sul | | Rest of Brazil | | Total Brazil |
	Income, p.c. (mil-réis)	Share of total population	Income, p.c. (mil-réis)	Share of total population	Income, p.c. (mil-réis)
Nominal					
1897*	11.3	0.381	9.2	0.619	10.0
1930	45.0	0.415	14.2	0.585	27.0
Real					
1897*	8.1	0.381	6.6	0.619	7.2
1930	18.7	0.415	5.9	0.585	11.2
Annual average growth (%)					
Nominal	4.2		1.3		3.0
Real	2.5		-0.3		1.4

Sources: Income per capita (nominal) and population distribution are taken from Topik 1987: Tables 3 & 4 (data from Brasil, IBGE, 1939-40 *Annuário estatístico*). Nominal per capita income are deflated by price index (Table A.10).

Note: *Population refers to 1890, year of the national census.

Table A.10 Economic Indicators

	Price index (1906 = 100)	Exchange rate (pence/mil-réis)	Coffee price (US¢/lb.)	Gross Domestic Product		Money Supply	
				Nominal (mil-réis, millions)	Real; index (1906 = 100)	Nominal M_2 (contos, thousands)	Real; index (1906 = 100)
1889	67.7	26.4	16.00	1778	60.2	323	61.2
1890	78.2	22.6	19.00	2096	61.4	689	80.9
1891	78.9	14.4	20.00	2959	85.9	1140	144.9
1892	99.0	12.0	14.00	3475	80.4	877	127.5
1893	122.1	11.3	16.40	3561	66.8	891	90.6
1894	142.0	10.1	14.70	3996	64.4	999	83.2
1895	143.8	9.9	16.60	4175	66.5	974	85.8
1896	131.2	9.0	11.10	4250	74.2	967	92.5
1897	139.6	7.7	7.50	4517	74.1	1094	92.3
1898	163.5	7.2	6.50	4900	68.6	1087	83.4
1899	170.9	7.4	6.70	4910	65.8	1058	78.5
1900	166.2	9.5	6.40	4560	62.8	849	71.7
1901	151.3	11.4	6.40	4013	60.7	770	66.9
1902	131.7	12.0	6.60	3810	66.3	729	71.2
1903	115.7	12.0	7.00	3932	77.8	713	78.0
1904	114.0	12.2	8.10	4372	87.8	783	82.1
1905	120.5	15.9	8.60	4088	77.7	768	80.5
1906	100.0	16.2	7.90	4366	100.0	831	100.0
1907	106.1	15.2	7.60	4963	107.1	953	105.2
1908	111.3	15.2	8.34	4818	99.2	935	106.1
1909	99.2	15.2	8.80	5252	121.3	1111	129.0
1910	97.9	16.2	10.40	5791	135.5	1257	151.3
1911	105.7	16.1	14.18	6204	134.4	1462	160.9
1912	117.7	16.1	16.00	6849	133.3	1513	158.1
1913	112.9	16.1	13.17	6631	134.6	1411	162.0

Year	Price index (1906 = 100)	Exchange rate (pence/mil-réis)	Coffee price (US¢/lb.)	Gross Domestic Product		Money Supply	
				Nominal (mil-réis, millions)	Real; index (1906 = 100)	Nominal M_2 (contos, thousands)	Real; index (1906 = 100)
1914	106.9	14.8	11.46	5630	120.6	1318	159.6
1915	110.5	12.6	9.57	6520	135.2	1448	156.6
1916	117.6	12.1	10.55	7740	150.7	1802	172.8
1917	129.5	12.8	10.16	9020	159.5	2068	186.9
1918	115.2	13.0	12.71	9670	192.2	2746	261.3
1919	150.9	14.5	24.78	11180	169.7	3088	241.8
1920	166.3	14.6	10.09	14900	205.2	3228	237.5
1921	169.9	8.4	10.38	12950	174.6	4287	276.7
1922	186.5	7.2	14.30	15110	185.5	4764	303.5
1923	205.5	5.4	14.84	21320	237.6	5240	304.4
1924	240.0	6.0	21.31	24130	230.3	5852	289.1
1925	256.6	6.1	24.55	28620	255.4	5336	272.7
1926	263.8	7.2	22.30	24790	215.3	5364	253.7
1927	270.9	5.9	18.68	27070	228.9	6649	277.4
1928	267.3	5.9	23.20	33310	285.4	7646	334.5
1929	244.7	6.0	22.00	32550	304.6	7583	389.2
1930	241.2	4.9	13.00	27210	258.4	7237	384.3

Sources:

Price Index: See Data Appendix.

Exchange rate: Brasil, IBGE, 1939/40, *Annuário estatística*, p. 1354.

Rates are the 90–day sight exchange rate drawn on London; annual average.

Coffee price: Fritsch, 1987: Table A.6.

Gross Domestic Product (nominal): Goldsmith, 1986 (Tables 3.1 and 4.2).

Real GDP index: deflated by price index (see Data Appendix).

Money supply: (year-end M_2) from Brasil, IBGE, 1990, *Estatísticas históricas*, Table 10.2.

Real money supply index: annual average money supply deflated by price index.

Table A.11　Growth Indices, Sectoral Comparisons, 1906–1930 (1906 = 100)

	Production			Coffee exports	Money supply	GDP (real)	Price index	Bank deposits			
	Total	Agricultural	Industrial					Private domestic	Foreign	Total private	Total
1906	100.00	100.00	100.00	100.00	100.00	100.00	100.00	100.00	100.00	100.00	100.00
1907	100.81	116.30	108.82	112.27	105.20	107.14	106.09	170.52	97.20	133.19	152.93
1908	97.58	100.83	108.82	90.63	106.10	99.15	111.30	161.76	102.05	131.35	173.49
1909	107.66	106.35	132.35	120.87	129.04	121.32	99.15	190.96	142.11	166.09	226.66
1910	110.48	111.33	138.24	69.63	151.31	135.51	97.88	223.53	170.36	196.46	273.27
1911	116.94	103.04	150.74	80.61	160.90	134.42	105.71	279.62	245.80	262.40	353.33
1912	125.00	114.36	166.91	86.50	158.12	133.28	117.70	298.14	265.25	281.39	366.16
1913	128.63	111.88	168.38	95.00	162.03	134.56	112.87	287.65	269.13	278.22	354.97
1914	127.02	119.34	153.68	80.70	159.62	120.60	106.93	307.69	258.11	282.44	350.10
1915	127.42	118.23	173.53	122.16	156.58	135.16	110.49	331.19	272.97	301.55	340.81
1916	128.63	123.20	193.38	93.36	172.83	150.72	117.62	408.09	313.78	360.07	390.57
1917	140.73	127.62	210.29	75.94	186.92	159.53	129.50	401.49	265.04	332.01	363.17
1918	137.90	131.49	208.09	53.22	261.27	192.19	115.24	585.40	409.02	495.59	527.70
1919	148.79	129.83	238.97	92.82	241.84	169.71	150.89	638.97	366.18	500.07	532.79
1920	167.34	147.24	251.47	82.52	237.51	205.18	166.33	742.53	417.22	576.88	621.60
1921	170.56	153.31	247.06	88.57	276.67	174.59	169.89	673.71	726.53	700.60	861.03
1922	183.87	154.14	293.38	90.74	303.50	185.54	186.53	699.52	658.04	678.40	959.33
1923	199.60	160.22	332.35	103.58	304.43	237.58	205.54	819.98	522.85	668.69	938.07
1924	202.42	161.88	328.68	101.86	289.08	230.29	239.99	797.02	372.47	580.85	790.54
1925	202.42	156.63	332.35	96.53	272.69	255.44	256.62	784.70	509.67	644.66	807.39
1926	212.90	161.60	340.44	98.46	253.74	215.28	263.75	762.52	529.03	643.63	815.78

Table A.11   Growth Indices, Sectoral Comparisons, 1906-1930 (1906 = 100) (continued)

| | Production | | | Coffee exports | Money supply | GDP (real) | Price index | Private domestic | Bank deposits | | |
	Total	Agricultural	Industrial						Foreign	Total private	Total
1927	235.89	179.01	377.21	108.23	277.38	228.89	270.88	813.26	500.08	653.79	920.94
1928	262.90	211.88	403.68	99.39	334.48	285.41	267.32	952.21	528.93	736.68	1136.53
1929	265.73	212.43	394.85	102.26	389.20	304.62	244.74	1002.31	546.42	770.18	1332.26
1930	260.08	214.92	368.38	109.47	384.34	258.41	241.18	855.03	535.79	692.48	1306.33

Sources:

Output: total: Haddad, 1974, Table 1; reprinted in Brasil, IBGE, 1990, *Estatísticas históricas*, Table 4.1. Agricultural and industrial: Haddad, 1974, Table 1.

Coffee exports: Brasil, IBGE, 1990, *Estatísticas históricas*, Table 6.43.

Money supply (real M₂): Brasil, IBGE, 1990, *Estatísticas históricas*, Table 10.2 (deflated by price index).

GDP: Goldsmith, 1986, Tables 3.1 and 4.2.

Prices and bank deposits: See Data Appendix.

Note: All data report annual average levels.

Table A.12 Fiscal Aggregates

	Debt service, % federal expense	Federal expense, % revenues	Sources of federal revenues (% of total revenues):				States, as % federal:	
			Tariff	Industrial tax	Income tax	Other	Revenues	Expenses
1889	—	115.75						
1890	24.70	113.01						
1891	23.00	96.35						
1892	18.50	122.70						
1893	19.70	115.69						
1894	13.00	140.63						
1895	17.50	112.03						
1896	16.10	106.56						
1897	17.10	125.02						
1898	53.20	206.17						
1899	21.60	92.06						
1900	41.50	140.80	53.57	11.92	0.00	34.51		
1901	27.50	109.85	53.23	10.37	0.00	36.40		
1902	28.50	86.59	53.98	9.88	0.00	36.14		
1903	25.30	87.43	45.61	8.52	0.00	45.87		
1904	23.30	104.67	44.67	7.99	0.00	47.34		
1905	25.90	93.48	55.87	8.79	0.00	35.34		
1906	24.90	98.08	57.49	10.08	0.00	32.44		
1907	20.70	97.42	53.59	8.95	0.00	37.46	38.55	43.14
1908	20.70	115.81	53.73	10.11	0.00	36.17	44.60	45.33
1909	24.60	115.20	51.81	10.17	0.00	38.02	54.11	48.79
1910	27.10	118.81	55.02	10.41	0.00	34.57	46.64	44.68

Table A.12 Fiscal Aggregates (continued)

	Debt service, % federal expense	Federal expense, % revenues	Sources of federal revenues (% of total revenues):				States, as % federal:	
			Tariff	Industrial tax	Income tax	Other	Revenues	Expenses
1911	20.40	121.00	56.37	10.61	0.00	33.03	42.57	38.94
1912	18.30	128.25	56.59	10.18	0.00	33.23	46.48	38.96
1913	21.60	116.59	52.62	9.95	0.00	37.43	41.27	44.34
1914	18.00	181.15	46.10	12.34	0.00	41.56	56.70	39.90
1915	24.70	170.31	37.75	16.80	0.00	45.45	70.25	42.88
1916	38.10	143.66	38.56	17.54	0.00	43.90	62.74	44.49
1917	37.40	149.12	29.47	21.90	0.00	48.63	59.37	41.01
1918	29.60	140.13	27.70	19.35	0.00	52.95	52.76	41.30
1919	26.70	148.89	33.99	21.08	0.00	44.93	63.45	43.14
1920	26.90	133.01	37.83	19.04	0.00	43.12	53.12	41.24
1921	20.50	133.48	35.78	17.30	0.00	46.92	55.87	44.63
1922	20.50	146.91	31.74	17.00	0.00	51.26	55.00	42.96
1923	29.60	111.68	37.20	20.54	0.00	42.25	56.73	56.97
1924	29.30	105.89	36.87	19.43	1.54	42.15	56.19	54.17
1925	26.60	102.45	42.11	18.22	1.99	37.68	62.30	63.53
1926	23.90	110.66	35.07	22.08	2.16	40.68	62.66	69.83
1927	30.70	98.49	39.82	19.75	3.00	37.43	57.38	72.71
1928	33.00	91.05	42.36	19.86	3.08	34.70	57.34	74.70
1929	30.20	92.71	38.68	17.78	3.16	40.38	60.05	80.12
1930	16.70	149.62	37.32	20.99	3.70	37.99	72.22	68.38

Sources:
Debt service, % federal revenue: Villela and Suzigan, 1973, Table 2.
Federal and state, revenues and expenses: Brasil, IBGE, 1990, *Estatísticas históricas*, Table 12.1.

Table A.13a Regression Results: Demand for Banking

DEMAND FUNCTIONS

Dependent variable: (Real) bank deposits of:

Independent variable:		Total Brazil β	(t)	Private domestic β	(t)	Foreign β	(t)	Total private β	(t)	State-subsidized β	(t)	Banco do Brasil β	(t)
Total prices	Prices	-2.40	(-2.85)	-2.61	(-1.89)	-4.43	(-2.40)	-2.03	(-2.54)	-9.53	(-1.66)	-11.58	(-1.42)
Total output	Output	1.27	(1.23)	1.69	(1.21)	1.63	(0.86)	0.96	(1.03)	7.71	(1.66)	5.83	(0.89)
	Constant	0.14	(2.53)	0.12	(1.60)	0.17	(1.66)	0.12	(2.28)	0.24	(1.10)	0.37	(1.16)
	R2	0.28		0.14		0.22		0.24		0.14		0.09	
Total prices	Prices	-2.27	(-2.68)	-1.89	(-1.50)	-3.92	(-2.76)	-1.82	(-2.54)	-17.65	(-0.89)	-12.54	(-1.37)
National income	Output	-0.03	(-0.09)	0.37	(0.92)	-0.48	(-0.84)	0.14	(0.45)	-2.17	(-0.55)	-2.10	(-0.88)
	Constant	0.19	(3.36)	0.14	(2.02)	0.23	(2.54)	0.14	(2.93)	0.93	(1.03)	0.72	(1.55)
	R2	0.28		0.21		0.27		0.29		0.04		0.08	
Total prices	Prices	-2.45	(-3.04)	-1.88	(-2.32)	-4.83	(-2.36)	-2.14	(-2.78)	-14.31	(-1.18)	-10.58	(-1.59)
Industrial output	Output	1.25	(1.95)	1.47	(2.33)	1.71	(1.27)	1.16	(1.98)	5.82	(0.98)	4.61	(1.20)
	Constant	0.13	(2.53)	0.08	(1.58)	0.15	(1.55)	0.10	(2.10)	0.41	(1.19)	0.31	(1.18)
	R2	0.31		0.25		0.21		0.28		0.06		0.11	
Industrial prices	Prices	-2.21	(-1.73)	-7.36	(-0.28)	-3.35	(-1.73)	-1.92	(-1.56)	-6.17	(-1.35)	-3.73	(-1.51)
Industrial output	Output	-2.87	(1.60)	9.48	(0.30)	3.82	(1.38)	2.54	(1.47)	7.42	(1.19)	4.69	(1.40)
	Constant	0.01	(-0.07)	-0.25	(-0.23)	-0.04	(-0.29)	-0.01	(-0.13)	-0.01	(-0.05)	-0.07	(-0.40)
	R2	0.14		0.01		0.14		0.12		0.09		0.11	

Table A.13a Regression Results: Demand for Banking (continued)

DEMAND FUNCTIONS		Dependent variable: (Real) bank deposits of:										
		Total Brazil		Private domestic		Foreign		Total private		State-subsidized		Banco do Brasil	
Independent variable:		β	(t)	β	(t)	β	(t)	β	(t)	β	(t)	β	(t)
Agricultural prices	Prices	-4.41	(-0.68)	2.00	(1.25)	-4.04	(-1.25)	-2.91	(-0.83)	-8.04	(-0.87)	-45.51	(-0.10)
Agricultural output	Output	0.65	(0.21)	0.27	(0.24)	-0.14	(-0.05)	0.21	(0.10)	2.72	(0.51)	2.91	(0.80)
	Constant	0.25	(0.78)	-0.02	(-0.18)	0.25	(1.14)	0.19	(0.97)	0.47	(0.93)	1.89	(0.10)
	R2	0.02		0.08		0.07		0.03		0.05		0.00	
Total prices	Prices	-2.37	(-2.76)	-2.60	(-1.83)	-4.14	(-2.62)	-1.89	(-2.58)	-17.07	(-0.97)	-12.49	(-1.36)
Coffee exports	Output	0.19	(0.90)	0.26	(0.90)	0.37	(1.05)	0.14	(0.79)	1.94	(0.78)	1.48	(0.99)
	Constant	0.19	(3.69)	0.18	(2.47)	0.22	(2.50)	0.15	(3.34)	0.82	(1.17)	0.63	(1.56)
	R2	0.27		0.14		0.25		0.25		0.04		0.08	
Coffee prices	Prices	1.32	(1.15)	0.72	(1.52)	7.70	(0.31)	1.35	(0.96)	3.36	(1.05)	3.41	(0.72)
Coffee exports	Output	0.05	(0.11)	0.00	(-0.02)	0.91	(0.22)	0.07	(0.16)	0.32	(0.27)	0.28	(0.22)
	Constant	0.00	(0.03)	0.02	(0.36)	-0.44	(-0.25)	-0.02	(-0.15)	-0.01	(-0.04)	-0.12	(-0.29)
	R2	0.07		0.11		0.01		0.05		0.05		0.03	

Sources:

Rates of change derived from indices of all output measures, total prices, coffee exports and bank deposits (Table A.11).

Rates of change derived from indices of agricultural and industrial prices: Brasil, IBGE 1990, *Estatísticas históricas*, Table 5.2. (Data series begins in 1908.)

Notes:

See Appendix, "Model of Demand and Supply of Banking," for a discussion of methodology and the two-stage least squares regression model. Prices in the supply function are derived from output in the associated demand model (Table A.13a).

ß: Correlation coefficient.

Table A.13b Regression Results: Supply of Banking

SUPPLY FUNCTIONS

Dependent variable: (Real) bank deposits of:

Independent variable:		Total Brazil β	(t)	Private domestic β	(t)	Foreign β	(t)	Total private β	(t)	State-subsidized β	(t)	Banco do Brasil β	(t)
Total, derived from Total output	Prices	0.70	(0.65)	0.84	(0.78)	0.30	(0.19)	0.98	(0.58)	0.52	(0.34)	0.27	(0.11)
	Cash	0.88	(2.59)	0.98	(2.71)	0.70	(2.60)	0.82	(1.61)	0.67	(5.09)	1.07	(3.37)
	Constant	0.01	(0.18)	-0.01	(-0.12)	0.02	(0.32)	-0.01	(-0.04)	0.09	(1.13)	0.03	(0.22)
	R^2	0.63		0.46		0.72		0.43		0.59		0.58	
Total, derived from national income	Prices	-1.88	(-0.48)	19.12	(0.12)	-1.39	(-1.02)	-2.91	(-0.91)	-2.99	(-0.88)	6.00	(0.78)
	Cash	0.11	(0.10)	6.37	(0.13)	0.43	(1.73)	-0.31	(-0.32)	0.54	(2.72)	1.63	(1.96)
	Constant	0.17	(0.70)	-1.04	(-0.11)	0.10	(1.44)	0.21	(1.14)	0.24	(1.54)	-0.25	(-0.63)
	R^2	0.33		0.01		0.61		0.17		0.49		0.31	
Total, derived from industrial output	Prices	1.29	(1.28)	0.73	(1.24)	1.78	(0.85)	1.84	(1.17)	-0.91	(-0.62)	0.56	(0.29)
	Cash	1.05	(3.19)	0.95	(3.88)	0.94	(2.59)	1.07	(2.17)	0.62	(5.08)	1.10	(4.15)
	Constant	-0.02	(-0.35)	...	(-0.05)	-0.04	(-0.42)	-0.05	(-0.55)	0.15	(1.99)	0.02	(0.15)
	R^2	0.55		0.48		0.53		0.32		0.64		0.59	
Industrial prices, derived from industrial output	Prices	0.32	(1.22)	0.30	(1.25)	0.50	(1.23)	0.45	(1.51)	-0.35	(-0.63)	0.07	(0.12)
	Cash	0.73	(4.82)	0.56	(3.38)	0.79	(5.23)	0.69	(4.03)	0.61	(4.74)	0.68	(2.91)
	Constant	0.03	(1.19)	0.03	(1.19)	0.02	(0.49)	0.02	(0.67)	0.14	(2.42)	0.04	(0.72)
	R^2	0.59		0.42		0.70		0.50		0.60		0.34	

Table A.13b Regression Results: Supply of Banking (continued)

SUPPLY FUNCTIONS

Dependent variable: (Real) bank deposits of:

Independent variable:		Total Brazil β	(t)	Private domestic β	(t)	Foreign β	(t)	Total private β	(t)	State-subsidized β	(t)	Banco do Brasil β	(t)
Agricultural prices, derived from agricultural output	Prices	-0.27	(-0.10)	-2.67	(-0.08)	0.00		-0.14	(-0.03)	1.93	(0.32)	-0.19	(-0.01)
	Cash	0.59	(1.53)	1.33	(0.14)	0.60	(7.39)	0.50	(0.50)	0.76	(1.78)	0.67	(2.57)
	Constant	0.06	(0.44)	0.10	(0.12)	0.04	(1.49)	0.05	(0.17)	0.03	(0.10)	0.05	(0.08)
	R²	0.56		0.03		0.73		0.46		0.38		0.36	
Total prices, derived from coffee exports	Prices	-0.40	(-0.43)	-0.27	(-0.27)	-0.94	(-0.91)	-0.60	(-0.65)	-1.19	(-0.72)	1.34	(0.58)
	Cash	0.55	(1.80)	0.66	(1.83)	0.50	(2.58)	0.36	(1.24)	0.61	(4.80)	1.18	(3.98)
	Constant	0.08	(1.28)	0.05	(0.86)	0.08	(1.47)	0.08	(1.47)	0.17	(1.98)	-0.02	(-0.16)
	R²	0.60		0.42		0.67		0.45		0.63		0.59	
Coffee prices, derived from coffee exports	Prices	0.77	(0.29)	0.76	(0.30)	0.81	(0.44)	0.73	(0.40)	1.01	(0.34)	0.03	(0.01)
	Cash	0.26	(0.20)	-0.04	(-0.02)	0.58	(2.21)	0.24	(0.31)	0.45	(0.73)	0.71	(1.15)
	Constant	0.02	(0.22)	0.02	(0.28)	-0.01	(-0.10)	0.01	(0.09)	0.08	(0.52)	0.04	(0.34)
	R²	0.18		0.10		0.34		0.16		0.30		0.43	

Sources:

Rates of change derived from indices of all output measures, total prices, coffee exports and bank deposits (Table A.11).

Rates of change derived from indices of agricultural and industrial prices: Brasil, IBGE 1990, Estatísticas históricas, Table 5.2. (Data series begins in 1908.)

Notes:

See Appendix, "Model of Demand and Supply of Banking," for a discussion of methodology and the two-stage least squares regression model. Prices in the supply function are derived from output in the associated demand model (Table A.13a).

β: Correlation coefficient.

223

Notes

Chapter 1

1. While this book does not attempt to construct a comparative study, it does use existing research to form its expectations and hypotheses.
2. Raymond W. Goldsmith, *Financial Structures and Development* (New Haven: Yale University Press, 1969), Table 1.3; Charles P. Kindleberger, *A Financial History of Western Europe*, 2d ed. (London and Boston: Allen & Unwin, 1993), 38 and Part II.
3. The classic formulations of these ideas derive from Mancur Olson, *The Logic of Collective Action: Public Goods and the Theory of Groups*, Harvard Economic Studies, vol. 124 (Cambridge, Mass.: Harvard University Press, 1971), Chapter 4; and Douglass C. North, *Structure and Change in Economic History* (New York: Norton, 1981), Chapter 3. Economic theories of the State are quite distinct from other sorts of explanations of the State, reflecting the different types of behavior under consideration. In recent historiography from the United States, the most contentious explorations of the State in Latin America concern themselves with the ability of "subaltern" peoples to affect the nature of the societies in which they live. See, for example, Gilbert M. Joseph and Daniel Nugent, eds., *Everyday Forms of State Formation: Revolution and the Negotiation of Rule in Modern Mexico* (Durham, N.C.: Duke University Press, 1994).
4. A "formed State" would be one in which the rules and expectations for public goods and property rights transcended changes of political regime. While the question of identifying a "formed State" is intriguing, it is not crucial for this book. No claim arises from this study that the Brazilian State was completely and successfully "formed" during the First Republic. In fact, much of Chapters 3 and 7 demonstrate that building the State was

a continuing concern in developing public policy related to banking—and that it did not succeed.

5. Christopher Clague, et al., "Institutions and Economic Performance: Property Rights and Contract Enforcement," in *Institutions and Economic Development: Growth and Governance in Less-Developed and Post-Socialist Countries,* ed. Christopher Clague (Baltimore: Johns Hopkins University Press, 1997), 67-90. This issue is explored in Chapter 6.

6. Kindleberger, *Financial History of Western Europe;* R. D. Richards, "The First Fifty Years of the Bank of England (1694-1744)," in *History of the Principal Public Banks,* ed. J. D. van Dillen (London: Frank Cass & Co. Ltd., 1964 [1934]), 201-72.

7. P. G. M. Dickson, *The Financial Revolution in England: A Study in the Development of Public Credit, 1688-1756* (Aldershot, Hampshire, England: Gregg Revivals; Brookfield, Vt.: distributed in the United States by Ashgate Publ. Co., 1993); Douglass C. North and Barry R. Weingast, "Constitutions and Commitment: The Evolution of Institutions Governing Public Choice in Seventeenth Century England," *Journal of Economic History* 49, no. 4 (December 1989): 803-32; Bray Hammond, *Banks and Politics in America, from the Revolution to the Civil War* (Princeton: Princeton University Press, 1957).

8. For consideration of these issues from a variety of perspectives with respect to the experiences of the United States, see Richard E. Sylla, *The American Capital Market, 1846-1914: A Study of the Effects of Public Policy on Economic Development,* Dissertations in American Economic History (New York: Arno Press, 1975); James Livingston, *Origins of the Federal Reserve System: Money, Class, and Corporate Capitalism, 1890-1913* (Ithaca, N.Y.: Cornell University Press, 1986); Eugene Nelson White, *The Regulation and Reform of the American Banking System, 1900-1929* (Princeton: Princeton University Press, 1983); Kenneth Ng, "Free Banking Laws and Barriers to Entry in Banking, 1838-1860," *Journal of Economic History* 48, no. 4 (December 1988): 877-89.

9. Robert G. King and Ross Levine, "Finance and Growth: Schumpeter Might Be Right," *Quarterly Journal of Economics* 108, no. 3 (August 1993): 717-37; Goldsmith, *Financial Structures,* Chapter 1; Rondo E. Cameron, ed., "Banking in the Early Stages," in *Banking in the Early Stages of Industrialization; a Study in Comparative Economic History,* with the collaboration of Olga Crisp, Hugh T. Patrick, and Richard Tilly (New York: Oxford University Press, 1967), 9-12.

10. North and Weingast, "Constitutions and Commitment."

11. Rondo Cameron, introduction to *Banking and Economic Development: Some Lessons of History,* ed. Rondo Cameron (Oxford: Oxford University Press, 1972), 1, offers this well-targeted phrase.

12. Joseph Alois Schumpeter, *The Theory of Economic Development: An Inquiry into Profits, Capital, Credit, Interest, and the Business Cycle,* trans. Opie Red-

vers, Harvard Economic Series, 46 (Cambridge, Mass.: Harvard University Press, 1934).

13. Alexander Gerschenkron, "Economic Backwardness in Historical Perspective," in *Economic Backwardness in Historical Perspective, a Book of Essays* (Cambridge, Mass.: Belknap Press of Harvard University Press, 1962), 5-30.

14. Cameron, "Banking in the Early Stages"; Cameron, "Banking and Economic Development." The chapters on Russia and Louisiana offer the most relevant direct comparisons with Brazil. Olga Crisp, "Russia, 1860-1914," in *Banking in the Early Stages of Industrialization; a Study in Comparative Economic History,* ed. Rondo E. Cameron, with the collaboration of Olga Crisp, Hugh T. Patrick, and Richard Tilly (New York: Oxford University Press, 1967), 183-238; George Green, "Louisiana, 1804-1861," in *Banking and Economic Development: Some Lessons of History,* ed. Rondo E. Cameron (Oxford: Oxford University Press, 1972), 199-231.

15. François Crouzet, *Capital Formation in the Industrial Revolution* (London: Methuen and Co., 1972); Pat Hudson, *The Genesis of Industrial Capital: A Study of the West Riding Wool Textile Industry, c. 1750-1850* (Cambridge: Cambridge University Press, 1986); Michael Collins, *Banks and Industrial Finance in Britain: 1800-1939,* Studies in Economic and Social History (London: The Economic History Society and Macmillan, 1991), are some of the best-known examples.

16. Duncan Ross, "Commercial Banking in a Market-Oriented Financial System: Britain Before the War," *Economic History Review* 49, no. 2 (May 1996): 314-35 is most useful for a succinct explanation of the differences in bank structure and their possible effect on economies.

17. Michael Collins, "English Bank Development Within a European Context, 1870-1939," *Economic History Review* 61, no. 1 (February 1998): 1-24; Caroline Fohlin, "*Fiduciari* and Firm Liquidity Constraints: The Italian Experience with German-Style Universal Banking," *Explorations in Economic History* 35, no. 1 (January 1998): 83-107.

18. Lance E. Davis, "The Investment Market, 1870-1914: The Evolution of a National Market," *Journal of Economic History* 25 (1965): 355-99; Richard Sylla, "Federal Policy, Banking Market Structure and Capital Mobility in the United States, 1863-1914," *Journal of Economic History* 29, no. 4 (December 1969): 657-86; John A. James, "Banking Market Structure, Risk and the Pattern of Local Interest Rates in the United States, 1893-1911," *Review of Economics and Statistics* 53, no. 4 (November 1976): 453-62; Kerry A. Odell, "The Integration of Regional and Interregional Capital Markets: Evidence from the Pacific Coast, 1883-1913," *Journal of Economic History* 49, no. 2 (June 1989): 297-309; Howard Bodenhorn, "A More Perfect Union: Regional Interest Rates in the United States, 1880-1960," in *Anglo-American Financial Systems: Institu-*

tions and Markets in the Twentieth Century, ed. Michael D. Bordo and Richard Eugene Sylla (Burr Ridge, Ill.: Irwin Professional Pub., 1995); Jane Knodell, "Interregional Financial Integration and the Banknote Market: The Old Northwest, 1815-1845," *Journal of Economic History* 48, no. 2 (June 1988): 287-98. The most important efforts to extend this research beyond the United States are: David F. Good, "Financial Integration in Late Nineteenth-Century Austria," *Journal of Economic History* 37, no. 4 (December 1977): 890-910; and Kenneth A. Lewis and Kozo Yamamura, "Industrialization and Interregional Interest Rate Structure; the Japanese Case: 1889-1925," *Explorations in Economic History* 8, no. 4 (summer 1971): 473-99.

19.   This formulation begs the question of defining economic development.

20.   John G. Gurley and E. S. Shaw, "Financial Aspects of Economic Development," *American Economic Review* 45, no. 4 (September 1955): 515-38.

21.   King and Levine, "Schumpeter Might Be Right"; Ross Levine, "Financial Development and Economic Growth: Views and Agenda," *Journal of Economic Literature* 35, no. 2 (June 1997): 688-726; Goldsmith, *Financial Structures,* 48.

22.   Christopher Clague, et al., "Contract-Intensive Money: Contract Enforcement, Property Rights and Economic Performance," University of Maryland Center Institutional Reform and the Informal Sector, Working Paper 151, College Park, Md.: 1997.

23.   The best recent examples are: Carlos Marichal, *A Century of Debt Crises in Latin America: From Independence to the Great Depression, 1820-1930* (Princeton: Princeton University Press, 1989); Barbara Stallings, *Banker to the Third World: U.S. Portfolio Investment in Latin America, 1900-1986,* Studies in International Political Economy, Vol. 18 (Berkeley and Los Angeles: University of California Press, 1987); Albert Fishlow, "Conditionality and Willingness to Pay: Some Parallels from the 1890s," in *The International Debt Crisis in Historical Perspective,* ed. Barry Eichengreen and Peter H. Lindert (Cambridge: MIT Press, 1989), 86-105; Eliana A. Cardoso and Rudiger Dornbusch, "Brazilian Debt Crises: Past and Present," in *The International Debt Crisis in Historical Perspective,* ed. Barry Eichengreen and Peter H. Lindert (Cambridge: MIT Press, 1989).

24.   Milton Friedman and Anna Jacobson Schwartz, *A Monetary History of the United States, 1867-1960* (Princeton: Princeton University Press for the National Bureau of Economic Research, 1963). On Latin America, see: Carlos Manuel Peláez and Wilson Suzigan, *História monetária do Brasil: Análise da política, comportamento e instituições monetárias,* Monografia no. 23 (Instituto de Planejamento Econômico e Social. Instituto de Pesquisas) (Rio de Janeiro: IPEA/INPES, 1976); and Paulo Neuhaus, "A Monetary History of Brazil, 1900-1945" (Ph.D. diss., University of Chicago, 1974), on Brazil. See, for example, Roberto Cortés Conde, *Dinero, deuda y crisis: Evolución fiscal y monetaria en la Argentina, 1862-*

1890 (Buenos Aires: Editorial Sudamericana, Instituto Torcuato di Tella, 1989); and Roberto Cortés Conde, *Los orígenes de la banca en la Argentina del siglo XIX* (Córdoba, R.A.: Centro de Estudios Históricos, 1995), on Argentina; see Banco de la República (Colombia), *El Banco de la República: Antecedentes, evolución y estructura* (Bogotá, D.F., Colombia: El Banco, 1990), on Colombia; Rolf Lüders, "A Monetary History of Chile" (Ph.D. diss., University of Chicago, 1968), on Chile.

25. For a selection, see: Leonor Ludlow and Carlos Marichal, eds., *Banca y poder en México, 1800-1925,* 1st ed., Colección Enlace (Mexico: Grijalbo, 1986); Robert A. Potash, *El Banco de Avió en México: El fomento a la industria 1821-1846* (México: Fondo de Cultura Económica, 1959); Flávio A. M. de Saes, *Crédito e bancos no desenvolvimento da economia paulista: 1850-1930* (São Paulo: Instituto de Pesquisas Econônomicas, 1986); Carlos Gabriel Guimarães, "A Casa Bancária Mauá, MacGregor & Cia. (1854-1866) e o império no Brasil" (paper presented at the Segundo Congresso Brasileiro de História Econômica, Universidade Federal Fluminense, Niterói, October 1996); Alfonso W. Quiroz, *Banqueros en conflicto: Estructura financiera y economía peruana, 1884-1930* (Lima, Peru: Centro de Investigación, Universidad del Pacífico, 1989); Alfonso W. Quiroz, *Domestic and Foreign Finance in Modern Peru, 1850-1950: Financing Visions of Development,* Pitt Latin America Series, ed. James M. Malloy (Pittsburgh: University of Pittsburgh Press, 1993); Charles Jones, "The Fiscal Motive for Monetary and Banking Legislation in Argentina, Australia and Canada Before 1914," in *Argentina, Australia and Canada: Studies in Comparative Development,* ed. D. C. M. Platt and Guido Di Tella (New York: St. Martin's Press, 1985); Charles Jones, "Commercial Banks and Mortgage Companies," in *Business Imperialism, 1840-1930: An Inquiry Based on British Experience in Latin America,* ed. D. C. M. Platt (Oxford: Clarendon Press, 1977), 17-52; Jones, "The Fiscal Motive"; Andrés Regalsky, "La evolución de la banca privada nacional en Argentina, 1860-1914: Una introducción a su estudio," in *La formación de los bancos centrales en España y América Latina,* ed. Pedro Tedde and Carlos Marichal (Madrid: Banco de España, Servicio de Estudios, 1994), 35-59. Business histories of British banks consider their presence in Latin America; with the exception of David Joslin, *A Century of Banking in Latin America; to Commemorate the Centenary in 1962 of the Bank of London & South America Limited* (New York: Oxford University Press, 1963), usually in passing. Geoffrey Jones, *British Multinational Banking 1830-1990* (Oxford: Clarendon Press, 1993). A more complete bibliography can be found in Carlos Marichal (ed.), "Banca," *América Latina en la historia económica. Boletín de Fuentes,* no. 3 (January-June 1995). Local and commissioned organizational histories of varying quality are available regionally.

26. Carlos Marichal, "Nation-Building and the Origins of Banking in Latin America, 1850-1900" (paper presented at the Economic History Seminar,

Columbia University, May 1998); Stephen Haber, "The Efficiency Conse-
quences of Institutional Change: Financial Market Regulation and Indus-
trial Productivity Growth in Brazil, 1866-1934," in *Latin America and the
World Economy in the Nineteenth and Twentieth Centuries,* ed. John H.
Coatsworth and Alan M. Taylor (Cambridge, Mass.: Harvard University
Press, 1998), 275-322; Anne Gerard Hanley, "Business Finance and the São
Paulo Bolsa, 1886-1917," in *Latin America and the World Economy in the
Nineteenth and Twentieth Centuries,* ed. John H. Coatsworth and Alan M.
Taylor (Cambridge: Harvard University Press, 1998); Anne Gerard Hanley,
"Capital Markets in the Coffee Economy: Financial Institutions and Eco-
nomic Change in São Paulo, Brazil, 1850-1905" (Ph.D. diss., Stanford Uni-
versity, 1995); Noel Maurer, "Banks and Entrepreneurs in Porfirian
Mexico: Inside Exploitation or Sound Business Strategy?" *Journal of Latin
American Studies* 31, no. 2 (May 1999): 331-62.

27. Here, I take the liberty of avoiding the debate about whether Brazil is,
in the late twentieth century, a developed country. For the sake of con-
venience, I simply assert that Brazil was not among the "earlier developing" countries that have come to be loosely understood as members of
the "first world."

28. See, for example, Peláez and Suzigan, *História monetária;* Annibal V. Villela
and Wilson Suzigan, *Política do governo e crescimento da economia brasileira,
1889-1945,* Instituto de Planejamento Econômico e Social. Instituto de
Pesquisas. Monografia, no. 10 (Rio de Janeiro: IPEA/INPES, 1973); Winston Fritsch, *External Constraints on Economic Policy in Brazil, 1889-1930*
(Pittsburgh: University of Pittsburgh Press, 1988).

29. Caio Prado Jr., *História econômica do Brasil* (São Paulo: Editora Brasilense,
1993 [1945]); Celso Furtado, *Formação econômica do Brasil,* 40th ed. (São
Paulo: Ed. Brasiliense, 1993 [1959]).

30. Fritsch, *External Constraints;* Steven Topik, *The Political Economy of the
Brazilian State, 1889-1930,* Latin American Monographs, Institute of Latin
American Studies, The University of Texas at Austin, no. 71 (Austin: Uni-
versity of Texas Press, 1987).

31. Richard Graham, *Patronage and Politics in Nineteenth-Century Brazil* (Stanford, Calif.: Stanford University Press, 1990) and Boris Fausto, *História
geral da civilização brasileira (III) o Brasil republicano (1) Estrutura de
poder e economia (1889-1930)* (Rio de Janeiro: Ed. Bertrand Brasil, 1989),
address regional political autonomy in the nineteenth and twentieth centuries.

32. Luiz Carlos T. D. Prado, "Commercial Capital, Domestic Market and Manufacturing in Imperial Brazil: The Failure of Brazilian Economic Development in the Nineteenth Century" (Ph.D. diss., University of London,
1991); Nathaniel H. Leff, *Underdevelopment and Development in Brazil,* 2
vols. (London and Boston: Allen & Unwin, 1982).

Chapter 2

1. Boris Fausto and Pedro Moacyr Campos, *Estrutura de poder e economia (1889-1930),* vol. 1 of *História geral da civilização brasileira* (São Paulo: Ed. Bertrand Brasil, 1989); Boris Fausto, "Society and Politics," in *Brazil, Empire and Republic,* ed. Leslie Bethell (Cambridge: Cambridge University Press, 1989), 257-308.

2. Covering memorandum to Edwin Montagu Commission Report, 1924, Bank of England Archive, Bank of England, London, File OV103/67 cf14.

3. The felicitous phrase "commodity lottery" is attributed to Carlos Alejandro-Díaz.

4. Celso Furtado, *Formação econômica do Brasil,* 40th ed. (São Paulo: Ed. Brasiliense, 1993 [1959]).

5. Thomas H. Holloway, *The Brazilian Coffee Valorization of 1906* (Madison: Wisconsin Historical Society, 1975); Antônio Delfim Netto, *O problema do café no Brasil,* Ensaios Econômicos, no. 16 (São Paulo: Instituto de Pesquisas Econômicas, 1981).

6. Richard Graham, *Patronage and Politics in Nineteenth-Century Brazil* (Stanford, Calif.: Stanford University Press, 1990); Linda Lewin, *Politics and Parentela in Paraíba: A Case Study of Family-Based Oligarchy in Brazil* (Princeton: Princeton University Press, 1987); Edgard Carone, *A República Velha,* Corpo e Alma do Brasil (São Paulo: Difusão Europeia do Livro, 1970), 153-58; Victor Nunes Leal, *Coronelismo: The Municipality and Representative Government in Brazil,* trans. June Henfrey, Cambridge Latin American Studies, vol. 28 (Cambridge: Cambridge University Press, 1977).

7. Stuart B. Schwartz, *Sugar Plantations in the Formation of Brazilian Society: Bahia 1550-1835,* Cambridge Latin American Studies, vol. 52 (Cambridge: Cambridge University Press, 1985); Thomas Flory, *Judge and Jury in Imperial Brazil, 1808-1871: Social Control and Political Stability in the New State,* Latin American Monographs, no. 53 (Austin: University of Texas Press, 1981); José Murilo de Carvalho, *Teatro de sombras: A política imperial,* Formação do Brasil, vol. 4 (Rio de Janeiro: IUPERJ; Vertice, 1988); Boris Fausto, *Crime e cotidiano: A criminalidade em São Paulo, 1880-1924* (São Paulo, Brasil: Brasiliense, 1984).

8. Even in areas and during periods of most intense agricultural exports, the plantation model of production may not have been as strong as often believed. See B. J. Barickman, *A Bahian Counterpoint: Sugar, Tobacco, Cassava, and Slavery in the Recôncavo, 1780-1860* (Stanford, Calif.: Stanford University Press, 1998); Michael Baud and Kees Koonings, "*A lavoura dos pobres:* Tobacco Farming and the Development of Commercial Agriculture in Bahia, 1870-1930," *Journal of Latin American Studies* 31, no. 2 (May 1999): 287-330; Schwartz, *Sugar Plantations.* According to these authors, most freed people lived and worked small plots of land; they

negotiated the access to land in a variety of arrangements; and they lived subsistent existences. Slaves often lived and worked on the small landholdings, in conditions similar to their impoverished owners. In cities, slaves often engaged in, and profited from, entrepreneurial endeavors. (João José Reis, *Slave Rebellion in Brazil: The Muslim Uprising of 1835 in Bahia*, trans. Arthur Brakel, Johns Hopkins Studies in Atlantic History and Culture [Baltimore: Johns Hopkins University Press, 1993]; Katia M. de Queiros Mattoso, *To Be a Slave in Brazil, 1550-1888*, trans. Arthur Goldhammer [New Brunswick, N.J.: Rutgers University Press, 1986]). Planters and merchants were often the same individuals, by necessity rather than by choice.

9. Eugene Ridings, *Business Interest Groups in Nineteenth-Century Brazil*, Cambridge Latin American Studies, vol. 78 (Cambridge: Cambridge University Press, 1994); Graham, *Patronage and Politics;* Darrell E. Levi, *The Prados of São Paulo, Brazil: An Elite Family and Social Change, 1840-1930* (Athens, Ga.: University of Georgia Press, 1987); Zelia Maria Cardoso de Mello, *Metamorfoses da riqueza, São Paulo, 1845-1895: Contribuição ao estudo da passagem da economia mercantil escravista a economia exportadora capitalista*, Estudos Históricos (São Paulo: Editora Hucitec: Prefeitura do Município de São Paulo, Secretária Municipal de Cultura, 1985).

10. Stephen H. Haber, ed., *How Latin America Fell Behind: Essays in the Economic Histories of Brazil and Mexico, 1800-1914* (Stanford, Calif.: Stanford University Press, 1997), Introduction, 1; Nathaniel H. Leff, *Underdevelopment and Development in Brazil*, 2 vols. (London and Boston: Allen & Unwin, 1982). Of course, one needs to be careful with this assessment, since its implicit comparison is the United States—and the more relevant characterization may be that the United States leapt ahead, rather than that Latin American economies fell behind.

11. Carlos Manuel Peláez, "A Comparison of Long-Run Monetary Behavior and Institutions in Brazil, Europe and the United States," *Journal of European Economic History* 5, no. 2 (fall 1976): 439-50; Carlos Manuel Peláez, "The Establishment of Banking Institutions in a Backward Economy: Brazil, 1800-1850," *Business History Review* 44, no. 4 (winter 1975): 446-72.

12. Leff, *Underdevelopment and Development;* Luiz Carlos T. D. Prado, "Commercial Capital, Domestic Market and Manufacturing in Imperial Brazil: The Failure of Brazilian Economic Development in the Nineteenth Century" (Ph.D. diss., University of London, 1991).

13. Stephen Haber, "Financial Markets and Industrial Development: A Comparative Study of Governmental Regulation, Financial Innovation and Industrial Structure in Brazil and Mexico, 1840-1930," in *How Latin America Fell Behind: Essays on the Economic Histories of Brazil and Mexico, 1800-1914,* ed. Stephen Haber (Stanford, Calif.: Stanford University

Press, 1997), 146-78; William Summerhill, "Transport Improvements and Economic Growth in Brazil and Mexico," in *How Latin America Fell Behind*, 93-117.

14. A comprehensive bibliography can be found in Ângela Pôrto, Lilian de A. Fritsch, and Sylvia F. Padilha, *Processo de modernização do Brasil: 1850-1930, Economia e sociedade, uma bibliografia,* Biblioteca CRESIFUL (Rio de Janeiro: Fundação Casa de Rui Barbosa, 1985). The standard historiographic references are Thomas E. Skidmore, "Historiography of Brazil, 1889-1964, Part I," *Hispanic American Historical Review* 55, no. 4 (November 1975): 716-48; and Thomas E. Skidmore, "Historiography of Brazil, 1889-1964, Part II," *Hispanic American Historical Review* 56, no. 1 (February 1976): 81-109. Many historians focus on common features of cultural and social organization arising from slavery that resulted in a Republic governed by personal and public hierarchies. Others conclude that the strength of the hierarchies resulted in more divisiveness than unity, because of the multiple and competing realms of power contained within hierarchies (Lewin, *Politics and Parentela*). Racial identification was another strong field for debating the definition of Brazil during these years. The unifying and separating experiences of European, African, and indigenous peoples, again under the pervasive reality of slavery, resulted in unending controversy in the racial identification of Brazilians. (Antonio Sérgio Alfredo Guimarães, "'Raça,' racismo e grupos de cor no Brasil," *Estudos Afro-Asiáticos* 27 [April 1995]: 45-63; Thomas E. Skidmore, *Black into White: Race and Nationality in Brazilian Thought* [Durham, N.C.: Duke University Press, 1993 (1974)].) Immigration of peoples from all over the world compounded this controversy: Jeffrey Lesser, *Negotiating National Identity: Immigrants and the Struggle for Ethnicity in Brazil* (Durham, N.C.: Duke University Press, 1999).

15. See Ângela de Castro Gomes and Marieta de Moraes Ferreira, "Primeira República: Um balanço historiográfico," *Estudos Históricos* 4, no. 2 (1989): 244-80. Pôrto, Fritsch, and Padilha's, *Processo de modernização* provides an extensive bibliography to the literature covering these issues.

16. Aspásia Camargo, "La federación sometida, nacionalismo desarrollista e inestabilidad democrática," in *Federalismos latinoamericanos: México, Brasil, Argentina,* ed. Marcello Carmagnani (México: Fondo de Cultura Económica, 1993), 301.

17. Graham, *Patronage and Politics,* and Fausto, "Society and Politics," discuss the nineteenth and twentieth centuries respectively.

18. See, for example, José Murilo de Carvalho, "Armed Forces and Politics in Brazil: 1930-1945," *Hispanic American Historical Review* 62, no. 2 (May 1982): 193-223; see Barbara Weinstein, "Not the Republic of Their Dreams: Historical Obstacles to Political and Social Democracy in Brazil," *Latin American Research Journal* 29, no. 2 (1994): 262-73, on the recent historiographic debates.

19. Hélio Silva, *O primeiro século da República* (Rio de Janeiro: J. Zahar Editor, 1987).

20. Fausto, "Society and Politics."

21. Edgard Carone, *A Primeira República (1889-1930),* 4th ed. (Rio de Janeiro: Editora Bertrand Brasil, 1988), 97-106.

22. Fausto, "Society and Politics," 272; E. Bradford Burns, *A History of Brazil* (New York: Columbia University Press, 1993), 290.

23. Fausto and Campos, *Estrutura de poder* Livro Primeiro. offers an overview of this characteristic of the political landscape.

24. That political interests remained regionally defined should not be interpreted to conclude that they were unchanging. The insightful regional studies by Love, Levine, Wirth, Pang, Ferreira, and others demonstrate dynamic evolution and professionalization of political elites. Joseph L. Love, *São Paulo in the Brazilian Federation, 1889-1937* (Stanford, Calif.: Stanford University Press, 1980); Robert M. Levine, *Pernambuco in the Brazilian Federation, 1889-1937* (Stanford, Calif.: Stanford University Press, 1978); John D. Wirth, *Minas Gerais in the Brazilian Federation, 1889-1937* (Stanford, Calif.: Stanford University Press, 1977); Eul-Soo Pang, *Bahia in the First Brazilian Republic: Coronelismo and Oligarchies, 1889-1934,* Latin American Monographs, 2d ser., vol. 23 (Gainesville, Fla.: University Press of Florida, 1979); Marieta de Moraes Ferreira, *Em busca da idade de ouro: As elites políticas fluminenses na Primeira República (1889-1930)* (Rio de Janiero: Editora UFRJ/Edições Tempo Brasileiro, 1994); Marieta de Moraes Ferreira, "A crise dos comissários de café de Rio de Janeiro" (Tese de mestrado, Niterói, Universidade Federal Fluminense, 1977).

25. Camargo, "Nacionalismo desarrollista," 301.

26. Love, *Brazilian Federation;* Wilson Cano, *Raízes da concentração industrial em São Paulo,* Corpo e Alma do Brasil, no. 53 (Rio de Janeiro: DIFEL/Difusão Editorial, S.A., 1977).

27. Pang, *Bahia,* vi.

28. Joseph L. Love, *Rio Grande do Sul and Brazilian Regionalism, 1882-1930* (Stanford, Calif.: Stanford University Press, 1971), 122.

29. Messrs. Rothschilds and Sons, Rothschilds Archive, London, XI/8/5, 1 September 1911.

30. Celso Castro, *Os militares e a república: Um estudo sobre cultura e ação política* (Rio de Janeiro: J. Zahar Editor, 1995).

31. Fausto, "Society and Politics," 289-301.

32. Wirth, *Minas Gerais;* Levine, *Pernambuco;* Love, *Brazilian Federation;* Love, *Brazilian Regionalism.*

33. Emilia Viotti da Costa, *The Brazilian Empire: Myths and Histories* (Chicago: University of Chicago Press, 1985).

34. On the demographic transitions of the Brazilian population, see Brasil, Instituto Brasileiro de Geografia e Estatística, *Estatísticas históricas do*

Brasil: Séries econômicas, demográficas e sociais 1550 a 1985, 2d ed., Séries Estatísticas Históricas do Brasil, 3, no. 2 (Rio de Janeiro: IBGE, 1990), Section I; Thomas William Merrick and Douglas H. Graham, *Population and Economic Development in Brazil, 1800 to the Present* (Baltimore: Johns Hopkins University Press, 1979). For considerations of modernity in the social and cultural realms, see Roberto da Matta, *The Brazilian Puzzle: Culture on the Borderlands of the Western World,* ed. David J. Hess (New York: Columbia University Press, 1995); Eduardo Jardim de Moraes, "Modernismo revisitado," *Estudos Históricos* 1, no. 2 (1988): 220-38; Carvalho, "The Force of Tradition." On the implications of changing patterns of work and labor organization, see George Reid Andrews, *Blacks & Whites in São Paulo, Brazil, 1888-1988* (Madison: University of Wisconsin Press, 1991); Joel Wolfe, *Working Women, Working Men: São Paulo and the Rise of Brazil's Industrial Working Class, 1900-1955* (Durham, N.C.: Duke University Press, 1993); John D. French, *The Brazilian Workers' ABC: Class Conflict and Alliances in Modern São Paulo* (Chapel Hill: University of North Carolina Press, 1992); Sheldon L Maram, *Anarquistas, imigrantes e o movimento operário brasileiro, 1890-1920,* Coleção Estudos Brasileiros, vol. 34 (Rio de Janeiro: Paz e Terra, 1979).

35. Derived from Winston Fritsch, *External Constraints on Economic Policy in Brazil, 1889-1930* (Pittsburgh: University of Pittsburgh Press, 1988), Table A.6.

36. Thomas H. Holloway, *Immigrants on the Land: Coffee and Society in São Paulo, 1886-1934* (Chapel Hill: University of North Carolina Press, 1980); Nelson Hideiki Nozoe, *São Paulo, Economia cafeeira e urbanização: Estudo da estrutura tributaria e das atividades econômicas na capital paulista (1889-1933),* Série Ensaios Econômicos/IPE/USP, no. 39 (São Paulo: IPE-USP, 1984). Certainly, modernity did not always entail improvement, as Peter L. Eisenberg, *The Sugar Industry in Pernambuco: Modernization without Change, 1840-1910* (Berkeley and Los Angeles: University of California Press, 1974), demonstrates in the case of sugar production practices in the Northeast.

37. Carvalho ("The Force of Tradition") emphasizes the countervailing forces impeding "modernizing" trends.

38. For an interesting recent methodological treatment of the impact of railroads, see William Roderick Summerhill III, "Railroads and the Brazilian Economy Before 1914," (Ph.D. diss., Stanford University, 1995), 289. On coffee price supports see Holloway, *Coffee Valorization;* Steven Topik, *The Political Economy of the Brazilian State, 1889-1930,* Latin American Monographs, Institute of Latin American Studies, The University of Texas at Austin, no. 71 (Austin: University of Texas Press, 1987), Chapter 3; Carlos Manuel Peláez, "Análise econômica do programa brasileiro de sustentação do café—1906-1945: Teoria, política e

medição," *Revista Brasileira de Economia* 25, no. 4 (October–December 1971): 5–211. On public health, see José Murilo de Carvalho, *Os bestializados: O Rio de Janeiro e a República que não foi,* 3d ed. (São Paulo: Cia. das Letras, 1989); Nancy Stepan, *Beginnings of Brazilian Science: Oswaldo Cruz, Medical Research and Policy, 1890-1920* (New York: Science History Publications, 1976).

39. Verena Stolcke, *Coffee Planters, Workers and Wives: Class Conflict and Gender Relations on São Paulo Coffee Plantations, 1850-1980,* St. Antony's/Macmillan Series (Basingstoke, Hampshire: Macmillan in association with St. Antony's College Oxford, 1988); Teresa Meade and Gregory Alonso Pirio, "In Search of the Afro-Amercan 'Eldorado': Attempts by North American Blacks to Enter Brazil in the 1920s," *Luso-Brazilian Review* 25, no. 1 (1988): 85-110.

40. Jeff Lesser, *Welcoming the Undesirables: Brazil and the Jewish Question* (Berkeley and Los Angeles: University of California Press, 1995), Appendix 2; Brasil, *Estatísticas históricas,* Tables 1.6 and 1.8. This represents a minimum estimate because the 1890 census significantly undercounted the population.

41. The majority of immigrants settled in these two states. Thomas H. Holloway, "Immigration in the Rural South," in *Modern Brazil,* ed. Michael L. Conniff and Frank D. McCann Jr. (Lincoln: University of Nebraska Press, 1989).

42. Ruthann Deutsch, "Charting the Archipelago: Urban Systems in Brazil's First Republic" (paper presented at University of Michigan Economic History Seminar, Ann Arbor, March 1994); Summerhill, "Railroads."

43. On the subsidization of European immigration see Lesser, *Negotiating National Identity;* for railroads, see Summerhill, "Railroads."

44. Nícia Villela Luz, *A luta pela industrialização do Brasil 1808-1930,* Corpo e Alma, no. 5 (São Paulo: Ed. Alfa Omega, 1978 [1960]).

45. It mattered little that only a very small share of the Brazilian population and territory participated immediately in this aspect of modernization. Considerations of the peasant millenarian uprisings throughout the First Republic offer excellent examples of the disjunction between exuberant expectations for the small class of rural and urban elite along the South Central littoral of Rio de Janeiro and São Paulo and the reality of life for many poor Brazilians away from developed coastal areas. The literary classic of this genre is Euclides da Cunha, *Rebellion in the Backlands,* trans. Samuel Putnam (Chicago: Phoenix Books, University of Chicago Press, 1944). See also Ralph della Cava, "Brazilian Messianism and National Institutions: A Reappraisal of Canudos and Joaseiro," *Hispanic American Historical Review* 48 (August 1968): 402-20; Todd A. Diacon, *Millenarian Vision, Capitalist Reality: Brazil's Contestado Rebellion, 1912-1916* (Durham, N.C.: Duke University Press, 1991); Robert M. Levine, *Vale of Tears: Revisiting the Canudos Massacre in Northeastern Brazil, 1893-1897* (Berkeley and Los Angeles: University of California Press, 1992).

46. Further, Coatsworth calculates that the gap of per capita income between Brazil and the United States did not change between 1900 and 1913. During these years, the most economically successful of the Republic, Brazilian per capita income remained at 10-11 percent of the U.S. level. John H. Coatsworth, "Economic and Institutional Trajectories in Nineteenth-Century Latin America," in *Latin America and the World Economy in the Nineteenth and Twentieth Centuries,* ed. John H. Coatsworth and Alan M. Taylor (Cambridge, Mass.: Harvard University Press, 1998), Table 1.1.

47. The domestic agriculture markets of the First Republic are surprisingly unexplored. Research suggests that coffee production under post-slavery land arrangements allowed for subsistence production by coffee-working immigrants and that some of this subsistence agriculture was distributed through market mechanisms (Stolcke, *Coffee Planters, Workers and Wives;* Holloway, *Immigrants*). However, these findings do not address local production and distribution outside of the coffee sector. This topic deserves more attention than it has received. Demographic characteristics (population growth and freed labor), industrialization, and urbanization suggest that increased domestic agricultural production (beyond the needs of coffee-producing markets), channeled through market distribution networks, were necessary.

48. Holloway, *Coffee Valorization;* Topik, *Political Economy,* Chapter 3.

49. Fritsch (*External Constraints,* Chapter 7) makes the case that Federal support for coffee only occurred when necessary to maintain revenues and policies sufficient to generate income to service international debt. Whether that was the motivation or not, coffee and rubber producers did receive Federal support (successful in the case of coffee, unsuccessful in the case of rubber) at their crisis points. Wilson Suzigan, *Indústria brasileira: Origem e desenvolvimento* (São Paulo: Brasiliense, 1986), Chapter 4, suggests that whether or not government price supports were economically efficient, they were important in protecting the prosperity of the coffee sector. Since much of the early impetus for industrialization came from coffee, price supports (which artificially sustained coffee revenues) may be viewed as indirect support for industrialization.

50. Robert H. Bates, *Open-Economy Politics: The Political Economy of the World Coffee Trade* (Princeton: Princeton University Press, 1997), Chapter 2.

51. On the development and demise of the rubber commerce, see Barbara Weinstein, *The Amazon Rubber Boom, 1850-1920* (Stanford, Calif.: Stanford University Press, 1983); Warren Dean, *Brazil and the Struggle for Rubber: A Study in Environmental History,* Studies in Environment and History (Cambridge: Cambridge University Press, 1987); Fernando Henrique Cardoso, "Dos governos militares a Prudente-Campos Sales," in

História geral: O Brasil republicano, vol. 2, ed. Boris Fausto (Rio de Janeiro: Ed. Bertrand Brasil, 1989), 15-50.

52. By most accounts, early stages of Brazilian industrial development could be detected by the late nineteenth century, and sustained industrialization was assured by the end of World War I (Suzigan, *Indústria brasiliera*). Although a wide variety of opinions remains on the questions of when and how industrialization became irreversible, scholars generally agree that this was the case by the end of the First Republic, and probably somewhat earlier. The major exception to the consensus that industrialization was entrenched in the Brazilian economy prior to 1930 is Werner Baer, *The Brazilian Economy: Growth and Development,* 4th ed. (Westport, Conn.: Praeger, 1995). He finds that Brazil was not industrializing until the State undertook large-scale, heavy manufacturing in the mid-1950s.

53. Flávio Rabelo Versiani, "Industrialização e economia de exportação antes de 1914," *Revista Brasileira de Economia* 34, no. 1 (January-March 1980): 3-40.

54. Topik, *Political Economy,* 148; Luz, *Luta,* 184-202.

55. Suzigan, *Indústria brasiliera;* Warren Dean, *The Industrialization of São Paulo, 1880-1945,* Latin American Monographs, no. 17 (Austin: Published for the Institute of Latin American Studies by the University of Texas Press, 1969); Cano, *Raízes.*

56. Suzigan, *Indústria brasiliera,* Chapter 4; Albert Fishlow, "Origins and Consequences of Import Substitution in Brazil," in *International Economics and Development: Essays in Honor of Raúl Prebisch,* ed. Luís Eugenio di Marco and Raúl Prebisch (New York: Academic Press, 1972), 311-65.
The value of currency affected the demand for manufactured goods directly through its effect on those deriving income through international trade, and indirectly through the effect on the price of locally produced goods in comparison to their imported alternatives.

57. Michael Bordo, Michael Edelstein, and Hugh Rockoff, "Was Adherence to the Gold Standard a 'Good Housekeeping Seal of Approval' during the Interwar Period?" (paper presented at the Symposium in Honor of Lance E. Davis, November 1998).

58. Joaquim Murtinho, *Idéias econômicas de Joaquim Murtinho: Cronologia, introdução, notas bibliográficas e textos selecionados,* edited by Nícia Villela Luz, Ação e Pensamento da República, no. 5 (Rio de Janeiro: Fundação Casa de Rui Barbosa, 1980). Also see Chapter 3 for a fuller discussion of this issue.

59. Brasil, Ministério da Fazenda, *Relatório apresentado ao Presidente da República dos Estados Unidos do Brasil pelo Ministro de Estado dos Negócios da Fazenda* (Rio de Janeiro: Imprensa Nacional), 1913, vii-x; 1916, 24-26 (hereafter MF, *Relatório*); Banco do Commércio e Indústria de São Paulo, *Relatório e contas da administração,* Banco do Commércio e Indústria de São Paulo que serão aprestedados aos accionistas, (São

Paulo: H. Puchetti), Banco do Commércio e Indústria de São Paulo Archive, São Paulo, 1914, 5; 1928, 3-4; Roberto Simonsen, "As finanças e a indústria" (Conferência realisada no Mackenzie College, São Paulo: 1930).

60. Estimates of the extent of industrialization during the First Republic involve tricky and unreliable extrapolation from data series that began in 1947 backward in time only to 1900. This exercise suggests the following distribution of production:

Percent of GDP in:

	Agriculture	Industry	Other
1900	39.3	13.0	47.7
1930	30.6	16.5	53.9

Note: "Other" includes such sectors as transportation and infrastructure, mining, constructions, and services that supported productive activity.

Extrapolated from Brasil, *Estatísticas históricas,* Table 4.21; Cláudio L.S. Haddad, "Growth of Brazilian Real Output 1900-1947" (Ph.D. diss., University of Chicago), 1974, Table 1. See also Suzigan, Indústria brasiliera, Chapter 4.

61. Suzigan, *Indústria brasiliera.* Topik, *Political Economy,* 149-52, also finds that much of the industrialization and industrial diversification during the 1920s was supported by an increased Federal role in industry through subsidies and industrial development laws. He cites Federal support of mineral exploration, railroads (expanding beyond coffee areas), steel mills, and caustic soda plants. Topik notes that, during the 1920s, specific efforts attracted direct investment by foreign companies. A steel mill law of 1924 and a 1921 revision of subsoil rights (which promoted the entry of Standard Oil of New Jersey and increased exploration of the Amazon) are the major expressions of this new approach by the government (which presages that of the Vargas years).

62. Joseph E. Sweigart, *Coffee Factorage and the Emergence of a Brazilian Capital Market, 1850-1888,* South American and Latin American Economic History (New York: Garland Pub., 1987); Ferreira, "A crise dos comissários."

63. Cláudio Pacheco, *História do Banco do Brasil,* 4 vols. (Rio de Janeiro: Banco do Brasil, 1973), passim; Dênio Nogueira and Carlos Manuel Peláez, "O sistema monetário brasileiro em perspectiva histórica (1800-1906)," in *A moderna história econômica,* ed. Carlos Manuel Peláez and Mircea Buescu (Rio de Janeiro: APEC, 1976), 59-72; Peláez, "Banking Institutions."

64. Peláez, "Long-Run Monetary Behavior," 445-47.

65. David Joslin, *A Century of Banking in Latin America; to Commemorate the Centenary in 1962 of the Bank of London & South America Limited* (New York: Oxford University Press, 1963), 101; Carlos Manuel Peláez and

Wilson Suzigan, *História monetária do Brasil: Análise da política, comportamento e instituições monetárias,* Monografia no. 23 (Instituto de Planejamento Econômico e Social, Instituto de Pesquisas) (Rio de Janeiro: IPEA/INPES, 1976), Chapter 3; Peláez, "Banking Institutions," 465-69.

66. Smaller, local, less-known organizations also established themselves as banks for short periods. The first privately owned Brazilian bank, (the first) Banco Comercial de Rio de Janeiro, organized in 1845.

67. Visconde de Mauá, Bankruptcy deposition, n.d., Autobiografia (Exposição aos credores); Carlos Gabriel Guimarães, "A Casa Bancária Mauá, MacGregor & Cia. (1854-1866) e o império no Brasil" (paper presented at the Segundo Congresso Brasileiro de História Econômica, Universidade Federal Fluminense, Niterói, October 1996).

68. Geoffrey Jones, *British Multinational Banking 1830-1990* (Oxford: Clarendon Press, 1993), 83, 86-87.

69. Stephen Haber, "The Efficiency Consequences of Institutional Change: Financial Market Regulation and Industrial Productivity Growth in Brazil, 1866-1934," in *Latin America and the World Economy in the Nineteenth and Twentieth Centuries,* ed. John H. Coatsworth and Alan M. Taylor (Cambridge, Mass.: Harvard University Press, 1998), 275-322; Haber, "Financial Markets"; Anne Gerard Hanley, "Business Finance and the São Paulo Bolsa, 1886-1917," in *Latin America and the World Economy in the Nineteenth and Twentieth Centuries,* ed. John H. Coatsworth and Alan M. Taylor (Cambridge, Mass.: Harvard University Press, 1998).

70. Gail D. Triner, "Banking and Brazilian Economic Development: 1906-1930" (Ph.D. diss., Columbia University, 1994), Chapter 6.

71. Maxwell J. Fry, *Money, Interest, and Banking in Economic Development,* 2d ed., The Johns Hopkins Studies in Development (Baltimore: Johns Hopkins University Press, 1995).

72. MF, *Relatório,* 1899, iv-v.

Chapter 3

1. Carlos Manuel Peláez and Wilson Suzigan, *História monetária do Brasil: Análise da política, comportamento e instituições monetárias,* Monografia no. 23, Instituto de Planejamento Econômico e Social. Instituto de Pesquisas (Rio de Janeiro: IPEA/INPES, 1976); Paulo Neuhaus, "A MonetaryHistory of Brazil, 1900-1945" (Ph.D. diss., University of Chicago, 1974).

2. Using monetary policy as a financing mechanism compromised its more usual and narrow purposes of managing price stability and (sometimes) managing growth.

3. On Europe, see Charles P. Kindleberger, *A Financial History of Western Europe,* 2d ed. (London and Boston: Allen & Unwin, 1993); Chapters 3 and 9, and the country studies of Part II, refer to these issues in specific settings.

4. Alexander Gerschenkron, *Economic Backwardness in Historical Perspective* (Cambridge, Mass.: Belknap Press of Harvard University Press, 1962); Rondo E. Cameron, ed., *Banking and Economic Development: Some Lessons of History* (New York: Oxford University Press, 1972); Rondo E. Cameron, ed., "Banking in the Early Stages," in *Banking in the Early Stages of Industrialization; a Study in Comparative Economic History,* with the collaboration of Olga Crisp, Hugh T. Patrick, and Richard Tilly (New York: Oxford University Press, 1967).

5. Douglass C. North, *Structure and Change in Economic History* (New York: Norton, 1981), especially Chapter 3; Yoram Barzel, *Economic Analysis of Property Rights* (Cambridge: Cambridge University Press, 1997), Chapters 6 and 9.

6. P. G. M. (Peter George Muir) Dickson, *The Financial Revolution in England: A Study in the Development of Public Credit, 1688-1756* (Aldershot, Hampshire, England: Gregg Revivals; Brookfield, Vt.: distributed in the United States by Ashgate Publ. Co., 1993); Douglass C. North and Barry R. Weingast, "Constitutions and Commitment: The Evolution of Institutions Governing Public Choice in Seventeenth Century England," *Journal of Economic History* 49, no. 4 (December 1989): 803-32; Bray Hammond, *Banks and Politics in America, from the Revolution to the Civil War* (Princeton: Princeton University Press, 1957).

7. Carlos Marichal, "Nation-Building and the Origins of Banking in Latin America, 1850-1900," paper presented at the Economic History Seminar, Columbia University, May 1998.

8. No comprehensive studies of Brazilian tax history exist. However, at least as early as 1898, attempts to introduce legislation for an income tax failed. Brasil, Ministério da Fazenda, *Relatório apresentado ao Presidente da República dos Estados Unidos do Brasil pelo Ministro de Estado dos Negócios da Fazenda* (Rio de Janeiro: Imprensa Nacional), 1898, 26 (hereafter MF, *Relatório*).

9. North, *Structure and Change;* Douglass C. North, *Institutions, Institutional Change, and Economic Performance* (Cambridge: Cambridge University Press, 1990).

10. For further detail on monetary history and the history of monetary policy in Brazil, see Peláez and Suzigan, *História monetária;* Carlos Manuel Peláez, "As conseqüências econômicas da ortodoxia monetária, cambial e fiscal no Brasil entre 1889-1945," *Revista Brasileira de Economia* 5, no. 3 (July-September 1971): 5-82; Neuhaus, "Monetary History"; Gustavo Henrique Barroso Franco, *Reforma monetária e instabilidade durante a transição republicana,* 2d ed. (Rio de Janeiro: Banco Nacional de Desenvolvimento Econômico e Social, 1987), 63-88; Winston Fritsch, *External Constraints on Economic Policy in Brazil, 1889-1930* (Pittsburgh: University of Pittsburgh Press, 1988).

11. Apólices were notes issued by the Treasury and traded in domestic money

markets; they were issued with perpetual maturity and fixed (5 percent) interest rates. Apólices were analogous to British consols. The apólice price data time series only begins in 1893; end-of-month prices are used to calculate the yield-to-maturity (Câmara Syndical dos Corretores de Fundos Públicos da Capital Federal, *Relatórios da Câmara Syndical dos Corretores de Fundos Públicos da Capital Federal,* Instituto Brasileiro de Mercados de Capitais [Rio de Janeiro: Imprensa Nacional], annually 1894-1931 [hereafter Câmara Syndical, *Relatório*]). The problems of working with the price data for long- term Brazilian debt traded in London—the more usual comparison—render the apólice data more reliable. Initial comparison of the available foreign and domestic debt data suggest that their differential remained relatively constant. Both instruments traded actively on the local money markets. Monthly British consol yields and U.S. treasury notes (from 1919, as a point of reference) are taken from the NBER Macro History Data Base, Series 13041 and 13033a, respectively. The yields-to-maturity on all of the price series have been used for comparative purposes.

12. For Brazil, London remained the source of debt flotation longer than it did for many other Latin American countries, and it remained the prominent source throughout the period.

13. Brasil, Instituto Brasileiro de Geografia e Estatística, *Estatísticas históricas do Brasil: Séries econômicas, demográficas e sociais 1550 a 1985,* 2d ed., Séries Estatísticas Históricas do Brasil, no. 3, Rio de Janeiro: IBGE, 1990, Table 10.2 provides these data. To estimate real growth, I derived a price index to cover the entire period. The size of the banking system (defined by sight plus term deposits) also comes from the estimated aggregated (and undocumented) IBGE, *Estatísticas históricas,* rather than the firm-level financial data for 1906 to 1930 that I use in subsequent chapters. Data availability for the years prior to 1906 governed this decision. For reasons of data consistency, M_2 (currency in circulation plus bank deposits) measures the money supply. Bank deposits include demand and term deposits. The Data Appendix more fully explains the data and procedures.

14. See Jeffry A. Frieden, *Debt, Development, and Democracy: Modern Political Economy and Latin America, 1965-1985* (Princeton: Princeton University Press, 1991), Chapter 2, for the skeletal political economy framework that much of this section follows. Frieden also suggests that "an attempt to apply the analytical arguments developed in Chapter 1 to Latin American history . . . would be too controversial" (Frieden, *Debt, Development, and Democracy,* 43). If only I had this insight when I began the project . . .

15. The concept of "the value" of the mil-réis is also problematic. As Leff points out, through the nineteenth, and decreasingly the twentieth century, no single exchange rate equilibrium prevailed for Brazil, given the enormous disparities between the Northeast and South-central economies (Nathaniel H. Leff, "Desenvolvimento econômico e desigualdade

regional: Origens do caso brasileiro," *Revista Brasileira de Economia* 26, no. 1 [January–March 1972]: 3–21). For our purposes here, the exchange rate will be the quoted exchange rate between the pound sterling and the milréis, quoted on the London markets. For practical purposes, that was the exchange rate prevailing in government transactions and international trade.

16. The Brazilian Treasury did not use a third potential approach to monetary policy, implementing capital controls. This was in keeping with international norms of the period and with the inability of the federal government to regulate international capital flows.

17. Robert H. Bates, *Open-Economy Politics: The Political Economy of the World Coffee Trade* (Princeton: Princeton University Press, 1997), Chapter 2; Barry J. Eichengreen, *Golden Fetters: The Gold Standard and the Great Depression, 1919-1939* (New York: Oxford University Press, 1992), 21.

18. Another possible tool of money management, requiring banks to hold in reserve at a central monetary authority a proportion of the deposit base, was not implemented until 1932. Neuhaus, "Monetary History," 114–15.

19. Michael D. Bordo and Hugh Rockoff, "The Gold Standard as a Good Housekeeping Seal of Approval," *Journal of Economic History* 56, no. 2 (1996): 389–428.

20. See Barry J. Eichengreen and Marc Flandreau, eds., *The Gold Standard in Theory and History,* 2d ed. (New York: University Paperbacks, Methuen, 1997), Introduction; Michael D. Bordo and Finn Kydland, "The Gold Standard as a Rule: An Essay in Exploration," *Explorations in Economic History* 32, no. 2 (1995): 423–64.

21. This is the logic by which one would expect an inverse relation between the yield differential and exchange rate.

22. Eichengreen, *Golden Fetters,* 23.

23. Development theories of the mid-twentieth century focused on this aspect of financial development. Ronald I. McKinnon, *Money and Capital in Economic Development* (Washington, D.C.: Brookings Institution, 1973).

24. The concept of a "war of attrition" in which heterogeneous economic groups with vested interests in the actions of the State contend for power in order to advance their interests can help to conceptualize the uses of monetary policy. The model suggests that the inability to establish a permanent "winner" in a war of attrition would delay the ability to stabilize government economic strategy. These delays, while detrimental to overall economic well-being, were rational from the perspective of specific interest groups. As long as the war of attrition in monetary policy remained unresolved, it created a path dependence that reinforced a fiscal war of attrition contending for the distribution and level of public expenditures and revenues, as well as inflationary tendencies. Its continuation served to

discourage investment because of perceived instability. With investment in government bonds low (and control over expenses also low), the State was under greater pressure to issue money (Alberto Alesina and Allen Drazen, "Why Are Stabilizations Delayed?" *American Economics Review* 81, no. 5 [December 1991]: 1170-88). I thank Eugene White for bringing this arti- cle to my attention and Roberto Cortés Conde for helping me to formu- late this context for a "war of attrition." This formulation of the interest groups involved in the war of attrition is somewhat unusual in that it spec- ifies the State as a participant, with identifiable interests, as well as being the "prize" in the war.

25. Eichengreen, *Golden Fetters,* 22-24; Jeffry A. Frieden, "The Dynamics of International Monetary Systems: International and Domestic Factors in the Rise, Reign, and Demise of the Classical Gold Standard," in *The Gold Standard in Theory and History,* ed. Barry J. Eichengreen and Marc Flandreau (New York: Methuen, 1997 [1985]), 207-27. Characterizing the interest groups as producers of tradables in opposition to nontradables is akin to the more traditional classification of debtors and creditors, respectively favoring floating and fixed exchange rates. However, the concerns of pro- ducers for different markets account for the underlying dynamics of the exchange rate debate and recognize that creditors could easily anticipate and circumvent their vulnerability to depreciating currency. I thank Jeff Frieden and the participants of the Yale University Economic History Workshop for these observations.

26. Bates, *Open-Economy Politics,* 36.

27. Frieden, "Dynamics of International Monetary Systems," 222.

28. Eichengreen, *Golden Fetters,* 23.

29. See for example Leopoldo de Bulhões, *Os financistas do Brasil,* Conferên- cia realisada na Biblioteca Nacional no dia 22 de dezembro de 1913 (Rio de Janeiro: Typ. de *Jornal do Commércio,* 1914), 38-39; Roberto Simonsen, "As crises no Brasil" (São Paulo: 1930).

30. Wilson Suzigan, *Indústria brasileira: Origem e desenvolvimento* (São Paulo: Brasiliense, 1986), Chapter 4; Flávio Rabelo Versiani, "Before the Depression: Brazilian Industry in the 1920's," in *Latin America in the 1930's: The Role of the Periphery in World Crisis,* ed. Rosemary Thorp (Oxford: Macmillan Press, 1984), 163-87; Albert Fishlow, "Origins and Consequences of Import Substitution in Brazil," in *International Eco- nomics and Development: Essays in Honor of Raúl Prebisch,* ed. Luís Euge- nio di Marco and Raúl Prebisch (New York: Academic Press, 1972), 311-65.

31. Fiduciary money was that issued by the State without a commitment to establish its intrinsic value with underlying real wealth (gold, hard cur- rency, or other assets). The difference between the "real" value of money and the amount designated on the note is "seigniorage." Economists refer to this implicit transfer of wealth from the public to the State as the

"seigniorage tax." The "inflation tax" or the inflation rate is the transfer implied by the eroding value of debt due to depreciated currency.

32. The interests of Brazilian banks, at the periphery of international capital markets, were in marked contrast to those of, for example, U.S. banks closer to the center of international markets, which had greater interest in and influence on international stability. Frieden, "Dynamics of International Monetary Systems," 220-21.

33. Frieden, "Dynamics of International Monetary Systems," 209, also makes this point.

34. Mancur Olson, *The Logic of Collective Action: Public Goods and the Theory of Groups,* Harvard Economic Studies, vol. 124 (Cambridge, Mass.: Harvard University Press, 1971), 34-39 and Chapter 2.

35. Messrs. Rothschilds and Sons, Rothschilds Archive, London, XI/111/3, 7 January 1907, and XI/8/5, 1 September 1911 (hereafter RAL).

36. Of course, the State faced a constraint in its preference for high exchange rates from the willingness of lenders to continue credit in an environment that they believed to embody overvalued exchange.

37. Neuhaus, "Monetary History," and Peláez and Suzigan, *História monetária.*

38. *Retrospecto Comercial de Journal do Commércio* (Rio de Janeiro: *Jornal de Commércio* de Rodrigues e Cia.), 1887, 14 (hereafter *RC*); Victor Viana, *O Banco do Brasil: Sua formação, seu engradecimento, sua missão nacional* (Rio de Janeiro: Typ. de *Journal do Commércio,* 1926), 27; Caio Prado Jr., *História econômica do Brasil* (São Paulo: Editora Brasilense, 1993 [1945]), Chapter 21.

39. Stephen Haber, "The Efficiency Consequences of Institutional Change: Financial Market Regulation and Industrial Productivity Growth in Brazil, 1866-1934," in *Latin America and the World Economy in the Nineteenth and Twentieth Centuries,* ed. John H. Coatsworth and Alan M. Taylor (Cambridge, Mass.: Harvard University Press, 1998), 283.

40. Rui Barbosa, *Finanças e política da República: Discursos e escriptos* (Rio de Janeiro: Companhia Impressora, 1892), 152, and Humberto Bastos, *Rui Barbosa, Ministro da independência econômica do Brasil (Aspectos econômicas da revolução repúblicana),* 2nd ed. (São Paulo: Liv. Martins Editora S.A., 1951). These initial reforms indicate a continuation of financial policy from the end of the Empire. Within the context of these few years, historiography has overemphasized the extent of rupture in economic policy. Maria Antonieta P. Leopoldi, "Industrial Associations and Politics in Contemporary Brazil: The Associations of Industrialists, Economic Policy-Making and the State with Special Reference to the Period 1930-61" (Ph.D. diss., Cambridge University, 1984), 167, makes the same point in a different context.

41. The banking reform of 1890 and its associated inflation have always been associated with the first Finance Minister of the Republic, Rui Barbosa. Despite his earlier liberal orthodox (and monarchical) policy inclinations,

Barbosa switched ideological leanings with the Republic. Rui Barbosa, *Correspondência de Rui: Seleção e notas* (Personal Correspondence), edited by Affonso Ruy, Coleção de Estudos Brasileiros, Autores Nacionais (Salvador: Centro de Estudos Baianos; Livraria Progresso, n.d.), 2 May 1889, letter to R. Dantas, 52–53; Peláez and Suzigan, *História monetária,* 143; Luís Viana Filho, *A vida de Rui Barbosa,* 11th ed. (Rio de Janeiro, RJ: Editora Nova Fronteira, 1987), 229–33. Leopoldi ("Industrial Associations and Politics," Chapter 5) examines the political narrative on exchange rate management, industrialization, and banking from 1889 to 1906.

42. Brasil, *Coleção das Leis e Decretos,* Decretos nos. 164 and 165; Carlos Manuel Peláez, "Conseqüências econômicas," 14; Franco, *Reforma monetária,* Chapter 4, 63–88. The reform measures signified a complete reversal of Barbosa's earlier ideological commitment to classical liberalism.

43. In the minds of policy makers in the Treasury, concerned with rapid domestic expansion, simply having sufficient currency to meet the requirements of commerce and wage payments was a binding problem. Barbosa, *Discursos,* 13, 156.

44. Peláez and Suzigan, *História monetária,* 144.

45. Steven Topik, *The Political Economy of the Brazilian State, 1889–1930,* Latin American Monographs, Institute of Latin American Studies, the University of Texas at Austin, no. 71 (Austin: University of Texas Press, 1987), 30–32, surveys the controversy of these policies between republicans and monarchists, as well as the generalized allegations of the fraudulent use of banks.

46. Despite the great imprecision of existing price indices prior to 1947, the available information conforms with the expectation that price changes were the inverse of exchange rate fluctuations—and prices were almost double in 1892 their level of 1889. Luis A. V. Catão, "A new wholesale price index for Brazil during the period 1870–1913," *Revista Brasileira de Economia* 46, no. 4 (October–December 1992): 519–33.

47. Eliana A. Cardoso and Rudiger Dornbusch, "Brazilian Debt Crises: Past and Present," in *The International Debt Crisis in Historical Perspective,* ed. Barry Eichengreen and Peter H. Lindert (Cambridge: MIT Press, 1989), 113. The contentious dissolution of the Chamber, currency depreciation with rampant inflation, and the impending crack of the Encilhamento contributed to the overthrow of Brazil's first republican government in 1891. Topik, *Political Economy,* 31.

48. Transactions on the Rio de Janeiro Bolsa de Valores increased by 84 percent, 88 percent, and 45 percent annually from 1889 to 1891, respectively. Eulália Maria Lahmeyer Lobo, "O Encilhamento," *Revista Brasileira de Mercado de Capitais* 2, no. 5 (May–August 1976): 269, 261–301. In 1890, 114 companies listed their shares on the Rio de Janeiro Bolsa, as compared to 58 in 1889 and 61 in 1891. Maria Bárbara Levy, *História da bolsa de valores do Rio de Janeiro* (Rio de Janeiro: IBMEC, 1977), 162–77, Table 17.

49. Levy, *História da bolsa de valores;* Maria Bárbara Levy, "O Encilhamento," in *Economia brasileira: Uma visão histórica,* ed. Paulo Neuhaus (Rio de Janeiro: Ed. Campus, 1980), 191-256. In June 1889, banks accounted for 44 percent of share trading on the Rio de Janeiro Bolsa; and in September 1892, they accounted for 88 percent. Although it would be short-sighted to see the Encilhamento as solely a speculative bubble, financial speculation was a prominent feature of the experience. Lobo, "Encilhamento"; Fishlow, "Origins and Consequences."

50. The Encilhamento is considered further in Chapter 4. Brazilian economic historiography has not tackled the relationship between the Encilhamento and the global recession (ignited by the Barings crisis of 1890 in Argentina). However, to the extent that a global recession impeded capital flows from core to periphery, clearly the diminished ability to sustain international capital in Brazil lessened incentives for remaining on the gold standard.

51. Franco, *Reforma monetária,* 128-30; *RC,* 1890, 1, 5, and 1891, 6. Barbosa (*Discursos,* 163-66) opposed the original organization of the Banco da República as overly restrictive.

52. The collapse of 1892 (the "crack" of the Encilhamento, in contemporary jargon) was not limited to banking. The domestic stock markets and international capital market dealings with Brazil also demonstrated the same collapse. Levy, *História da bolsa de valores,* Chapter 4; Franco, *Reforma monetária.*

53. Franco, *Reforma monetária,* 135-37.

54. Franco, *Reforma monetária,* 129.

55. MF, *Relatório,* 1905, xxii-xxviii; Carlos Manuel Peláez, "The Establishment of Banking Institutions in a Backward Economy: Brazil, 1800-1850," *Business History Review* 44, no. 4 (winter 1975): 446-72.

56. These efforts included trying to require an increased ratio of gold reserves to back banknotes in 1893. Levy, "Encilhamento," 218.

57. Political histories of the First Republic cover these episodes. See, for example, Boris Fausto and Pedro Moacyr Campos, *Estrutura de poder e economia (1889-1930),* vol. 1 of *História geral da civilização brasileira* (São Paulo: Ed. Bertrand Brasil, 1989); Edgard Carone, *A República Velha,* Corpo e Alma do Brasil, no. 31 (São Paulo: Difusão Europeia do Livro, 1970).

58. From 1900 to 1906, a period when Brazil was not involved in international military conflict, military expenditures accounted for 10-15 percent of federal expenses (Brasil, *Estatísticas históricas,* Tables 10.1 and 10.2. Data are not available prior to 1900). National military forces were invoked against the civilian population and in suppressing local uprisings.

59. Thomas H. Holloway, *The Brazilian Coffee Valorization of 1906* (Madison: Wisconsin Historical Society, 1975); Steven Topik, *Political Economy,* Chapter 3; Winston Fritsch, *External Constraints,* Table A.6. Despite the

depression in coffee export profits, the trade balance improved, largely because of the short-lived boom in the price and volume of rubber exports during these years.

60. Banco do Brasil [Banco da República], *Relatório do Banco do Brasil apresentado à Assembléia Geral dos accionistas na sessão ordinaria,* Banco do Brasil Archives, Rio de Janeiro, 1896, 12 (hereafter BB, Relatório).

61. Fausto and Campos, *Estrutura de poder,* Chapters 1 and 2.

62. *RC,* 1898, 19.

63. Joaquim Murtinho, *Idéias econômicas de Joaquim Murtinho: Cronologia, introdução, notas bibliográficas e textos selecionados,* Ação e Pensamento da República, no. 5, ed. Nícia Villela Luz (Rio de Janeiro: Fundação Casa de Rui Barbosa, 1980), editor's introduction. Murtinho's economic ideology was substantially influenced by J. P. Wileman, the longtime British economic observer in Brazil. J. P. Wileman, *Brazilian Exchange: The Study of an Inconvertible Currency* (New York: Greenwood Press, 1969 [1896]), offered the most detailed assessment of his views on Brazilian finance.

64. One measure that Murtinho took to induce deflation was to simply burn currency. Bulhões, *Financistas do Brasil,* 36.

65. *RC,* 1900, 14-15, and 1901, 9, 21-22.

66. Neuhaus, "Monetary History," 11.

67. Fritsch, *External Constraints,* 10.

68. *O Diario Popular,* 26 January 1899 and 20 February 1899 (cited in Flávio A. M. de Saes, *Crédito e bancos no desenvolvimento da economia paulista: 1850-1930* [São Paulo: Instituto de Pesquisas Econômicas, 1986], 133).

69. Holloway, *Coffee Valorization,* 32.

70. Bates, *Open-Economy Politics,* 37.

71. Even so, the difficulties of merging state political interests left the coffee price-support scheme a program of the state government of São Paulo.

72. Marcelo de Paiva Abreu, "A dívida pública externa do Brasil, 1824-1931," *Estudos Econômicos,* Instituto de Pesquisas Econômicas, Universidade de São Paulo, 15, no. 2 (1985): Tables A.1-A.4.

73. MF, *Relatório,* 1906, 83; Bank of London and South America, Letters from London to Rio de Janeiro, Archives of the Bank of London and South America, University College, London, G3/9, 30 July 1908 and 28 January 1909 (hereafter BOLSA, Letters).

74. Peláez and Suzigan, *História monetária,* 164.

75. Peláez, "Conseqüências econômicas," 22.

76. When this occurred in 1908, the office suspended operations between May and September and the rate rose to 18 pence/mil-réis. After this experience, the office's funding was increased, as was the official parity (from 15 to 16 pence/mil-réis).

77. This interpretation of the Banco do Brasil's activities is clearly different from Fritsch's, which focused on the bank's role in public finance with suf-

ficient intensity that it did not serve any counter-cyclical purpose. Fritsch, *External Constraints*, 17-18.

78. Steven Topik, "A emprêsa estatal em um regime liberal: o Banco de Brasil—1905-1930," *Revista Brasileira de Mercado Capitais* 7, no. 19 (1981): 70-83.

79. *RC*, 1905, 79; MF, *Relatório*, 1904, x, and 1906, vi; Edmond Théry, *Projecto de reforma monetária e de creação dum banco emissor no Brasil* (Rio de Janeiro: Typ. D'os Annaes-Revista de Litteratura, Arte, Sciencia e Indústria, 1905), 69-71; Topik, *Political Economy*, 39. The functions that the bank took on included: depository for (gold) tariffs and sole agent for conducting foreign exchange transactions for the Treasury (including the foreign exchange transactions of the Conversion Office).

80. MF, *Relatório*, 1905, 74-79; *RC*, 1905, 78-82. The bank's role as a lender of last resort was informal at this time.

81. Individual states governed and regulated banks chartered within their own states. Foreign banks established before 1905 also had national banking rights; but their activities were somewhat more constrained than the Banco do Brasil's, because they were strictly commercial in nature. Domestic banks could establish themselves in multiple states by acquiring charters and allocating reserves and capital to branches in different states. Some banks did this during the First Republic.

82. These activities were also sources of revenue for the bank.

83. BB, *Relatório*, 1905, 5.

84. BB, *Relatório*, 1905.

85. MF, *Relatório*, 1906.

86. Table A.12 and Abreu, "Dívida pública," Tables A.1-A.4.

87. Here, I only introduce the topic in order to substantiate that the Banco do Brasil profoundly affected the structure of private banking. The actual business structure and practices of banking are discussed in Chapters 4-6.

88. Neuhaus, "Monetary History," 32.

89. International borrowing had quite heavily supported infrastructure investment during the previous years. RAL, XI/111/44, 31 December 1909 and 22 February 1911; Abreu, "Dívida pública"; Neuhaus, "Monetary History," 31.

90. MF, *Relatório*, 1920, 122.

91. While exports began to recover, slowly from 1915, imports continued to decline. In fact, the nominal value of imports did not reach their 1912 level again until 1927. Brasil, *Estatísticas históricas*, Table 11.2.

92. Peláez, "Conseqüências econômicas," 50; Peláez and Suzigan, *História monetária*, 164; Annibal V. Villela and Wilson Suzigan, *Política do governo e crescimento da economia brasileira, 1889-1945*, Instituto de Planejamento Econômico e Social. Instituto de Pesquisas. Monografia, no. 10 (Rio de Janeiro: IPEA/INPES, 1973), 123; Neuhaus, "Monetary History," 34.

93. Bordo and Kydland, "Rule"; Bordo and Rockoff, "Seal of Approval."
94. RAL, 1914, XI/111/65.
95. *RC*, 1914, 136-38. Neuhaus ("Monetary History," 34) states that the widespread acceptance of the concept of the gold standard, because of the continuing reaction against the government-induced inflation of the Encilhamento, delayed its suspension beyond a reasonable period.
96. These effects on financial markets influenced the debate among economic historians of whether the external shock of World War I stimulated industrialization in Brazil (and elsewhere in Latin America). While the volume of industrial output may have increased, due to invoking previously underutilized plant capacity, the closing of capital markets inhibited the ability to construct new industrial capacity. Suzigan, *Indústria brasiliera,* Chapter 4.
97. MF, *Relatório,* 1913, vi-x.
98. Neuhaus, "Monetary History," 35-42; Peláez and Suzigan, *História monetária,* 206-07; Villela and Suzigan, *Política do governo,* 140-42. As it would turn out, inconvertible currency issues continued until 1926.
99. *RC*, 1914, 94.
100. *RC*, 1914, 140.
101. In November 1915, the Treasury issued 350,000 contos to cover its operating expense deficits; 50,000 contos of the amount were placed with the Banco do Brasil at 3 percent interest to fund the rediscount facility, for the purpose of lending to "develop national production" (BB, *Relatório,* 1915, 15; see also *RC*, 1915, 148). Neuhaus identifies this policy as the beginning of credit regulation by the bank (Neuhaus, "Monetary History," 32). Fritsch (*External Constraints,* 39) finds that the

> . . . government's view began to reflect the growing complaints about what contemporaries referred to as the private banks system's 'inelasticity,' i.e., its limited capacity for credit creation resulting from the high reserve ratios and its inadequate response to the financial needs of the real sector. . . . The legacy of these complaints, from 1915 onwards, was the notion that the Banco do Brasil could play an important part in minimizing the inadequacies of the private banking system by implementing the still unused central banking powers conferred by its 1905 statutes [i.e., rediscounting and branching].

102. Peláez and Suzigan (*História monetária,* 165) point to the support of the textile industry in this move.
103. *RC*, 1916, 22.
104. *RC*, 1919, 138; MF, *Relatório,* 1916, 24-26; 1918, viii; 1919, xxxiv-xxxv.
105. MF, *Relatório,* 1921.
106. This experience has earned the moniker the "dance of the millions," and it affected nearly all economies that derived significant revenues from

exporting primary commodities. Carlos Marichal, *A Century of Debt Crises in Latin America: From Independence to the Great Depression, 1820-1930* ([Princeton: Princeton University Press, 1989], Chapter 7). In Brazil, the aftereffects of the dance of the millions had been exacerbated by an inflationary purchase of the domestic gold output by the federal government in 1918. Neuhaus, "Monetary History," 50.

107. Sandra Jatahy Pesavento, *O cotidiano da República: Elites e povo na virada do século,* Síntese Rio-Grandense, no. 3 (Porto Alegre, R.S.: Editora da Universidade, Universidade Federal do Rio Grande do Sul, 1990), 19.

108. Whitaker had been a founder of the Banco Commercial do Estado de São Paulo in 1912. Saes, *Crédito e bancos,* 138, 149.

109. *RC,* 1916, 23.

110. Banco do Brasil, Cartas Particulares dos Presidentes, Banco do Brasil Archives, Rio de Janeiro, 20 October 1922 (hereafter BB, Cartas).

111. As a very rough estimate, deficits represented 3 percent of Brazilian GDP. Some historians have advanced arguments that supporting coffee prices and government expenditure *was* developmentalist in nature, but that was not evident to contemporaries (nor is it universally accepted among historians). Fishlow, "Origins and Consequences"; Suzigan, *Indústria brasiliera.*

112. BB, Cartas, 20 June 1921.

113. MF, *Relatório,* 1920, 141-42. The original funding limit of the Rediscount Office was 100,000 contos (approximately £4 million).

114. Topik, *Political Economy,* 48-49. With an eye to fiscal austerity, the government also introduced the first income tax in 1923, with the first tax collections in 1924. Even so, the income tax remained an effective means for funding State expenditure; by the end of the Republic, it funded less than 3 percent of the federal government's expenditure. See also BOLSA, Letters, G3/12, 1 June 1923.

115. MF, *Relatório,* 1923, 292-93.

116. The exchange rate was 5.94 pence/mil-réis in January 1923, and it declined during the year (BB, *Relatório,* 1923, 5-18 and 21; MF, *Relatório,* 1922, 126; *RC,* 1923, 144; Neuhaus, "Monetary History," 65). Another important reform with large and interesting monetary implications, the transfer of coffee price supports from federal responsibility to the state of São Paulo, will be discussed in Chapter 7.

117. Banco do Brasil, *Estátutos do Banco do Brasil,* Banco do Brasil Archives, Rio de Janeiro (Rio de Janeiro: Imprensa Nacional) 1922, Arts. 9 and 11 (hereafter BB, *Estatútos*); *RC,* 1923, 48.

118. The directors of the Issue and Exchange Offices and the president of the bank were political appointments of the president of Brazil.

119. Peláez and Suzigan (*História monetária,* 184-89) and Neuhaus ("Monetary History," 79) find a fundamental difference of goals between the president of Brazil, whose objective was monetary stability, and the Treasury minister and president of the Banco do Brasil, who were committed to

instituting a monetary and banking system responsive to the demand for "real bills" in the private sector.

120. *RC,* 1922, 29; Cincinato Braga, *Brasil novo,* vol. 2 (Rio de Janeiro: Imprensa Nacional, 1930), Chapter 8; BOLSA, Letters, G3/12, 16 August 1923; Neuhaus, "Monetary History," 78.

121. Bank of London and South America, Telegrams between London and Rio de Janeiro, Archives of the Bank of London and South America, University College, London, G3/12, 1 February 1923 and 7 December 1923; Bank of England, Bank of England Archives, London (hereafter BoE), OV 130/67 cf14, 1923 (cover memorandum for the Montagu Report). Continuing political uncertainty of a different nature was also expressed in an uprising in São Paulo in 1924. In all, the federal government had only shaky claims to national political control.

122. Neuhaus finds that the deflationary goal of the president of Brazil and the goal to implement a real bills doctrine in banking of the minister of Finance and the president of the Banco do Brasil were the source of the difference between rhetoric and results at this time. Neuhaus, "Monetary History," 65-68.

123. *RC,* 1920, 116-18, and 1923, 31.

124. RAL, 111/309 (British Financial Mission, by Edwin Montagu and the members of the mission, Report by British Financial Mission to Brazil to Messrs. Rothschild, Messrs. Baring Bros. & Co Ltd. and Messrs. J. Henry Schroder & Co). Fritsch (*External Constraints,* Chapter 5) and Winston Fritsch ("1924," *Pesquisa e Planejamento Econômica* 10, no. 3 [(December 1980)]: 713-44) conclude that the British mission headed by Edwin Montagu imposed onerous deflationary conditions on Brazilian monetary and fiscal policies as the conditions necessary for new borrowing in the London market. The mission occurred in association with efforts to undertake new borrowing. Consistent with this goal, its recommendations were strongly deflationary in nature. However, the conditions also accorded closely with Bernardes's policy preferences. Their only point of serious disagreement was the privatization of the Banco do Brasil. Given this broad base of acceptance and the timing of the invitation to the mission from Brazil, a conclusion that the Montagu Mission served to validate, and give credibility to, existing policy preferences seems at least as justifiable as a conclusion of the imposition of external constraints. A revised conclusion that the Bernardes government relied upon the Montagu commission to lend credibility for its desired policy direction is very similar to Drake's conclusions with respect to other missions by money doctors in Latin America, notably those of Edwin Kemmerer. Paul W. Drake, *The Money Doctor in the Andes: The Kemmerer Missions, 1923-1933* (Durham, N.C.: Duke University Press, 1989).

125. Carlos Inglez de Souza, *A solução da crise econômica brasileira,* Conferência realisado em 18 de julho de 1925. Associação Commercial de São

Paulo (São Paulo: Casa Editora "A Renascença," 1925), 4-5. By the mid-1920s, the intensity and importance of popular political interests increased. Michael L Conniff, *Urban Politics in Brazil: The Rise of Populism, 1925-1945,* Pitt Latin American Series (Pittsburgh: University of Pittsburgh Press, 1981).

126. The transfer of responsibility for coffee price supports from the federal level to the state of São Paulo was the major contribution to diminished federal expenditure. The profound political implications of this transfer are discussed in Chapter 7.

127. In 1924 and 1925 total production was virtually stagnant, and industry (especially textiles) suffered the most serious slowdown. The increase in bankruptcies continued at high levels into 1926. *RC,* 1924, 17-19, 24; Peláez and Suzigan, *História monetária,* 185.

128. Neuhaus, "Monetary History," 71-74.

129. Peláez and Suzigan, *História monetária,* 183-84. International monetary practices also gave support to this move. The economies of major capital-exporting countries tried to reestablish the pre–World War I gold standard mechanisms and capital market structure. These efforts to reinstitute prior practices were seen as measures to reestablish their financial and political credibility. Eichengreen, *Golden Fetters,* Chapter 2.

130. Neuhaus, "Monetary History," 81-82.

131. Banco do Brasil, Atas dos Directores, Banco do Brasil Archives, Rio de Janeiro, 10 October 1929.

132. Neuhaus ("Monetary History," 81-82) argues, without specific data, that the credit contraction at the Banco do Brasil in 1928 triggered the recession. Credit data presented in Chapter 4 find that the (real) volume of Banco do Brasil credit expanded by 12 percent during 1928.

133. BB, *Relatório,* 1929; *RC,* 1930.

134. This led to another house call from a British money doctor in 1930. Otto Niemeyer led a mission that once again offered the orthodox prescription of balanced budgets, privatization of public concerns, an independent central bank, and currency convertibility. Otto Niemeyer, *Reorganization of Brazilian National Finance; Report Submitted to the Brazilian Government* (Rio de Janeiro: British Chamber of Commerce, 1931); BoE, OV9/294 cf. 7, letter dated 23 March 1931 from Otto Niemeyer to Minister of Finance José Maria Whitaker. Between the time of inviting the mission and the receipt of its report, the world depression had begun and Getúlio Vargas's "revolution" had ended the Republic. Vargas's experience as Treasury minister during the previous effort to establish the gold standard and his personal history (from Rio Grande do Sul, a state not tied to export wealth as intently as São Paulo) reinforced his initial statements supporting orthodox monetary policy.

135. Marcelo de Paiva Abreu, "Crise, crescimento e modernização autoritária: 1930-1945," in *A ordem do progresso: Cem anos de política econômica*

republicana, 1889-1989 (Rio de Janeiro: Ed. Campus, 1990), 74; Neuhaus, "Monetary History," 90-95.

136. Abreu, "Crise, crescimento e modernização"; Fishlow, "Origins and Consequences." Expansive programs continued through the early years of the Vargas regime. In 1932 and 1933 (partly in response to a serious political uprising in São Paulo), however, three measures inserted federal regulation into banking even more emphatically than previously. The Banking Mobilization Office (Caixa de Mobilização Bancária, or CAMOB) opened within the Banco do Brasil to serve as a lender of last resort for failing banks. Further, a usury rate of 12 percent was legislated; it became illegal (until 1964) to charge any higher interest rate for credit. Finally, in 1933, the Treasury imposed reserve requirements on banks. Banks were required to maintain a proportion of their deposits in reserve accounts with the central monetary authority, initially the Banco do Brasil. These last two measures counterbalanced other expansionary programs.

137. The implications for regional political economy of these changes were important, and they will be considered in Chapter 7.

138. Braga, *Brasil novo,* vol. 2, Chapter 12; Gustavo Barroso, *Brasil: Colonia de banqueiro (História dos emprestimos de 1824 a 1934),* 2d ed. (Rio de Janeiro: Civilização Brasileira, S.A., 1934).

139. RAL, XI/111/29, 16 July 1914, and XI/142/12, 9 January 1914; Peláez and Suzigan, *História monetária,* 165.

Chapter 4

1. The available firm-level data represent approximately 90-95 percent of the total banking system, according to the available estimates. See Data Appendix.

2. Carlos Manuel Peláez and Wilson Suzigan, *História monetária do Brasil: Análise da política, comportamento e instituições monetárias,* Monografia no. 23, Instituto de Planejamento Econômico e Social. Instituto de Pesquisas (Rio de Janeiro: IPEA/INPES, 1976); Gustavo Henrique Barroso Franco, *Reforma monetária e instabilidade durante a transição republicana,* 2d ed. (Rio de Janeiro: Banco Nacional de Desenvolvimento Econômico e Social, 1987).

3. Stephen Haber, "The Efficiency Consequences of Institutional Change: Financial Market Regulation and Industrial Productivity Growth in Brazil, 1866-1934," in *Latin America and the World Economy in the Nineteenth and Twentieth Centuries,* ed. John H. Coatsworth and Alan M. Taylor (Cambridge, Mass.: Harvard University Press, 1998), 275-322; Steven Topik, "Brazil's Bourgeois Revolution?" *The Americas* 48, no. 2 (October 1991): 245-71; Albert Fishlow, "Origins and Consequences of Import Substitution in Brazil," in *International Economics and Development:*

Essays in Honor of Raúl Prebisch, ed. Luís Eugenio di Marco and Raúl Prebisch (New York: Academic Press, 1972), 311-65.

4. Maria Bárbara Levy, *História da bolsa de valores do Rio de Janeiro* (Rio de Janeiro: IBMEC, 1977), 171; Câmara Syndical dos Corretores de Fundos Públicos da Capital Federal, *Relatórios da Câmara Syndical dos Corretores de Fundos Públicos da Capital Federal,* Instituto Brasileiro de Mercados de Capitais (Rio de Janeiro: Imprensa Nacional), 1905 (hereafter Câmara Syndical, *Relatório*).

5. The Commercial Code of 1890 (Brasil, *Coleção das Leis e Decretos,* Decretos 164 of January 1890 and 434 of July 1891 [hereafter Leis e Decretos]) provided for limited-liability corporations, without legislative approval. It also mandated regularly published financial statements (balance sheets and income statements). The limitation of shareholder liability to the amount of the value of the investment, rather than risking the full amount of personal worth, was an incentive for investment from a wider pool of participants than the traditional family and friends. The ability to sell shares without the firm's consent was a further incentive. Although these activities of dynamic capital markets were slow to develop, in practice, they were of fundamental institutional importance. Anne Gerard Hanley, "Business Finance and the São Paulo Bolsa, 1886-1917," in *Latin America and the World Economy in the Nineteenth and Twentieth Centuries,* ed. John H. Coatsworth and Alan M. Taylor (Cambridge, Mass.: Harvard University Press, 1998), 115-38; Gail D. Triner, "Banking and Brazilian Economic Development: 1906-1930" (Ph.D. diss., Columbia University, 1994), Chapter 6. See Levy, *História da bolsa de valores,* Chapter 4, for an enumeration of the increase in incorporated companies on the Rio de Janeiro Bolsa de Valores.

6. Haber, "Efficiency Consequences," 283.

7. Câmara Syndical, *Relatório,* 1905, 28.

8. The purchase of stocks and bonds funded the corporate enterprises of banks' founders and fueled general speculation.

9. That Treasury-funded banks might have used idle resources to purchase apólices is no small irony.

10. The major arbitrage opportunities for Brazilians occurred in price differentials between the pound sterling/mil-réis exchange rate in the London and Rio de Janeiro markets.

11. The exchange rate fell steadily from 23 pence/mil-réis in November 1990 to a low of 10.2 pence in July 1892 (Table A.10). As early as February 1892, the Federal Treasury was preparing to provide support to banks. *Retrospecto Comercial de Journal do Commércio* (Rio de Janeiro: *Jornal de Commércio* de Rodrigues e Cia.) 1892, 6 (hereafter *RC*).

12. Under this arrangement, an investor would subscribe to acquire shares but would be required to pay into the corporation only a fixed percentage of the price at which the shares were issued. Although legally committed to

pay the remainder when "called," the ability to call in capital effectively diminished for a failing organization, as investors became increasingly reluctant to risk additional resources. *RC,* 1891, 7; Câmara Syndical, *Relatório,* 1896, 44-47.

13. For example, the Banco Commércio e Indústria de São Paulo (Comind) issued two capital calls during 1892. They were successful enough to sustain the bank through the Encilhamento, though some shareholders forfeited their shares when unable to make payment to the bank. Banco do Commércio e Indústria de São Paulo, *Relatório e contas da administração Banco do Commércio e Indústria de São Paulo que serão aprestendados aos accionistas,* (São Paulo: H. Puchetti), Banco do Commércio e Indústria de São Paulo Archive, São Paulo, 1892, 4 (hereafter Comind, *Relatório*).

14. Brasil, Ministério da Fazenda, *Relatório apresentado ao Presidente da República dos Estados Unidos do Brasil pelo Ministro de Estado dos Negócios da Fazenda* (Rio de Janeiro: Imprensa Nacional), 1898, 195 (hereafter MF, *Relatório*).

15. Banco do Brasil, Atas dos Directores, Banco do Brasil Archives, Rio de Janeiro, 14 February 1899 (hereafter BB, Atas).

16. As two examples, the Banco da República acquired the credit portfolio of Banco Industrial Brasileiro and equity shares of Banco do Brasil e Norte Americano. BB, Atas, 14 September 1898 and 21 October 1898.

17. Leis e Decretos, Decretos Nos.1359, 354, and 359, April 1893, 16 and 30 December 1895, respectively.

18. MF, *Relatório,* 1907, xvi; Câmara Syndical, *Relatório,* 1899, 7-11 (and most subsequent years); Levy, *História da bolsa de valores,* 193-262, passim; Eulália Maria Lahmeyer Lobo, "O Encilhamento," *Revista Brasileira de Mercado de Capitais* 2, no. 5 (May-August 1976): 261-301; Franco, *Reforma monetária,* Chapter 4.

19. Exchange brokers actively lobbied to maintain this protection; debate continued throughout the First Republic on this issue. The topic is prominent in their first annual reports. Câmara Syndical, *Relatório,* 1894, 15-16, and 1895, 13-14, and it reappears almost every year throughout the period.

20. The support provided to failing banks by the purchase of illiquid assets by the Banco da República is discussed below.

21. Joaquim Murtinho, *Idéias econômicas de Joaquim Murtinho: Cronologia, introdução, notas bibliográficas e textos selecionados,* Ação e Pensamento da República, no. 5. ed. Nícia Villela Luz (Rio de Janeiro: Fundação Casa de Rui Barbosa, 1980), Introduction, 34-40.

22. MF, *Relatório,* 1899, iv-v, and 1901, xxvii.

23. The Banco Hypothecário had consolidated the failed mortgage portfolios of the (third) Banco do Brasil and the Banco dos Estados Unidos do Brasil in 1890.

24. *RC,* 1900, 12-15; MF, *Relatório,* 1900, vi-vii, and 1901, xliii-xliv; Banco do Brasil [Banco da República], *Relatório do Banco da República apresentado à Assembléia Geral dos accionistas na sessão ordinaria,* Banco do Brasil Archives, Rio de Janeiro, 1900-01, 50-55, 68 (hereafter BB, Relatório). The Banco da República, *Relatório,* attributes the failure to deficiencies in the structure of the 1892 merger. The liquidity problems of the Banco da República had been recurrent. In March 1899, the Treasury had lent the bank money in order to liquidate its debt, and in April 1899, trading of Banco da República's shares on the stock exchange had been halted. "Exposição do Ministro da Fazenda," 1899; Annex to BB, [Banco da República], *Relatório,* 1899.

25. Câmara Syndical, *Relatório,* 1901, 12-15; Leopoldo de Bulhões, *Os financistas do Brasil,* Conferência realisada na Biblioteca Nacional no dia 22 de dezembro de 1913 (Rio de Janeiro: Type de *Jornal do Commércio,* 1914); U.S. Consular Reports, 21 September 1900, no.115. See also Winston Fritsch, *External Constraints on Economic Policy in Brazil, 1889-1930* (Pittsburgh: University of Pittsburgh Press, 1988), 8-9; Paulo Neuhaus, "A Monetary History of Brazil, 1900-1945" (Ph.D. diss., University of Chicago, 1974), 5-6.

26. Of course, this interpretation of the failure of the Banco da República as a liquidity crisis is something of a tautology. A bankruptcy is, by its strict definition, the inability to meet current payment obligations. Therefore, all bankruptcies could be viewed as liquidity crises during which creditors lose patience.

27. Rafael Luís Vieira Souto, "O último relatório da Fazenda, 1899," in *Idéias econômicas de Joaquim Murtinho,* ed. Nícia Villela Luz (Rio de Janeiro: Fundação Casa de Rui Barbosa, 1980), 438-39.

28. BB [Banco da República], *Relatório,* 1900/01 (combined), 82.

29. Felisbello Freire, *História do Banco do Brasil* (Rio de Janeiro: O Economist, 1907), 201.

30. Approximating the significance of this problem, as a proportion of their total credit, the share of the Banco da República's and Banco do Brasil's illiquid assets was:

Banco da República	1898	66%
	1899	72%
Banco do Brasil	1906	46%
	1907	18%
Average	1906-30	7%

Source: derived from BB, *Relatório,* 1906-30 and BB [Banco da República], *Relatórios,* 1898 and 1899.

31. The value of selected income earning assets of the Banco da República (par vs. market value, in thousands of contos), as of 31 October 1900, was:

	Par	Current Market	Market, % Par
Investment securities & apólices in reserve fund	106.4	66.9	62.9
Discounted notes	25.1	16.2	64.5
Guaranteed operating loans	73.0	28.2	38.6
Industrial loans	39.2	23.6	60.2
Total of above	243.7	134.9	55.4

Source: BB [Banco da República], *Relatório*, 1900/01, 82.

32. BB [Banco da República], *Relatório,* 1900/01, 82.
33. No board of directors meetings occurred between 16 October 1900 and 4 July 1906; at least no minutes from directors meetings have been preserved.
34. *RC,* 1903, 51-54, 72.
35. *RC,* 1903, 72.
36. MF, *Relatório,* 1904.
37. Campos Sales's considerable personal wealth derived from extensive family coffee-plantation holdings in São Paulo. María Zelia de Camargo de Villegas, *El gobierno de Manuel Ferraz de Campos Salles, el restaurador de las finanzas (1898-1902)* (Caracas: Instituto de Altos Estudios de América Latina, Centro Abreu e Lima de Estudios Brasileños; Universidad Simon Bolivar, 1993).
38. *RC,* 1905, 78. Expectations of failure on the part of British bankers, due to anticipated incompetence and lack of resources, emphasized the institutional fragility of these arrangements. Bank of London and South America, Letters from London to Rio de Janeiro, Archives of the Bank of London and South America, University College, London, G3/8, 13 February 1907 (hereafter BOLSA, Letters).
39. *RC,* 1906, 80.
40. *RC,* 1917, 100.
41. MF, *Relatório,* 1923, xvi.
42. Roberto Simonsen, "As finanças e a indústria," Conferência realisada no Mackenzie College, São Paulo, 1930.
43. *RC,* 1926, 43.
44. Duncan Ross, "Commercial Banking in a Market-Oriented Financial System: Britain Before the War," *Economic History Review* 49, no. 2 (May 1996): 314-34, offers a good discussion on the types of banks and the differences in the businesses they conducted.

45. The rights and subsidies that some state governments accorded to the major banks within their states in order to promote agricultural and mortgage lending were an important exception to the constraint against long-term lending. I take up this subject in Chapter 7.

46. Comind, *Relatório*, 1894, 5-6; Anne Gerard Hanley, "Capital Markets in the Coffee Economy: Financial Institutions and Economic Change in São Paulo, Brazil, 1850-1905" (Ph.D. diss., Stanford University, 1995), Chapter 3.

47. Banco do Brasil, *Estátutos do Banco do Brasil,* Banco do Brasil Archives, Rio de Janeiro (Rio de Janeiro: Imprensa Nacional) 1905 Título III, Art. 5 (nos. 4 and 8) continued in amended *Estátutos* of 1916 and 1921, Arts. 2 and 3 (no. 1) (hereafter BB, *Estátutos*). After 1921 the restriction on loans was "subject to bank policy"; the restrictions on notes remained for four months. See also BB, Atas, 12 April 1909. Banco de Crédito Real de Minas Gerais, *Livros das Atas dos Assembléias Gerais,* Crédito Real Archive, Juiz de Fora, Minas Gerais, 6 September 1912, identifies the bank's credit maturity guidelines (which were the same as the Banco do Brasil's) and establishes the right for the bank to exercise its discretion to renew credit. See also Banco de Crédito Real de Minas Gerais, "Estátutos do Banco de Crédito Real de Minas Gerais, de Accôrdo com as Modificações.," Juiz de Fora 1916, Capítulo IV, Art. 20. The "Contracto celebrado entre o Estado de Minas Gerais e o Banco . . ." of 1926 (Art. 5), limited both notes and loans for general commercial purposes to a maturity of six months. Banco de Crédito Hypothecário e Agrícola do Estado de São Paulo and Banco do Estado de São Paulo, *Atas das Assembléias Gerais,* Banco do Estado de São Paulo Library, São Paulo, 31 December 1913 and Banco do Commércio e Indústria de São Paulo, *Estátutos,* Banco do Commércio e Indústria de São Paulo Archive, São Paulo, 1917, Art. 7.

48. Instances of renewing credit instruments upon their expiration were frequently documented in the Atas of both the Banco do Brasil and the Banco de Credit Real de Minas Gerais. For a sample of the British experience in this regard, see BOLSA, Letters, G3/10, 23 March 1911; G3/11, 28 May 1918; G3/12, 5 April 1923. (Lending to the debtor in this citation continues at least through the remainder of the First Republic.) See also British Consular Reports, 1908, Report No. 4054, 5.

49. BB, *Estátutos*, 1905, Art. 7.

50. *RC,* 1905, 20; see also MF, *Relatório*, 1915, 15.

51. BOLSA, Letters, G3/12, 31 January 1923; *RC,* 1909, 24.

52. Lloyds Bank, Personnel and training notes of Bank of London and South America held by the Lloyds Bank Archive, London, Internal memorandum between directors ("Beane Report"), 1933, Statistical Annex; Gail D. Triner, "British Banking in Brazil During the First Republic" (paper presented at the Conference on Latin American History, New York, January 1997), 17.

53. MF, *Relatório*, 1906; Triner, "British Banking," 10.

54.   BB, *Estátutos,* 1905, Art. 10; 1916, Art. 10; 1922, Art. 4; 1930, Art. 15.

55.   BB, *Relatório,* 1906–30, passim.

56.   See, for example, Banco do Estado de São Paulo, *Relatórios e contas de administração do BCHASP que serão submetidos à approvação dos acçionistas do mesmo banco em reunião annual,* Banco do Estado de São Paulo Library, São Paulo, 1926 (hereafter Bchasp/Banespa, *Relatório*); Banco de Crédito Real de Minas Gerais, *Livros das Atas da Diretória,* Crédito Real Archive, Juiz de Fora, Minas Gerais, Livro 1, Atas, 22 October 1923 and 9 January 1926.

57.   Simonsen, "Finanças e a indústria," 1930.

58.   Bchasp/Banespa, *Relatório,* 1914, 5; Comind, *Relatório,* 1913, 5, 1920, 4–5, and 1922, 10.

59.   The domicile of capital registration (i.e., country in which equity shares were originally listed) defines the domestic and foreign ownership characterization. This categorization is less clear-cut than one might assume. For example, the Banco de Crédito Hypothecário e Agrícola de São Paulo was originally a French bank; it was capitalized in French francs and managed by French nationals. The bank's subsidy and mortgage charter from the state government of São Paulo characterized it as a state-subsidized bank. In another case, the Banco Commerciale Italiano di São Paulo (a Brazilian bank) became a foreign bank when the Banque Francesse et Italiano (French, headquartered in Paris) took it over.

60.   Hereafter, for lack of a better phrase, I will refer to these as state-subsidized, or public-sector, banks.

61.   The Herfindahl Index, a standard measure of concentration, is calculated as the sum of the squared market share of each participant. Each bank's share of total deposits measures its market share. In Figure 4.1, I have calculated indices for the total banking system, all privately owned banks, and domestic and foreign privately owned banks.

62.   The freezing of German banking activities during World War I resulted in the anomalous trend of the foreign banks.

63.   *RC,* 1906, 79; MF, *Relatório,* 1906, xxvi; BB, *Relatório,* 1906, 7, and 1908, 5–11.

64.   Gail D. Triner, "Banks, Regions and Nation in Brazil, 1889–1930," *Latin American Perspectives* 26, no. 1 (January 1999): 129–50.

65.   The regression of the change in the share of private-sector deposits held by the five largest banks, as a function of the change in the share held by the Banco do Brasil, for the period 1906–30 was:

$$FIVE = -1.32 - .59BB$$
$$(-.59)\quad (-3.92)$$
$$R^2 = .41\ \text{Durbin-Watson} = 2.10\ n=24$$

66. The share of foreign bank deposits in 1906, 47 percent, appears abnormally high, and it reflects the diminished banking system prior to the opening of the Banco do Brasil. The trends of foreign banking presented here are somewhat different than those presented in Triner, "British Banking," because of the change in the composition of the database. The changes do not alter the conclusions.

67. Triner, "British Banking."

68. Triner, "British Banking."

69. Lloyds Bank, Beane Report. See also Geoffrey Jones, *British Multinational Banking 1830-1990* (Oxford: Clarendon Press, 1993), 141.

70. For example, in 1921 the president of the Banco do Brasil mentioned to the minister of the Treasury that one of the goals of the Rediscount Office was to allow banks to maintain lower cash ratios (BB, Atas, 11 December 1920; Banco do Brasil, Cartas Particulares dos Presidentes, Banco do Brasil Archives, Rio de Janeiro, 14 December 1921 [hereafter BB, Cartas]). See also Neuhaus, "Monetary History," 21 and 35-42; Steven Topik, *The Political Economy of the Brazilian State, 1889-1930,* Latin American Monographs, Institute of Latin American Studies the University of Texas at Austin, no. 71 (Austin: University of Texas Press, 1987), 44.

71. Bank of London and South America, Telegrams between London and Rio de Janeiro, Archives of the Bank of London and South America, University College, London, G3/12, 9 February 1923 (hereafter BOLSA, Telegrams).

72. These contractions, and their effects on money supply and monetary policy, are examined in Peláez and Suzigan, *História monetária,* 199-216 and 231-37; Fritsch, *External Constraints,* 38-45 and 138-42; and Neuhaus, "Monetary History," 39-89. Wilson Suzigan, *Indústria brasileira: Origem e desenvolvimento* (São Paulo: Brasiliense, 1986), 44-66, provides a good overview of what is known of the effects of these contractions in the productive sectors of the economy.

73. As through the nineteenth century, foreign banks faced no consistent regulatory disadvantage in Brazil during the First Republic. Foreign banks were distinguished from domestic organizations by: their client bases, composed largely (but not exclusively) of their compatriot businessmen; their ability to freely conduct foreign exchange and speculation (denied to domestic banks after 1893); their ability to obtain a national, rather than state, charter; and the possibility of financial support from an overseas headquarters.

74. Brasil, Instituto Brasileiro de Geografia e Estatística, *Estatísticas históricas do Brasil: Séries econômicas, demográficas e sociais 1550 a 1985,* 2d ed., Séries Estatísticas Históricas do Brasil, no. 3, Rio de Janeiro: IBGE, 1990, Table 11.10.

75. BB, Cartas, 14 December 1921. A decline in bank reserve ratios would

have indicated an increased willingness to commit a larger share of their total financial resources to (risky) income-producing investments. Persistent complaints about banks' high cash holdings were common.

76. The stubbornly high cash holdings of banks also remained a serious concern to merchants at the time. *Jornal do Commércio,* (Rio de Janeiro: Rodrigues e Cia), 18 July 1921. As a counterargument, the sharp increase of foreign bank liquidity might suggest that the Rediscount Office prevented an impending contraction in the real volume of credit that banks otherwise would have invoked.

77. The delayed implementation of reductions in deposits (demonstrated below) supports my initial conclusion that the slow response was a circumvention of policy, rather than an inability to implement it. BB, *Relatório,* 1924, 7; Waldemar Falcão, *O empirismo monétario no Brasil* (São Paulo: Cia. Editora Nacional, 1931); Neuhaus, "Monetary History," 72.

78. Leveraging liabilities to create credit is a common practice of banks in the late twentieth century, and it was common for U.S. and European banks in the late nineteenth century.

79. Further, because banks did not measure their capital and reserves in a way that allowed them to use these funds to leverage their portfolios in an informed manner, they did not have many options to expand credit. See the Data Appendix for discussions of capital and reserves.

80. The second period, 1924, experienced the greatest discord between the political goals of the president of Brazil and the economic goals of other high-level financial policy makers.

81. Comind, *Relatório,* 1922, 10, and 1929, 3.

82. Banks' cost structures and their loss experience explain the difference between the measures of interest rates from the perspective of banks and their borrowers. Over time, the patterns of fluctuation should resemble each other. For the time-series data available here, they do follow consistent trends.

83. Further, while the data do not allow calculation of the net profitability of foreign-bank credit, neither logic nor the contemporary rhetoric would support expectations of lower interest rates for foreign banks. Triner, "British Banking."

84. *RC,* 1915, 3-4; Comind, *Relatório,* 1915, 4-5.

85. This finding, of course, begs the question of whether the emerging stability among privately owned banks owed something to the fluctuations absorbed by the Banco do Brasil.

86. BB, Cartas, 20 June 1921.

87. Extending the rediscounting facility to the Treasury negatively affected the Banco do Brasil's earnings by the differential between commercial lending rates and the discount rate to the Treasury (Fritsch, *External Constraints,* 62-65). While it would not be unusual that the federal government borrowed from banks at lower rates than the private sector, his assertion is not

quantified. In addition, it is not clear that there was an unmet demand for credit in the private sector at the time.

88. Since the Treasury owned 25 percent of the Banco do Brasil at this time, the differential in returns can be viewed as a means of transferring a portion of the cost of rediscounting to 75 percent of Banco do Brasil shareholders.

Chapter 5

1. Rondo E. Cameron, "Banking in the Early Stages," in *Banking in the Early Stages of Industrialization; a Study in Comparative Economic History,* ed. Rondo E. Cameron, with the collaboration of Olga Crisp, Hugh T. Patrick, and Richard Tilly (New York: Oxford University Press, 1967); Alexander Gerschenkron, *Economic Backwardness in Historical Perspective, A Book of Essays* (Cambridge, Mass.: Belknap Press of Harvard University Press, 1962); François Crouzet, *Capital Formation in the Industrial Revolution* (London: Methuen and Co., 1972); P. L. Cottrell, *Industrial Finance: 1830-1914:The Finance and Organization of English Manufacturing Industry* (London: Methuen and Co., 1979); Pat Hudson, *The Genesis of Industrial Capital: A Study of the West Riding Wool Textile Industry, c. 1750-1850* (Cambridge: Cambridge University Press, 1986), offer some of the most prominent studies.

2. Alexander Gerschenkron, "Economic Backwardness in Historical Perspective," in *Economic Backwardness in Historical Perspective, a Book of Essays* (Cambridge, Mass.: Belknap Press of Harvard University Press, 1962), 5-30.

3. I thank Rory Miller for pushing me to articulate this point.

4. Some of the sources covering these issues are: George Reid Andrews, *Blacks and Whites in São Paulo, Brazil, 1888-1988* (Madison: University of Wisconsin Press, 1991); Joel Wolfe, *Working Women, Working Men: São Paulo and the Rise of Brazil's Industrial Working Class, 1900-1955* (Durham, N.C.: Duke University Press, 1993); John D. French, *The Brazilian Workers' ABC: Class Conflict and Alliances in Modern São Paulo* (Chapel Hill: University of North Carolina Press, 1992); Maria Antonieta P. Leopoldi, "Industrial Associations and Politics in Contemporary Brazil: The Associations of Industrialists, Economic Policy-Making and the State with Special Reference to the Period 1930-61" (Ph.D. diss., Cambridge University, 1984); Eulália Maria Lahmeyer Lobo, Lia A. Carvalho, and Myrian Stanley, *Questão habitacional e o movimento operário* (Rio de Janeiro: Editora UFRJ, 1989); Domingos Giroletti, *Fábrica, convento, disciplina* (Belo Horizonte: Impr. Oficial de Minas Gerais, 1991).

5. Extrapolated from Brasil, Instituto Brasileiro de Geografia e Estatística, *Estatísticas históricas do Brasil: Séries econômicas, demográficas e sociais 1550 a 1985,* 2d ed., Séries Estatísticas Históricas do Brasil, 3 (Rio de Janeiro:

IBGE, 1990), Table 4.2; and Cláudio L. S. Haddad, "Growth of Brazilian Real Output 1900-1947" (Ph.D. diss., University of Chicago, 1974), Table 1.

6. Derived from Haddad, "Brazilian Real Output," Table 1.

7. Good reviews and considerations of this historiography are in Wilson Suzigan, *Indústria brasileira: Origem e desenvolvimento* (São Paulo: Brasiliense, 1986); Flávio Rabelo Versiani, "Before the Depression: Brazilian Industry in the 1920's," in *Latin America in the 1930's: The Role of the Periphery in World Crisis,* ed. Rosemary Thorp (Oxford: Macmillan Press, 1984), 163-87; Flávio Rabelo Versiani and José Roberto Mendonça de Barros, *Formação econômica do Brasil: A expêriencia da industrialização,* Série ANPEC de Leituras de Economia (São Paulo: Edição Saraiva, 1977).

8. Warren Dean, *The Industrialization of São Paulo, 1880-1945,* Latin American Monographs, no. 17 (Austin: Published for the Institute of Latin American Studies by the University of Texas Press, 1969); Nícia Villela Luz, *A luta pela industrialização do Brasil 1808-1930,* Corpo e Alma, no. 5 (São Paulo: Ed. Alfa Omega, 1978 [1960]).

9. See also the Data Appendix. The constraints to extending the data further back in time to the beginning of the Republic impede their usefulness here, as they did in Chapter 4.

10. Paulo Neuhaus, "A Monetary History of Brazil, 1900-1945" (Ph.D. diss., University of Chicago, 1974), 15-16; José Eduardo Marques Mauro, "Os primórdios do desenvolvimento econômico brasileiro (1850-1930)," in *A moderna história econômica,* ed. Carlos Manuel Peláez and Mircea Buescu (Rio de Janeiro: APEC, 1976), 145-46; Steven Topik, *The Political Economy of the Brazilian State, 1889-1930,* Latin American Monographs, Institute of Latin American Studies the University of Texas at Austin, no. 71 (Austin: University of Texas Press, 1987), 52. Carlos Manuel Peláez, "The Establishment of Banking Institutions in a Backward Economy: Brazil, 1800-1850," *Business History Review* 44, no. 4 (winter 1975): 446-72, addresses Brazil's under-banked status during the nineteenth century.

11. Raymond W. Goldsmith, *Financial Structures and Development* (New Haven: Yale University Press, 1969), 26 and Chapter 2; Cameron, "Banking in the Early Stages," 300-05 and Tables 9.1 and 9.2; John G. Gurley and E. S. Shaw, "Financial Aspects of Economic Development," *American Economic Review* 45, no. 4 (September 1955): 515-38; Robert G. King and Ross Levine, "Finance and Growth: Schumpeter Might Be Right," *Quarterly Journal of Economics* 108, no. 3 (August 1993): 720-23, 717-37.

12. Cameron, "Banking in the Early Stages," 300.

13. This measure represents an unrealistic lower bound of the influence of banking, since the credit captured on the balance sheets is to private-sector borrowers. However, to the large extent that they include credit under public programs, this conservative measure eliminates effects of public

financing and subsidy programs from the consideration of financial depth.

14. Figure 3.3 illustrates the fundamental reversal in the composition of money from 1906. As in Chapter 3, M_2 measures the money supply as currency in circulation plus bank demand deposits plus bank term deposits.

15. This data relies on the firm-level aggregation of bank deposits (Data Appendix and Brasil, *Estatísticas históricas,* Table 10.2). Traditional analyses of money supply confirm the increasing influence of banking in monetary management (Neuhaus, "Monetary History"). This approach assumes that the factors explaining the demand for money were stable. There are strong reasons to suspect that substantive changes in the demand for money occurred during the period under consideration. One indication of a shift in demand for bank deposits is found within the money supply data themselves: the secularly declining ratio of currency held by the public. Further, the compositional analysis of money supply ignores the effects of price inflation on the productive economy. Rapid price changes were common during the First Republic, and they largely resulted from changes in the money supply. Severe price changes could affect the productive sectors through shifts in both prices and price expectations. The relationship between economic structure and the demand for banking and money is of more relevance here.

16. The exact timing of this process remains unclear. Albert Fishlow, "Origins and Consequences of Import Substitution in Brazil," in *International Economics and Development: Essays in Honor of Raúl Prebisch,* ed. Luís Eugenio di Marco and Raúl Prebisch, (New York: Academic Press, 1972), credits the disruptions of the Encilhamento for the earliest import substituting industrialization. Dean (*Industrialization of São Paulo*) looks to the prosperity of the coffee sector as the motor of industrial expansion. Suzigan (*Indústria brasiliera*) takes a more subtle and gradualist interpretation, but he finds earliest introduction of industrial manufacturing shortly prior to the fall of the Empire in 1889 and concludes that Brazil was self-sufficient in the manufacture of consumer goods by 1919. The only major analyst to advance a conclusion of significant industrialization not beginning until *after* the First Republic is Werner Baer, *The Brazilian Economy: Growth and Development,* 4th ed. (Westport, Conn.: Praeger, 1995), Chapters 3 and 4. He identifies the construction of large-scale capital-goods industries after World War II as the beginning of the industrialization process. Based on a more sociologically oriented historical analysis, Font is the only author to find that industrialization was in "counterpoint with the *fazenda* coffee economy." Maurício Font, *Coffee, Contention, and Change in the Making of Modern Brazil,* Studies in Social Discontinuity (Cambridge, Mass.: B. Blackwell, 1990), 107, and more generally, Chapter 4.

17. Dean, *Industrialization of São Paulo.*

18. Carlos Manuel Peláez, "As conseqüências econômicas da ortodoxia mon-

etária, cambial e fiscal no Brasil entre 1889-1945," *Revista Brasileira de Economia* 5, no. 3 (July-September 1971): 5-82, concluded that orthodox monetary policy delayed development and industrialization because of the support provided to the coffee sector.

19. Suzigan, *Indústria brasiliera.*

20. These results differ from those presented in Gail D. Triner, "Banking, Economic Growth and Industrialization: Brazil, 1906-1930," *Revista Brasileira de Economia* 50, no. 1 (January 1996): 135-54, because of differences in the criteria by which the banks were grouped and the extension of the database. The direction and substance of the results do not change.

21. The statistical representations of these statements are the positive values for the correlation coefficients (ß) associated with the production variables and the negative correlation coefficients, with higher absolute value of *t* (an assessment of statistical reliability).

22. Suzigan, *Indústria brasiliera,* especially Chapter 4.

23. See, for example, Flávio A. M. de Saes, *Crédito e bancos no desenvolvimento da economia paulista: 1850-1930* (São Paulo: Instituto de Pesquisas Econômicas, 1986).

24. This finding would suggest that coffee merchants benefited; it does not indicate whether coffee planters, field workers, or anyone else in the production cycle benefited.

25. This finding needs to be viewed with extreme caution. The output and price data for agriculture appear to combine domestic and export agriculture (with their very different economic dynamics).

26. An industrial price series is available from 1908 (Brasil, *Estatísticas históricas,* Table 5.2). This specification of the model gives weaker results, largely because of difficulties with the industrial price series.

27. Granger-Sims tests, regressing the rate of change of real deposits on the change in real deposits lagged for four periods and on the change in output lagged for four periods, to try to determine the antecedence of banking or income growth, give indeterminate results.

28. Banco do Commércio e Indústria de São Paulo, *Relatório e contas da administração* Banco do Commércio e Indústria de São Paulo que serão apresentados aos accionistas, (São Paulo: H. Puchetti), Banco do Commércio e Indústria de São Paulo Archive, São Paulo, 1890, 4-5 (hereafter Comind, *Relatório*).

29. Unless otherwise cited, information on the background and formation of Comind is from Darrell E. Levi, *The Prados of São Paulo, Brazil: An Elite Family and Social Change, 1840-1930* (Athens, Ga.: University of Georgia Press, 1987), 69-84 and 141-47.

30. In a unique form of organization, the São Paulo affiliate was separately organized and capitalized; it operated according to its own, local, statutes.

31. Martinho da Silva Prado was one of the original owners. The genealogical relationship is unclear. From piecing together information from Levi

(*Prados of São Paulo*) and Saes (*Crédito e bancos*), this Martinho da Silva Prado could have been Antônio's son or grandson.

32. Saes, *Crédito e bancos,* 77.

33. Saes, *Crédito e bancos,* 134. Saes documents extensive interlocking directorships among paulista banks and their owners' other enterprises.

34. Financial data for individual banks come from the database described in the Data Appendix.

35. The bank failed in a fraud scandal in the 1980s.

36. José de Souza Martins, *Conde Matarazzo, o empresário e a emprêsa; Estudo de sociologia do desenvolvimento,* Coleção Estudos Brasileiros, vol. 1, 2d ed., (São Paulo: HUCITEC, 1976), provides the information on Matarazzo. Dean (*Industrialization of São Paulo*) rests much of his conclusion that the source of paulista industrialization lay largely with immigrant merchants on the experiences of a few exceptional entrepreneurs, of whom Matarazzo figures prominently.

37. Between 1886 and 1934, 4.1 million immigrants arrived in Brazil; about 56 percent of them settled in São Paulo, with the intention of participating in the massive coffee boom. Thomas H. Holloway, *Immigrants on the Land: Coffee and Society in São Paulo, 1886-1934* (Chapel Hill: University of North Carolina Press, 1980), 40.

38. Documents and reporting on this are absent; this conclusion is derived from the reporting of bank data in the Estado de São Paulo, Repartição de Estatística e Arquivo do Estado. *Annuário estatístico do Estado de São Paulo.* São Paulo: Typ. *Diário Official,* 1902-1928 (hereafter Estado de São Paulo, *Annuário estatístico*).

39. Estado de São Paulo, *Annuário estatístico,* 1910; Bank of London and South America, Letters from London to Rio de Janeiro, Archives of the Bank of London and South America, University College, London, G3/10, 27 October 1910 (hereafter BOLSA, Letters).

40. The history of Banco Pelotense is in Eugenio Lagemann, *O Banco Pelotense e o sistema financeiro regional,* Série Documenta 19 (Porto Alegre, RS: Mercado Aberto, 1985), Chapter 3.

41. Share ownership did not diversify through the remainder of the bank's life.

42. Lagemann, *Banco Pelotense,* 104-05, Tables 15 and 16.

43. Lagemann, *Banco Pelotense,* 107-08. Lagemann does not explain the organizational procedures by which Pelotense opened branches in Santa Caterina and Minas Gerais. My understanding of the law and procedures is that, absent a national charter, the bank would have had to incorporate in the states in which it operated. This procedure would have required filing operating statutes and obtaining a charter with the state governments, and allocating financial resources, capital and reserves, in the state.

44. Lagemann, *Banco Pelotense,* 166.

45. According to Lagemann, who leaves the specifics unexplained, the bank also suffered serious management problems that were independent of

the incremental pressures of the Depression. Lagemann, *Banco Pelotense,* 129-32.

46. Teresa Cristina de Novaes Marques, "O setor bancário privado carioca entre 1918 e 1945: Os Bancos Boavista e Português do Brasil–Um estudo de estratégias empresariais" (Tese de mestrado, Rio de Janeiro, Universidade Federal de Rio de Janeiro, 1998), 19 n.38; and Marques, personal communication, 24 October 1998.

47. Information on Banco Português do Brasil is drawn from Marques, "Setor bancário privado carioca," 104-38.

48. Estátutos do Banco Português do Brasil, 1918, cap. 1, art. 3, no. 8; as cited in Marques, "Setor bancário privado carioca," 111 n.178.

49. Marques, "Setor bancário privado carioca," 135.

50. Only in the very anomalous year of 1920 was the Banco Português do Brasil among the five largest Brazilian banks (Table A.7).

51. Business historians and those interested in the institutional dynamics that determine business development may benefit from considering the extent to which diversified share ownership impelled the bank to conform to the standards of the period and may have served as an oversight of the directors' investments funded by the bank.

52. Information on Boavista is from Marques, "Setor bancário privado carioca," 160-89.

53. The Guinle family built and established the Palace Hotel and the Copacabana Palace; they also leased the Hotel Glória.

54. Light, as it has been commonly called, was responsible for much early Brazilian urban electrification.

55. The short period of the bank's operations at the end of the First Republic impedes the value of considering the trajectory of its financial statements.

56. BOLSA, Letters, G3/10, 27 October 1910.

57. U.S. Bureau of Foreign and Domestic Commerce, "Banking and Credit in Argentina, Brazil, Chile and Peru," by Edward S. Hurley, U.S. Bulletin of the Department of Commerce, Special Agents Series no. 90 (Washington, D.C.: GPO, 1914), 7 and 50; BOLSA Letters, G3/11, 8 October 1918; David Joslin, *A Century of Banking in Latin America; to Commemorate the Centenary in 1962 of the Bank of London & South America Limited* (New York: Oxford University Press, 1963), 108-10; Levy "Foreign Capital," 364-65.

58. Gail D. Triner, "British Banking in Brazil During the First Republic" (paper presented at the Conference on Latin American History, New York, 1997), 19.

59. Barbara Stallings, *Banker to the Third World: U.S. Portfolio Investment in Latin America, 1900-1986,* Studies in International Political Economy no. 18 (Berkeley and Los Angeles: University of California Press, 1987), and Carlos Marichal, *A Century of Debt Crises in Latin America: From*

Independence to the Great Depression, 1820-1930 (Princeton: Princeton University Press, 1989), discuss the importance of these issues for Latin America as a whole.

60. One German bank, the Brasiliensche Deutsche, had been an early arrival in Brazil. It is surprising that these two participants did not open offices in Brazil earlier, since both were present in other locations in Latin America from the nineteenth century, and Germany was the second largest importer of Brazilian coffee. Nevertheless, their balance sheets did not appear in the Brazilian financial press until 1911. The assets of German banks were frozen during World War I.

61. U.S. Department of Commerce, *Financial Developments in South American Countries,* by William H. Lough, Special Agent of the Department of Commerce (Washington, D.C.: GPO, 1915), 44. The only requirement specific to foreign banks was that they maintain a fixed share of their capital in Brazil. However, administrative and reporting requirements did monitor foreign banks separately, and more closely, than their domestic counterparts (Brasil, *Coleção das Leis e Decretos,* Decreto no. 434, 4 July 1891). At times, foreigners apparently perceived discrimination against their position in commerce (Messrs. Rothschilds and Sons, Rothschilds Archive, London, 111/309; and "British Financial Mission, by Edwin Montagu and the members of the mission, 1924, Report by British Financial Mission to Brazil to Messrs. Rothschild, Messrs. Baring Bros. & Co. Ltd. and Messrs. J. Henry Schroder & Co."). Despite the absence of specific regulations discriminating for or against foreign banks, currency trading regulations prohibiting purely speculative transactions did serve to give foreign banks access to a line of business and profits beyond that of their domestic competitors. Triner, "British Banking," 12-13.

62. Anne Gerard Hanley, "Business Finance and the São Paulo Bolsa, 1886-1917," in *Latin America and the World Economy in the Nineteenth and Twentieth Centuries,* ed. John H. Coatsworth and Alan M. Taylor (Cambridge, Mass.: Harvard University Press, 1998).

63. Marques, "Setor bancário privado carioca," 160-65.

64. This concords with Zelia Maria Cardoso de Mello, *Metamorfoses da riqueza, São Paulo, 1845-1895: Contribuição ao estudo da passagem da economia mercantil escravista a economia exportadora capitalista,* Estudos Históricos (São Paulo: Editora Hucitec; Prefeitura do Município de São Paulo, Secretária Municipal de Cultura, 1985). She found, for São Paulo, that planters (and merchants) increasingly invested in industrial and financial endeavors.

65. Anne Gerard Hanley, "Capital Markets in the Coffee Economy: Financial Institutions and Economic Change in São Paulo, Brazil, 1850-1905" (Ph.D. diss., Stanford University, 1995), 105-13, and Saes, *Crédito e bancos,* 120, arrive at the same findings with respect to São Paulo.

66. Naomi R. Lamoreaux, *Insider Lending: Banks, Personal Connections, and*

Economic Development in Industrial New England (Cambridge: Cambridge University Press, 1994). Lamoreaux concludes that it provided security for lending in early New England. See also Noel Maurer, "Banks and Entrepreneurs in Porfirian Mexico: Inside Exploitation or Sound Business Strategy?" *Journal of Latin American Studies* 31, no. 2 (May 1999): 331-62; Richard Tilly, "Germany, 1815-1870," in *Banking in the Early Stages of Industrialization; a Study in Comparative Economic History,* ed. Rondo E. Cameron, with the collaboration of Olga Crisp, Hugh T. Patrick, and Richard Tilly (New York: Oxford University Press, 1967), 151-82. Nathaniel H. Leff, "Capital Markets in the Less Developed Countries: The Group Principle," in *Money and Finance in Economic Growth and Development,* ed. Ronald I. McKinnon (New York: Dekker, 1976), discusses this same phenomenon with respect to a later period of Brazilian history.

67. Roberto Simonsen, "As finanças e a indústria," Conferência realisada no Mackenzie College, São Paulo, 1930.

68. Comind, *Relatório,* 1921, 5-6.   Banco de Crédito Real de Minas Gerais, *Livros das Atas da Diretória,* Crédito Real Archive, Juiz de Fora, Minas Gerais, Livros 1-2, 1889-1930, passim, and Banco do Brasil, Atas dos Directores, Banco do Brasil Archives, Rio de Janeiro, passim, recognize this with numerous "roll-overs" of short-term debt. Further, the growth of the Bolsa de Valores as an organizational mechanism for issuing stocks and debentures (long-term bonds) attests to the resourcefulness of Brazilian entrepreneurs to structure flexible institutions and instruments to generate financing. Hanley, "São Paulo Bolsa"; Triner, "Banking and Brazilian Economic Development," Chapter 6.

69. In this respect, Brazilian banking appears similar to the Gerschenkronian characterization of the State as an entrepreneurial force motivating late development. Gerschenkron, "Economic Backwardness."

Appendix to Chapter 5

1. This approach follows Marie Elizabeth Sushka, "The Antebellum Money Market and the Economic Impact of the Bank War," *Journal of Economic History* 36, no. 4 (1976): 809-35.

2. The model uses the contemporaneous variables and does not incorporate lagged estimates. The extent of fluctuation, especially for prices, was sufficient that the rate of change in a prior year's measure would not generate expectations of continuation of change at the same rate, or even in the same direction from one year to the next (see Table A.10). Tests of regressions including the lagged variables confirmed that they were not statistically significant in explaining the succeeding year's rate of change.

3. Agricultural and industrial price series are available from 1908 (Brasil, *Estatísticas históricas,* Table 5.2). Using these series gives weaker results, largely because of difficulties with the sectoral price series.

4. For the methodology, see Peter Kennedy, *A Guide to Econometrics,* 3d ed. (Cambridge, Mass.: MIT Press, 1993).

5. The statistics measuring autocorrelation (Durbin-Watson) and the probability that the independent variables (t-ratios) and the dependent variables (F and significance of F) are statistically valid within acceptable ranges.

6. These results differ from those presented in Gail D. Triner, "Banking, Economic Growth, and Industrialization: Brazil, 1906-1930," *Revista Brasileira de Economia* 50, no. 1 (January 1996): 135-54, because of differences in the criteria by which the banks were grouped and the expansion of the overall database. The substance of the results has not changed.

Chapter 6

1. Banco do Brasil, Cartas Particulares dos Presidentes, Banco do Brasil Archives, Rio de Janeiro, 7 January 1911 (hereafter BB, Cartas).

2. Banco do Brasil, Atas dos Directores, Banco do Brasil Archives, Rio de Janeiro, 17 November 1911 (hereafter BB, Atas).

3. Banco do Brasil, *Relatório do Banco do Brasil apresentado à Assembléia Geral dos accionistas na sessão ordinaria,* Banco do Brasil Archives, Rio de Janeiro, 1911, 6 and Income Statement (hereafter BB, Relatório).

4. Christopher Clague et al., "Institutions and Economic Performance: Property Rights and Contract Enforcement," in *Institutions and Economic Development: Growth and Governance in Less-Developed and Post-Socialist Countries,* ed. Christopher Clague (Baltimore: Johns Hopkins University Press, 1997), 67-90; Christopher Clague and others, "Contract-Intensive Money: Contract Enforcement, Property Rights and Economic Performance," University of Maryland Center Institutional Reform and the Informal Sector, Working Paper 151, College Park, Md.: 1997.
The specific measure of contract-intensive money is $(M_2 - C)/M_2$.
M_2 is the measure of the money supply and is consistent with the measures used elsewhere in this study; C is currency held outside of banks. In First Republican Brazil, $(M_2 - C)$ equaled bank demand and term deposits (those captured in this study). Therefore, contract-intensive money is the ratio of bank deposits to M_2.

5. Clague et al., "Contract-Intensive Money."

6. Clague et al. ("Contract-Intensive Money," 4) suggest that financial transactions may accrue especially large gains from secure property rights because "transactions in capital markets are not usually self-enforcing; they typically require either enforcement of loan contracts or enforcement of rules."

7. Douglass C. North, *Institutions, Institutional Change, and Economic Performance* (Cambridge: Cambridge University Press, 1990), Chapter 1.

8. These highly capsulized summaries are distilled from Douglass C. North, *Structure and Change in Economic History* (New York: Norton, 1981);

North, *Institutions;* Yoram Barzel, *Economic Analysis of Property Rights* (Cambridge: Cambridge University Press, 1997).

9. Barzel, *Economic Analysis of Property Rights,* 4.

10. Marieta de Moraes Ferreira, "A crise dos comissários de café de Rio de Janeiro" (Tese de mestrado, Niterói, Universidade Federal Fluminense, 1977), found, in fact, that by the end of the Empire, commercial banking in the province of Rio de Janeiro found a strong impetus in the desire of coffee merchants to extricate themselves from the financial risks of dealing with coffee producers. Producers had been increasingly "in decline" as the weight of the sector shifted to São Paulo, and they became unreliable credits for merchants.

11. An especially good example is:

> At the beginning of the second semester we began to note a large surge. In our business with the [financial] market we noticed a relative scarcity of currency, which was soon noticed in all the [financial] markets, with an increase in discount rates, and a general decline of deposits. As a consequence, we have not increased our operations, but maintained them at the same—or even reduced— level, to the extent possible. We are always trying to maintain our good relations with old clients. As a credit establishment, the duty to punctually honor the orders of our depositors, as always, was imposed upon us. . . . Effectively, this shortage of currency was clearly demonstrated; and expressed itself first in its withdrawal from interior regions of the country . . . (BB, *Relatório,* 1919, 8).

12. Any of the bank archival sources used for this project offer good examples of this: BB, *Relatórios,* Atas, and Cartas; Banco de Crédito Real de Minas Gerais, *Relátorio apresentado à Assembléia Geral dos Accionistas do Banco de Crédito Real de Minas Gerais* na sua Reunião Ordinária, Crédito Real Archive, Juiz de Fora, Minas Gerais (Juiz de Fora: Typ. Pereira, hereafter Crédito Real, *Relatório*) and Banco de Crédito Real de Minas Gerais, *Livros das Atas da Diretória,* Crédito Real Archive, Juiz de Fora, Minas Gerais, Livros 1-2 (hereafter Crédito Real, Atas); Banco de Crédito Hypothecário e Agrícola do Estado de São Paulo and Banco do Estado de São Paulo, *Relatórios e contas de administração do BCHASP que serão submetidos à approvação dos acçionistas do mesmo banco em reunião annual,* Banco do Estado de São Paulo Library, São Paulo (hereafter Bchasp/Banespa, *Relatório*); and Banco do Commércio e Indústria de São Paulo, *Relatório e contas da adminstração* Banco do Commércio e Indústria de São Paulo que serão aprestendados aos accionistas, (São Paulo: H. Puchetti), Banco do Commércio e Indústria de São Paulo Archive, São Paulo, (hereafter Comind, *Relatório*). The annual reports (*relatórios*) generally began with an overview of economic conditions. Comind,

Relatório, provided some of the best-informed economic analysis during the 1920s.

13. The inequality of confidence that banks exhibited with respect to the two sides of their balance sheets was demonstrated in bank statutes, minutes of directors' meetings, and in the financial press. Bank statutes were very specific about credit criteria and procedures, and very brief on deposit-taking activity See, for example, Banco do Brasil, *Estátutos do Banco do Brasil,* Banco do Brasil Archives, Rio de Janeiro (Rio de Janeiro: Imprensa Nacional) 1905, 1916 titulo 3, arts. 5-7, 1922, arts. 2-3 (hereafter BB, *Estátutos*); Banco de Crédito Real de Minas Gerais, *Estátutos do Banco de Crédito Real de Minas Gerais, de Accôrdo com as Modificações,* Crédito Real Archive, Juiz de Fora, Minas Gerais, 1914 and 1919, capítulos 3-5 (hereafter Crédito Real, *Estátutos*); Banco do Commércio e Indústria de São Paulo, *Estátutos,* Banco do Commércio e Indústria de São Paulo Archive, São Paulo, 1917, art. 7 (hereafter Comind, *Estátutos*). Boards of directors managed credit portfolios at a very detailed level. Especially at the beginning of the period under consideration, individual credits, and the settlement of individual credits, were decided by the board. Decisions were often taken weekly. (For a good example during periods of severe credit contractions, see Crédito Real, Atas: 14 August 1926, June 1929, October 1929, and January 1930.)

14. Brasil, Ministério da Fazenda, *Relatório apresentado ao Presidente da República dos Estados Unidos do Brasil pelo Ministro de Estado dos Negócios da Fazenda* (Rio de Janeiro: Imprensa Nacional), 1901, xxvii (hereafter MF, *Relatório*).

15. See, for example, Comind, *Relatório,* 1919, 4-5.

16. None of the protections used were exclusive to the Brazilian experience.

17. Nathaniel H. Leff, "Capital Markets in the Less Developed Countries: The Group Principle," in *Money and Finance in Economic Growth and Development,* ed. Ronald I. McKinnon (New York: Dekker, 1976), 97-122, offers an early and persuasive discussion on the importance and limitations of the "group principle." Noel Maurer, "Banks and Entrepreneurs in Porfirian Mexico: Inside Exploitation or Sound Business Strategy?" *Journal of Latin American Studies* 31, no. 2 (May 1999): 331-62, applies the concept to banking development in porfirian Mexico. The country studies in Carlos Dávila and Rory Miller, eds., "Business History in Latin America," in *Business History in Latin America: The Experience of Seven Countries,* Liverpool Latin American Studies, New Series, 1 (Liverpool: Liverpool University Press, 1999), emphasize the importance of small personal groups in business formation throughout Latin America.

18. Naomi R. Lamoreaux, "Information Problems and Banks' Specialization in Short-Term Lending: New England in the Nineteenth-Century," in *Inside the Business Enterprise: Historical Perspectives on the Use of Information,* ed. Peter Temin (Chicago: University of Chicago Press, 1991), 161-95, and

Naomi R. Lamoreaux, *Insider Lending: Banks, Personal Connections, and Economic Development in Industrial New England* (Cambridge: Cambridge University Press, 1994), establish these ideas and build this case with respect to banking in New England.

19. Bank of London and South America, Letters from London to Rio de Janeiro, Archives of the Bank of London and South America, University College, London, G3/8, 13 February 1907 (hereafter BOLSA, Letters).

20. BOLSA Letters, G3/8, 26 September 1907.

21. Fairly few of these corporations existed in 1900. In addition, Brazilians had experienced widespread failure and losses among these organizations during the Encilhamento and had become very wary of them.

22. The Commercial Code of 1890 (as elucidated in the subsequent Decree no. 434 of 1891) may have provided the basis for this problem (Brasil, *Coleção das Leis e Decretos,* Decreto 434, 4 July 1891, capítulo 8, art. 3 [hereafter Leis e Decretos]). Joint-stock limited-liability companies could not be declared bankrupt, though they could be forced into compulsory liquidation. Given the extent of Brazilian legal historiography, I have been unable to clarify the practical importance of these provisions. Companies did go into bankruptcy and the difference of outcome between a bankruptcy and a compulsory liquidation is unclear. By 1902, a new law (Leis e Decretos, Lei 859, 16 August 1902) providing for corporate bankruptcies superseded the previous law. But many concepts, procedures, and practices remain murky, as discussed below.

23. BB (Banco da República), *Relatório,* 1900–01, 135–36. This was, of course, while the bank itself was in the process of failing; so, it may be prudent to question the wisdom of the practice.

24. BB, Atas, 31 July 1907.

25. At least partially, bond markets filled this need. By issuing long-term debt directly to private lenders, the acceptance of new forms of corporate organizations was transferred to agents other than banks. Further understanding of the relationships between various private capital and money markets would be a useful project.

26. Personal relations between principals of corporations and bankers also played a large role in establishing credit for incorporated firms.

27. Corporate financial disclosure was slow to develop commonly applied standards. Nevertheless, annually published financial reports were required for registering and trading equity shares; these requirements did advance the availability of information.

28. Anne Gerard Hanley, "Capital Markets in the Coffee Economy: Financial Institutions and Economic Change in São Paulo, Brazil, 1850–1905" (Ph.D. diss., Stanford University, 1995), 93, finds that, in São Paulo, "The credit instruments represented by discounts were a remnant of the days of personal financial intermediation." My findings suggest otherwise; they suggest that discounted notes served as a flexible credit instrument that

accommodated the short-term transactional needs of merchants, while simultaneously responding to many of the credit-risk concerns of lenders.

29. BB, *Estátutos,* 1905, título 3, art. 5 (nos. 4 and 8), continued in amended *Estátutos,* 1916 and 1922 (arts. 2 and 3 [no. 1]). After 1921, the restriction on loans was "subject to bank policy"; the restrictions on notes remained for four months (See also BB, Atas, 12 April 1909). Crédito Real, Atas, 6 September 1912, identifies the bank's credit maturity guidelines (which were the same as the Banco do Brasil's) and establishes the right of the bank to exercise its discretion to renew credit; see also Crédito Real, *Estátutos,* 1916, capítulo 4, art. 20. The "Contracto celebrado entre o Estado de Minas Gerais e o Banco . . ." of 1926 (art. 5) limited both notes and loans for general commercial purposes to a maturity of six months. See also Bchasp/Banespa, *Relatório,* 31 December 1913; Comind, *Estátutos,* 1917, art. 7.

30. For analogous procedures in early U.S. banking, see Lamoreaux, "Information Problems," 161-95.

31. Instances of renewing credit instruments upon their expiration were frequently documented in the Atas of both the Banco do Brasil and the Banco de Credit Real de Minas Gerais. Banks' directors often discussed continually renewed short-term credit. See, for example, BB, Atas, 26 July 1911, 27 March 1912, 31 May 1916. The Crédito Real Atas often recorded debates on restricting or extending roll-overs of discounted notes (e.g., 6 September 1912, and almost constantly through 1920 and 1921). See Comind, *Relatório,* 1921, 5, for a succinct expression of concern on this circumstance.

32. *Retrospecto Comercial de Journal do Commércio* (Rio de Janeiro: *Jornal de Commércio* de Rodrigues e Cia.) 1920, 6 (hereafter *RC*).

33. For example, the Banco do Brasil, as the only creditor to a coffee merchant in Santos, restructured the debt of Roxy e Companhia and accepted personal assets of the firm's principles as security on the corporate debt, in order to avoid Roxy e Cia.'s bankruptcy (BB, Cartas, September-November 1912). Other specific examples are documented prior to the restructuring of the Banco da República (e.g., BB (Banco da República), Atas, 15 October 1898), and references continue sporadically (e.g., BB, Atas, through July 1909; BB, Cartas, 3 August 1915 and 18 June 1922). By the 1920s, these actions may have diminished or, more likely, been resolved at a level below that of the directors and president, since they are not documented by specific action. However, the issues are addressed in directors' meetings. See also BB, Atas, 20 October 1927, when the directors discuss attempts to maintain the value of collateral when the collateralized goods were commodities with severely depressed market prices.

34. Comind, *Relatório,* 1920, 5-6.

35. For example, BB, Atas, 1, 7, and 15 July 1909, continuing for several weeks, documents the Banco do Brasil's attempts to settle the debts of Widow

Bento's husband, although they had not previously been at risk. Similarly, the bank monitored roll-overs of Lloyd Brasileiro debt carefully while the company struggled. BB, Atas, 11 May 1909 and 12 August 1909; BB, *Relatório,* 1912, 3-4.

36. BOLSA, Letters, G3/09 & G3/10, passim. See especially 3 November 1910.

37. Comind, *Relatório,* passim; Crédito Real, Atas, passim.

38. BB, Cartas (to the Treasury minister), 22 October 1921. See also BB, Cartas (also to the Treasury minister), 29 May 1929.

39. BB, *Estátutos,* 1905, título 3, art. 5 (nos. 4 and 8). Each amendment of the statutes continued these provisions. Crédito Real, *Estátutos* (as amended 1919, and subsequent amendments), capítulo 4, art. 29 (b-g). Bchasp/Banespa, *Relatório,* 31 December 1913. BB, Atas, 4 November 1909 and 10 October 1929; BB, Cartas, 28 May 1921, provide good examples of discussions about varying interpretations of the collateralization provisions. Crédito Real, Atas, 5 November 1912, documents the same concerns within the Minas bank. For the banks granting mortgage credit, the collateral was the property being financed (again, at a discount from its appraised value). Concerns about adequate appraisal were addressed in statutes (see Bchasp/Banespa and Crédito Real references above); higher collateral was required for rural property than for urban real estate.

40. See, for example, Crédito Real, Atas, 25 September 1915 and 12 December 1923.

41. See references in note 39, above.

42. See, for example, BB, Atas, 30 November 1927 and 20 May 1929; Crédito Real, Atas, 2 September 1916. Such a circumstance could severely limit a borrower's total access to credit. Since the same property could not be offered as security for more than one debt, total borrowing capacity could be constrained by the amount of collateral available.

43. BB, Cartas, 3 August 1918.

44. Crédito Real, Atas, June 1928. The Board of Directors agreed to "discount a promissory note for 743 contos of the Botelo Ironworks Company for six months, guaranteed by bonds it issued and the signature of the directors."

45. Mortgage credit did not need to be reserved for rural real estate, but the problems impeding its availability resonated most strongly in the rural sector. The supply of mortgage credit was also an important concern in financing urban development. The issues of valuation and collateralization had the effect of favoring urban mortgage lending. To preserve mortgage credit for rural concerns, a 1913 reform of Bchasp statutes set a limit of 25 percent of its capital plus long-term debt that could finance urban mortgages and limited urban mortgages to the cities of São Paulo and Santos (Banco de Crédito Hypothecário e Agrícola do Estado de São Paulo and Banco do Estado de São Paulo, *Atas das Assembléias Gerais,* Banco do

Estado de São Paulo Library, São Paulo, 31 December 1913 [hereafter Bchasp/Banespa Atas]). Rural mortgages required higher levels of collateral than urban mortgages. Urban real estate was easier to value and monitor, valuation and possession (when required) were more certain than for rural property. These provisions are documented in the Estado de São Paulo, Secretário da Fazenda, *Relatório apresentado ao Presidente do Estado pelo Secretário da Fazenda,* (São Paulo), various years, and as early as 1899 for the Banco de Crédito Real de São Paulo (capítulo 2 of the contract between the State and the bank), (hereafter Secretário da Fazenda [São Paulo], *Relatório*). They are repeated in the original statutes of Bchasp (as reprinted in Secretário da Fazenda [São Paulo], *Relatório,* 1909, 565-69), and remain in each of the amendments to the statutes of Bchasp/ Banespa. Even so, in São Paulo (where the data are available) mortgage credit did seem to end up in its targeted uses. Gail D. Triner, "Banking and Brazilian Economic Development: 1906-1930" (Ph.D. diss., Columbia University, 1994), Table 3.5.

46. Stuart B. Schwartz, *Sugar Plantations in the Formation of Brazilian Society: Bahia 1550-1835,* Cambridge Latin American Studies, no. 52 (Cambridge: Cambridge University Press, 1985), offers one of the most informative discussions in English of colonial merchant/planter relations and conflicts.

47. The issues surrounding property rights are not well documented in Brazilian historiography. A discussion of colonial property rights and laws is found in Schwartz, *Sugar Plantations,* 202-44. Warren Dean, "Latifundia and Land Policy in Nineteenth-Century Brazil," *Hispanic American Historical Review* 51, no. 44 (November 1971): 606-25, discusses land rights during the Empire.

48. Bchasp/Banespa, Atas, 21 December 1913 and 22 December 1927; Crédito Real, *Estátutos,* as amended 1918, arts. 28 and 44-48.

49. Crédito Real, *Estátutos,* as amended 1918, art. 44. This provision was included in subsequent amendments to the statutes, and similar provisions were included in the statutes of all banks that undertook or contemplated mortgage lending.

50. The specification of "urban" buildings was important. Urban buildings were integral parts of productive units less often than rural buildings (such as mills, processing or storage facilities, etc.).

51. Crédito Real, Atas, 15 November 1912.

52. Crédito Real, Atas, 25 September 1915 and 15 April 1916.

53. Bchasp/Banespa, *Relatório,* 1925, 5.

54. Even before the Republic these efforts began with some of the liberalizing moves of the late Empire (*RC,* 1887, 14). The most specific proposal was published by Visconde Rodrigues D'Oliveira, *O crédito agrícola no Brasil* (Rio de Janeiro: Typ. D'os Annaes/Revista de Litteratura, Arte, Sciencia e Indústria, 1905). Further proposals were considered throughout the remain-

der of the First Republic (see, for example, BB, Atas, 23 August 1922). Previous efforts for mortgage-lending institutions were not sustainable. One of the largest such efforts, the Banco Hypothecário do Brasil, failed (MF, *Relatório,* 1912, vol. 1, 116). A major reason for its failure in 1892 was a lack of investors in the bank's mortgage notes, which would have provided long-term funding for the bank (MF, *Relatório,* 1913, vii-xv). Brazilian banks were not unique in their aversion to mortgage credit. In the United States, the Sherman Act of 1863 prohibited nationally chartered banks from holding real estate as collateral, for essentially the same reasons that Brazilian banks shied away from it. On the United States, see Richard E. Sylla, *The American Capital Market, 1846-1914: A Study of the Effects of Public Policy on Economic Development,* Dissertations in American Economic History (New York: Arno Press, 1975), 52-54.

55. D'Oliveira, *Crédito agrícola;* BB, *Estátutos,* 1922.

56. MF, *Relatório,* 1912, 116-26, and 1913, viii-x. Finally, in 1936 the Department of Agricultural and Industrial Credit opened. Stanley E. Hilton, "Vargas and Brazilian Economic Development, 1930-1945: A Reappraisal of His Attitude Toward Industrialization and Planning," *Journal of Economic History* 35, no. 4 (1975): 754-78.

57. Winston Fritsch, *External Constraints on Economic Policy in Brazil, 1889-1930* (Pittsburgh: University of Pittsburgh Press, 1988), Table A.6.

58. As determined by the dates and content of banks' Atas.

59. Routine examples of managing credit authorization limits include BB, Atas, 28 January 1925 and 4 February 1925; Crédito Real, Atas, 16 September 1916, 9 January 1926, June 1929, and January 1930.

60. Crédito Real's directors began establishing credit limits for branches in 1916 and revised the limits periodically, as business conditions merited (Crédito Real, Atas, 16 September 1916, 3 August 1918, 21 September 1918, and periodically thereafter). At Crédito Real, the Board of Directors maintained an active though diminishing role in the discussion of individual credits. The Banco do Brasil's directors distanced themselves more from ongoing credit decisions. Branch lending limits were established in 1911 (BB, Atas, 18 January 1911). In 1912, some branch managers were given wider discretion over discount rates in order to accommodate local conditions (BB, Atas, 31 January 1912). In 1915, branch lending limits were loosened for the purpose of expanding credit (BB, Atas, 12 January 1915). By 1915, the Banco do Brasil's Board of Directors involved itself with individual credits only on an exceptional basis.

61. *Jornal do Commércio,* (Rio de Janeiro: Rodrigues e Cia), 22 December 1922 (hereafter *JC*); based on a report by the Rio de Janeiro Commercial Association.

62. BB, Atas, 8 January 1915; Crédito Real, Atas, 29 December 1917. By the mid-1920s, Banco do Brasil branches with an excess of credit relative to deposits rediscounted notes with the head office, subject to

preestablished limits. This had the same effect as interbranch deposit transfers. BB, Atas, 4 February 1925.

63. These payments were bookkeeping entries. The rate paid on interbranch transfers was somewhat lower than the deposit rate.

64. While it is unclear whether it charged a transfer price to its offices and branches for reallocating funds, the Bank of London and South America also showed signs of competition between locations for access to idle funds, especially during periods of recession. The bank's London head office often mediated the negotiations for funds transfers. See, for example, Bank of London and South America, Telegrams between London and Rio de Janeiro, Archives of the Bank of London and South America, University College, London, B14/3, 31 August 1927 and 5 September 1929 (hereafter BOLSA, Telegrams).

65. BB, Atas, 6 October 1910.

66. BB, Atas, 27 March 1912; Crédito Real, Atas, 6 September 1912.

67. BB, Cartas—examples include 8 June 1922 and 20 October 1922. These letters are abundant from 1921 to 1926.

68. Leis e Decretos, Decreto 434, 4 July 1891.

69. The development of the banking and accounting professions are sometimes taken as benchmarks in the formation of modern urban middle classes. Sidney Pollard, *The Genesis of Modern Management: A Study of the Industrial Revolution in Great Britain.* (Harmondsworth, Mddx.: Penguin Books 1968). I thank Rory Miller for this reference.

70. Associação de Bancos no Estado do Rio de Janiero, *Os dez primeiros Anos de ABERJ (Associação de Bancos no Estado do Rio de Janeiro),* (Rio de Janeiro: ABERJ (Associação de Bancos no estado do Rio de Janeiro), n.d.

71. Maria Antonieta P. Leopoldi, "Industrial Associations and Politics in Contemporary Brazil: The Associations of Industrialists, Economic Policy-Making and the State with Special Reference to the Period 1930-61" (Ph.D. diss., Cambridge University, 1984), offers the fullest discussion of this phenomenon with respect to industrialization in Brazil.

72. The published bank income statements do not offer this level of detail for expenses for enough organizations to make such an assessment feasible. Further, the methodology of such an assessment would take the study too far afield from its main purpose.

73. A transatlantic telephone call between the head office and the Rio de Janeiro office of the Bank of London and South America during the "Revolution of 1930" merited a notation about the medium of communication (BOLSA, Telegrams, B14/4, 14 October 1930).

74. Two seminal examples of the theoretical literature on the relationship between property rights and economic growth are North, *Structure and Change,* and William B. Scott, *In Pursuit of Happiness: American Conceptions of Property from the Seventeenth to the Twentieth Century* (Bloomington: Indiana University Press, 1977).

75. *RC,* 1898, 20-21, and 1901, 22; U.K. Foreign Office, *Diplomatic and Consular Reports on Trade and Finance,* Annual Series (London: Harrison & Sons, 1895-1914), no. 2080 [1897], 19, no. 2747 [1900], 11-2, and no. 3713 [1905], 7-8.

76. Honório Fernandes Monteiro, "Effeitos da sentença declaratória de fallência sobre o contracto de conte corrente, quanto ás remessas com a clausula 'Salvo em Bolsa.'" Dissertação apresentada à congregação de Faculdade de Direito de São Paulo para concurso á doencia livre de direito commercial, São Paulo, Emp. Graphica de *Revista do Tribunaes,* 1929.

77. At times bankrupted parties did continue to have access to these accounts. The funds would otherwise have been available to settle the bankruptcy. Monteiro, "Effeitos da sentença declaratória de fallência."

78. An early example of the inability to easily settle a bankruptcy, and the threat of non-pro rata settlements, was the case of the Banco de Crédito Commercial. BB (Banco da República), *Atas;* 14 February 1899.

79. Leis e Decretos, Decreto 859, 16 August 1902, art. 5. This paragraph is based on the provisions of this law, which were in effect until December 1929. A substantially complete draft version of the law is also summarized in U.K. Foreign Office, *Diplomatic and Consular Reports,* vol. 105 (1901), 11-2.

80. M. A. de S. Sa Vianna, *Das fallências* (Rio de Janeiro: Hildbrant, 1907), 117-18.

81. Sa Vianna, *Fallências,* 148-51. During the First Republic, it became commonly accepted that corporate entities could be treated similarly to individuals.

82. Sa Vianna, *Fallências,* 97.

83. Sa Vianna, *Fallências,* 103. Sa Vianna cites this as a reason that bankruptcies were typically only called when it became clear that debtors were severely undercapitalized and had little likelihood of achieving solvency in the foreseeable future. Late payments were not cause for invoking proceedings that could result in bankruptcy. The Bank of London and Brazil was particularly blunt in describing these accommodations; see, for example, BOLSA, Letters, G3/9, 12 March 1908 and 3 December 1908.

84. U.S. Bureau of Foreign and Domestic Commerce, "Banking and Credit in Argentina, Brazil, Chile and Peru," by Edward S. Hurley, U.S. Bulletin of the Department of Commerce, Special Agents Series no. 90 (Washington, D.C.: GPO, 1914), 41-42. The last sentence of the quotation referred to the high interest rate charged to borrowers in reflection of their poor creditworthiness. When, and if, debt payments resumed, the recovering businessman was faced with a higher debt burden to cover his special borrowing needs. If bankruptcy was not avoided, lenders would probably not recover the full value in settling the account.

85. BOLSA, Letters, G3/7, 9 March 1905.

86. BOLSA, Letters, G3/12, 23 March 1923, 25 January 1924, 29 May 1924,

25 June 1924, and 4 July 1924; BOLSA, Telegrams, B14/2, 23 July 1925, and B14/4, 20 November 1929.

87. As of 1929, this relationship was continuing and unresolved, although the firm seemed to move closer to declaring a bankruptcy. My archival notes do not document a settlement of the firm's business or problems.

88. Sa Vianna, *Falências,* 99–100. I would like to have studied bankruptcies of banks. This would have provided a very interesting perspective on the full range of issues with respect to identifying, defining, and distributing financial assets. However, after the crisis of 1900-01, important banks did not fail; the difficulties of finding sufficient information prevented this course of research.

89. Another interesting example occurred when National City Bank tried to withdraw from the ongoing support of P. J. Nicolson orchestrated by the Bank of London and South America. BOLSA, Telegrams, 29 May 1924 and 22 August 1925.

90. BB, Atas, 21 September 1915 and 24 November 1915.

91. BOLSA, Telegrams, B14/2, 18 September 1925.

92. BOLSA, Telegrams, B4/4, 1 February 1929.

93. Comind, *Relatório,* 1928, 3.

94. BB, Atas, 2 August 1928; BB, *Relatório,* 1928, 13-4.

95. BB, Atas, 23 July 1927, 7 October 1927, 20 October 1927, and 30 November 1927.

96. BB, Atas, 19 December 1929 and 19 December 1930.

97. The provisions for the process of declaring and settling bankruptcies continued with the amendment of the bankruptcy laws. Leis e Decretos, Lei 5746, 9 December 1929.

98. Dr. N. Eizerik, interview, 18 October 1991. According to Dr. Eizerik, discomfort with the concepts of financial property, as compared to real property, continues to impede financial development and the day-to-day ability to settle financial disputes and to specify complex financial transactions.

99. Leis e Decretos, Decreto 13110, 19 July 1918.

100. MF, *Relatório,* 1922, 512-22.

101. MF, *Relatório,* 1920, 140-41. Also, at the time, banks maintained reserves on their own of 40-50 percent, and up to 70 percent.

102. MF, *Relatório,* 1922, 513.

103. Leff, "The Group Principle," 104-06.

104. RC, 1928, 3.

105. RC, 1928, 12.

Chapter 7

1. Nathaniel H. Leff, *Underdevelopment and Development in Brazil,* 2 vols. (London and Boston: Allen & Unwin, 1982); Luiz Carlos T. D. Prado,

"Commercial Capital, Domestic Market and Manufacturing in Imperial Brazil: The Failure of Brazilian Economic Development in the Nineteenth Century" (Ph.D. diss., University of London, 1991).

2. Aspásia Camargo, "La federación sometida, nacionalismo desarrollista e inestabilidad democrática," in *Federalismos latinoamericanos: México, Brasil, Argentina,* ed. Marcello Carmagnani (México: Fondo de Cultura Económica, 1993), 303.

3. Joseph L. Love, "Federalismo y regionalismo en Brasil, 1889-1937," in *Federalismos latinoamericanos: México, Brasil, Argentina,* ed. Marcello Carmagnani (México: Fondo de Cultura Económica, 1993), 180-220; Thomas H. Holloway, *The Brazilian Coffee Valorization of 1906* (Madison: Wisconsin Historical Society, 1975).

4. Banco do Brasil, Atas dos Directores, Banco do Brasil Archives, Rio de Janeiro, 10 September 1900 (hereafter BB, Atas); Brasil, Ministério da Fazenda, *Relatório apresentado ao Presidente da República dos Estados Unidos do Brasil pelo Ministro de Estado dos Negócios da Fazenda* (Rio de Janeiro: Imprensa Nacional), 1907, xix (hereafter MF, *Relatório*); Gustavo Henrique Barroso Franco, *Reforma monetária e instabilidade durante a transição republicana,* 2d ed. (Rio de Janeiro: Banco Nacional de Desenvolvimento Econômico e Social, 1987), 77-91.

5. Raymond W. Goldsmith, *Brasil 1850-1984: Desenvolvimento financeiro sob um século de inflação* (São Paulo: Banco Bamerindus e Ed. Harper Row do Brasil, 1986), 100; Banco do Brasil, *Relatório do Banco do Brasil apresentado à Assembléia Geral dos accionistas na sessão ordinaria,* Banco do Brasil Archives, Rio de Janeiro, 1915, 41-42, and 1922, 10-11(hereafter BB, Relatório).

6. BB, *Relatório,* 1927, 5-6.

7. Bank of London and South America, Letters from London to Rio de Janeiro, Archives of the Bank of London and South America, University College, London, G3/8, 5 September 1907; G3/10, 20 January 1910 (hereafter BOLSA, Letters).

8. BOLSA, Letters, G3/9, 15 July 1908.

9. The only other financial institution with national representation was the Rio de Janeiro Bolsa de Valores, which slowly acquired a national character by listing and trading the shares of companies from geographically separate areas of Brazil.

10. Interstate branching began slowly, with cumbersome regulatory arrangements, in the 1920s.

11. Financial mechanisms supporting rubber commerce have been the target of very little research. Barbara Weinstein, *The Amazon Rubber Boom, 1850-1920* (Stanford, Calif.: Stanford University Press, 1983), is the best source for a background on rubber production and commerce.

12. This branch was instrumental in the transfer of funds associated with the second coffee valorization of 1917.

13. BB, *Relatório,* 1915, 41–42.

14. *Retrospecto Comercial de Journal do Commércio* (Rio de Janeiro: *Jornal de Commércio* de Rodrigues e Cia.) 1917, 103–04 (hereafter *RC*).

15. BB, *Relatório,* 1922, 10.

16. Banco do Brasil, Cartas Particulares dos Presidentes, Banco do Brasil Archives, Rio de Janeiro, 26 October 1921 (hereafter BB, Cartas).

17. BB, *Relatório,* 1928, 12–13. In 1928, the bank reported the cumulative operating loss of the branches to be 3,232 contos.

18. Financial statements for individual branches are only available from 1908 to 1916. BB, *Relatório,* 1908–16 annually; Gail D. Triner, "Banking and Brazilian Economic Development: 1906–1930" (Ph.D. diss., Columbia University, 1994), Table 3.7.

19. BB, *Relatório,* 1909–16.

20. In 1910 and 1915, the net transfers to all of the branches were in excess of the credit they extended.

21. While unable to liquidate the bank's rubber losses, Banco do Brasil branches reached 10 percent of total Brazilian credit. BB, *Relatório,* Financial statements, 1908–16.

22. BB, *Relatório,* 1921, 11, and 1922, 10–11.

23. BB, Cartas, 8 July 1921, 26 August 1921, and 16 September 1921; Triner, "Banking and Brazilian Economic Development," Table 3.6.

24. BB, Cartas, 8 July 1921.

25. *Jornal do Commércio,* (Rio de Janeiro: Rodrigues e Cia), 22 August 1923 (hereafter *JC*).

26. BB, *Relatório,* 1922–30, annually. Correspondent balances are not included in credit and deposit volumes.

27. In 1930, these four geographic areas accounted for approximately 80 percent of Brazil's industrial production and 85 percent of banking assets (broadly defined), and provided 80 percent of State revenues. (Steven Topik, *The Political Economy of the Brazilian State, 1889–1930,* Latin American Monographs, Institute of Latin American Studies the University of Texas at Austin, no. 71 [Austin: University of Texas Press, 1987], Table 4). While it would be interesting to consider the extent to which finance incorporated more "peripheral" regions into larger capital markets, data constraints render such an analysis infeasible. This chapter begins from an even more fundamental perspective, by exploring the integration of the largest and richest areas. Empirical data on state economies during the First Republic are extraordinarily scarce.

28. Lance E. Davis, "The Investment Market, 1870–1914: The Evolution of a National Market," *Journal of Economic History* 25 (1965): 355–99; Richard Sylla, "Federal Policy, Banking Market Structure and Capital Mobility in the United States, 1863–1914," *Journal of Economic History* 29, no. 4 (December 1969): 657–86; Gene Smiley, "Interest Rate Movements in the United States, 1888–1913," *Journal of Economic History* 35

(September 1975): 591-620; John A. James, "Banking Market Structure, Risk and the Pattern of Local Interest Rates in the United States, 1893-1911," *Review of Economics and Statistics* 53, no. 4 (November 1976): 453-62; Kerry A. Odell, "The Integration of Regional and Interregional Capital Markets: Evidence from the Pacific Coast, 1883-1913," *Journal of Economic History* 49, no. 2 (June 1989): 297-309; Howard Bodenhorn, "Capital Mobility and Financial Integration in Antebellum America," *Journal of Economic History* 52, no. 3 (September 1992): 585-610; Howard Bodenhorn, "A More Perfect Union: Regional Interest Rates in the United States, 1880-1960," in *Anglo-American Financial Systems: Institutions and Markets in the Twentieth Century,* ed. Michael D. Bordo and Richard Eugene Sylla (Burr Ridge, Ill.: Irwin Professional Pub., 1995); Howard Bodenhorn and Hugh Rockoff, "Regional Interest Rates in Antebellum America," in *Strategic Factors in Nineteenth Century American Economic History: A Volume to Honor Robert Fogel,* ed. Claudia Goldin and Hugh Rockoff (Chicago: University of Chicago Press and National Bureau of Economic Research, 1992), 159-88.

29. Davis, "Investment Market"; James, "Banking Market Structure"; Odell, "Integration of Regions"; Bodenhorn, "Capital Mobility and Financial Integration in Antebellum America"; and Bodenhorn and Rockoff, "Regional Interest Rates," examine various arguments on capital mobility in the United States increasingly supporting converging conditions for money, and hence, converging interest rates. Sylla ("Banking Market Structure") otherwise argues that the interest rate differentials did not capture real capital immobility or hinder economic growth during the nineteenth century in the United States. Smiley ("Interest Rate Movements"), on the other hand, finds little or no evidence of financial integration for the period 1888-1913, the period when most economic historians of the United States look for it.

30. Odell, "Integration of Regions."

31. Sylla, "Banking Market Structure."

32. James R. Malley, "Dynamic Specification in Econometric Estimation," *Journal of Agricultural Economics Research* 42, no. 2 (1990): 52-55 and Peter Kennedy, *A Guide to Econometrics,* 3d ed. (Cambridge, Mass.: MIT Press, 1993), 250-54, offer further discussion of the technical aspects of the model. More sophisticated time-series and factor-analysis models can also test these hypotheses. However, the nature, quantity, and specificity of the currently available data mitigate their usefulness. (I thank Leonard Nakamura for these ideas.) The tests used here do not follow the usual procedures for integration, using an error correction model to test for a unit root, because I am not testing for the existence of an integrated market. I do not hypothesize that markets were fully integrated at this time. Here, I am testing for trends toward integration—a much more modest expectation.

33. Governor Júlio Prestes, campaigning in 1929 for the presidency of Brazil,

cited in Joseph L. Love, *São Paulo in the Brazilian Federation, 1889-1937* (Stanford, Calif.: Stanford University Press, 1980), 36. The term paulista refers to being from São Paulo.

34. Warren Dean, *The Industrialization of São Paulo, 1880-1945*, Latin American Monographs, no. 17 (Austin: Published for the Institute of Latin American Studies by the University of Texas Press, 1969); Nelson Hideiki Nozoe, *São Paulo, economia cafeeira e urbanização: Estudo da estrutura tributária e das atividades econômicas na capital paulista (1889-1933)*, Série Ensaios Econômicos/IPE/USP, no. 39 (São Paulo: IPE/USP, 1984).

35. Wilson Suzigan, *Indústria brasileira: Origem e desenvolvimento* (São Paulo: Brasiliense, 1986); Dean, *Industrialization of São Paulo.*

36. Wilson Cano, *Raízes da concentração industrial em São Paulo*, Corpo e Alma do Brasil, no. 53 (Rio de Janeiro: DIFEL/Difusão Editorial, S.A., 1977).

37. The share of deposits from São Paulo declined to 20 percent of the total banking system while the Rediscount Office was open and financing Treasury expenditure.

38. The low absolute value of the coefficient for CONVERGE (0.22, Table 7.1) suggests the slow rate of convergence.

39. Attempts early in the Republic to revitalize cane production and sugar refining also failed to revitalize commercial agriculture. Marieta de Moraes Ferreira, *Em busca da idade de ouro: As elites políticas fluminenses na Primeira República (1889-1930)* (Rio de Janiero: Editora UFRJ/Edições Tempo Brasileiro, 1994), Chapter 3; Marieta de Moraes Ferreira, "A crise dos comissários de café de Rio de Janeiro" (Tese de mestrado, Niterói, Universidade Federal Fluminense, 1977).

40. These issues are addressed indirectly in Ferreira, "A crise dos comissários"; Ferreira, *Busca da idade de ouro;* Eulália Maria Lahmeyer Lobo, *História do Rio de Janeiro: do capital comercial ao capital industrial e financeiro*, 2 vols. (Rio de Janeiro: IBMEC, 1978); José Murilo de Carvalho, *Os bestializados: O Rio de Janeiro e a República que não foi*, 3d ed. (São Paulo: Cia. das Letras, 1989); Jeffrey D. Needell, *A Tropical Belle Epoque: Elite Culture and Society in Turn-of-the-Century Rio de Janeiro*, Cambridge Latin American Studies, no. 62 (Cambridge: Cambridge University Press, 1987); Maria Bárbara Levy, *A indústria do Rio de Janeiro através de suas sociedades anônimas: esboços de história empresarial*, Coleção Biblioteca Carioca (Rio de Janeiro: Editora UFRJ: Prefeitura da Cidade do Rio de Janeiro, Secretária Municipal de Cultura, Departamento Geral de Documentação e Informação Cultural, Divisão de Editoração, 1988 [published posthumously 1994]).

41. Lobo, *História do Rio de Janeiro*, Chapter 4.

42. Levy, *Indústria do Rio de Janeiro*, Chapter 6.

43. Two short breaks in the interest rate history, due to data availability problems, occurred for carioca banks.

44. Fernando Nogueira da Costa, "Bancos em Minas Gerais (1889-1964)" (Tese de mestrado, Brasil, Universidade Estadual de Campinas, 1978), 22, 64; John D. Wirth, *Minas Gerais in the Brazilian Federation, 1889-1937* (Stanford, Calif.: Stanford University Press, 1977), Chapter 2. Wirth takes a much more pessimistic position about the mineiro economy than many others.

45. Da Costa, "Minas Gerais," 34.

46. Da Costa, "Minas Gerais," 58-70.

47. Laird W. Bergad, *Slavery and the Demographic and Economic History of Minas Gerais, Brazil, 1720-1888,* Cambridge Latin American Studies 85 (Cambridge and New York: Cambridge University Press, 1999).

48. Da Costa, "Minas Gerais," 53; Wirth, *Minas Gerais,* 32-51; Werner Baer, *The Brazilian Economy: Growth and Development,* 4th ed. (Westport, Conn.: Praeger, 1995), 32-35. Wirth, *Minas Gerais,* 32-33, suggests the First Republic as a whole to have been a period of relative decline for Minas Gerais. His point of comparison is São Paulo.

49. M. C. Eakin, "From Planters to Industrialists: Textile Manufacturing and the Origins of Industrialization in Belo Horizonte, Brazil, 1890s-1940s" (paper presented at the Latin American Studies Association Conference, Washington, D.C., September 1995).

50. Da Costa, "Minas Gerais," 78-88. Apparently, the traditional political rivalry between the states of Rio de Janeiro, São Paulo, and Minas Gerais motivated the development of state-level financial involvement; da Costa finds evidence of prominent mineiro politicians accusing the Banco do Brasil of hurting mineiro interests for political reasons.

51. Proxy interest rate information is not available for Rio Grande do Sul. It is only available for the Banco de Crédito Real in Minas Gerais. After 1911, when other limited-liability banks began to appear, the Crédito Real retained an average of about 50 percent of bank deposits in Minas Gerais for the remainder of the period; therefore, its interest rates determined prevailing rates in the state. However, since it became a state-owned bank, and this transition occurred relatively early, I prefer to discuss the interest rate experience of the Crédito Real in that context below.

52. I could find no discussion or legislative evidence to inform the conditions and terms on which a private, out-of-state bank opened in Minas Gerais. Neither did other out-of-state domestic banks (other than the Banco do Brasil) seem to open branches in Minas Gerais.

53. Banco Hipotecário e Agrícola de Minas Gerais opened a branch in São Paulo in 1921 (again, under unclear arrangements), demonstrating the importance of São Paulo to the mineiro economy. Flávio A. M. de Saes, *Crédito e bancos no desenvolvimento da economia paulista: 1850-1930* (São Paulo: Instituto de Pesquisas Econômicas, 1986), 106.

54. Wirth (*Minas Gerais,* Chapter 2) cites the Minas Gerais economy as second in size to São Paulo in industry and agriculture (Table 2.2).

55. Eugenio Lagemann, *O Banco Pelotense e o sistema financeiro regional,* Série Documenta no. 19 (Porto Alegre, RS: Mercado Aberto, 1985), 28.

56. Pedro Cezar Dutra Fonseca, "A transição capitalista no Rio Grande do Sul: A economia gaúcha na Primeira República," *Estudos Econômicos* 15, no. 2 (May–August 1985): 263-89.

57. Fonseca, "Transição capitalista," 270.

58. Fonseca, "Transição capitalista," 271.

59. Joseph L. Love, *Rio Grande do Sul and Brazilian Regionalism, 1882-1930* (Stanford, Calif.: Stanford University Press, 1971), 129, suggests that growth in Rio Grande do Sul exceeded that of Minas Gerais in the 1920s.

60. Lagemann (*Banco Pelotense,* 65-71 and Table 24) suggests that foreign bank presence in Rio Grande do Sul did not exceed 10-12 percent of deposits in the state after 1906.

61. Other states also opened and subsidized mortgage banks during the 1920s. The banks in São Paulo and Minas Gerais were the largest and most important, and probably the most successful. Other states also attempted smaller state-supported agricultural banks; for example, in Paraná a state bank opened in 1914 (*RC,* 1914, 144). During the 1920s, other state-owned banks opened in Rio Grande do Sul, Paraíba, and Piauí (Baer, *Brazilian Economy,* 276). Chapter 6 considers the institutional problems of long-term lending and funding.

62. In the case of the Banco de Crédito Real de Minas Gerais, the notes had a life of 30 years. It was the only bank to publicly issue and trade these notes on the Rio de Janeiro Bolsa de Valores for a sustained period during the First Republic (*JC,* various issues, 1889-1930, monthly trading tables for the Bolsa de Valores). The Banco do Estado de São Paulo also issued mortgage notes in 1928.

63. In addition, both banks held bonds issued by the state in their asset portfolios as collateral against the mortgage notes they issued. These were not the types of income-earning assets that Brazilian banks typically chose as investments. Bonds lacked the liquidity that banks tried to maintain in their portfolios, and they probably incurred an opportunity cost in comparison to other investments. The bonds lacked liquidity since their maturity matched that of the mortgage notes, which was significantly in excess of the four to six month exposure of commercial credit instruments. The bonds serving as collateral in each instance were issued by the respective state governments, at reduced interest rates.

64. These provisions in Minas Gerais are specified in Banco de Crédito Real de Minas Gerais, *Estátutos do Banco de Crédito Real de Minas Gerais, de Accôrdo com as Modificações,* Crédito Real Archive, Juiz de Fora, Minas Gerais, August, 1898 (hereafter Crédito Real, *Estátutos*), and the contract between the bank and the State, 18 December 1908. For São Paulo, see Banco de Crédito Hypothecário e Agrícola do Estado de São Paulo and Banco do Estado de São Paulo, *Relatórios e contas de administração do*

BCHASP que serão submetidos a approvação dos acçionistas do mesmo banco em reunião annual, Banco do Estado de São Paulo Library, São Paulo, 1912, 6; 1924, 5-6; 1926, 1-3; 1927, 3-4 (hereafter Bchasp/Banespa, *Relatório*); and the contract between Bchasp and the State of São Paulo, 24 January 1924. Early attempts of the State of São Paulo to encourage mortgage lending through the (failed) Banco de Crédito Real de São Paulo are documented in the Estado de São Paulo, Secretário da Fazenda, *Relatório apresentado ao Presidente do Estado pelo Secretário da Fazenda,* (São Paulo), 1898-1903 (hereafter Secretário da Fazenda [São Paulo], *Relatório*).

65. Da Costa also notes that, initially, Bchasp had significant private-bank participation in share ownership; for example, Comind owned 28 percent of the bank's original capital. Fernando Nogueira da Costa, "Banco do Estado: O Caso Banespa" (Tese de doutoramento, Universidade Estadual de Campinas, 1988), 53.

66. Saes, *Crédito e bancos,* 126.

67. Secretário da Fazenda (São Paulo), *Relatório,* 1925, viii.

68. Winston Fritsch, *External Constraints on Economic Policy in Brazil, 1889-1930* (Pittsburgh: University of Pittsburgh Press, 1988), 137; da Costa, "Banespa," Chapters 2 and 3.

69. Robert H. Bates, *Open-Economy Politics: The Political Economy of the World Coffee Trade* (Princeton: Princeton University Press, 1997), 45-47; Fritsch, *External Constraints,* 107-10.

70. Fritsch, *External Constraints,* 107-09; Carlos Manuel Peláez, "As conseqüências econômicas da ortodoxia monetária, cambial e fiscal no Brasil entre 1889-1945," *Revista Brasileira de Economia* 5, no. 3 (July-September 1971): 59.

71. See Chapter 3. An explanation with more logical and historical consistency for the transfer of coffee price supports and accompanying monetary mechanisms to the state of São Paulo is that it placed the cost and operation of the programs with the group deriving the most benefit from them. The attendant transfer of political and economic power was more obvious ex-post than ex-ante.

72. This question deserves more empirical research.

73. Carlos Manuel Peláez, "Análise econômica do programa brasileiro de sustentação do café—1906-1945: Teoria, política e medição," *Revista Brasileira de Economia* 25, no. 4 (October-December 1971): 72-76.

74. Bchasp/Banespa, *Relatório,* 1927, 1-2; Secretário da Fazenda (São Paulo), *Relatório,* 1920; 1925, viii; and 1926, vii and x.

75. Bchasp/Banespa, *Relatório,* 1927, 3-4; 1928, 4; and 1929, 3. Institutional histories of these banks, and their relationships with their states, can be found in da Costa, "Minas Gerais"; da Costa, "Banespa."

76. Da Costa, "Banespa"; Peláez, "Análise econômica," 79-81.

77. Da Costa, "Banespa," Chapter 4, 159; Paulo Neuhaus, "A Monetary History of Brazil, 1900-1945" (Ph.D. diss., University of Chicago, 1974), 92.

78. Increased real deposits were 254,000 contos and 393,000 contos for Banespa and the Banco do Brasil, respectively, during each relevant two-year period.
79. Da Costa, "Banespa," 146.
80. Bates, *Open-Economy Politics,* 41-47.
81. Da Costa, "Minas Gerais," 76-79.
82. In addition to the Banco de Crédito Real de São Paulo failure in 1904 (Saes, *Crédito e bancos,* 128), the Banco do Lavouro e Commércio in Rio de Janeiro was also in receivership by the bank reforms of 1906.
83. Banco de Crédito Real de Minas Gerais, *Livros das Atas dos Assembléias Gerais,* Crédito Real Archive, Juiz de Fora, Minas Gerais, 5 January 1918 (hereafter Crédito Real Atas AG).
84. In 1911, the state treasury funded a second mortgage bank in Belo Horizonte, the Banco Hipotecário e Agrícola de Minas Gerais. The new bank faltered, but it served as the intermediary through which the state of Minas Gerais began acquiring shares of the Crédito Real. Da Costa, "Minas Gerais," Chapter 2.
85. Banco de Crédito Real de Minas Gerais, *Livros das Atas da Diretória,* Livros 1-2, Crédito Real Archive, Juiz de Fora, Minas Gerais, August 1912 (hereafter Crédito Real, Atas).
86. Crédito Real, Atas, 3 August 1918; Crédito Real, Atas AG, 8 July 1928.
87. See, for example, Crédito Real, Atas AG, 18 February 1922.
88. Banco de Crédito Real de Minas Gerais, *Relátorio apresentado à Assembléia Geral dos Accionistas do Banco de Crédito Real de Minas Gerais* na sua Reunião Ordinária, Crédito Real Archive, Juiz de Fora, Minas Gerais (Juiz de Fora: Typ. Pereira), 1924; Crédito Real, Atas, 8 July 1926 and 9 October 1926.
89. Da Costa, "Minas Gerais," 75-78.
90. Da Costa, "Minas Gerais," Table 11.
91. This shift from low rates at Crédito Real (and by extension in Minas Gerais) is even more notable when the interest rate is approximated with the gross income measure. Under the alternative measure, the bank ends the Republic as a *high* interest rate organization. The difference between these two measures reflects the revenue and expense structure of the bank, and this implies that Crédito Real had a higher level of expenses (operating and interest expenses) than was the Brazilian norm. Not enough information is available to determine whether the difference was due to inefficient management, corruption/favoritism, or high costs of raising funds (interest expense on deposits).
92. This corresponds with the experience in the western United States of higher rate differentials and lower sensitivity to fluctuations in the financially developed center. Odell, "Integration of Regions," 306.
93. The cases of Banespa in the early 1990s significantly increasing public-sector indebtedness, and of the state of Minas Gerais threatening to not

honor its debt obligations to the Central Bank in January 1999, offer very good cases in point for the late twentieth century. The experience of the mineiro treasury in January 1999 was associated with the Central Bank abandoning its policy of maintaining an exchange rate fixed to the U.S. dollar, and the subsequent devaluation of the real. See, for example, multiple articles in *The Economist* (London: Economist Newspaper Ltd., 16 January 1999): "Itamar Franco Takes His Revenge," "Brazil on the Slide," and "Storm Clouds from Brazil." Any news or business magazine from this date would provide similar stories.

Chapter 8

1. Whitaker had been president of the Banco do Brasil from 1920 to 1922, leading the bank during its largest rediscounting program. This experience with domestic monetary protection served him well as Treasury minister at the onset of the Depression. Augusto de Bulhões, *Ministros da Fazenda do Brasil, 1808-1954* (Rio de Janeiro, Brasil: Departamento de Impr. Nacional, 1955).

2. *Retrospecto Comercial de Journal do Commércio* (Rio de Janeiro: *Jornal de Commércio* de Rodrigues e Cia.) 1930, 29 (hereafter *RC*); Bank of London and South America, Telegrams between London and Rio de Janeiro, Archives of the Bank of London and South America, University College, London, B14/4, 3 October–13 November 1930 (hereafter BOLSA, Telegrams); Paulo Neuhaus, "A Monetary History of Brazil, 1900-1945" (Ph.D. diss., University of Chicago, 1974), 96-97.

3. Wilson Suzigan, *Indústria brasileira: origem e desenvolvimento* (São Paulo: Brasiliense, 1986).

4. This study has suggested a variety of explanations for the formation of the most important of the state-level banks, Banespa. These explanations have competing implications for the political economy. Specific research could valuably inform this topic.

5. As, in the early example of the Brasil, Ministério da Fazenda, *Relatório apresentado ao Presidente da República dos Estados Unidos do Brasil pelo Ministro de Estado dos Negócios da Fazenda* (Rio de Janeiro: Imprensa Nacional), 1901, xxvii and xliii-v (hereafter MF, *Relatório*): "If the banks accomplished their business, trying to harmonize their interests with those of the nation that gave them such generous concessions, they would find favorable profits by continuously distributing notes. . . . Unfortunately this is not the case; [and] it is facilitating speculation."

6. Banco do Commércio e Indústria de São Paulo, *Relatório e contas da administração* Banco do Commércio e Indústria de São Paulo que serão apresentados aos accionistas, (São Paulo: H. Puchetti), Banco do Commércio e Indústria de São Paulo Archive, São Paulo, 1920, 10 (hereafter Comind, *Relatório*).

7. See, for example, various essays in Alfred C. Stepan, *The Military in Politics: Changing Patterns in Brazil* (Princeton: Princeton University Press, 1971), and Thomas E. Skidmore, *Politics in Brazil, 1930-1964: An Experiment in Democracy* (New York: Oxford University Press, 1967).

8. Antônio Delfim Netto, *O problema do café no Brasil*, Ensaios Econômicos, no. 16 (São Paulo: Instituto de Pesquisas Econômicas, 1981); William Summerhill, "Transport Improvements and Economic Growth in Brazil and Mexico," in *How Latin America Fell Behind: Essays on the Economic Histories of Brazil and Mexico, 1800-1914*, ed. Stephen Haber (Stanford, Calif.: Stanford University Press, 1997), 93-117; Werner Baer, *The Brazilian Economy: Growth and Development*, 4th ed. (Westport, Conn.: Praeger, 1995), Chapter 11.

9. Boris Fausto, *A revolução de 1930: Historiografia e história* (São Paulo: Editora Brasiliense, 1989 [1970]) is a standard, if somewhat dated, source on the revolution of 1930.

10. Baer, *Brazilian Economy*, Chapters 3 and 4.

11. Geraldo de Beauclair Mendes de Oliveira, "A evolução do sistema financeiro na época Vargas" (Tese de mestrado, Niterói, Universidade Federal Fluminense, 1974).

12. Brasil, Instituto Brasileiro de Geografia e Estatística, *Estatísticas históricas do Brasil: Séries econômicas, demográficas e sociais 1550 a 1985*, 2d ed., Séries Estatísticas Históricas do Brasil, 3 (Rio de Janeiro: IBGE, 1990), Tables 4.3-4.8 and 5.4-5.5; Raymond W. Goldsmith, *Brasil 1850-1984: Desenvolvimento financeiro sob um século de inflação* (São Paulo: Banco Bamerindus e Ed. Harper Row do Brasil, 1986), Chapters 4-6; Baer, *Brazilian Economy*, Chapters 4-9.

13. Carlos Manuel Peláez, *História econômica do Brasil: Um elo entre a teoria e a realidade econômica*, 1st ed. (São Paulo: Atlas, 1979), Chapter 5. As the economy industrialized, the tone of the debates about monetary policy and the interdependencies of domestic and international markets changed somewhat, but their underlying concerns were consistent with those of the First Republic. The composition of exports had shifted to include manufactured goods as well as primary products, and the Brazilian position in world coffee markets had eroded. However, international debt and trade remained crucial to Brazilian finances. The strong Brazilian participation in articulating dependency theory from the post–World War II years to the mid-1970s is firmly rooted to this long-term and deeply entrenched controversy. (Gail D. Triner, "The Delayed Development of Early Brazilian Financial Historiography, 1889-1930," *Revista de Historia Económica* 17, special issue [1999]: 53-76). Subsequent political economy trends of "globalization" reflect the same concerns, though radically different judgments; Brazilians continue to have leading roles in these debates.

14. The cruzeiro replaced the mil-réis in 1941. Since then, the Brazilian currency has been redefined a number of times with successive inflation-control programs. Most recently, the *real* was introduced in 1994.

15. In addition to the economic discussions of inflation in Baer, *Brazilian Economy,* Chapters 5 and 7, and Goldsmith, *Brasil 1850-1984,* see the interesting interdisciplinary consideration of the effects of long-term inflation on Brazilian society and culture in José Ribas Vieira, et al., eds., *Na corda bamba: Doze estudos sobre a cultura da inflação* (Rio de Janeiro, RJ: Relume Dumará, 1993).

16. See, for example, Albert Fishlow, "Some Reflections in Post-1964 Brazilian Economic Policy," in *Authoritarian Brazil: Origins, Policies, and Future,* ed. Alfred C. Stepan (New Haven: Yale University Press, 1973), 69-118.

17. See John H. Welch, *Capital Markets in the Development Process: The Case of Brazil,* Pitt Latin American Series (Pittsburgh: University of Pittsburgh Press, 1993), Chapter 3, on the nature of the banking and capital market reforms of 1964. The economic historiography follows the periodization of political history: 1946-64, 1964-85, and 1985-present. As such, the political economy of the institution of the Central Bank is not well understood. (Baer, *Brazilian Economy;* Goldsmith, *Brasil 1850-1984;* Carlos Manuel Peláez and Wilson Suzigan, *História monetária do Brasil: Análise da política, comportamento e instituições monetárias,* Monografia no. 23 [Instituto de Planejamento Econômico e Social, Instituto de Pesquisas] [Rio de Janeiro: IPEA/INPES, 1976].) As this project and others have pointed out, some Brazilians had expressed a desire for an independent central bank since the end of the nineteenth century. The ability to constitute one in 1964 and the historical trajectory of the particular form it took would make an interesting project. I have not seen in the financial historiography a consideration of the effects of military coup and government. However, the economic historiography and political economy literature have noted the military's concern for the very high inflation rates during the early 1960s and its authoritarian implementation of very restrictive domestic monetary policy. Fishlow, "Some Reflections"; Albert Fishlow, "Brazilian Size Distribution of Income," *American Economic Review* 62, no. 2 (1972): 391-402.

18. State banks remain prominent in Brazil. Their main functions evolved to financing state governments, acting as local development banks, and offering commercial and consumer banking facilities. Francis A. Lees, James M. Botts, and Rubens Penha Cysne, *Banking and Financial Deepening in Brazil* (Houndmills, Basingstoke, Hampshire: Macmillan, 1990) 143-47.

19. Welch, *Capital Markets,* 79-81.

20. Public-sector "savings banks" had, in fact, opened in the late nineteenth century. They remained tiny and were not involved in credit creation. Savings banks, until the 1964 reforms, gathered deposits from "small depositors." These deposits were then transferred to the Banco do Brasil. They provided a very small source of additional deposits to the bank and instituted a mechanism for individuals of tiny means to be able to access the benefits of saving money within the banking system. Caixas Econômicas

did not have a significant effect on either the banking system or the savings practices of the general population during the First Republic.

21. Ricardo Alberto Bielschowsky, "Bancos e acumulação de capital na industrialização brasilieira—uma introductória (1935-1962)" (Tese de mestrado, Brasília, Universidade de Brasília, 1975). This practice appears to be a continuation of the "group principle" articulated by Leff Nathaniel H. Leff, "Capital Markets in the Less Developed Countries: The Group Principle," in *Money and Finance in Economic Growth and Development,* ed. Ronald I. McKinnon (New York: Dekker, 1976), 97-122, and indicates continuing constraints to the development of property rights in finance. Without more study, I am not clear on the influence of privately owned commercial banks on the political debates about the organization of the financial system or on monetary policy.

Appendix

1. The data used in this study are expanded, in terms of the banks included, from that used for previous publications (Gail D. Triner, "Banking and Brazilian Economic Development: 1906-1930" [Ph.D. diss., Columbia University, 1994], and Gail D. Triner, "The Formation of Modern Brazilian Banking, 1906-1930: Opportunities and Constraints Presented by the Public and Private Sectors," *Journal of Latin American Studies* 28 [February 1996]: 49-74). I have also separated out the two banks that became state-owned organizations (and always had subsidies from their state treasuries), Banespa and Crédito Real de Minas Gerais, from the privately owned banks in the sample. These changes in data treatment explain the differences in specific data points. However, in no instance has the expanded coverage resulted in changed conclusions from earlier work.

2. Analytic needs have counseled against using the few alternatives of published aggregated data that are available. The Finance Ministry and *Retrospecto Comercial* published statewide bank balance aggregations from 1916. These sources are undocumented and inflexible in their structure. Collecting data at the level of individual firms allows for the aggregation of banks to suit the analytic needs at hand, and to assess individual bank balances when desired. Also, the database chronologically extends back to 1906, which I identify in Chapter 3 as the institutional origin of the modern banking system.

3. Brasil, Instituto Brasileiro de Geografia e Estatística, *Estatísticas históricas do Brasil: Séries econômicas, demográficas e sociais 1550 a 1985,* 2d ed., Séries Estatísticas Históricas do Brasil, 3 (Rio de Janeiro: IBGE, 1990).

4. The banks included in this study differ from those in Flávio A. M. de Saes, *Crédito e bancos no desenvolvimento da economia paulista: 1850-1930* (São Paulo: Instituto de Pesquisas Econômicas, 1986). Saes included privately owned *casas bancárias,* credit unions, and cooperatives (as reported

in Estado de São Paulo, Repartição de Estatística e Arquivo do Estado, *Annuário estatístico do Estado de São Paulo,* annual series, [São Paulo: Typ. *Diário Official.* Hereafter Estado de São Paulo, *Annúario estátistico*]).

5. Steven Topik, *The Political Economy of the Brazilian State, 1889-1930,* Latin American Monographs, Institute of Latin American Studies the University of Texas at Austin, no. 71 (Austin: University of Texas Press, 1987), Table 4.

6. Estado de São Paulo, *Annuário estatístico.*

7. *Minas Gerais: Orgão official do governo mineiro,* Annual Series (Belo Horizonte: Imprensa Official, 1905-1930).

8. Eugenio Lagemann, *O Banco Pelotense e o sistema financeiro regional,* Série Documenta, no. 19 (Porto Alegre, R.S.: Mercado Aberto, 1985).

9. Jones Correia Filho, *Guia prática para o ensino de contabilidade bancária,* 1st ed. (Rio de Janeiro: Banco do Brasil/Flores e Mano, 1929). This text focuses on the mechanics of accounting entries, more than the economic characteristics of financial instruments.

10. The financial ratios that are derived from the data are calculated from annual average balance levels (the average from year-end of the prior year to year-end of the current year). Growth rates are calculated as the change (natural-log difference) from year-end to year-end.

11. Gustavo Henrique Barroso Franco, *Reforma monetária e instabilidade durante a transição republicana,* 2d ed. (Rio de Janeiro: Banco Nacional de Desenvolvimento Econômico e Social, 1987), 77-91; Brasil, Ministério da Fazenda, *Relatório apresentado ao Presidente da República dos Estados Unidos do Brasil pelo Ministro de Estado dos Negócios da Fazenda* (Rio de Janeiro: Imprensa Nacional), 1907, xiv.

12. Banespa's inclusion of interbank deposits is also a change in the bank's accounting procedures from earlier years.

13. By 1921, many banks reliably reported the distribution of their deposits according to whether or not they paid interest for demand deposits, and the distribution between demand and term deposits was widely reported through most of the period.

14. Limited deposits provided a small volume of lower cost funds to banks, while encouraging savings and investment among a segment of the population that had not previously saved. The Banco do Brasil provides the fullest discussion of provisions for limited deposits (Banco do Brasil, Cartas Particulares dos Presidentes, Banco do Brasil Archives, Rio de Janeiro, 15 May 1909; Banco do Brasil, Atas dos Directores, Banco do Brasil Archives, Rio de Janeiro, 12 November 1909; also *Retrospecto Comercial de Journal do Commércio* [Rio de Janeiro: *Jornal de Commércio* de Rodrigues e Cia.], 1909, 23-24). It is not clear what limited deposits provided to the small-scale savers, since popular savings banks (Caixas Econômicas) provided the same service to the same population and were located in the same regions as banks offering limited deposits.

These deposits, however, were presumably of interest to banks, since they lowered the cost of funding by a small amount.

15. These were referred to as *depósitos judiceais* and *depósitos committentes.*

16. According to current accounting practices, banks measure their capital as the difference between assets and liabilities. This is actively used to determine if banks maintain adequate amounts of credit.

17. The allocation of reserves may also have been related to policies with regard to the distribution of profits. I found instances of capital increases being financed by distribution of reserves to existing shareholders. For example, the capital increase of Banco de Commércio e Indústria de São Paulo increased its capital in January 1928 in this manner. (Banco do Commércio e Indústria de São Paulo, *Relatório e contas da administração* Banco do Commércio e Indústria de São Paulo que serão aprestendados aos accionistas, [São Paulo: H. Puchetti], Banco do Commércio e Indústria de São Paulo Archive, São Paulo, 1928, 31-33.) This suggests that bank policies with respect to capital and reserves retained a great deal of flexibility.

18. Contrary to current accounting standards, such assets were reported at book value, rather than at market or depreciated value. This was less distortive for banks than other types of firms, since banks tended to have relatively low levels of real assets. Nevertheless, their exclusion eliminates one possible source of distortion.

19. However, as a measure of increasing levels of exchange transactions conducted through markets, these categories can yield interesting information.

20. Because retained earnings and gains and losses were added to balances semiannually, it was impossible, and extraordinarily unreliable, to make any assumptions based on six-month data.

21. Very little detail of bank expenses is available. After 1912, bank income statements did not identify expenses by category unless the expense carried over into the balance sheet (the change in reserves, dividend payments, gains and losses, and sometimes directors' fees). Therefore interest and personnel expenses are not available. As with other Brazilian enterprises of the period, banks did not account for depreciation of fixed assets over their useful lives. This, however, does not represent a serious distortion, since banks do not own significant amounts of plant and equipment. However, not adjusting for depreciation carries the implicit assumption that the proportion of assets accounted for by bank real estate (office buildings and rent) was approximately equal among banks.

22. Gains and losses are not averaged to smooth out unusual occurrences. This does not appear to affect the results to a noticeable extent.

23. The data from these banks simply required more accumulating resources than I had available. With effort, I believe that they can be found.

24. Only one other attempt at constructing a time series of domestic interest rates exists. Paulo Neuhaus, "A Monetary History of Brazil, 1900-1945" (Ph.D. diss., University of Chicago, 1974), Table 40, presents apólice yields

(domestic debt instruments of the Federal government, structured like consuls). Neuhaus is not entirely clear on how the data have been constructed: for the early portion of that time series he reports semiannual yields, but he reports annual yields from 1922. The data are from a variety of sources. Neuhaus calculates the gains and losses from price change in his yield calculation (without giving the time period of the underlying data). To my knowledge, the Neuhaus data have not been used in analytic work.

25. On some of the difficulties encountered in estimating interest rates in the U.S., see John A. James, "Banking Market Structure, Risk and the Pattern of Local Interest Rates in the United States, 1893-1911," *Review of Economics and Statistics* 53, no. 4 (November 1976): 453-62; Lance E. Davis, "The Investment Market, 1870-1914: The Evolution of a National Market," *Journal of Economic History* 25 (1965): 355-99; Howard Bodenhorn and Hugh Rockoff, "Regional Interest Rates in Antebellum America," in *Strategic Factors in Nineteenth Century American Economic History: A Volume to Honor Robert Fogel,* ed. Claudia Goldin and Hugh Rockoff (Chicago: University of Chicago Press and National Bureau Economic Research, 1992), 159-88.

26. Earning assets, rather than credit, constitutes the denominator for two reasons. The practical reason is that banks did not report earnings relative to specific types of assets (except for some banks reporting implicit revenues on discounted notes for a short period). The substantive reason for determining rates relative to earning assets is that bankers were concerned about the composition of their entire portfolio of assets from which they could derive revenues.

27. Davis ("Investment Market," 357) also tackles these questions in early research of U.S. financial history. He finds the ratio of gross revenues to average earning assets an acceptable proxy measure for interest rates.

28. Davis, "Investment Market," 357; Bodenhorn and Rockoff, "Regional Interest Rates," 161.

29. Sensitivity testing of the two measures confirms their robust nature. The proxy rates based on gross revenues and net profits generally conform to each other in terms of the relative rankings of rate levels and the direction and magnitude of change.

30. Averages are calculated as the simple arithmetic average from the end date of the preceding semester to the end date of the current semester.

31. This also has the effect of constructing two semester averages to smooth short-term unusual anomalies. Much of the research on the United States has incorporated three-semester averaging.

32. The adjustment to calculate "real" (price-adjusted) balances does not apply to interest rate calculations.

33. Luis A. V. Catão, "A new wholesale price index for Brazil during the period 1870-1913," *Revista Brasileira de Economia* 46, no. 4 (October-December 1992): 519-33.

34. Cláudio R. Contador and Cláudio L. Haddad, "Produto real, moeda e preços: A experiência brasileira no período 1861–1970," *Revista Brasileira de Estatística* 143, no. 36 (1975): 407–40; Brasil, *Estatísticas históricas,* 151–52 and Table 5.2.

35. Raymond W. Goldsmith, *Brasil 1850–1984: Desenvolvimento financeiro sob um século de inflação* (São Paulo: Banco Bamerindus e Ed. Harper Row do Brasil, 1986), Tables 3-3 and 4-7.

36. Eulália Maria Lahmeyer Lobo, "O Encilhamento," *Revista Brasileira de Mercado de Capitais* 2, no. 5 (May–August 1976): 261–301; Raymond W. Goldsmith, *Premodern Financial Systems: A Historical Comparative Study* (Cambridge: Cambridge University Press, 1987).

37. Another method for combining the indices, based on regression results for predicting an extrapolated Catão index from the estimated correlation coefficients when regressing the Catão index on the Contador-Haddad price series (William Roderick Summerhill III, "Railroads and the Brazilian Economy Before 1914" [Ph.D. diss., Stanford University, 1995], 84–86), yielded clearly unrealistic results. These results reflected the peculiarities of extrapolating for an extended series (17 years, or data points) that began at a historically low level.

38. Calculated according to Edward I. Altman, *Financial Handbook,* 5th ed. (New York: Wiley, 1981), Chapter 31, Section 17.

39. Câmara Syndical dos Corretores de Fundos Públicos da Capital Federal, *Relatórios da Câmara Syndical dos Corretores de Fundos Públicos da Capital Federal,* Instituto Brasileiro de Mercados de Capitais (Rio de Janeiro: Imprensa Nacional), 1894–1931.

40. For the period to 1914, see Michael D. Bordo and Hugh Rockoff, "The Gold Standard as a Good Housekeeping Seal of Approval," *Journal of Economic History* 56, no. 2 (1996): 389–428.

41. Monthly British consol yields and U.S. treasury notes (from 1919, as a point of reference) are taken from the NBER Macro History Data Base, Series 13041 and 13033a, respectively. All instruments were traded actively on the local money markets.

Bibliography

ARCHIVAL SOURCES AND SERIES (FREQUENTLY CITED)

Banco do Brasil. Banco do Brasil Archives, Rio de Janeiro
———. Atas dos Directores, Livros 009-17, 1897-1930.
———. Cartas Particulares dos Presidentes, 1909-30.
———. *Estátutos do Banco do Brasil*. Banco do Brasil Archives, Rio de Janeiro. Rio de Janeiro: Imprensa Nacional, various years.
———. *Relatório do Banco do Brasil apresentado à Assembléia Geral dos accionistas na sessão ordinária*, 1889-1932.
Banco do Commércio e Indústria de São Paulo. Privately Held, São Paulo. São Paulo: H. Puchetti.
———. *Estátutos* do Banco do Commércio e Indústria de São Paulo, various years.
———. *Relatórios e contas da administração* Banco do Commércio e Indústria de São Paulo que serão apresentados aos accionistas, 1890-1931.
Banco de Crédito Hypothecário e Agrícola do Estado de São Paulo and Banco do Estado de São Paulo. Banespa Library, São Paulo.
———. *Atas das Assembléias Gerais,* Annual Series, 1911-30.
———. *Estátutos,* 1909, 27 January 1925, 4 November 1926, 22 September 1927, 22 March 1928.
———. *Relatórios e contas de administração do BCHASP que serão submetidos à approvação dos acçionistas do mesmo banco em reunião annual; Relatórios e contas de administração do Banco do Estado de São Paulo que serão submetidos à approvação dos acçionistas do mesmo banco em reunião annual*, São Paulo. São Paulo, 1911-31.
Banco de Crédito Real de Minas Gerais. Banco de Crédito Real de Minas Gerais Archives, Juiz de Fora, Minas Gerais
———. *Livros das Atas da Diretória*, Livros 1-2, 1889-1940.
———. *Livros das Atas dos Assembléias Gerais,* Livro 1, 1898-1930.

————. *Estátutos do Banco de Crédito Real de Minas Gerais, de accôrdo com as modificações.*

————. *Relátorio apresentado à Assembléia Geral dos accionistas do Banco de Crédito Real de Minas Gerais na sua reunião ordinária,* Annual Series, 1898-1931.

Bank of England. Bank of England Archive, London.

Bank of London and South America. Archives of the Bank of London and South America, University College, London.

————. Internal correspondence.

————. Letters from London to Rio de Janeiro, 1905-24.

————. Telegrams between London and Rio de Janeiro, 1924-1930.

Brasil

Leis e Decreto. Brasil. *Coleção das Leis e Decretos.* 1889-1930.

————. Ministério da Fazenda. *Relatório apresentado ao Presidente da República dos Estados Unidos do Brasil pelo Ministro de Estado dos Negócios da Fazenda.* Annual Series, Rio de Janeiro: Imprensa Nacional 1898-1929.

Câmara Syndical dos Corretores de Fundos Públicos da Capital Federal. Instituto Brasileiro de Mercados de Capitais, Annual Series.

————. *Relatórios da Câmara Syndical dos corretores de fundos públicos da Capital Federal, 1894-1931.* Rio de Janeiro, Imprensa Nacional.

Messrs. Rothschilds and Sons. Rothschilds Archive, London 1887-1918.

Serials:

————. *Jornal do Commércio.* Annual Series, 1893-1930. Rio de Janeiro: Rodrigues e Cia.

————. *Retrospecto Comercial de Jornal do Commércio.* Annual Series, 1887-1932. Rio de Janeiro: *Jornal de Commércio* de Rodrigues e Cia.

CONTEMPORANEOUS MONOGRAPHS, PUBLICATIONS, ETC.

Alvarenga, Manuel Augusto de. *Consolidação das leis hypothecárias.* São Paulo: Typ. Andrade, Mello and Comp., 1899.

Amaral, Angelo do. *O accôrdo financeiro.* 1898 Funding Loan. Rio de Janeiro: Libraria Brasileira, n.d.

Amaral, Francisco Eugenio de, ed. *A moratória e o decreto de emissão de papel moeda.* Coleção de Pareceres. São Paulo: Livraria Magalhães, 1914.

Autran, Manõel Godofredo de Alincastro. *Bancos e sociedades anônimas, a consolidação das leis e regulamentos respectivos segunda Decreto No. 434 de 4 julho de 1891, conveniente anotada.* Rio de Janeiro: Laemmert and Cia, 1892.

Banco do Brasil. (Como banco emissor e futuro banco de estado: A reforma monetária; medidas econômicas e financeiras complementares.) Rio de Janeiro, Typ. de *Jornal de Commércio,* 1915.

Bank of London and Brazil. *Annual Report to Shareholders.* Annual Series. London: 1888-1930.

Bank of London and River Plate. *Annual Report to Shareholders.* Annual Series. London: 1888-1930.

Barbosa, Juscelino. *Banco do Brasil: Explicações para o povo*. Artigos publicados no *Minas Gerais: Orgão official do governo mineiro*. Belo Horizonte: Imprensa Official, 1924.

Barbosa, Rui. *Correspondência de Rui: Seleção e notas*. Edited by Affonso Ruy. Coleção de Estudos Brasileiros, Autores Nacionais. Salvador: Centro de Estudos Baianos; Livraria Progresso, n.d.

————. *Finanças e política da República: Discursos e escriptos*. Rio de Janeiro: Companhia Impressora, 1892.

Barroso, Gustavo. *Brasil: Colonia de banqueiro (História dos empréstimos de 1824 a 1934)*. 2d ed. Rio de Janeiro: Civilização Brasileira, S.A., 1934.

Braga, Cincinato. *Brasil novo*. 2 vols. Rio de Janeiro: Imprensa Nacional, 1930.

Brasil. Ministério da Fazenda. *Retrospectivo administrativo (1912-1922): Exposição feito pelo Dr. Homero Baptista ao transmittir a pasta da Fazenda ao seu substituto Dr. Sampaio Vidal*. Rio de Janeiro: Imprensa Nacional, 1922.

British Bank of Brazil. *Annual Report to Shareholders*. Annual Series. London: 1888-1930.

British Financial Mission By Edwin Montagu and the members of the mission, 1924. Report by British Financial Mission to Brazil to Messrs. Rothschilds, Messrs. Baring Bros. & Co Ltd. and Messrs. J. Henry Schroder & Co. Rothschilds Archive, London, File 111/309.

Bulhões, Leopoldo de. *Os financistas do Brasil*. Conferência Realisada no Biblioteca Nacional no dia 22 de dezembro de 1913. Rio de Janeiro: Typ. de *Jornal do Commércio*, 1914.

Cabral, Dr. João Chrysostomo de Rocha. *Das fallências e respecto processo*. Recife: Imprensa Nacional, 1902.

Calógeras, J. Pandiá. *A política monetária do Brasil*. Translated by Thomaz Newlands Neto. Brasiliana, Grande Formato, 18. São Paulo: Ed. Nacional, 1960 (1910).

Carvalho, de Mendonça, J. X. *Banco do Brasil: Pareceres de 10/20/22 a 20/10/30*. Edição privada. Rio de Janeiro: A. Coelho Branco, 1941.

Colin, Oswaldo Roberto. Personal interview. Jan. 28, 1992. (President of Banco do Brasil, 1979-1985).

Correia Filho, Jones. *Guia prática para o ensino de contabilidade bancária*. 1st ed. Rio de Janeiro: Banco do Brasil/Flores e Mano, 1929.

D'Oliveira, Visconde Rodrigues. *O crédito agrícola no Brasil*. Rio de Janeiro: Typ. D'os Annaes/Revista de Litteratura, Arte, Sciencia e Indústria, 1905.

Estado de Minas Gerais. Secretária da Agrícola. Serviço de Estatística Geral. *Annuário estatística*. Ano I (1920), vol. 1, 3, 4; Ano II (1922-25), Ano III (1949). Juiz de Fora.

Estado de São Paulo. Repartição de Estatística e Arquivo do Estado. *Annuário estatístico do Estado de São Paulo*. Annual Series. São Paulo: Typ. *Diário Official*, 1902-28.

————. Secretário da Fazenda. *Relatório apresentado ao Presidente do Estado pelo Secretário da Fazenda*. Annual Series. São Paulo, 1898-1930.

Falcão, Waldemar. *O empirismo monetário no Brasil*. São Paulo: Cia. Editora Nacional, 1931.

Franco, Bernardo de Souza. *Os bancos do Brasil: Sua história, defeitos da organização actual e reforma do sistema bancário.* Rio de Janeiro: Typ. Nacional, 1848.

Freire, Felisbello. *História do Banco do Brasil.* Rio de Janeiro: O Economist, 1907.

Inglez de Souza, Carlos. *Restauração de moeda no Brasil.* São Paulo, Typ. da Casa Garraux: 1925.

————. *A solução da crise econômica brasileira.* Conferência realisado em 18 de julho de 1925. Associação Commercial de São Paulo. São Paulo: Casa Editora "A Renascença," 1925.

Leães, Sobrinho. *O Banco do Brasil: Serviço público federal.* São Paulo, 1944.

Legislação bancária e assumptos cambiaes. Typewritten Copy. Banco do Brasil Archives, Rio de Janeiro, 1937.

Lloyds Bank. Internal memoranda between directors. Personnel and Training Notes of Bank of London and South America, Held by the Lloyds Bank Archive, London.

London and Brazilian Bank. *Trade Reports from South America and Portugal.* London, 1918.

Minas Gerais: Orgão official do governo mineiro. Annual Series. Belo Horizonte: Imprensa Official, 1898–1930.

Monteiro, Honório Fernandes. "Effeitos da sentença declaratória de fallência sobre o contracto de conte corrente, quanto as remessas com a clausula 'salvo em bolsa.'" Dissertação apresentada a congregação de Faculdade de Direito de São Paulo para concurso a Doencia Livre de direito commercial. São Paulo. Emp. Gráphica de *Revista do Tribunaes, 1929.*

Murtinho, Joaquim. *Idéias econômicas de Joaquim Murtinho: Cronologia, introdução, notas bibliográficas e textos selecionados.* Edited by Nícia Villela Luz. Ação e Pensamento da República, no. 5. Rio de Janeiro: Fundação Casa de Rui Barbosa, 1980.

Niemeyer, Otto. *Reorganization of Brazilian National Finance; Report Submitted to the Brazilian Government.* Rio de Janeiro: British Chamber of Commerce, 1931.

Ouro Preto, Affonso Celso de Assis (Visconde de Figueiredo). *Finanças e riqueza pública.* 2d ed. Rio de Janeiro: n.d.

Ribeiro, João. *Bancos.* Memória apresentado ao Congresso Industrial de Minas Gerais. Juiz de Fora: Typ. Central, 1903.

Ribeiro de Andrade, Antônio Carlos. *Bancos de emissão no Brasil.* Rio de Janeiro: Liv. Leite Ribeiro, 1923.

Rivadavia Corrêa. "A verdade sobre a situação financeira do Brasil em 1914." Discurso proferido no Senado Federal ao 28 dezembro de 1918. Rio de Janeiro: Imprensa Nacional, 1919.

Sa Vianna, M. A. de S. *Das fallências.* Rio de Janeiro: Hildbrant, 1907.

Serzedello, Innocencio Corrêa. *O problema econômico do Brasil.* Compilation of articles from *A Tribuna.* Rio de Janeiro: Imprensa Nacional, 1903.

Simonsen, Roberto. "As crises no Brasil." São Paulo: 1930.

————. "As finanças e a indústria." Conferência realisada no Mackenzie College. São Paulo: 1930.

————. "A situação econômica e financeira do Brasil atravez da mensagem do

Presidente da República. Entrevista que ao 'Boletim Medeiros' concedeu o Dr. Roberto Simonsen." São Paulo: Centro das Indústrias do Estado do São Paulo, 1928.

Théry, Edmond. *Projecto de reforma monetária e de creação dum banco emissor no Brasil.* Rio de Janeiro: Typ. D'os Annaes-Revista de Litteratura, Arte, Sciencia e Indústria, 1905.

U.K. Department of Overseas Trade. *Financial, Commercial and Economic Conditions in Brazil.* London: H.M.S., 1938.

U.K. Foreign Office. *Diplomatic and Consular Reports on Trade and Finance.* Annual Series. London: Harrison & Sons, 1895-1914.

U.S. Bureau of Foreign and Domestic Commerce. "Banking and Credit in Argentina, Brazil, Chile and Peru." By Edward S. Hurley, U.S. Bulletin of the Department of Commerce, Special Agents Series, no. 90. Washington, D.C.: GPO, 1914.

———. "Brazil: A Study of Economic Conditions Since 1913." By Arthur Redfield. Miscellaneous Series, no. 86. Washington, D.C.: GPO, 1920.

———. *Handbook of Foreign Currency and Exchange.* By James Raider Mood, Prepared in the Division of Statistical Research. Trade Promotion Series, no. 102. Washington, D.C.: GPO, 1930.

U.S. Department of Commerce. *Financial Developments in South American Countries.* By William H. Lough, special agent of the Department of Commerce. Washington, D.C.: GPO, 1915.

U.S. Department of State. *Dispatches from U.S. Consuls in Rio de Janeiro.* Washington, D.C.: General Services Administration, National Archives and Records Services, 1888-1930.

Viana, Victor. *O Banco do Brasil: Sua formação, seu engradecimento, su missão nacional.* Rio de Janeiro: Typ. de *Journal do Commércio,* 1926.

Vieira Souto, Rafael Luís. "Caixa de Conversão: Parecer apresentado pelo Dr. Vieira Souto." Centro Industrial do Brasil. Rio de Janeiro: Typ. do *Jornal do Commércio,* 1906.

———. "A situação econômica." Rio de Janeiro: 1901.

———. "O último relatório da Fazenda, 1899." In *Idéias econômicas de Joaquim Murtinho.* Edited by Nícia Villela Luz. Rio de Janeiro: Fundação Casa de Rui Barbosa, 1980 [1899].

Visconde de Mauá. Autobiografia (Exposição Aus Credores [Bankruptcy deposition]), n.d.

Wileman, J. P. "Brazilian Exchange." In *Brazilian Exchange: The Study of an Inconvertible Currency.* New York: Greenwood Press, 1969 [1896].

SECONDARY SOURCES

Abreu, Marcelo de Paiva. "Argentina and Brazil in the 1930's: The Impact of British and American International Economic Policies." In *Latin America in the 1930's:*

The Role of the Periphery in World Crisis. Edited by Rosemary Thorp, 144-62. Oxford: Macmillan Press, 1984.

———. "Crise, crescimento e modernização autoritária: 1930-1945." In *A ordem do progresso: Cem anos de política econômica republicana, 1889-1989*, 73-104. Rio de Janeiro: Ed. Campus, 1990.

———. "A dívida pública externa do Brasil, 1824-1931." *Estudos Econômicos* (Instituto de Pesquisas Econômicas, Universidade de São Paulo 15, no. 2 (1985): 167-89.

Albert, Bill. *South America and the First World War: The Impact of the War on Brazil, Argentina, Peru and Chile*. Cambridge: Cambridge University Press, 1983.

———. *South America and the World Economy from Independence to 1930*. London: Macmillan, 1983.

Alesina, Alberto and Allen Drazen. "Why Are Stabilizations Delayed?" *American Economics Review* 81, no. 5 (December 1991): 1170-88.

Altman, Edward I. *Financial Handbook*. 5th ed. New York: Wiley, 1981.

Alvim, Zuleika M. F. *Brava gente!: Os italianos em São Paulo, 1870-1920*. São Paulo: Brasiliense, 1986.

Andrews, George Reid. *Blacks and Whites in São Paulo, Brazil, 1888-1988*. Madison: University of Wisconsin Press, 1991.

Associação de Bancos no Estado do Rio de Janeiro. *Os dez primeiros anos de ABERJ (Associação de Bancos no Estado do Rio de Janiero)*. Rio de Janeiro: ABERJ, n.d.

Azevedo, Thales de and E. Q. Vieira Lins. *História do Banco da Bahia, 1858-1958*. Rio de Janeiro: Liv. José Olympio Editóra, 1969.

Baer, Werner. *The Brazilian Economy: Growth and Development*. 4th ed. Westport, Conn.: Praeger, 1995.

———. *The Development of the Brazilian Steel Industry*. Nashville, Tenn.: Vanderbilt University Press, 1969.

Baer, Werner and Larry Samuelson. "Editors' Introduction." Special issue: Latin America in the Post-Import-Substitution Era. *World Development* 5, nos. 1 and 2 (January-February 1977): 1-6.

Bairoch, Paul. *Economics and World History: Myths and Paradoxes*. New York: Harvester Wheatsheaf, 1993.

Baklanoff, Eric N., ed. *The Shaping of Modern Brazil*. Essays from the 1967 LSU Colloquium on the Modernization of Brazil. Baton Rouge: Published for the Latin American Studies Institute by Louisiana State University Press, 1969.

Banco de la República (Colombia). *El Banco de la República: Antecedentes, evolución y estructura*. Bogotá, D.E.: Colombia: El Banco, 1990.

Barickman, B. J. *A Bahian Counterpoint: Sugar, Tobacco, Cassava, and Slavery in the Recôncavo, 1780-1860*. Stanford, Calif.: Stanford University Press, 1998.

Barman, Roderick J. *Brazil: The Forging of a Nation, 1798-1852*. Stanford, Calif.: Stanford University Press, 1988.

Barzel, Yoram. *Economic Analysis of Property Rights*. Cambridge: Cambridge University Press, 1997.

Bastos, Humberto. *Rui Barbosa, ministro da independência econômica do Brasil (Aspectos econômicas da revolução repúblicana).* 2d ed. São Paulo: Liv. Martins Editora S.A., 1951.

Bates, Robert H. *Open-Economy Politics: The Political Economy of the World Coffee Trade.* Princeton: Princeton University Press, 1997.

Baud, Michael and Kees Koonings. "*A Lavoura dos Pobres:* Tobacco Farming and the Development of Commercial Agriculture in Bahia, 1870-1930." *Journal of Latin American Studies* 31, no. 2 (May 1999): 287-330.

Beauclair Mendes de Oliveira, Geraldo de. "A evolução do sistema financeiro na época Vargas." Tese de mestrado, Niterói, UFF, 1974.

Bello, José Maria. *A History of Modern Brazil, 1889-1964.* Stanford, Calif.: Stanford University Press, 1966.

Bennett, Douglas and Kenneth Sharpe. "The State as Banker and Entrepreneur: The Last Resort Character of the Mexican State's Economic Intervention, 1917-1970." In *Brazil and Mexico: Patterns in Late Development.* Edited by Sylvia Ann Hewlett and Richard S. Weinert, 169-212. Inter-American Politics Series, no. 3. Philadelphia: Institute for the Study of Human Issues, 1982.

Bergad, Laird W. *Slavery and the Demographic and Economic History of Minas Gerais, Brazil, 1720-1888.* Cambridge Latin American Studies, no. 85. Cambridge: Cambridge University Press, 1999.

Bethell, Leslie. *Brazil, Empire and Republic: 1822-1930.* Cambridge: Cambridge University Press, 1989.

Bielschowsky, Ricardo Alberto. "Bancos e acumulação de capital na industrialização brasileira—uma introductória (1935-1962)." Tese de mestrado. Brasília: Universidade de Brasília, 1975.

Bodenhorn, Howard. "Capital Mobility and Financial Integration in Antebellum America." *Journal of Economic History* 52, no. 3 (September 1992): 585-610.

———. "A More Perfect Union: Regional Interest Rates in the United States, 1880-1960." In *Anglo-American Financial Systems: Institutions and Markets in the Twentieth Century.* Edited by Michael D. Bordo and Richard Eugene Sylla. Burr Ridge, Ill.: Irwin Professional Pub., 1995.

Bodenhorn, Howard and Hugh Rockoff. "Regional Interest Rates in Antebellum America." In *Strategic Factors in Nineteenth Century American Economic History: A Volume to Honor Robert Fogel.* Edited by Claudia Goldin and Hugh Rockoff, 159-88. Chicago: University of Chicago Press and National Bureau Economic Research, 1992.

Bordo, Michael, Michael Edelstein, and Hugh Rockoff. "Was Adherence to the Gold Standard a 'Good Housekeeping Seal of Approval' during the Interwar Period?" Paper presented at the Symposium in Honor of Lance E. Davis, November, 1998.

Bordo, Michael D. and Finn Kydland. "The Gold Standard as a Rule: An Essay in Exploration." *Explorations in Economic History* 32, no. 2 (1995): 423-64.

Bordo, Michael D. and Hugh Rockoff. "The Gold Standard as a Good Housekeeping Seal of Approval." *Journal of Economic History* 56, no. 2 (1996): 389-428.

Bouças, Valentim F. *História de dívida externa*. 2d ed. Rio de Janeiro: Edições Financeiras, 1950.

Brandão, Alonso Caldas. *Legislação bancária*. 2 vols. Rio de Janeiro: Coelho Branco, 1954.

Brasil, Instituto Brasileiro de Geografia e Estatística. *Estatísticas históricas do Brasil: Séries econômicas, demográficas e sociais 1550 a 1985*. 2d ed. Séries Estatísticas Históricas do Brasil vol. 3, Rio de Janeiro: IBGE, 1990.

Brasil, Instituto Brasileiro de Geografia e Estatística. Conselho Nacional de Estatística. *Annuário estatístico do Brasil*. Ano V. Rio de Janeiro, 1939–40.

Broz, J. Lawrence. "The Origins of Central Banking: A Collective Action Account." Paper presented at the American Political Science Association. San Francisco, August, 1996.

Buescu, Mircea. *300 anos de inflação*. Rio de Janeiro: APEC, 1973.

Bulhões, Augusto de. *Ministros da Fazenda do Brasil, 1808-1954*. Rio de Janeiro: Impr. Nacional, 1955.

Bulmer-Thomas, Victor. *The Economic History of Latin America since Independence*. Cambridge Latin American Studies 77. Cambridge: Cambridge University Press, 1994.

Burns, E. Bradford. *A History of Brazil*. New York: Columbia University Press, 1993.

Camargo, Aspásia. "La federación sometida, nacionalismo desarrollista e inestabilidad democrática." In *Federalismos latinoamericanos: México, Brasil, Argentina*. Edited by Marcello Carmagnani, 300–57. México: Fondo de Cultura Económica, 1993.

Cameron, Rondo E. "Banking in the Early Stages." In *Banking in the Early Stages of Industrialization; a Study in Comparative Economic History*. With the collaboration of Olga Crisp, Hugh T. Patrick, and Richard Tilly. New York: Oxford University Press, 1967.

Cameron, Rondo E. Introduction to *Banking and Economic Development: Some Lessons of History*. Edited by Rondo Cameron. Oxford: Oxford University Press, 1972.

Cameron, Rondo E., ed. *Banking and Economic Development: Some Lessons of History*. New York: Oxford University Press, 1972.

Cano, Wilson. *Disequilíbrios regionais e concentração industrial no Brasil: 1930-1970*. Campinas: Ed. da Universidade Estadual de Campinas, 1985.

———. *Raízes da concentração industrial em São Paulo*. Corpo e Alma do Brasil, no. 53. Rio de Janeiro: DIFEL/Difusão Editorial, S.A., 1977.

Cardoso, Eliana A. and Rudiger Dornbusch. "Brazilian Debt Crises: Past and Present." In *The International Debt Crisis in Historical Perspective*. Edited by Barry Eichengreen and Peter H. Lindert, 106–40. Cambridge, Mass.: MIT Press, 1989.

Cardoso de Mello, Zelia Maria. *Metamorfoses da riqueza, São Paulo, 1845-1895: Contribuição ao estudo da passagem da economia mercantil escravista a economia exportadora capitalista*. Estudos Históricos. São Paulo: Editora Hucitec: Prefeitura do Município de São Paulo, Secretária Municipal de Cultura, 1985.

Carone, Edgard. *A Primeira República (1889-1930)*. 4th ed. Rio de Janeiro: Editora

Bertrand Brasil, 1988.

————. *A República Velha*. Corpo e Alma do Brasil, no. 31. São Paulo: Difusão Europeia do Livro, 1970.

Carvalho, José Murilo de. "Armed Forces and Politics in Brazil: 1930-1945." *Hispanic American Historical Review* 62, no. 2 (May 1982): 193-223.

————. *Os bestializados: O Rio de Janeiro e a República que não foi*. 3d ed. São Paulo: Cia. das Letras, 1989.

————. "Brazil 1870-1914: The Force of Tradition." *Journal of Latin American Studies* 24, Supplement (1992): 145-62.

————. "Political Elites and State Building: The Case of Nineteenth-Century Brazil." *Comparative Studies in Society and History* 24, no. 3 (July 1982): 378-99.

————. *Teatro de sombras: A política imperial*. Formação do Brasil, no. 4. Rio de Janeiro: IUPERJ, Vertice, 1988.

Castro, Celso. *Os militares e a República: Um estudo sobre cultura e ação política*. Rio de Janeiro: J. Zahar Editor, 1995.

Catão, Luis A.V. "Constraints to Balanced Long-Term Growth: The Cases of Brazil and Mexico, 1870-1913." Mimeo. University of São Paulo and PUC-Rio de Janeiro, May, 1990.

————. "A new wholesale price index for Brazil during the period 1870-1913." *Revista Brasileira de Economia* 46, no. 4 (October-December 1992): 519-33.

Cavalcante, José Cândido Marquês. *Dicionário inglês-português para economistas*. Rio de Janeiro: Liv. Freitas Bastos, S.A., 1960.

Clague, Christopher, et al. "Contract-Intensive Money: Contract Enforcement, Property Rights and Economic Performance." University of Maryland Center Institutional Reform and the Informal Sector. Working Paper 151. College Park, Md.: 1997.

————. "Institutions and Economic Performance: Property Rights and Contract Enforcement." In *Institutions and Economic Development: Growth and Governance in Less-Developed and Post-Socialist Countries*. Edited by Christopher Clague, 67-90. Baltimore: Johns Hopkins University Press, 1997.

Coatsworth, John H. "Economic and Institutional Trajectories in Nineteenth-Century Latin America." In *Latin America and the World Economy in the Nineteenth and Twentieth Centuries*. Edited by John H. Coatsworth and Alan M. Taylor, 23-54. Cambridge, Mass.: Harvard University Press, 1998.

————. "Obstacles to Economic Growth in Nineteenth-Century Mexico." *American Historical Review* 83, no. 1 (February 1978): 80-100.

Cohen, Jon S. "Institutions and Economic Analysis." In *Economics and the Historian*. Edited by Thomas G. Rawski, 60-84. Berkeley and Los Angeles: University of California Press, 1995.

Collins, Michael. *Banks and Industrial Finance in Britain: 1800-1939*. Studies in Economic and Social History. London: The Economic History Society and Macmillan, 1991.

————. "English Bank Development Within a European Context, 1870-1939." *Economic History Review* 61, no. 1 (February 1998): 1-24.

Conniff, Michael L. *Urban Politics in Brazil: The Rise of Populism, 1925-1945.* Pitt Latin American Series. Pittsburgh, Pa.: University of Pittsburgh Press, 1981.

Contador, Cláudio R. and Cláudio L. Haddad. "Produto real, moeda e preços: A experiência brasileira no período 1861-1970." *Revista Brasileira de Estatística* 143, no. 36 (1975): 407-40.

Cortés Conde, Roberto. *Dinero, deuda y crisis: Evolución fiscal y monetaria en la Argentina, 1862-1890.* Buenos Aires: Editorial Sudamericana, Instituto Torcuato di Tella, 1989.

———. *Los orígenes de la banca en la Argentina del siglo XIX.* Córdoba, R.A.: Centro de Estudios Históricos, 1995.

Cortés Conde, Roberto and Stanley J. Stein, eds. *Latin America: A Guide to Economic History, 1830-1930.* Berkeley: University of California Press, 1977.

Cottrell, P. L. *Industrial Finance: 1830-1914: The Finance and Organization of English Manufacturing Industry.* London: Methuen and Co., 1979.

Crisp, Olga. "Russia, 1860-1914." In *Banking in the Early Stages of Industrialization; a Study in Comparative Economic History.* Edited by Rondo E. Cameron with the collaboration of Olga Crisp, Hugh T. Patrick, and Richard Tilly, 183-238. New York: Oxford University Press, 1967.

Crouzet, François. *Capital Formation in the Industrial Revolution.* London: Methuen and Co., 1972.

Cunha, Euclides da. *Rebellion in the Backlands.* Translated by Samuel Putnam. Chicago: Phoenix Books, University of Chicago Press, 1944.

da Costa, Emilia Viotti. *The Brazilian Empire: Myths and Histories.* Chicago: University of Chicago Press, 1985.

da Costa, Fernando Nogueira. "Banco do estado: O caso Banespa." Tese de doutoramento, Universidade Estadual de Campinas, 1988.

———. "Bancos em Minas Gerais (1889-1964)." Tese de mestrado, Brasil, Universidade Estadual de Campinas, 1978.

da Matta, Roberto. *The Brazilian Puzzle: Culture on the Borderlands of the Western World.* Edited by David J. Hess. New York: Columbia University Press, 1995.

Dávila, Carlos and Rory Miller, eds. *Business History in Latin America: The Experience of Seven Countries.* Liverpool Latin American Studies, New Series, no. 1. Liverpool: Liverpool University Press, 1999.

Davis, Lance E. "The Investment Market, 1870-1914: The Evolution of a National Market." *Journal of Economic History* 25 (1965): 355-99.

Davis, Lance Edwin, Douglass Cecil North, and Calla Smorodin. *Institutional Change and American Economic Growth.* Cambridge: Cambridge University Press, 1971.

Dean, Warren. *Brazil and the Struggle for Rubber: A Study in Environmental History.* Studies in Environment and History. Cambridge: Cambridge University Press, 1987.

———. *The Industrialization of São Paulo, 1880-1945.* Latin American Monographs, no. 17. Austin: Published for the Institute of Latin American Studies by the University of Texas Press, 1969.

————. "Latifundia and Land Policy in Nineteenth-Century Brazil." *Hispanic American Historical Review* 51, no. 44 (November 1971): 606-25.

Delfim Netto, Antônio. *O problema do café no Brasil.* Faculdade de Ciências Econômicas e Administrativas, Boletim, no. 5; Cadeira 3, no. 1. São Paulo: Universidade de São Paulo, 1959.

della Cava, Ralph. "Brazilian Messianism and National Institutions: A Reappraisal of Canudos and Joaseiro." *Hispanic American Historical Review* 48 (August 1968): 402-20.

Deutsch, Ruthann. "Charting the Archipelago: Urban Systems in Brazil's First Republic." Paper presented at University of Michigan Economic History Seminar. Ann Arbor, March 1994.

Diacon, Todd A. *Millenarian Vision, Capitalist Reality: Brazil's Contestado Rebellion, 1912-1916.* Durham, N.C.: Duke University Press, 1991.

Dickson, P. G. M. (Peter George Muir). *The Financial Revolution in England: A Study in the Development of Public Credit, 1688-1756.* Aldershot, Hampshire, England: Gregg Revivals; Brookfield, Vt.: distributed in the United States by Ashgate Publ. Co., 1993.

Drake, Paul W. *The Money Doctor in the Andes: The Kemmerer Missions, 1923-1933.* Durham, N.C.: Duke University Press, 1989.

Eakin, Marshall C. "The Formation of a Business Elite: Belo Horizonte, Brazil, 1890s-1940s." Paper presented at the Conference on Latin American History. New York, January, 1997.

————. "From Planters to Industrialists: Textile Manufacturing and the Origins of Industrialization in Belo Horizonte, Brazil, 1890s-1940s." Paper presented at the Latin American Studies Association Conference. Washington, D.C., September, 1995.

Edelstein, Michael. *Overseas Investment in the Age of High Imperialism.* New York: Columbia University Press, 1982.

Eichengreen, Barry J. *Golden Fetters: The Gold Standard and the Great Depression, 1919-1939.* NBER Series on Long-Term Factors in Economic Development. New York: Oxford University Press, 1992.

Eichengreen, Barry J. and Marc Flandreau, eds. *The Gold Standard in Theory and History.* 2d ed. New York: Routledge, 1997 (1985).

Eisenberg, Peter L. *The Sugar Industry in Pernambuco: Modernization without Change, 1840-1910.* Berkeley and Los Angeles: University of California Press, 1974.

Fabozzi, Frank J. *Foundations of Financial Markets and Institutions.* Englewood Cliffs, N.J.: Prentice Hall, 1994.

Faoro, Raymundo. *Os donos do poder: Formação do patronato político brasileiro.* 2 vols. Pôrto Alegre: Editôra Globo, 1958.

Fausto, Boris. *Crime e cotidiano: A criminalidade em São Paulo, 1880-1924.* São Paulo: Brasiliense, 1984.

————. *História geral da civilização brasileira (III) o Brasil republicano (1) Estrutura de poder e economia (1889-1930).* Rio de Janeiro: Ed. Bertrand Brasil, 1989.

————. *A revolução de 1930: Historiografia e história*. São Paulo: Editora Brasiliense, 1989 [1970].

————. "Society and Politics." In *Brazil, Empire and Republic*. Edited by Leslie Bethell, 257-308. Cambridge: Cambridge University Press, 1989.

Fausto, Boris and Pedro Moacyr Campos. *Estrutura de poder e economia (1889-1930)*. Vol. 1 of *História geral da civilização brasileira*. São Paulo: Ed. Bertrand Brasil, 1989.

Fernandes, Florestan. *A integração do negro na sociedade de classes*. Ciencias Sociais Dominus, no. 3. São Paulo: Dominus Editora, 1965.

Ferreira, Marieta de Moraes. *Em busca da idade de ouro: As elites políticas fluminenses na Primeira República (1889-1930)*. Rio de Janiero: Editora UFRJ/Edições Tempo Brasileiro, 1994.

————. "A crise dos comissários de café do Rio de Janeiro." Tese de mestrado, Niterói, Universidade Federal Fluminense, 1977.

Fishlow, Albert. "Brazilian Development in Long-Term Perspective." *American Economic Review* 70, no. 2 (May 1980): 102-08.

————. "Brazilian Size Distribution of Income." *American Economic Review* 62, no. 2 (1972): 391-402.

————. "Conditionality and Willingness to Pay: Some Parallels from the 1890s." In *The International Debt Crisis in Historical Perspective*. Edited by Barry Eichengreen and Peter H. Lindert, 86-105. Cambridge, Mass.: MIT Press, 1989.

————. "Origins and Consequences of Import Substitution in Brazil." In *International Economics and Development: Essays in Honor of Raúl Prebisch*. Edited by Luís Eugenio di Marco and Raúl Prebisch, 311-65. New York: Academic Press, 1972.

————. "Some Reflections in Post-1964 Brazilian Economic Policy." In *Authoritarian Brazil: Origins, Policies, and Future*. Edited by Alfred C. Stepan, 69-118. New Haven: Yale University Press, 1973.

Flory, Thomas. *Judge and Jury in Imperial Brazil, 1808-1871: Social Control and Political Stability in the New State*. Latin American Monographs, no. 53. Austin: University of Texas Press, 1981.

Fohlin, Caroline. "*Fiduciari* and Firm Liquidity Constraints: The Italian Experience with German-Style Universal Banking." *Explorations in Economic History* 35, no. 1 (January 1998): 83-107.

Fonseca, Pedro Cezar Dutra. "A transição capitalista no Rio Grande do Sul: A economia gaúcha na Primeira República." *Estudos Econômicos* 15, no. 2 (May-August 1985): 263-89.

Font, Maurício. *Coffee, Contention, and Change in the Making of Modern Brazil*. Studies in Social Discontinuity. Cambridge, Mass.: B. Blackwell, 1990.

Franco, Gustavo Henrique Barroso. *Reforma monetária e instabilidade durante a transição republicana*. 2d ed. Rio de Janeiro: Banco Nacional de Desenvolvimento Econômico e Social, 1987.

————. "Taxa de câmbio e oferta de moeda: 1880-1897: Uma análise econométrica." *Revista Brasileira de Economia* 40, no. 1 (January-March 1986): 63-88.

French, John D. *The Brazilian Workers' ABC: Class Conflict and Alliances in Modern São Paulo.* Chapel Hill: University of North Carolina Press, 1992.

Frieden, Jeffry A. *Debt, Development, and Democracy: Modern Political Economy and Latin America, 1965-1985.* Princeton: Princeton University Press, 1991.

———. "The Dynamics of International Monetary Systems: International and Domestic Factors in the Rise, Reign, and Demise of the Classical Gold Standard." In *The Gold Standard in Theory and History.* Edited by Barry J. Eichengreen and Marc Flandreau, 207-27. New York: Methuen, 1997 [1985].

Friedman, Milton and Anna Jacobson Schwartz. *A Monetary History of the United States, 1867-1960.* Princeton: Princeton University Press for the National Bureau of Economic Research, 1963.

Fritsch, Winston. *External Constraints on Economic Policy in Brazil, 1889-1930.* Pittsburgh: University of Pittsburgh Press, 1988.

———. "Brazilian Economic Policy during the Post-War Boom and Slump." PUC/RJ Discussion Paper, no. 20. November 1981.

———. "1924." *Pesquisa e Planejamento Econômica* 10, no. 3 (December 1980): 713-44.

Fry, Maxwell J. *Money, Interest, and Banking in Economic Development.* 2d ed. The Johns Hopkins Studies in Development. Baltimore: Johns Hopkins University Press, 1995.

Furtado, Celso. *Formação econômica do Brasil.* 40th ed. São Paulo: Ed. Brasiliense, 1993 (1959).

Gebara, Ademir and José Roberto do Amaral Lapa, et al. *História política da República.* Tempo e Memoria. Campinas, São Paulo: Papirus Editora, 1990.

Gerschenkron, Alexander. *Economic Backwardness in Historical Perspective.* Cambridge, Mass.: Belknap Press of Harvard University Press, 1962.

Gille, Bertrand. "Banking and Industrialization in Europe: 1730-1914." In *Fontana Economic History of Europe: The Industrial Revolution.* Edited by Carlo M. Cipolla, vol. 3, 255-99. London: Fontana/Collins, 1972.

Giroletti, Domingos. *Fábrica, convento, disciplina.* Belo Horizonte: Impr. Oficial de Minas Gerais, 1991.

Glade, William. *The Latin American Economies: A Study of Their Institutional Evolution.* New York: American Book, 1969.

Goldsmith, Raymond W. *Brasil 1850-1984: Desenvolvimento financeiro sob um século de inflação.* São Paulo: Banco Bamerindus e Ed. Harper Row do Brasil, 1986.

———. *Financial Structures and Development.* New Haven: Yale University Press, 1969.

———. *Premodern Financial Systems: A Historical Comparative Study.* Cambridge: Cambridge University Press, 1987.

Gomes, Ângela de Castro. *História e historiadores.* Rio de Janeiro: Ed. Fundação Getúlio Vargas, 1996.

Gomes, Ângela de Castro and Marieta de Moraes Ferreira. "Primeira República: Um balanço historiográfico." *Estudos Históricos* 4, no. 2 (1989): 244-80.

Good, David F. "Financial Integration in Late Nineteenth-Century Austria." *Journal of Economic History* 37, no. 4 (December 1977): 890-910.

Graham, Richard. *Patronage and Politics in Nineteenth-Century Brazil.* Stanford, Calif.: Stanford University Press, 1990.

Green, George. "Louisiana, 1804–1861." In *Banking and Economic Development: Some Lessons of History.* Edited by Rondo Cameron, 199–231. Oxford: Oxford University Press, 1972.

Guedes, Beatriz C. de Oliveira. "Dicionário de mercado de capitais e bolsa de valores." Rio de Janeiro: IBMEC, n.d.

Guimarães, Carlos Gabriel. "A Casa Bancária Mauá, MacGregor & Cia. (1854–1866) e o império no Brasil." Paper presented at Segundo Congresso Brasileiro de História Econômica. Universidade Federal Fluminense, Niterói, October 1996.

Gurley, John G. and E. S. Shaw. "Financial Aspects of Economic Development." *American Economic Review* 45, no. 4 (September 1955): 515–38.

Haber, Stephen. "The Efficiency Consequences of Institutional Change: Financial Market Regulation and Industrial Productivity Growth in Brazil, 1866–1934." In *Latin America and the World Economy in the Nineteenth and Twentieth Centuries.* Edited by John H. Coatsworth and Alan M. Taylor, 275–322. Cambridge, Mass.: Harvard University Press, 1998.

———. "Financial Markets and Industrial Development: A Comparative Study of Governmental Regulation, Financial Innovation and Industrial Structure in Brazil and Mexico, 1840–1930." In *How Latin America Fell Behind: Essays on the Economic Histories of Brazil and Mexico, 1800-1914.* Edited by Stephen Haber, 146–78. Stanford, Calif.: Stanford University Press, 1997.

———. "Industrial Concentration and the Capital Markets: Brazil, Mexico and the United States, 1840–1930." *Journal of Economic History* 51, no. 3 (September 1991): 559–80.

———. "Lucratividade industrial e a Grande Depressão no Brasil: Evidências da indústria têxtil de algodão." *Estudos Econômicos* 21, no. 2 (May–August 1991): 241–70.

———, ed. *How Latin America Fell Behind: Essays in the Economic Histories of Brazil and Mexico, 1800-1914.* Stanford, Calif.: Stanford University Press, 1997.

Haddad, Cláudio L. S. "Growth of Brazilian Real Output 1900–1947." Ph.D. diss., University of Chicago, 1974.

Hahner, June. "Jacobinos versus Galegos: Urban Radicals versus Portuguese Immigrants in Rio de Janeiro in the 1890s." *Journal of Interamerican Studies and World Affairs* 18, no. 2 (1976): 125–54.

Hammond, Bray. *Banks and Politics in America, from the Revolution to the Civil War.* Princeton: Princeton University Press, 1957.

Hanley, Anne Gerard. "Business Finance and the São Paulo Bolsa, 1886–1917." In *Latin America and the World Economy in the Nineteenth and Twentieth Centuries.* Edited by John H. Coatsworth and Alan M. Taylor. Cambridge, Mass.: Harvard University Press, 1998.

———. "Capital Markets in the Coffee Economy: Financial Institutions and Economic Change in São Paulo, Brazil, 1850–1905." Ph.D. diss., Stanford University, 1995.

Hewlett, Sylvia Ann. "Poverty and Inequality in Brazil." In *Brazil and Mexico: Patterns in Late Development*. Edited by Sylvia Ann Hewlett and Richard S. Weinert, 317-38. Inter-American Politics Series, no. 3. Philadelphia: Institute for the Study of Human Issues, 1982.

Hilton, Stanley E. "Vargas and Brazilian Economic Development, 1930-1945: A Reappraisal of His Attitude toward Industrialization and Planning." *Journal of Economic History* 35, no. 4 (1975): 754-78.

Hirschman, Albert O. "A Generalized Linkage Approach to Development with Special Reference to Staples." *Economic Development and Cultural Change,* no. 25, Supplement (1977): 67-98.

Holloway, Thomas H. *The Brazilian Coffee Valorization of 1906*. Madison: Wisconsin Historical Society, 1975.

———. "Immigration in the Rural South." In *Modern Brazil*. Edited by Michael L. Conniff and Frank D. McCann Jr. Lincoln: University of Nebraska Press, 1989.

———. *Immigrants on the Land: Coffee and Society in São Paulo, 1886-1934*. Chapel Hill: University of North Carolina Press, 1980.

Horwitz, Morton J. *The Transformation of American Law, 1780-1860*. Cambridge, Mass.: Harvard University Press, 1977.

Hudson, Pat. *The Genesis of Industrial Capital: A Study of the West Riding Wool Textile Industry, c. 1750-1850*. Cambridge: Cambridge University Press, 1986.

James, John A. "Banking Market Structure, Risk and the Pattern of Local Interest Rates in the United States, 1893-1911." *Review of Economics and Statistics* 53, no. 4 (November 1976): 453-62.

———. "The Development of the National Money Market, 1893-1914." *Journal of Economic History* 36, no. 4 (December 1976): 878-97.

Jenks, Leland Hamilton. *The Migration of British Capital to 1875*. Borzoi Political Science Texts. New York: A. A. Knopf, 1927.

Jones, Charles. "Commercial Banks and Mortgage Companies." In *Business Imperialism, 1840-1930: An Inquiry Based on British Experience in Latin America*. Edited by D. C. M. Platt, 17-52. Oxford: Clarendon Press, 1977.

———. "The Fiscal Motive for Monetary and Banking Legislation in Argentina, Australia and Canada Before 1914." In *Argentina, Australia and Canada: Studies in Comparative Development*. Edited by D. C. M. Platt and Guido Di Tella. New York: St. Martin's Press, 1985.

Jones, Geoffrey. *British Multinational Banking 1830-1990*. Oxford: Clarendon Press, 1993.

Joseph, Gilbert M. and Daniel Nugent, eds. *Everyday Forms of State Formation: Revolution and the Negotiation of Rule in Modern Mexico*. Durham, N.C.: Duke University Press, 1994.

Joslin, David. *A Century of Banking in Latin America; to Commemorate the Centenary in 1962 of the Bank of London & South America Limited*. New York: Oxford University Press, 1963.

Kafka, Alexandre. "Brazil." In *Banking Systems*. Edited by Benjamin H. Beckhart, 49-118. New York: Columbia University Press, 1954.

Kelejian, Harry H. and Wallace E. Oates. *Introduction to Econometrics: Principles and Applications.* New York: Harper & Row, 1981.

Kemmerer, E. W. "Economic Advisory Work for Governments." *American Economic Review* 17 (1927): 1-12.

Kennedy, Peter. *A Guide to Econometrics.* 3d ed. Cambridge, Mass.: MIT Press, 1993.

Keremitsis, Eileen. "The Early Industrial Worker in Rio de Janeiro." Ph.D. diss., Columbia University, 1982.

Kindleberger, Charles P. *A Financial History of Western Europe.* 2d ed. London and Boston: Allen & Unwin, 1993.

————. *The World in Depression, 1929-1939.* History of the World Economy in the Twentieth Century, vol. 4. Berkeley and Los Angeles: University of California Press, 1986.

King, Robert G. and Ross Levine. "Finance and Growth: Schumpeter Might Be Right." *Quarterly Journal of Economics* 108, no. 3 (August 1993): 717-37.

Knodell, Jane. "Interregional Financial Integration and the Banknote Market: The Old Northwest, 1815-1845." *Journal of Economic History* 48, no. 2 (June 1988): 287-98.

Knox, John. *Dicionário de economia, finanças, sociologia, comércio e relações sindicais.* Rio de Janeiro: Liv. Freitas, n.d.

Krasner, Stephen D. "Manipulating International Commodity Markets: Brazilian Coffee Policy 1906 to 1962." *Public Policy* 21, no. 4 (fall 1973): 493-523.

Lacombe, Américo Jacobina. *À sombra de Rui Barbosa.* Brasiliana, vol. 365. São Paulo: Companhia Editora Nacional/MEC, 1984 (1978).

Lafer, Horácio. *O crédito e o sistema bancário no Brasil.* Rio de Janeiro: Imprensa Nacional, 1948.

Lagemann, Eugenio. *O Banco Pelotense e o sistema financeiro regional.* Série Documenta, no. 19. Porto Alegre, R.S.: Mercado Aberto, 1985.

Lamoreaux, Naomi R. "Banks, Kinship and Economic Development: The New England Case." *Journal of Economic History* 46, no. 3 (September 1986): 647-67.

————. "Information Problems and Banks' Specialization in Short-Term Lending: New England in the Nineteenth Century." In *Inside the Business Enterprise: Historical Perspectives on the Use of Information.* Edited by Peter Temin, 161-95. Chicago: University of Chicago Press, 1991.

————. *Insider Lending: Banks, Personal Connections, and Economic Development in Industrial New England.* Cambridge: Cambridge University Press, 1994.

Leal, Victor Nunes. *Coronelismo: The Municipality and Representative Government in Brazil.* Translated by June Henfrey. Cambridge Latin American Studies, no. 28. Cambridge: Cambridge University Press, 1977.

Lees, Francis A., James M. Botts, and Rubens Penha Cysne. *Banking and Financial Deepening in Brazil.* Houndmills, Basingstoke, Hampshire: Macmillan, 1990.

Leff, Nathaniel H. *The Brazilian Capital Goods Industry, 1929-1964.* Cambridge, Mass.: Harvard University Press, 1968.

————. "Capital Markets in the Less Developed Countries: The Group Principle."

In *Money and Finance in Economic Growth and Development.* Edited by Ronald I. McKinnon, 97-122. New York: Dekker, 1976.

―――. "Desenvolvimento econômico e desigualidade regional: Origens do caso brasileiro." *Revista Brasileira de Economia* 26, no. 1 (January-March 1972): 3-21.

―――. "Economic Retardation in Nineteenth-Century Brazil." *Economic History Review* 2d ser., 25, no. 3 (August 1972): 489-507.

―――. "Estimativa da renda provável no Brasil no século XIX com base nos dados sobre a moeda." *Revista Brasileira de Economia* 26, no. 2 (April-June 1972): 45-61.

―――. *Underdevelopment and Development in Brazil.* 2 vols. London and Boston: Allen & Unwin, 1982.

Leopoldi, Maria Antonieta P. "Industrial Associations and Politics in Contemporary Brazil: The Associations of Industrialists, Economic Policy-Making and the State with Special Reference to the Period 1930-61." Ph.D. diss., Cambridge University, 1984.

Lesser, Jeffrey. *Negotiating National Identity: Immigrants and the Struggle for Ethnicity in Brazil.* Durham, N.C.: Duke University Press, 1999.

―――. *Welcoming the Undesirables: Brazil and the Jewish Question.* Berkeley and Los Angeles: University of California Press, 1995.

Levi, Darrell E. *The Prados of São Paulo, Brazil: An Elite Family and Social Change, 1840-1930.* Athens, Ga.: University of Georgia Press, 1987.

Levine, Robert M. *Pernambuco in the Brazilian Federation, 1889-1937.* Stanford, Calif.: Stanford University Press, 1978.

―――. *Vale of Tears: Revisiting the Canudos Massacre in Northeastern Brazil, 1893-1897.* Berkeley and Los Angeles: University of California Press, 1992.

―――. *The Vargas Regime; the Critical Years, 1934-1938.* New York: Columbia University Press, 1970.

Levine, Ross. "Financial Development and Economic Growth: Views and Agenda." *Journal of Economic Literature* 35, no. 2 (June 1997): 688-726.

Levy, Maria Bárbara. "A acumulação de capital comercial na economia cafeeira (século XIX)." *Revista do Comércio de Café* (April 1974): 29-34.

―――. "The Banking System and Foreign Capital in Brazil." In *International Banking, 1870-1914.* Edited by Rondo Cameron and V. I. Bovykin, 351-70. New York: Oxford University Press, 1991.

―――. "O Encilhamento." In *Economia brasileira: Uma visão histórica.* Edited by Paulo Neuhaus, 191-256. Rio de Janeiro: Ed. Campus, 1980.

―――. *História dos bancos comerciais no Brasil (Estudo preliminar).* Rio de Janeiro: IBMEC, 1972.

―――. *História da Bolsa de Valores do Rio de Janeiro.* Rio de Janeiro: IBMEC, 1977.

―――. "A indústria de Rio de Janeiro—através de suas sociedades anônimas (Esboços de história empresarial)." Coleção Biblioteca Carioca Rio de Janeiro: Editora UFRJ: Prefeitura da Cidade do Rio de Janeiro, Secretária Municipal de Cultura, Departamento Geral de Documentação e Informação Cultural, Divisão de Editoração, 1988 (published posthumously, 1994).

Levy, Maria Bárbara and Ana Maria Ribeiro de Andrade. "Fundamentos do sistema bancário no Brasil: 1834-1860." *Estudos Econômicos* 15 (1985): 17-48.

———. "A gestão monetária na formação do estado nacional." *Revista Brasileira de Mercado de Capitais* 6, no. 17 (May-August 1980): 138-52.

Lewin, Linda. *Politics and Parentela in Paraíba: A Case Study of Family-Base Oligarchy in Brazil.* Princeton: Princeton University Press, 1987.

Lewis, Kenneth A. and Kozo Yamamura. "Industrialization and Interregional Interest Rate Structure; the Japanese Case: 1889-1925." *Explorations in Economic History* 8, no. 4 (summer 1971): 473-99.

Lima, Heitor Ferreira. *Tres industrialistas brasileiros, Mauá, Rui Barbosa, Roberto Simonsen.* Biblioteca Alfa-Omega de Ciencias Sociais. História; ser. 1a, vol. 12. São Paulo: Editora Alfa-Omega, 1976.

Livingston, James. *Origins of the Federal Reserve System: Money, Class, and Corporate Capitalism, 1890-1913.* Ithaca, N.Y.: Cornell University Press, 1986.

Lobo, Eulália Maria Lahmeyer. "O Encilhamento." *Revista Brasileira de Mercado de Capitais* 2, no. 5 (May-August 1976): 261-301.

———. *História do Rio de Janeiro: Do capital comercial ao capital industrial e financeiro.* 2 vols. Rio de Janeiro: IBMEC, 1978.

Lobo, Eulália Maria Lahmeyer, Lia A. Carvalho, and Myrian Stanley. *Questão habitacional e o movimento operário.* Rio de Janeiro: Editora UFRJ, 1989.

Love, Joseph L. "Federalismo y regionalismo en Brasil, 1889-1937." In *Federalismos Latinoamericanos: México, Brasil, Argentina.* Edited by Marcello Carmagnani, 180-220. México: Fondo de Cultura Económica, 1993.

———. *Rio Grande do Sul and Brazilian Regionalism, 1882-1930.* Stanford, Calif.: Stanford University Press, 1971.

———. *São Paulo in the Brazilian Federation, 1889-1937.* Stanford, Calif.: Stanford University Press, 1980.

Love, Joseph L. and Nils Jacobsen, eds. *Guiding the Invisible Hand: Economic Liberalism and the State in Latin American History.* New York: Praeger, 1988.

Lüders, Rolf. "A Monetary History of Chile." Ph.D. diss., University of Chicago, 1968.

Ludlow, Leonor and Carlos Marichal, eds. *Banca y poder en México, 1800-1925.* 1st ed. Colección Enlace. Mexico: Grijalbo, 1986.

Luz, Nícia Villela. "A história econômica do Brasil no período de 1830-1930—abordagens e problemas: Um ensaio bibliográfico." In *A moderna história econômica.* Edited by Carlos Manuel Peláez and Mircea Buescu, 203-12. Rio de Janeiro: APEC, 1976.

———. *A luta pela industrialização do Brasil 1808-1930.* Corpo e Alma, no. 5. São Paulo: Ed. Alfa Omega, 1978 [1960].

Luz, Nícia Villela and Carlos Manuel Peláez. "Economia e história: O encontro entre os dois campos de conhecimento." *Revista Brasileira de Economia* 26, no. 3 (1972): 273-301.

McKinnon, Ronald I. *Money and Capital in Economic Development.* Washington, D.C.: Brookings Institution, 1973.

Malley, James R. "Dynamic Specification in Econometric Estimation." *Journal of Agricultural Economics Research* 42, no. 2 (1990): 52-55.

Manchester, Alan Krebs. *British Preeminence in Brazil, Its Rise and Decline; a Study in European Expansion.* Chapel Hill: University of North Carolina Press, 1933.

Maram, Sheldon L. *Anarquistas, imigrantes e o movimento operário brasileiro, 1890-1920.* Coleção Estudos Brasileiros, vol. 34. Rio de Janeiro R.J.: Paz e Terra, 1979.

Marichal, Carlos. *A Century of Debt Crises in Latin America: From Independence to the Great Depression, 1820-1930.* Princeton: Princeton University Press, 1989.

———. "Nation-Building and the Origins of Banking in Latin America, 1850-1900." Paper presented at the Economic History Seminar. Columbia University, May 1998.

———, ed. "Banca." *América Latina en la historia económica. Boletín de fuentes,* no. 3 (January-June 1995).

———, ed. *Las inversiones extranjeras en América Latina, 1850-1930: Nuevos debates y problems en historia económica comparada.* Edited by Alicia Hernández Chávez. Fideicomiso Historia de las Américas. México: Colegio de México, 1995.

Marques, Teresa Cristina de Novaes. "O setor bancário privado carioca entre 1918 e 1945: Os Bancos Boavista e Português do Brasil—Um estudo de estratégias empresariais." Tese de mestrado. Rio de Janeiro: Universidade Federal de Rio de Janeiro, 1998.

Martins, José de Souza. *Conde Matarazzo, o empresário e a emprêsa; Estudo de sociologia do desenvolvimento.* Coleção Estudos Brasileiros, vol. 1, 2d ed. São Paulo: HUCITEC, 1976.

Martins, Roberto and A. Martins Filho. "Slavery in a Nonexport Economy: Nineteenth-Century Minas Gerais Revisited." *Hispanic American Historical Review* 63, no. 3 (1983): 537-90.

Martins Filho, Amilcar Vianna. *A economia política do café com leite, 1900-1930.* Série Dissertações e Teses, no. 2. Belo Horizonte: UFMG/PROED, 1981.

Mattoon Jr., Robert H. "Railroads, Coffee and the Growth of Big Business in São Paulo, Brazil." *Hispanic American Historical Review* 57, no. 2 (May 1977): 273-95.

Mattoso, Katia M. de Queiros. *To Be a Slave in Brazil, 1550-1888.* Translated by Arthur Goldhammer. New Brunswick, N.J.: Rutgers University Press, 1986.

Maurer, Noel. "Banks and Entrepreneurs in Porfirian Mexico: Inside Exploitation or Sound Business Strategy?" *Journal of Latin American Studies* 31, no. 2 (May 1999): 331-62.

Mauro, Frederico. *La preindustrialisation du Bresil: Essais sur une economie en transition.* Paris: Editions du Centre National de la Recherche Scientifique, 1984.

Mauro, José Eduardo Marques. "Os primórdios do desenvolvimento econômico brasileiro (1850-1930)." In *A moderna história econômica.* Edited by Carlos Manuel Peláez and Mircea Buescu, 133-48. Rio de Janeiro: APEC, 1976.

Meade, Teresa and Gregory Alonso Pirio. "In Search of the Afro-American 'Eldorado': Attempts by North American Blacks to Enter Brazil in the 1920s." *Luso-Brazilian Review* 25, no. 1 (1988): 85-110.

Merrick, Thomas William and Douglas H. Graham. *Population and Economic Development in Brazil, 1800 to the Present*. Baltimore: Johns Hopkins University Press, 1979.

Michie, R. "The Finance of Innovation in Late Victorian and Edwardian Britain: Possibilities and Constraints." *Journal of European Economic History* 17, no. 3 (winter 1988): 491-530.

————. *The London and New York Stock Exchanges, 1850-1914*. London and Boston: Allen & Unwin, 1987.

Miller, Rory. *Britain and Latin America in the Nineteenth and Twentieth Centuries*. Studies in Modern History. Edited by John Morrill and David Cannadine. London: Longman, 1993.

————. "Latin American Manufacturing and the First World War: An Exploratory Essay." *World Development* 9, no. 8 (August 1981): 707-16.

Minella, Ary Cesar. *Banqueiros: Organização e poder político no Brasil*. Rio de Janeiro: Espaco e Tempo: ANPOCS, 1988.

Mints, Lloyd W. *A History of Banking Theory in Great Britain and the United States*. Chicago: University of Chicago Press, 1945.

Monteiro, Ana Maria Ferreira da Costa. "Emprendedores e investidores em indústria têxtil no Rio de Janeiro: 1878-1895; Uma contribuição do capitalismo no Brasil." Tese de mestrado, Niterói, Universidade Federal Fluminense, 1985.

Moraes, Eduardo Jardim de. "Modernismo revisitado." *Estudos Históricos* 1, no. 2 (1988): 220-38.

National Bureau of Economic Research, Macro History Database; Yield on Consols, Series m13041c; http://www.nber.org/databases/macrohistory/data/13/m13041c.db; Cambridge, Mass.

National Bureau of Economic Research, Macro History Database; Yield on Long-term United States Bonds, Series m13033a; http://www.nber.org/databases/macrohistory/data/13/m13033a.db; Cambridge, Mass.

Needell, Jeffrey D. *A Tropical Belle Epoque: Elite Culture and Society in Turn-of-the-Century Rio de Janeiro*. Cambridge Latin American Studies, no. 62. Cambridge: Cambridge University Press, 1987.

Neuhaus, Paulo. "A doctrina de crédito legítimo e o primeiro banco central brasileiro." *Revista Brasileira de Mercado Capitais* 1, no. 1 (January-April 1975): 157-75.

————. "A Monetary History of Brazil, 1900-1945." Ph.D. diss. University of Chicago, 1974.

Ng, Kenneth. "Free Banking Laws and Barriers to Entry in Banking, 1838-1860." *Journal of Economic History* 48, no. 4 (December 1988): 877-89.

Nogueira, Dênio and Carlos Manuel Peláez. "O sistema monetário brasileiro em perspectiva histórica (1800-1906)." In *A moderna história econômica*. Edited by Carlos Manuel Peláez and Mircea Buescu, 59-72. Rio de Janeiro: APEC, 1976.

Normano, João Frederico. *Brazil, a Study of Economic Types*. Chapel Hill: University of North Carolina Press, 1935.

North, Douglass C. *Institutions, Institutional Change, and Economic Performance*. Cambridge: Cambridge University Press, 1990.

————. *Structure and Change in Economic History*. New York: Norton, 1981.

North, Douglass C. and Barry R. Weingast. "Constitutions and Commitment: The Evolution of Institutions Governing Public Choice in Seventeenth Century England." *Journal of Economic History* 49, no. 4 (December 1989): 803-32.

Nozoe, Nelson Hideiki. *São Paulo, economia cafeeira e urbanização: Estudo da estrutura tributária e das atividades econômicas na capital paulista (1889-1933)*. Série Ensaios Econômicos/IPE/USP 39. São Paulo: IPE/USP, 1984.

Odell, Kerry A. "The Integration of Regional and Interregional Capital Markets: Evidence from the Pacific Coast, 1883-1913." *Journal of Economic History* 49, no. 2 (June 1989): 297-309.

Olson, Mancur. *The Logic of Collective Action: Public Goods and the Theory of Groups*. Harvard Economic Studies, vol. 124. Cambridge, Mass.: Harvard University Press, 1971.

Pacheco, Cláudio. *História do Banco do Brasil*. 4 vols. Rio de Janeiro: Banco do Brasil, 1973.

Pang, Eul-Soo. *Bahia in the First Brazilian Republic: Coronelismo and Oligarchies, 1889-1934*. Latin American Monographs, 2d ser., no. 23. Gainesville, Fla.: University Press of Florida, 1979.

Patrick, Hugh. "Financial Development and Economic Growth in Underdeveloped Countries." *Economic Development and Cultural Change* 14, no. 2 (January 1966): 174-89.

Peláez, Carlos Manuel. "Análise econômica do programa brasileiro de sustentação do café—1906-1945: Teoria, política e medição." *Revista Brasileira de Economia* 25, no. 4 (October-December 1971): 5-211.

————. "A Comparison of Long-Run Monetary Behavior and Institutions in Brazil, Europe and the United States." *Journal of European Economic History* 5, no. 2 (fall 1976): 439-50.

————. "As conseqüências econômicas da ortodoxia monetária, cambial e fiscal no Brasil entre 1889-1945." *Revista Brasileira de Economia* 5, no. 3 (July-September 1971): 5-82.

————. "The Establishment of Banking Institutions in a Backward Economy: Brazil, 1800-1850." *Business History Review* 44, no. 4 (winter 1975): 446-72.

————. *História econômica do Brasil: Um elo entre a teoria e a realidade econômica*. São Paulo: Atlas, 1979.

————. "The Theory and Reality of Imperialism in the Coffee Economy of Nineteenth-Century Brazil." *Economic History Review* 2d ser., 29, no. 2 (May 1976): 276-90.

————, ed. *Essays on Coffee and Economic Development*. Translated by Magnolia Maciel Peláez. Rio de Janeiro: Instituto Brasileiro do Café by the Fundação Getúlio Vargas Pub. Service, 1973.

Peláez, Carlos Manuel and Wilson Suzigan. *História monetária do Brasil: Análise da política, comportamento e instituições monetárias*. Monografia, no. 23 (Instituto de

Planejamento Econômico e Social. Instituto de Pesquisas). Rio de Janeiro: IPEA/INPES, 1976.

Pesavento, Sandra Jatahy. *O cotidiano da República: Elites e povo na virada do século.* Síntese Rio-Grandense, no. 3. Porto Alegre, R.S.: Editora da Universidade, Universidade Federal do Rio Grande do Sul, 1990.

Platt, D. C. M., ed. *Business Imperialism, 1840-1930: An Inquiry Based on British Experience in Latin America.* Oxford: Clarendon Press, 1977.

———. *Latin America and British Trade, 1806-1914.* Merchant Adventurers. London: A. and C. Black, 1972.

Pollard, Sidney. *The Genesis of Modern Management: A Study of the Industrial Revolution in Great Britain.* Harmondsworth, Mddx.: Pelican Books of Penguin Books, 1968.

Pôrto, Ângela, Lilian de A. Fritsch, and Sylvia F. Padilha. *Processo de modernização do Brasil: 1850-1930, economia e sociedade, uma bibliografia.* Biblioteca CRESIFUL. Rio de Janeiro: Fundação Casa de Rui Barbosa, 1985.

Potash, Robert A. *El Banco de Avió en México: El fomento a la industria 1821-1846.* México: Fondo de Cultura Económica, 1959.

Prado, Luiz Carlos T. D. "Commercial Capital, Domestic Market and Manufacturing in Imperial Brazil: The Failure of Brazilian Economic Development in the Nineteenth Century." Ph.D. diss., University of London, 1991.

Prado, Maria Lígia Coelho and Maria Helena Rolim Capelato. "A borracha na economia brasileira da Primeira República." In *História geral: O Brasil republicano; vol. 2.* Edited by Boris Fausto, 285-307. Rio de Janeiro: Ed. Bertrand Brasil, 1989.

Prado Jr., Caio. *História econômica do Brasil.* São Paulo: Editora Brasiliense, 1993 (1945).

Quiroz, Alfonso W. *Banqueros en conflicto: Estructura financiera y economía peruana, 1884-1930.* 1st ed. Lima, Perú: Centro de Investigación, Universidad del Pacífico, 1989.

———. *Domestic and Foreign Finance in Modern Peru, 1850-1950: Financing Visions of Development.* Pitt Latin American Series. James M. Malloy, gen. ed. Pittsburgh: University of Pittsburgh Press, 1993.

———. *La deuda defraudada: Consolidación de 1850 y dominio economico en el Perú.* Lima, Peru: Instituto Nacional de Cultura: Editorial y Productora Grafica "Nuevo Mundo," 1987.

Regalsky, Andrés. "La evolución de la banca privada nacional en Argentina, 1860-1914: Una introducción a su estudio." In *La formación de los bancos centrales en España y América Latina.* Edited by Pedro Tedde and Carlos Marichal, 35-59. Madrid: Banco de Espana, Servicio de Estudios, 1994.

Reis, João José. *Slave Rebellion in Brazil: The Muslim Uprising of 1835 in Bahia.* Translated by Arthur Brakel. Johns Hopkins Studies in Atlantic History and Culture. Baltimore: Johns Hopkins University Press, 1993.

Ribas Vieira, José, et al., *Na corda bamba: Doze estudos sobre a cultura da inflação.* Rio de Janeiro: Relume Dumará, 1993.

Ribeiro, Benito and Mário Mazzei Guimarães. *História dos bancos e do desenvolvimento fincanceiro do Brasil: History of Brazilian Banking and Financial Development.* Translated by George Ree. São Paulo: Pro-Service, 1967.

Richards, R. D. "The First Fifty Years of the Bank of England (1694-1744)." In *History of the Principal Public Banks.* Edited by J. D. van Dillen, 201-72. London: Frank Cass & Co. Ltd., 1964 (1934).

Ridings, Eugene. *Business Interest Groups in Nineteenth-Century Brazil.* Cambridge Latin American Studies, no. 78. Cambridge: Cambridge University Press, 1994.

———. "The Foreign Connection: A Look at the Business Elite of Rio de Janeiro in the Nineteenth Century." *New Scholar* 7, nos. 1-2 (1979): 167-81.

Rippy, J. Fred. *British Investments in Latin America, 1822-1949: A Case Study in the Operations of Private Enterprise in Retarded Regions.* Minneapolis: University of Minnesota Press, 1959.

Rosenberg, Emily S. *Financial Missionaries to the World: The Politics and Culture of Dollar Diplomacy, 1900-1930.* Cambridge, Mass.: Harvard University Press, 1999.

Ross, Duncan. "Commercial Banking in a Market-Oriented Financial System: Britain Before the War." *Economic History Review* 49, no. 2 (May 1996): 314-34.

Saes, Decio. *A formação do estado burguês no Brasil (1888-1891).* Coleção Estudos Brasileiros, vol. 86. Rio de Janeiro: Paz e Terra, 1985.

Saes, Flávio A. M. de. *Crédito e bancos no desenvolvimento da economia paulista: 1850-1930.* São Paulo: Instituto de Pesquisas Econômicas, 1986.

———. "Banco: Fontes para a história dos bancos no Brasil (o caso de São Paulo: 1850-1930)." *América Latina en la Historia Económica. Boletín de fuentes,* no. 3 (January-June 1995): 63-72.

———. *A grande emprêsa de serviços públicos na economia cafeeira.* São Paulo: Ed. Hucitec, 1986.

Scheiber, Harry N. "Economic Liberty and the Constitution." In *Essays in the History of Liberty: Seaver Institution Lectures at the Huntington Library,* 75-99. San Marino, Calif.: Huntington Library, 1988.

———. "Public Rights Law and the Rule of Law in American Legal History." *California Law Review* 72 (1984): 217-51.

Schumpeter, Joseph Alois. *The Theory of Economic Development: An Inquiry into Profits, Capital, Credit, Interest, and the Business Cycle.* Translated by Opie Redvers. Harvard Economic Series, 46. Cambridge, Mass.: Harvard University Press, 1934.

Schwartz, Stuart B. *Sugar Plantations in the Formation of Brazilian Society: Bahia 1550-1835.* Cambridge Latin American Studies, no. 52. Cambridge: Cambridge University Press, 1985.

Schwartzman, Simon. *São Paulo e o estado nacional.* Corpo e Alma do Brasil, 42. São Paulo: Difel, 1975.

Scott, William B. *In Pursuit of Happiness: American Conceptions of Property from the Seventeenth to the Twentieth Century.* Bloomington: Indiana University Press, 1977.

Silva, Hélio. *O primeiro século da República.* Rio de Janeiro: J. Zahar Editor, 1987.

Simonsen, Mário Henrique. "Inflation and the Money and Capital Markets of

Brazil." In *The Economy of Brazil.* Edited by Howard S. Ellis, 133-61. Berkeley and Los Angeles: University of California Press, 1969.

Singer, Paul. "O Brasil no contexto do capitalismo internacional, 1889-1930." In *História geral da civilização brasileira,* vol. 3. Edited by Sergio Buarque de Holanda, 345-414. São Paulo: Difusão Europeia do Livro, 1960.

————. *Desenvolvimento econômico e evolução urbana.* São Paulo: 1968.

Skidmore, Thomas E. *Black into White: Race and Nationality in Brazilian Thought.* Durham, N.C.: Duke University Press, 1993 (1974).

————. "Historiography of Brazil, 1889-1964, Part I." *Hispanic American Historical Review* 55, no. 4 (November 1975): 716-48.

————. "Historiography of Brazil, 1889-1964, Part II." *Hispanic American Historical Review* 56, no. 1 (February 1976): 81-109.

————. *Politics in Brazil, 1930-1964: An Experiment in Democracy.* New York: Oxford University Press, 1967.

Smiley, Gene. "Interest Rate Movements in the United States, 1888-1913." *Journal of Economic History* 35 (September 1975): 591-620.

Somogyi, Flavio. "Un exemple de la présence economique français au Brésil: 'L'empire Bouilloux-Lafont'." In *Transport et commerce en Amérique Latine.* Edited by Frédéric Mauro and Soline Alemany. Paris, n.d.

Spiegel, Henry W. *The Brazilian Economy; Chronic Inflation and Sporadic Industrialization.* Philadelphia: Blakiston Co., 1949.

Spindel, Cheywa R. *Homens e maquinas na transição de uma economia cafeeira.* Rio de Janeiro: 1980.

Stallings, Barbara. *Banker to the Third World: U.S. Portfolio Investment in Latin America, 1900-1986.* Studies in International Political Economy, no. 18. Berkeley and Los Angeles: University of California Press, 1987.

Stein, Stanley J. *The Brazilian Cotton Manufacture: Textile Enterprise in an Underdeveloped Area, 1850-1950.* Studies in Entrepreneurial History. Cambridge, Mass.: Harvard University Press, 1957.

————. *Vassouras, a Brazilian Coffee County, 1850-1900.* Harvard Historical Studies, vol. 69. Cambridge, Mass.: Harvard University Press, 1957.

Stein, Stanley J. and Shane J. Hunt. "Principal Currents in the Economic Historiography of Latin America." *Journal of Economic History* 31, no. 1 (March 1971): 222-53.

Stepan, Alfred C. *The Military in Politics: Changing Patterns in Brazil.* Princeton, N.J.: Princeton University Press, 1971.

Stepan, Nancy. *Beginnings of Brazilian Science: Oswaldo Cruz, Medical Research and Policy, 1890-1920.* New York: Science History Publications, 1976.

Stolcke, Verena. *Coffee Planters, Workers and Wives: Class Conflict and Gender Relations on São Paulo Coffee Plantations, 1850-1980.* St. Antony's/Macmillan Series. Basingstoke, Hampshire: Macmillan in association with St. Antony's College Oxford, 1988.

Stone, Irving. "British Direct and Portfolio Investment in Latin America Before 1914." *Journal of Economic History* 37, no. 3 (September 1977): 690-722.

Summerhill, William. "Railroads and the Brazilian Economy Before 1914." Ph.D. diss., Stanford University, 1995.

———. "Transport Improvements and Economic Growth in Brazil and Mexico." In *How Latin America Fell Behind: Essays on the Economic Histories of Brazil and Mexico, 1800-1914.* Edited by Stephen Haber, 93-117. Stanford, Calif.: Stanford University Press, 1997.

Sushka, Marie Elizabeth. "The Antebellum Money Market and the Economic Impact of the Bank War." *Journal of Economic History* 36, no. 4 (1976): 809-35.

Sushka, Marie Elizabeth and W. Brian Barrett. "Banking Structure and the National Capital Market, 1869-1914." *Journal of Economic History* 54, no. 2 (June 1984): 463-77.

Suzigan, Wilson. *Indústria brasileira: Origem e desenvolvimento.* São Paulo: Brasiliense, 1986.

Suzigan, Wilson and Tamás Szmrecsányi. "Os investimentos estrangeiros no início da industrialização do Brasil." In *História econômica da Primeira República.* Coletânea de Textos apresentados no I Congresso Brasileiro de História Econômica. Edited by Tamás Szmrecsányi and Silva Sérgio, 261-83. São Paulo: Hucitec, 1996.

Swartz, W. R. "Codification in Latin America: The Brazilian Commercial Code of 1850." *Texas International Law Review* 10 (1975): 347-56.

Sweigart, Joseph E. *Coffee Factorage and the Emergence of a Brazilian Capital Market, 1850-1888.* South American and Latin American Economic History. New York: Garland Pub., 1987.

Sylla, Richard E. *The American Capital Market, 1846-1914: A Study of the Effects of Public Policy on Economic Development.* Dissertations in American Economic History. New York: Arno Press, 1975.

———. "Federal Policy, Banking Market Structure and Capital Mobility in the United States, 1863-1914." *Journal of Economic History* 29, no. 4 (December 1969): 657-86.

———. "The United States: 1863-1914." In *Banking and Economic Development: Some Lessons of History.* Edited by Rondo Cameron, 232-62. New York: Oxford University Press, 1972.

Sylla, Richard, John B. Legler, and John J. Wallis. "Banks and State Public Finance in the New Republic: The United States, 1790-1860." *Journal of Economic History* 47, no. 2 (June 1987): 391-403.

Szmrecsányi, Tamás and José Roberto do Amaral Lapa, eds. *História econômica da independência e do império.* Coletânea de Textos apresentados no I Congresso Brasileiro de História Econômica. São Paulo: Hucitec, 1996.

Szmrecsányi, Tamás and Sérgio Silva, eds. *História econômica da Primeira República.* Coletânea de Textos apresentados no I Congresso Brasileiro de História Econômica. São Paulo: Hucitec, 1996.

Taunay, Afonso de Escragnolle. *História do café no Brasil.* Rio de Janeiro: Departamento Nacional do Café, 1939.

Thorp, Rosemary, ed. *Latin America in the 1930s: The Role of the Periphery in World*

Crisis. Studies in Monetary History. London: Macmillan in association with St. Antony's College, Oxford, 1984.

Tilly, Richard. "German Banking, 1850-1914: Development Assistance for the Strong." *Journal of European Economic History* 15, no. 1 (spring 1986): 113-52.

———. "Germany, 1815-1870." In *Banking in the Early Stages of Industrialization; a Study in Comparative Economic History.* Edited by Rondo E. Cameron with the collaboration of Olga Crisp, Hugh T. Patrick, and Richard Tilly, 151-82. New York: Oxford University Press, 1967.

Topik, Steven. "Brazil's Bourgeois Revolution?" *Americas* 48, no. 2 (October 1991): 245-271.

———. "Capital estrangeiro e o estado no sistema bancário brasileiro, 1889-1930." *Revista Brasileira de Mercado Capitais* 5, no. 15 (1979): 395-421.

———. "The Economic Role of the State in Liberal Regimes: Brazil and Mexico Compared, 1889-1910." In *Guiding the Invisible Hand: Economic Liberalism and the State in Latin American History.* Edited by Joseph L. Love and Nils Jacobsen, 117-44. New York: Praeger, 1988.

———. "A emprêsa estatal em um regime liberal: O Banco de Brasil—1905-1930." *Revista Brasileira de Mercado Capitais* 7, no. 19 (1981): 70-83.

———. *The Political Economy of the Brazilian State, 1889-1930.* Latin American Monographs, Institute of Latin American Studies the University of Texas at Austin, no. 71. Austin: University of Texas Press, 1987.

———. "The State's Contribution to the Development of Brazil's Internal Economy, 1850-1930." *Hispanic American Historical Review* 65, no. 2 (1982): 203-28.

Triner, Gail D. "Banking and Brazilian Economic Development: 1906-1930." Ph.D. diss., Columbia University, 1994.

———. "Banking, Economic Growth and Industrialization: Brazil, 1906-1930." *Revista Brasileira de Economia* 50, no. 1 (January 1996): 135-54.

———. "Banks, Regions and Nation in Brazil, 1889-1930." *Latin American Perspectives* 26, no. 1 (January 1999): 129-50.

———. "British Banking in Brazil during the First Republic." Paper presented at the Conference on Latin American History. New York, January, 1997.

———. "The Delayed Development of Early Brazilian Financial Historiography, 1889-1930." *Revista de Historia Económica* 17, Special issue (1999): 53-76.

———. "The Formation of Modern Brazilian Banking, 1906-1930: Opportunities and Constraints Presented by the Public and Private Sectors." *Journal of Latin American Studies* 28, no. 1 (February 1996): 49-74.

Versiani, Flávio Rabelo. "Before the Depression: Brazilian Industry in the 1920's." In *Latin America in the 1930's: The Role of the Periphery in World Crisis.* Edited by Rosemary Thorp, 163-87. Oxford: Macmillan Press, 1984.

———. "Industrial Development in an 'Export' Economy: The Brazilian Experience Before 1914." *Journal of Development Economics* 7, no. 3 (September 1980): 307-31.

———. "Industrialização e economia de exportação antes de 1914." *Revista Brasileira de Economia* 34, no. 1 (January-March 1980): 3-40.

Versiani, Flávio Rabelo and José Roberto Mendonça de Barros. *Formação econômica do Brasil: A expêriencia da industrialização.* Série ANPEC de Leituras de Economia. São Paulo: Edição Saraiva, 1977.

Viana Filho, Luís. *A vida de Rui Barbosa.* 11th ed. Rio de Janeiro: Editora Nova Fronteira, 1987.

Villela, Annibal V. and Wilson Suzigan. *Política do governo e crescimento da economia brasileira, 1889-1945.* Instituto de Planejamento Econômico e Social. Instituto de Pesquisas. Monografia, no. 10. Rio de Janeiro: IPEA/INPES, 1973.

Wagley, Charles. *An Introduction to Brazil.* New York: Columbia University Press, 1971.

Weid, Elisabeth von der, Ana Marta Rodrigues Bastos, and Francisco Carlos Elia. *O fio da meada: Estratégia de expansão de uma indústria textil: Companhia América Fabril, 1878-1930.* Prefácio de Maria Bárbara Levy. Rio de Janeiro: Fundação Casa Rui Barbosa, 1986.

Weinstein, Barbara. *The Amazon Rubber Boom, 1850-1920.* Stanford, Calif.: Stanford University Press, 1983.

———. "Not the Republic of Their Dreams: Historical Obstacles to Political and Social Democracy in Brazil." *Latin American Research Journal* 29, no. 2 (1994): 262-73.

Welch, John H. *Capital Markets in the Development Process: The Case of Brazil.* Pitt Latin American Series. James M. Malloy, gen. ed. Pittsburgh: University of Pittsburgh Press, 1993.

White, Eugene Nelson. *The Regulation and Reform of the American Banking System, 1900 -1929.* Princeton, N.J.: Princeton University Press, 1983.

Wilkie, James W. and Stephen Haber. *Statistical Abstract of Latin America.* Los Angeles: Latin American Center, University of California, 1981.

Wirth, John D. *Economic Nationalism: Trade and Steel under Vargas.* Stanford, Calif.: Stanford University Press, 1969.

———. *Minas Gerais in the Brazilian Federation, 1889-1937.* Stanford, Calif.: Stanford University Press, 1977.

Wolfe, Joel. *Working Women, Working Men: São Paulo and the Rise of Brazil's Industrial Working Class, 1900-1955.* Durham, N.C.: Duke University Press, 1993.

Index